F ollowing each story, an **Expanded Meanings** section focuses on the teaching principles, science ideas, and science standards illustrated by the narrative. The pedagogy features:

The Teaching Ideas Behind This Story focuses on the teaching principles that are demonstrated by the science story.

The Science Ideas Behind This Story focuses on the science concepts to help grasp the science story fully.

The Science Standards Behind This Story focuses on national science standards that the science story illustrates.

Questions for Further Exploration provide probing questions that encourage further investigation.

Resources for Further Exploration provide additional resources for the ideas explored in the science story.

EXPANDING MEANINGS

■ **The Teaching Ideas Behind This Story**

■ When students simply repeat answers they have heard, we cannot be sure that there is any deep meaning in this knowledge. The students in Ms. Hudson's class all agreed that the bottle contained air. Nevertheless, I could tell that many were not comfortable with this idea. For some, it

● **The Science Ideas Behind This Story**

● Although air is all around us and seeps into everything, it is a difficult concept for young students to understand. They can blow air onto their hands, feel the force of a breeze—but, still, it is a tricky concept.

● Air that is warmed expands. Its particles move faster and become farther apart. Because its particles are farther apart, this warmed air is now less dense. In the experiment in Ms. Hudson's class, the colder air above—denser, with its particles closer together—dropped down, pushing the warm air upward.

● The method by which heat energy travels in liquids and gases is called *convection*. You can read more about convection in the chapter "Science Content and Curriculum." Ms. Hudson or I could have introduced this term and asked the students to memorize the definition. But even after learning the term, they might have been unable to relate it to the balloon and the bottle.

✔ **The Science Standards Behind This Story**

STANDARDS

The story of Ms. Hudson's class reflects the following portions of the National Science Education Standards (National Research Council, 1996):

✔ *Teaching Standard B:* "Teachers of science . . . encourage and model the skills of scientific inquiry, as well as the curiosity, openness to new ideas and data, and skepticism that characterize science" (p. 32).

✔ *Content Standard B, Grades K–4 (Physical Science):* "The children . . . have intuitive notions of energy. . . . Teachers can build on the intuitive notions of students without requiring them to memorize technical definitions" (p. 126).

Questions for Further Exploration

■ How is *convection* of heat energy in the balloon experiment different from the *conduction* of heat that occurs when you touch a hot stove?

Resources for Further Exploration

ELECTRONIC RESOURCES

Building an Understanding of Constructivism (1994). *Classroom Compass,* 1(3), http://www.sedl.org/scimath/compass/v01n03/2.html. This article from the third issue of the online journal *Classroom Compass* offers a fine overview of constructivism.

Crowther, David T. (1997). The constructivist zone. *The Electronic Journal of Science Education.* http://unr.edu/homepage/jcannon/ejse/ejse.html. Follow the links to volume 2, number 2, of this electronic journal. Crowther's editorial offers a historical perspective on constructivism and an overview of its impact on current practice. The issue as a whole is devoted to the "science wars"—the controversy over methods of teaching science.

PRINT RESOURCES

Duckworth, E. (1996). *The Having of Wonderful Ideas and Other Essays on Teaching and Learning,* 2d ed. New York: Teachers College Press.
Gallas, K. (1995). *Talking Their Way into Science.* New York: Teachers College Press.
Kaner, E. (1989). *Balloon Science.* Reading, MA: Addison-Wesley.
Logan, J. (1997). *Teaching Stories.* New York: Kodansha International.

Science Stories

Science Methods for Elementary and Middle School Teachers

THIRD EDITION

Janice Koch

Hofstra University

Houghton Mifflin Company   Boston New York

In memory of Beatrice Deutsch

Vice President and Publisher: *Patricia Coryell*

Senior Sponsoring Editor: *Sue Pulvermacher-Alt*

Senior Development Editor: *Lisa Mafrici*

Editorial Associate: *Sara Hauschildt*

Senior Project Editor: *Jane Lee*

Senior Art and Design Coordinator: *Jill Haber*

Senior Photo Editor: *Jennifer Meyer Dare*

Senior Composition Buyer: *Sarah Ambrose*

Senior Designer: *Henry Rachlin*

Manufacturing Manager: *Florence Cadran*

Marketing Manager: *Jane Potter*

Marketing Assistant: *Erin Lane*

Cover image: © Getty Images

Acknowledgment is made to the following sources for permission to reprint selections from copyrighted material:

The Montillation of Traxoline, p. 12: Reprinted by permission of the author, Judith Lanier. **Definition, p. 3:** Copyright © 2000 by Houghton Mifflin Company. Reproduced by permission from *The American Heritage Dictionary of the English Language*, Fourth Edition. **Drawing (left), p. 39:** Reprinted by permission. **Drawing (right), p. 39:** Reprinted by permission. **Excerpt, p. 116:** Reprinted by permission. **Excerpts, pp. 216–218:** Reprinted by permission. **Excerpt, p. 271:** Reprinted by permission of Geerat Vermeij. **Excerpt, p. 273:** From Greg Stefanich, *Science Teaching in Inclusive Classrooms: Models and Applications*. Copyright © 2001. Reprinted by permission of the author. **Classroom Survey: How Accessible Is Your Classroom?, p. 274:** Adapted from G. Stefanich, M. Fetters, E. Pyle, D. Pickard, and J. Ellis, *Making Science Accessible and Inclusive: Strategies for Teachers in Science Education*, © 2003 (preconference workshop presented at the Association for the Education of Teachers of Science International Conference, St. Louis, MO, January 2003). Used with permission. **Table 13.1, p. 304:** Table 6.8 and Table 6.9 taken from National Research Council, *National Science Education Standards*. Washington, DC: National Academy Press, 1996, pp. 109–110. **Excerpt, pp. 357–358:** Reprinted with permission from D. P. Shepardson and S. Britsch (1997), "Children's Science Journals," *Science and Children*, Vol. 35 (2), p. 13ff.

Printed in the U.S.A.

Library of Congress Control Number: 2003110104

ISBN: 0-618-37647-X

123456789—CRS—08 07 06 05 04

Brief Contents

PREFACE   xix

Part One: The Scientist Within   1

1   An Invitation to Teaching Science   2

2   Locating Your Scientific Self   33

Part Two: Doing Science with Students: Inquiry in Practice   55

3   The Teacher as Mediator   56

4   The Science Circus: Using the Skills of Scientific Study   86

5   Making Connections: Science in the Students' Own Environment   104

6   Science Is Not Neat: Explorations of Matter   126

7   Sustained Inquiry: Explorations of Living Things   141

8   Spiraling Curriculum: Explorations of Density   172

9   Making Models: Explorations of the Solar System   201

10   Expanding the Science "Box": Explorations of Electricity and Atoms   223

Part Three: Creating the Science Experience in Your Classroom   253

11   Planning for Science: Lesson Plans and Instructional Strategies   254

12   Science and Technology: A Seamless Connection   280

13   Science Content and Curriculum: The Big Ideas and Your Scientific Self   302

14   What's the Big Idea? Assessing What Students Know and Are Able to Do   350

15   Pulling It All Together: Reflection and Self-Assessment   376

MORE RESOURCES FOR TEACHERS   387

GLOSSARY   397

REFERENCES   411

INDEX   419

Contents

PREFACE   xix

Part One: The Scientist Within   1

1 An Invitation to Teaching Science 2

FOCUSING QUESTIONS   2

What Is Science, and Why Teach It?   3
Science as a Process, a Set of Ideas, and a Set of Attitudes   3
The Nature of Science   6
The Value of Teaching Science   7

How Do Students Learn Science?   8
Key Tenets of Constructivist Theory   8
Implications for Teaching   12
SCIENCE STORY: Listening to Students' Ideas   14
SCIENCE STORY: The Search for Understanding:
                         A Toaster Story   16

Standards for Science Education   19

Issues of Diversity   21
Questions to Ask About Your Students   21
Connecting Science to All Students   22

The Role of Technology   24
Technology Education Standards   25
Ways of Using Technology   26
Issues of Technology Access   27

Structure of This Book   28
Part One: The Scientist Within   28
Part Two: Doing Science with Students: Inquiry in Practice   28
Part Three: Creating the Science Experience in Your Classroom   29

Becoming a Science Teacher   30
KEY TERMS   30   RESOURCES FOR FURTHER EXPLORATION   31

2 Locating Your Scientific Self   33

FOCUSING QUESTIONS   33

SCIENCE STORY: Why the Balloon Doesn't Pop:
                        An Experience for New Teachers   33

Teachers as Scientists   35

Beliefs About Science: We Teach What We Think   36

What Is a Scientist? Stereotype Versus Reality   38

Drawing a Scientist   38
Interviewing a Scientist   41

Reflective Practice I: Your Science Autobiography   44

Writing Your Science Autobiography   45
Reflecting on Your Science Autobiography   45

Reflective Practice II: Keeping a Science Journal   46

A Bird Story: Sample Entries from a Science Journal   47
Learning from Your Science Journal   51
Some Guidelines for Your Own Science Journal   52

The Inner Scientist   52

KEY TERMS   53   RESOURCES FOR FURTHER EXPLORATION   53

Part Two: Doing Science with Students:
            Inquiry in Practice   55

3 The Teacher as Mediator   56

FOCUSING QUESTIONS   56

SCIENCE STORY: The Bottle and the Balloon   57

EXPANDING MEANINGS   58
The Teaching Ideas Behind This Story   58
The Science Ideas Behind This Story   59
The Science Standards Behind This Story   59
Questions for Further Exploration   59
Resources for Further Exploration   60

Helping Students Construct Meaning   60

Prior Knowledge   61
Valuing the Students' Thinking   61
Mediating the Students' Learning   62

SCIENCE STORY: Icicles   64

The Next Day: From Icicles to Ice Cubes   69

| EXPANDING MEANINGS   69

The Teaching Ideas Behind This Story   69

The Science Ideas Behind This Story   70

The Science Standards Behind This Story   71

Questions for Further Exploration   72

Resources for Further Exploration   72

Mediation and Alternative Conceptions   73

SCIENCE STORY: The "Skin" of Water   73

An Experiment to Explore Shondra's Question   75

Further Experiments and Discussion   78

More Challenges   79

| EXPANDING MEANINGS   81

The Teaching Ideas Behind This Story   81

The Science Ideas Behind This Story   82

The Science Standards Behind This Story   83

Questions for Further Exploration   83

Resources for Further Exploration   83

Students as Knowers   84

KEY TERMS   85

4 The Science Circus: Using the Skills of Scientific Study   86

FOCUSING QUESTIONS   86

The Science Circus   87

SCIENCE STORY: The Circus Comes to Mount Holly   88

An Old Log   88

The Soda Can   90

Crazy Rocks   91

The Leaky Faucet   91

The Penny in the Pie Pan   93

Three Types of Soil   94

The Weather Station   95

| EXPANDING MEANINGS   96

The Teaching Ideas Behind This Story   96

The Science Ideas Behind This Story   97

The Science Standards Behind This Story   98

Questions for Further Exploration   99
Resources for Further Exploration   100

Science in the Classroom and in Everyday Life   101

Family Science Night   101

KEY TERMS   103

5 *Making Connections: Science in the Students' Own Environment*   104

FOCUSING QUESTIONS   104

Diversity Within and Without   105

Seeing the Larger Picture: Content Plus Context   105
From Alienation to Inclusion   107

Science Corners   108

Making the Science Corner an Interactive Experience   108
Connections to Literature and Other Subjects   111
Sample Science Corners from Around the Country   113
Field Trips   115

SCIENCE STORY: *Making Connections, Inside and Outside the Classroom*   117

The Osage   117

A Snow Story   118

Two Seashores   118

Investigating a Natural Disaster   120

Coconuts Outside the Door   120

EXPANDING MEANINGS   121
The Teaching Ideas Behind These Stories   121
The Science Ideas Behind These Stories   122
The Science Standards Behind These Stories   123
Questions for Further Exploration   123
Resources for Further Exploration   124

The Daily Life of the Classroom   125

KEY TERMS   125

6 *Science Is Not Neat: Explorations of Matter*   126

FOCUSING QUESTIONS   126

Classifying   126

SCIENCE STORY: *Exploring Solids, Liquids, and Gases*   127

SCIENCE STORY: *Mysterious Matter*   132

| **EXPANDING MEANINGS**   133
| The Teaching Ideas Behind These Stories   133
| The Science Ideas Behind These Stories   134
| The Science Standards Behind These Stories   135
| Questions for Further Exploration   135
| Resources for Further Exploration   135

If It's So Messy, Can It Be Science?   137
Messiness in the Classroom   137
Messiness in the Categories   139
KEY TERMS   140

7 **Sustained Inquiry: Explorations of Living Things**   141

FOCUSING QUESTIONS   141
SCIENCE STORY: **What Does It Mean to Be Alive?**   142
What Makes a Rabbit Real?   142
Are Plants Alive?   143

| **EXPANDING MEANINGS**   144
| The Teaching Ideas Behind These Stories   144
| The Science Ideas Behind These Stories   144
| The Science Standards Behind These Stories   145
| Questions for Further Exploration   145
| Resources for Further Exploration   145

Plants and Animals in Your Science Corner   146
SCIENCE STORY: **From Seed to Plant: A Failed Experiment**   146
SCIENCE STORY: **What's Inside a Seed?**   148
The Following Days: Germination Bags   150

| **EXPANDING MEANINGS**   154
| The Teaching Ideas Behind These Stories   154
| The Science Ideas Behind These Stories   155
| The Science Standards Behind These Stories   156
| Questions for Further Exploration   156
| Resources for Further Exploration   156
SCIENCE STORY: **Planting in a Vacant Lot**   157
SCIENCE STORY: **When Is a Vegetable a Fruit?**   157

> **EXPANDING MEANINGS**   160
>> The Teaching Ideas Behind These Stories   160
>> The Science Ideas Behind These Stories   161
>> The Science Standards Behind These Stories   161
>> Questions for Further Exploration   161
>> Resources for Further Exploration   162

A Classroom Invertebrate   162

SCIENCE STORY: *A Book of Snails*   163

> **EXPANDING MEANINGS**   167
>> The Teaching Ideas Behind This Story   167
>> The Science Ideas Behind This Story   167
>> The Science Standards Behind These Stories   168
>> Questions for Further Exploration   168
>> Resources for Further Exploration   168

Working Together to Conduct Investigations Over Time   169
> KEY TERMS   170

8   *Spiraling Curriculum: Explorations of Density*   172

FOCUSING QUESTIONS   172

SCIENCE STORY: *Looking at Liquids*   173

The Next Day: Building Science Toys to Illustrate Density   177

> **EXPANDING MEANINGS**   178
>> The Teaching Ideas Behind This Story   178
>> The Science Ideas Behind This Story   178
>> The Science Standards Behind This Story   180
>> Questions for Further Exploration   180
>> Resources for Further Exploration   180

SCIENCE STORY: *Delving Deeper into Density*   181

The Floating Egg   181

> **EXPANDING MEANINGS**   182
>> The Teaching Ideas Behind This Story   182
>> The Science Ideas Behind This Story   183
>> The Science Standards Behind This Story   183
>> Questions for Further Exploration   183
>> Resources for Further Exploration   183

Extending Curriculum: Taking Advantage of Emerging Relevance   184

SCIENCE STORY: *Floating and Sinking Fruits*   185

EXPANDING MEANINGS   188
The Teaching Ideas Behind This Story   188
The Science Ideas Behind This Story   188
The Science Standards Behind This Story   188
Questions for Further Exploration   189
Resources for Further Exploration   189

Looking Back to Look Ahead   189
SCIENCE STORY: *Apples, Potatoes, and Density*   190
The Following Days: Further Tests and Measurements   195

EXPANDING MEANINGS   197
The Teaching Ideas Behind This Story   197
The Science Ideas Behind This Story   197
The Science Standards Behind This Story   198
Questions for Further Exploration   199
Resources for Further Exploration   199

"Replacement" of Understandings   200
KEY TERMS   200

9 Making Models: Explorations of the Solar System   201

FOCUSING QUESTIONS   201

The Usefulness of Models   202
SCIENCE STORY: *An Edible Solar System*   203

EXPANDING MEANINGS   208
The Teaching Ideas Behind This Story   208
The Science Ideas Behind This Story   208
The Science Standards Behind This Story   210
Questions for Further Exploration   210
Resources for Further Exploration   210

Models and Meaning   211
SCIENCE STORY: *A Model Orbit*   212

EXPANDING MEANINGS   214
The Teaching Ideas Behind This Story   214
The Science Ideas Behind This Story   214
The Science Standards Behind This Story   214
Questions for Further Exploration   215
Resources for Further Exploration   215

SCIENCE STORY: *Shapes of the Moon*   215

Modeling the Moon Phases   217

> **EXPANDING MEANINGS**   218
>
> The Teaching Ideas Behind This Story   218
>
> The Science Ideas Behind This Story   218
>
> The Science Standards Behind These Stories   219
>
> Questions for Further Exploration   219
>
> Resources for Further Exploration   220

Using Moon-Phase Journals   221

> **KEY TERMS**   221

10 Expanding the Science "Box": Explorations of Electricity and Atoms   223

FOCUSING QUESTIONS   223

SCIENCE STORY: *Batteries, Bulbs, and Wires*   224

SCIENCE STORY: *Batteries, Bulbs, and Wires Revisited*   226

The Next Day: Lighting a Shoebox House   232

> **EXPANDING MEANINGS**   234
>
> The Teaching Ideas Behind These Stories   234
>
> The Science Ideas Behind These Stories   234
>
> The Science Standards Behind These Stories   235
>
> Questions for Further Exploration   236
>
> Resources for Further Exploration   236

Thinking About Teaching and Learning   236

SCIENCE STORY: *Making Models of Atoms*   238

Exploring the History of Atomic Theory   239

Mystery Boxes   241

Discussing the Nucleus   241

The Periodic Table   243

The Atom Design Challenge   243

> **EXPANDING MEANINGS**   247
>
> The Teaching Ideas Behind This Story   247
>
> The Science Ideas Behind This Story   248
>
> The Science Standards Behind This Story   249
>
> Questions for Further Exploration   249
>
> Resources for Further Exploration   249

Design Technology   250

> **KEY TERMS**   251

Part Three: Creating the Science Experience in Your Classroom   **253**

11 Planning for Science: Lesson Plans and Instructional Strategies   254

FOCUSING QUESTIONS 254

An Activity Is Not a Lesson 254

Planning the Lesson 255

A Planning Guide 256
If I Know It, Do I Have to Write It? 259
Time Allotment 259
After the Planning, the Letting Go! 260

The Role of Questioning 261

Types of Questions 261
A Word About Wait Time 263

Science Learning Groups: Creating an Environment for Cooperative Learning 264

Cooperative Learning Groups 264
Constructivism and Small-Group Learning 265
Scientific Investigation and Group Learning 267
Structuring Cooperative Learning Groups in Your Classroom 267

Inclusive Science Education 270

Science and the Inclusion Model 271
Classroom Strategies for Doing Science with Students with Disabilities 272

Questions for Your Own Reflection 276

KEY TERMS 277   **RESOURCES FOR FURTHER EXPLORATION** 277

12 Science and Technology: A Seamless Connection   280

FOCUSING QUESTIONS 280

The Meanings and Uses of Technology 281

The National Educational Technology Standards 282
Integrating Technology with Instruction and Learning 283
The Need to Know 284

Making Observations and Gathering Data   285

Obtaining Information from the Web   285
Instruments with Computer Interfaces   288
Video Cameras: Extending Our Senses   289

Internet Projects and Collaboration   290

Web-Based Projects   290

SCIENCE STORY: *A WebQuest on Marine Organisms*   291

Underwater Adventure   291
Mission   291
Resources   293
Conclusion   294
Extending Student Collaboration Through Email   294

Using Commercial Software for Science Instruction   295

Evaluating Software   295

Internet Resources for Teachers   296

Gateway Sites   296
Lesson Plans on the Web   297

Technology and Learning: Some Concluding Thoughts   299

KEY TERMS   300   RESOURCES FOR FURTHER EXPLORATION   300

13 Science Content and Curriculum: The Big Ideas and Your Scientific Self   302

FOCUSING QUESTIONS   302

Making Big Ideas Your Own Ideas   303

Ways of Thinking About Science Topics   304

Systems   306

The Solar System   306
Thinking About Systems: The Interconnection of Parts   309
Human Body Systems   310
Thinking About Systems: Noticing Similarities and Differences   316
Simple Machines   316
Thinking About Systems: Simple Machines as Systems   320
Thinking About Systems: The Benchmarks for Science Literacy   322

Interactions and Patterns of Change   322

Heat Energy and Matter   323
Thinking About Interactions: Chemical and Physical Changes   325
Thinking About Interactions:
Links Between Interactions and Systems   328

Electricity   329
Light   331
Thinking About Interactions: Making Connections:
From Electricity to Heat and Light   333
Sound   335
Thinking About Interactions: Sound Energy and
Musical Instruments   337
Magnetism   337

From Content to Curriculum   339
Who Creates the Curriculum? National
Influence and Local Control   340
MST (Mathematics, Science, and Technology) Curriculum   341
Other Interdisciplinary Trends   343

Developing Curriculum Units   344
Aligning a Unit of Study with the Standard   345
Selecting Activities   345
What Is Missing?   346
A Checklist for the Science Curriculum   346
KEY TERMS   347   RESOURCES FOR FURTHER EXPLORATION   347

14 **What's the Big Idea?
Assessing What Students
Know and Are Able to Do**   350

FOCUSING QUESTIONS   350

Assessment and Testing   351

Assessment and the Instructional Context   352

Using Science Journals for Assessment   353
A Sample Structure for a Science Journal   353
Integrating Technology with Science Journals   356
Drawing Pictures and Telling Stories   357
Evaluating Student Journals   357

Using Science Portfolios for Assessment   358
Evaluating Student Portfolios   359

Using Science Conversations for Assessment   360

Using Technology to Assess Understanding   361
Concept Maps   362
Concept Cartoons   363
Electronic Presentations   364

Multiple Types of Performances   366
SCIENCE STORY: *Third Graders Enact the Water Cycle*   367
SCIENCE STORY: *Second Graders Do a Station
                Assessment for a Unit on Matter*   368

Assessment and National Standards   370

Teaching, Learning, and Assessing   373
KEY TERMS   374   RESOURCES FOR FURTHER EXPLORATION   374

15 *Pulling It All Together:
Reflection and Self-Assessment*   376

FOCUSING QUESTIONS   376

Your Scientific Self   376

Becoming a Reflective Teacher   379
Developing a Personal Philosophy   379

Professional Development   380
Networking in the Profession   380
Promotion and Certification Requirements   380
Further Means of Professional Development   382

How Am I Doing? A Guide to Self-Evaluation   383

**Looking Back to Look Ahead: A New Chapter
in Your Science Autobiography**   383
KEY TERMS   386   RESOURCES FOR FURTHER EXPLORATION   386

MORE RESOURCES FOR TEACHERS   387

GLOSSARY   397

REFERENCES   411

INDEX   419

Preface

For the elementary or middle school teacher, teaching science is frequently a challenging task, and sometimes it can even be intimidating. This book is an invitation to elementary and middle school science. Or, to put it another way, the book is a welcome mat for future teachers, welcoming them to the world of science and inspiring them to teach it.

I have written this book so that it can be used as a core text in a science methods course for preservice or inservice teachers. But its approach and content are forged from my own struggles to find material that would address the school science experience as a natural part of the classroom's daily life. In my experience, I have observed that many future teachers are apprehensive about teaching science. They don't believe that they themselves are "scientific" or that they can teach students to think like "scientists." Often, like many others in our society, they have a culturally constructed stereotype of the scientist: a kind of mad genius in a white lab coat who does strange, inexplicable things with test tubes. Unfortunately, many conventional texts do little to counter these preconceptions, and when teachers begin to work with students, they often convey the same apprehension and the same brand of stereotype. This book attempts to break the cycle by showing teachers that they do indeed have a "scientist within." By discovering their own scientific selves, teachers can reawaken the joy and wonder of unraveling the mysteries of the natural world, and they can share that experience with their students.

This Book's Approach to Science Teaching and Learning

In addition to deliberate efforts to awaken the reader's scientific self, this book relies on three other key elements: (1) the use of Science Stories derived from classroom experiences; (2) an emphasis on constructivist principles of learning; and (3) frequent connections to the *National Science Education Standards*.

Science Stories: Narrative as a Tool for Science Teaching and Learning

Sixteen years ago, when I began to teach the science methods course at a major metropolitan university, I started telling stories about my own experiences in doing science with children. I found that the stories helped my students understand both what "science" is and how they could facilitate science experiences in their own classrooms.

At about the same time, I was traveling to various school districts to help teachers create science experiences in their classrooms. I spent many months visiting schools and modeling science lessons. As I learned a great deal from the students and their teachers, I realized that their stories had important implications for my teacher education classes. Thus my repertoire of stories naturally expanded.

The use of narrative is not new to teacher education, but it is a fresh approach to the science methods course. This book presents much of its theory and its practical advice by way of stories about students and teachers actually doing science together. Rather than imbibing generalities out of context, readers can see what the principles mean in typical classroom situations.

To supplement its narratives, this book uses many strategies to encourage readers to reflect on these classroom scenarios. The stories themselves are set in a framework of discussion that helps readers to see the larger picture. Following each story or set of stories, an **Expanding Meanings** section focuses on the teaching principles, science ideas, and science standards illustrated by the narrative. These sections also offer questions and resources that challenge readers to explore further on their own.

Perhaps the most important thing to be said about this contextualized, narrative approach is that I have seen it work in my own courses. Many of my former students have gone on to become excellent teachers who inspire children to engage in remarkable science explorations. My experience with these science stories leads me to believe that they are an important teacher education tool. And as students begin their field work, they will create more science stories.

A Constructivist Foundation

This book is deeply rooted in constructivism and in the constructivist approach to teaching and learning science. Chapter 1 presents some key tenets of constructivism to provide a solid theoretical base, and later chapters develop and illustrate these important principles. The emphasis throughout is not just on science ideas but on *how* students learn such ideas—how they construct their own meanings. The science stories illustrate many different aspects of this making of meaning, demonstrating how teachers can best mediate the process.

Besides advocating a constructivist approach, this book attempts to model it as well. Readers are continually challenged not to absorb the text passively, but to make their own meaning from it—to think about and extend the concepts and examples it presents. I encourage readers to reflect on their own science experiences as well as on their interactions with their students. The book envisages the study of science as a lifelong journey of exploration and inquiry. Getting this journey started is perhaps the most important task for science educators.

Meaningful Links to the *National Science Education Standards*

Throughout the text, I refer to various aspects of the *National Science Education Standards* (NSES) and to the instructional practices that they imply. Key points of the NSES are emphasized, including the following:

■ the skills of scientific inquiry

■ active learning

■ extended investigations and problem solving

■ collaborative and cooperative learning

■ integrating technology fully into teaching and learning

■ making connections to students' lived experiences

■ responding to and learning from student diversity

Coverage of standards is now highlighted throughout the text by the use of marginal icons.

New Features of the Third Edition

Although revisions have been made throughout the text, the principal changes in this third edition of *Science Stories* fall into four categories:

■ **Broadening of the text to include middle school.** The first two editions of *Science Stories* focused on teaching science in elementary school. For the sake of teacher education courses that combine middle school and elementary science in a single methods course, this edition also includes science stories from grades six through eight, and the corresponding text passages address concepts and issues relevant to middle school students.

■ **Increased emphasis on design technology and other activities in which students use technological tools.** Chapter 10, for example, has a new science story about a design challenge, and Chapter 12 includes an assessment rubric for a WebQuest. Throughout the text, technology is emphasized as a seamless connection to the science learning context. We want to prepare students to access and generate information using all of the appropriate technologies.

■ **Expanded discussion of the National Educational Technology Standards (NETS) and new Standards icons.** In Chapter 1, Chapter 12, and elsewhere, this edition devotes increased attention to the technology standards developed by the International Society for Technology in Education (ISTE). These standards suggest guidelines for what both teachers and students should be able to do with technological tools. Standards coverage is now highlighted with new marginal icons.

■ **Guidelines for teaching diverse learners.** Although previous editions stressed the point that students bring a wide range of backgrounds and experiences to school, this third edition presents more explicit suggestions (especially in Chapter 11) for teaching diverse learners.

Learning Features of This Text

In addition to the science stories, the vital theoretical background, and the frequent links to the national standards, this book provides readers with important tools to help them use the material effectively. These tools include:

Focusing Questions. At the beginning of each chapter, the reader is asked to reflect on a few key questions. These questions are not simply a disguised summary of the chapter content. Rather, they try to make a personal connection to the reader in a way that invites thought about the chapter topics.

Expanding Meanings. As mentioned earlier, the science stories in this book are followed by a section titled "Expanding Meanings." Designed to stimulate reflection, Expanding Meanings sections include five parts:

The Teaching Ideas Behind This Story. A list of the science teaching ideas that are demonstrated by the science story. In this section the reader comes to understand the reasoning behind the techniques modeled by the teacher in the story.

The Science Ideas Behind This Story. An explanation of specific science concepts that the reader should understand in order to grasp the science story fully.

The Science Standards Behind This Story. Description of particular national standards that the science story illustrates.

Questions for Further Exploration. Probing questions that set readers thinking about matters that range beyond the specific story.

Resources for Further Exploration. Electronic and print resources that expand on the ideas explored in the story. In the chapters that do not include science stories, the resources appear at the end of the chapter.

Key Terms. At the end of each chapter is a list of key terms; each term is referenced to the page where it is defined.

Marginal Notes. Short phrases in the page margins reinforce important points throughout the text. Many are deliberately designed to provoke the reader's reflection.

Two sections at the back of the book also provide significant resources for the reader:

More Resources for Teachers. This section provides a wealth of useful information that encourages readers to go beyond this book into their own explorations of science and science teaching.

Glossary. The Glossary provides clear, concise definitions of key scientific and pedagogical concepts.

Companion Web site

A **companion web site** (accessible from **http://college.hmco.com/education**) contains many valuable resources for both students and instructors using the text. The site features additional science stories about teaching and learning science in real classrooms, as well as a set of authentic projects based on my experience with *The Mathematics, Science, and Technology* (MST) project research and investigations. Also included on the web site are chapter-by-chapter discussion questions, links to national standards and state frameworks, connections to Houghton Mifflin's Science Center site, and much more.

For instructors who use *Science Stories* in a course, the web site offers sample course syllabi, chapter-by-chapter instructional resources, and assessment approaches.

Acknowledgments

The "seeds" for this book were planted many years ago when I began working with Peggy McIntosh, co-director of the National S.E.E.D. (Seeking Educational Equity and Diversity) Project, a faculty development initiative on inclusive curriculum. At Peggy's urging, I began to tell my science stories with the remarkable precollege teachers of the S.E.E.D. project. Moreover, through my association with my S.E.E.D. colleagues, Judy Logan, author of *Teaching Stories* (1997), and the late Cathy Nelson, co-editor of *Seeding the Process of Multicultural Education* (1998), I learned the value of telling our stories and the promise that these stories hold for teachers. I thank them with all my heart for their vision, their friendship, and their wonderful, authentic work.

Clearly, there would be no stories to tell without the teachers from many different areas who invited me into their classrooms and shared their students with me. I want to express my thanks to the teachers from Deer Isle, Maine; from the Unquowa School in Fairfield, Connecticut; from Somerville Elementary School in Ridgewood, New Jersey; from the districts of Port Chester, Tarrytown, and Somers in New York State; and from Beth Am Day School in South Miami, Florida. I appreciate my local Long Island schools, where I visited many times and observed many wonderful science experiences. My special thanks as well to the teachers of the Munsey Park School in Manhasset, who let me use their new science room and allowed me to work with engaging, interesting students for a whole semester. Thana Giradhar from Ridgewood Public Schools and Heather Stoller, Lorraine Amdur, Ilana Johnston, and Marie Ciota from Somers Public Schools are well represented in this textbook. Marcella Slobodzian and her students from Northport Middle School were an inspiration for much of the work in this edition.

The third edition is also informed by my work in Central Queensland, Australia, specifically at St. Anthony's School and Central Queensland University in Rockhampton. Living and working on the east coast of Queensland provided me with a renewed understanding of science as a way of knowing the world and as a universal constant for motivating and inspiring the lives of elementary and middle school students. It also reaffirmed my conviction that, wherever you are and wherever you live, good science teaching is meaningful and constructivist, honors the learner, and shares the natural world with *all* students. My friends and colleagues Ken Appleton and Jan Bulman of Rockhampton greatly influenced my thinking for this third edition. Their stories and approaches to science education inspired me. Thanks, too, to Kon and Rhonda Staples for providing me with a flat in which to work on the third edition, 12,000 miles from home.

My students at Hofstra University and Central Queensland University are another inspiration for the science stories. With their candor and their insight, they have helped me to understand that they need a different kind of science methods book. They have also shown me that stories work! My graduate students in Mathematics, Science, and Technology contributed new stories to this third edition. My Hofstra mentors, Maureen Miletta and Jane Goldman, were a constant source of encouragement and support. Although it is possible for me to remember where the ideas for the text originated, it would have been impossible to turn them into a science methods textbook without the vision of Loretta Wolozin, then a senior sponsoring editor at Houghton Mifflin. She traveled to Long Island one day to convince me that these stories could make a textbook that would speak to the preservice teacher in a way no other science methods textbook could. Loretta was convincing, and I will always be grateful for her persistence, support, and vision. To help me along, she solicited the services of a creative developmental editor, Doug Gordon, who understood from the outset that *Science Stories* was different and important. It would never have become a book without Doug Gordon, and he has mentored the third edition as well.

My sincere appreciation also goes to Lisa Mafrici, who was there from the beginning of my relationship with Houghton Mifflin and continued to work with me for the second and third editions, and to the talented project editor, Jane Lee, whose production skills helped me handle the countless tedious tasks of creating a usable, reader-friendly text. Several reviewers also offered important guidance and feedback for the third edition. Sincere thanks in particular to Catherine Cavanaugh, University of North Florida; Gregory Coverdale, St. Cloud State University; and

Suneetha S. deSilva, Rocky Mountain College. Thanks also to the reviewers of the previous editions, who contributed to the shaping of this book: Elizabeth L. Dershimer, Stetson University; Daniel C. Dobey, State University of New York at Fredonia; Chuck Downing, Point Loma Nazarene University; Susan A. Everett, University of Iowa; Pamela Fraser-Abder, New York University; Samuel Hausfather, Berry College, Georgia; Robin McGrew-Zoubi, Sam Houston State University; David M. Moss, University of New Hampshire; Donna Gail Shaw, University of Alaska Anchorage; Roderick M. Thronson, Carroll College; Deborah J. Tippins, University of Georgia; and Robert E. Yager, University of Iowa.

At the very beginning, it was my mother, Beatrice Deutsch, who encouraged my own scientific self to develop and flourish. Today, it is my husband, Bob Koch, my children, Robin and Brian Tarantino and Betsy Koch, and my granddaughters, Kayley Elizabeth Tarantino and Sydney Reese Tarantino, who nurture my present-day scientific self with their own appreciation of the natural world.

Janice Koch

The Scientist Within

Where I grew up, in an inner-city neighborhood of New York, summertime recreation was usually afforded by the local park. In addition to playgrounds and sprinklers, there were grassy fields and trees. I often occupied myself by lying in the grass and watching the insects on their journey through the grass and clover. Sometimes an ant would crawl up onto my hand and explore my fingers, my palm, and my wrist. In amazement I would watch this ant as it worked feverishly to find familiar ground, knowing it was not on grassy turf.

The park held many other fascinations. In the early fall, I collected acorns from the huge oak trees, as well as "polly noses," the winged seeds from maple trees found in the northeastern part of the United States. Often I would lie on a blanket, looking up in the sky, and make up stories about the clouds. Their formations became animals or dragons, depending on the day.

On occasions when my family and I visited a restaurant, I would always mix the salt, pepper, sugar, and ketchup into the complimentary glass of water on the table. "Ugh," my father would exclaim, "she's making such a mess." "Don't be silly, dear," remarked my mother. "She is exploring. Maybe she will grow up to be a scientist."

As you can see from this story, my mother, although not herself a scientist, had a feeling about what scientists do, and she "coded" my early explorations as "scientific." You, too, are probably more of a scientist than you realize. The chapter on "Locating Your Scientific Self" will help you explore your scientific self, especially your personal "science baggage"—the experiences that helped shape your beliefs about science and scientists. You'll write about and reflect on those experiences and start your own science journal. These exercises will underscore the relationship between doing science with students and feeling scientific about yourself.

First, however, the chapter, "An Invitation to Teaching Science," will give you an overview of what science and science teaching are all about.

1 An Invitation to Teaching Science

FOCUSING QUESTIONS

- When you were a child, did you wonder about how things in nature worked? Did you ever try to find out by exploring the world around you?
- If you hear that someone is a "scientist," what does that suggest to you?
- How do you think people learn to understand scientific concepts? And why do so many people have difficulty understanding such concepts?

Thinking back to your childhood, you may remember wondering about the world around you—wondering what things were and how they worked. I remember being puzzled, for instance, about how people could fit into airplanes because the planes looked like tiny birds in the sky. I also wondered why we never found a tiny chick when we cracked open chicken eggs. Perhaps you wondered why the sky appears blue, why leaves change colors in some regions in the fall, or why cracks in the pavement appear after an icy winter.

If you and I had such thoughts about the world around us, it stands to reason that other children must have had them as well. In fact, I believe there is a childhood scientist in each of us who is waiting to be awakened. Ever curious about their surroundings, children have an instinct to explore, take apart, and experiment with the things around them. In this way, they propel themselves toward their own important discoveries.

Unfortunately, too often these early instincts are buried by later experiences, including what can feel like the chore of learning science in school. You may have some vivid memories of sitting in a classroom and being bored or stifled by science. If you're lucky, you'll also remember one or more science classrooms that inspired you to think and investigate.

I firmly believe that it is the task of elementary and middle school science to nurture children's instincts for exploration. If you plan to teach, this book is designed to help you discover and develop the budding scientist in each of your students. It will help you to rethink your ideas about science and science learning. You'll see that all the "why" and "how" questions that students have about their world can wend their way into our classrooms and enrich our teaching of science. And I hope you'll come to understand that science can be a highly personal and engaging experience, for students and teacher alike.

This book has a lot to say about personal experiences. I want to take you as directly as possible into classrooms so you can see how science involves teachers and students learning together. Before I do though, you should know some key ideas that will help you to make the best possible use of this book.

What Is Science, and Why Teach It?

How do you think of "science"?

> *It might seem unfair to reward a person for having so much pleasure over the years, asking the maize plant to solve specific problems and then watching its responses.*
> —BARBARA McCLINTOCK, ON RECEIVING THE NOBEL PRIZE FOR PHYSIOLOGY AND MEDICINE (1983)

What do you think of when you think of "science"? Reactions to this question vary. Many new teachers, making word associations, think "test tubes," "laboratories," or "white coats." There are actually many ways to think about the subject of science. For example, we can think of science as a way to explore nature. Some people think of it as a subject that holds the key to understanding the secrets of the universe. That sounds exciting—and a bit mysterious as well. Many people think about a long list of facts to be memorized—a common notion of school science.

Whatever our associations, we should remember that science is basically an area of knowledge created by people—men and women—who devote much of their energies to exploring some part of nature and trying to make sense of it. In this sense, human societies have a long tradition of scientific exploration. Ever since the dawn of civilization, people have studied nature and tried to understand it.

Science as a Process, a Set of Ideas, and a Set of Attitudes

Defining science

To me, the best definition of science takes account of three different facets of the subject. Science can be described as a *process*, a *set of ideas*, and *a set of attitudes*.

The middle part of that definition, the "set of ideas," is probably familiar to you. The mention of science typically conjures up images of biology, chemistry, physics, geology, and earth science—the subjects commonly taught as science in schools.

Scientific method

The notion of science as a process may be harder to grasp. Yet this part of the definition has important implications for the "set of ideas" part of the definition of science. As they explore nature, scientists go through a series of steps that help them to learn more about their area of study. This process is sometimes called the **scientific method.** In fact, there are many scientific methods, but they all have some principles in common.

What Is This Thing Called Science?

Over the years, scientists and many others have written about the distinguishing characteristics of science. There is no one absolute definition of science, but here are a few interesting attempts to describe what makes science different from other ways of studying the world:

science The observation, identification, description, experimental investigation, and theoretical explanation of phenomena.

—*American Heritage Dictionary of the English Language* (2001)

Contrary to popular belief, scientists are not detached observers of nature and the facts they discover are not simply inherent in the natural phenomena they observe. Scientists construct facts by constantly making decisions about what they will consider significant, what experiments they should pursue, and how they will describe their observations.

—Ruth Hubbard and Elijah Wald (1993, p. 7)

Science is the belief in the ignorance of experts.

—Richard P. Feynman (1968, p. 319)

Science advances, not by the accumulation of new facts . . . but by the continuous development of new concepts.

—James B. Conant (1966, p. 25)

Science is the process of "finding out." It is the art of interrogating nature, a system of inquiry that requires curiosity, intellectual honesty, skepticism, tolerance for ambiguity, and openness to new ideas and the sharing of knowledge.

—Roberta H. Barba (1998, p. 227)

Science is forming questions about the way things work and trying to answer these questions through experimentation and observation. It is having an open mind and rejoicing when the outcome is a surprise.

—Meryl Rosenblum, elementary school teacher (1996)

What do these statements have in common? How do they match your own conception of science?

The Process   Science as process refers to the ways in which scientists go about their work. They usually begin by exploring the questions about nature that engage them. The questions themselves are not necessarily obscure. Your early wonderings that I spoke about at the beginning of this chapter could in fact lead to a scientific question. This is true of many children's wonderings.

What is a "scientific" question?

Then what makes a question a *scientific* question? A question is considered scientific when, in order to find the answer, people usually go through these steps:

- Make careful observations.

- Set up an experiment and explore the results.

■ Test their ideas through further experimentation.

■ Ask others to repeat the experiments.

These steps are what we mean by the process of science. Scientists collect information through careful observation of nature and natural phenomena. They explore and test their ideas by setting up experiments (and, sometimes, by trial and error). Others repeat their experiments in the search for consistent outcomes. To help make one set of results comparable to another set, different scientists follow similar procedures in their investigations.

This process is what sets science apart from other ways of knowing the world. Using the process involves a particular set of skills that are often called **process skills.** Observing is an example of a process skill. So are predicting and making inferences, classifying, and planning an experiment, to name a few.

We use process skills every day.

It's important to realize that the process skills come into play not just in science labs, but in all areas of life in our increasingly complex world. Often we use science process skills without even "coding" them as science. Every day, for example, you make observations about the weather and decide what to wear on the basis of your observations. In doing this, you are using two of the basic process skills. In later chapters of this book, we will explore these skills in detail.

A Set of Ideas   Through the process of observation, experimentation and exploration, and repetition, scientists develop concepts about the natural world. These concepts are referred to in this book as "science ideas." To put it simply, they are understandings about the natural world. Most high school science textbooks are filled with these understandings.

What are science ideas?

Science ideas include definitions and explanations of natural phenomena. For example, in science, energy is defined as the ability to do work. Science books define work as the process by which a force moves a given mass through a distance. Energy, therefore, is anything that can make matter move. Scientists calculate the amounts of energy that are required to do different kinds of work in nature. As this example shows, the language of science sometimes uses terms differently from the way they are used in everyday life.

You can see that science's set of ideas is inseparable from science as process. Without the process, there could be no ideas. Without ideas to spur more questions, there would be no need for further processes.

One way of thinking about science ideas or concepts is to classify them into three major areas of science: life science, earth science, and physical science. Another way of classifying science ideas is according to certain overarching conceptual categories. For example, science helps us to understand systems such as human body systems and the solar system. Science also helps us understand interactions and patterns of change, such as the ones we see in the life cycles of animals and plants and in the relationships between matter and energy. In the chapter "Science Content and Curriculum," and in many of the science stories throughout the text, you'll see how science ideas relate to the conceptual categories of systems and interactions, as well as to the more traditional areas of life, earth, and physical science.

Scientific attitudes

A Set of Attitudes Another facet of science includes a set of attitudes or dispositions that encourage people to engage in scientific study. Scientific attitudes evolve when children are engaged in the processes of science. These attitudes include a curiosity and sense of wonder about how the natural world works, as well as an excitement about the journey of discovery. Science is actually much more about "trying to find things out" than it is about "knowing answers." Scientific attitudes therefore include persistence and a desire to find evidence to support statements, an open-mindedness and willingness to change one's mind when confronted with new evidence, and a willingness to cooperate and collaborate with others.

The Nature of Science

What science knows and how it knows

The "nature of science" is a subject much discussed by many researchers in both science education and professional science as well as by philosophers and historians of science (Lederman, 1992). Understanding the nature of science includes knowing both *what* science knows and *how* science knows what it knows—the science ideas, the processes, and the attitudes that influence the processes. In schools, we often teach only what a specific field of science knows, not the genuine nature of science itself.

Consider this example of a nature-of-science activity. A class of twenty college students is divided into five groups. Each group of four students receives an identical set of sixteen canceled checks from the same family. The checks are in sealed envelopes, and each group is allowed to randomly select four checks at a time. After each round of check selection, group members are asked to record the ideas they have developed about the family as a result of exploring their canceled checks. After all sixteen checks have been analyzed in relation to the others, the group recorder writes down—on a large piece of poster paper for all to see—the tentative conclusions that the group has reached about the family.

When the students review all the conclusions, they find that each group's story varies in some ways from the others—except for three or four main ideas about the family. The class members decide that these three or four ideas are ones that they can begin to call their *theories* about this family. They suggest ways to explore their family theories further. How do they know they are right? They ask me, their professor, if I know the right answer. I do not. I am an explorer, too.

How does this story relate to the nature of science? The canceled-check activity is an excellent metaphor for the way scientists work:

- Just like the student groups, several scientists often explore the same problem, with identical evidence, but in different sequences.

- The order in which the students select their checks from the envelopes influences their story. Similarly, scientists often find that the sequence in which they have encountered their evidence influences their developing ideas.

- The discussion each student group has about the evidence also influences the outcomes. Scientists, too, work in groups and confer about their evidence regularly.

- Finally, unlike many school science experiences you may have had, real science proceeds to find answers where no previous answers exist. Similarly, the students in our example developed theories based on how they saw the evidence and what their own experiences told them. They did not pursue preexisting "right" or "wrong" answers.

Such is the nature of science: a quest for new knowledge based on repeated efforts to explore the evidence and draw conclusions within a social community of workers.

The Value of Teaching Science

Lurking in the back of your mind may be a question about why we teach science before high school. The answer has three parts, corresponding to our three-part definition of science.

What's the point of teaching science in elementary and middle school?

First, the set of ideas that we are calling science ideas is increasingly vital in our technologically oriented society. Many educators, cultural commentators, and leaders of industry have often stated that knowing what science is about is crucial for everyone. Many of today's jobs require some scientific knowledge, and even our everyday decisions—from what to eat to which vehicle to buy—can be affected by our scientific understanding or lack of it. In today's world, it's never too early to begin learning science, and elementary and middle schools are expected to do their part. A good science program teaches science ideas, processes, and attitudes that prepare students for further, more complex studies in science.

Second, the skills that students acquire by engaging in the scientific processes are useful in many fields other than science. In fact, studies show that science in the early grades has the potential to help children to become critical thinkers, to reason carefully, to solve problems, and to make informed decisions (AAAS, 1993). Elementary and middle school students who engage in scientific activities in their classroom build confidence in themselves as thinkers.

Third, by cultivating scientific attitudes, we can help students improve their abilities to explore a problem from many perspectives, confer with their classmates and their teacher, and become knowledge builders and meaning makers.

In all these ways, science learning prepares students not just for biology and chemistry, but for English, history, and social studies as well—and, in the most fundamental sense, for life. In later chapters of this book, you will learn more about science skills and attitudes and their all-important relationship to science content.

How Do Students Learn Science?

Learning about learning is one of the tasks associated with becoming a teacher. In particular, understanding how students *learn* science is vital to becoming an effective science teacher. This intricate and complex subject is one of the most exciting challenges in teaching. As you prepare for your chosen profession, you have the opportunity to learn about the ways students learn, not just from books and lectures, but directly from and with their classmates.

Major influences on this book

First, though, it will help you to have some grounding in the ideas of other professionals who have studied the subject. Many individuals have made important contributions to our understanding of how students learn. The scholars, philosophers, and learning theorists who have most influenced this book are John Dewey, Jean Piaget, Jerome Bruner, Lev Vygotsky, and Ernst von Glaserfeld. Although these thinkers did not always agree completely, I have developed my own model of teaching science based on much of their thinking. This model is particularly influenced by a family of theories about knowledge and learning called constructivism.

Key Tenets of Constructivist Theory

Basic to **constructivism** is the idea that all knowledge is *constructed*. This means that knowledge is not passively received. Rather, it is actively constructed by the learner as he or she comes to experience the world.

Do you have a new idea? Or do you construct it?

This sounds like a simple notion, but, in fact, it is not. It describes a complex and recursive process by which learners engage in experiences, think about those experiences, see how they fit in with their prior constructions, and then, sometimes, formulate new constructions. Figure 1.1 illustrates this pattern in the way our minds work.

Piaget and Bruner   One of the key contributors to this understanding of the learning process was the Swiss scholar and scientist Jean Piaget. Beginning in the 1920s, Piaget conducted countless interviews and research studies with children of varying ages. He was able to describe *stages of cognitive development* that the children passed through—that is, specific times in the children's development when different mental structures began to emerge. Although he recognized that children vary, he pegged his stages of development to general age ranges (see Table 1.1). For example, he believed that most children are in the sensorimotor stage when they are between eighteen months and two years of age and in the preoperational stage when they are between two and seven. He also believed that a child's

Piaget: Stages in a child's mental growth

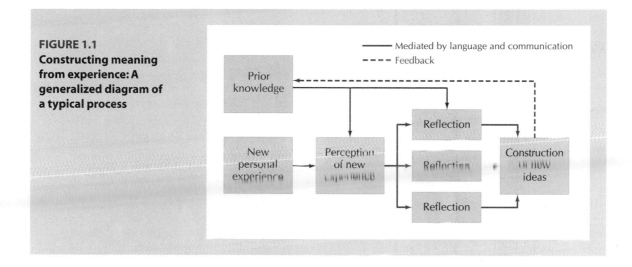

FIGURE 1.1
Constructing meaning from experience: A generalized diagram of a typical process

progress through the stages is biologically determined. Most important for our purposes, Piaget concluded that the growth of knowledge is the result of individual constructions made by the learner. In other words, Piaget decided that knowledge is not passively received but is actively built up by the learner—a process of invention or creation, not reception. As he recognized, this gives tremendous responsibility to the learner.

In describing the stages of cognitive development, Piaget demonstrated that at each stage of maturation, the child is ready for a different type of learning. That is, the types of ideas that learners construct vary with each maturational stage. Some critics of Piaget's stages assert that children can be in several stages at the same time and that the stages cannot be neatly defined by specific ages.

Bruner: Discovery learning

Jerome Bruner, a leading supporter of Piaget's work, suggested that at any given stage of cognitive development, teaching should proceed in a way that allows children to discover ideas for themselves. His work became known as **discovery learning.** He differed from Piaget in one important respect. Whereas Piaget believed that readiness for a particular type of learning depended on a child's stage of cognitive development, Bruner noticed that children are always ready to learn a concept *at some level*. Realizing this, Bruner emphasized the importance of returning to science topics at various ages, of revisiting them at different stages of the child's development (Bruner, 1960). This produces a *spiraling* of science curriculum topics, as the same broad topics are revisited at higher grade levels. For science topics that educators and scientists see as meaningful and relevant for students' lives, this practice has become an important part of curriculum planning.

For many years, Piaget's stages of development and Bruner's discovery learning ideas were the basis for teaching science. Common to these theorists' views is the understanding that:

TABLE 1.1	Piaget's Stages of Human Cognitive Development	
Stage	**Age Range**	**Characteristics**
Sensorimotor	18 months to 2 years	Infants explore their environment with their physical senses. They construct such basic concepts as object permanence (the fact that an object can continue to exist even when they do not perceive it).
Preoperational	2–7 years	Children learn language and classify objects into groups, assigning names and categories. They begin to see logical relationships.
Concrete operations	7–11 years	Children build their simple categories into more general categories and apply these in mental operations. Gradually, their thinking evolves from the concrete toward the abstract.
Formal operations	Beginning at 11–15 years	Learners can draw abstract conclusions and master complicated, higher-order processes.

■ Children are active knowers.

■ Children construct their ideas on the basis of their experiences of the world.

■ Children's *prior knowledge*—that is, what they have learned from all their previous experiences—plays a crucial role in determining how they integrate a new concept.

Prior knowledge

This last concept, concerning children's prior knowledge, warrants further reflection. It demands that we recognize that all students come to the classroom with funds of knowledge based on their past experiences. In fact, students arrive at our doors with varying ranges of experiences and therefore varying types of prior knowledge. It is fascinating to discover how students think about new experiences on the basis of where they have been and how they have lived before we met them.

Students are knowers—even before we teach them anything.

This way of understanding learning requires us to view our students as "knowers"—even before we teach them anything. Indeed, they *are* knowers. Young as they may be, they have lived several years and acquired many experiences before meeting us. Their experiences have led them to construct their own ideas about the world. These ideas become the framework on which they try to "fit in" new ideas. It is as though the students ask themselves, "How does this match my prior thinking? Where can I place it?"

Indeed, perhaps the most important thing to know about your students is what they already know! We need to understand students' existing beliefs in order to help them construct new ideas. As you will see later in this book, having conversations with your students about their prior understandings helps both you and them gain insight into their thinking.

Vygotsky and the Social Context   Piaget's work, which dealt in detail with the individual learner, was criticized for not taking into account the learner's social context. Constructing an understanding of the world does

Children learn in a particular environment.

not happen in a social or cultural vacuum. The Russian psychologist Lev Vygotsky demonstrated how social contexts influence the ideas that individuals construct as they communicate with each other. For instance, the teacher and students in a classroom use language that is socially and culturally accepted in their specific environment. This language may include slang, regional dialects, or other special usages. The ideas that students construct in the classroom conform to these socially accepted usages and meanings. Brooks and Brooks (1999) put it this way: "Coming to know one's world is a function of caring about one's world. Caring about one's world is fostered by communities of learners involved in trying to answer similar . . . problems" (p. 30).

Three Roles of Constructivism   As we explore constructivism as a learning theory, we will see that it has important implications for the way we teach science. Even though the idea that students construct new knowledge by attaching meaning to their prior knowledge sounds simple, creating teaching practice around this theory is quite complex. This is because constructivism is really more than one thing; it conceives the learner as playing three distinct roles. Understanding these roles is important to understanding how science educators use this learning theory to develop their teaching strategies.

The philosopher D. C. Phillips (1995) identified three roles of constructivism—the active learner, the social learner, and the creative learner:

A learner's three roles

- The role of *active learner* relates to knowledge and understanding as something actively acquired. Constructivism generally casts the learner in an active role. Instead of just passively listening, reading, and working on routine exercises, the learner is engaged in some sort of activity.

- The role of *social learner* relates to knowledge and understanding as social constructs. Ideas are not constructed in isolation; we construct ideas in dialogue with others—they are, in a sense, "co-constructed." You will see this when you read the stories of teachers and students doing science in later chapters.

- The role of creative learner refers to knowledge and understanding as something created or re-created by the learner. This means that we need to create and sometimes re-create understandings for ourselves by going over ideas, acting them out, and doing experiments related to these ideas. In the chapter "Science Content and Curriculum," we explore some science concepts, and I invite you to become actively engaged in re-creating these concepts for yourself.

Implications for Teaching

You may wonder why constructivism has become a major influence in contemporary science education. It is because researchers have found that traditional methods of instruction are inadequate to help students form deep meanings and thoughtful understandings of ideas. We have come to understand that the stimuli we receive are simply not enough to convey meaning—that, for example, merely reading this book is not sufficient for gaining understanding. (To demonstrate this point for yourself, see the feature "Traditional Science Instruction.") To some extent, the individual must construct or reconstruct what things mean (Perkins, 1999).

It makes sense, therefore, to think about organizing our teaching practice to reflect this understanding. By that, I mean that we can translate this theory of knowing and learning into a theory of teaching practice. A number

Traditional Science Instruction

Imagine that you receive the following reading assignment in a science class:

The Montillation of Traxoline

Traxoline is a new form of zionter. It is montilled in Ceristanna. Ceristannians gristerlate large amounts of fevon and then bracter it to montil traxoline. It is very important to learn about traxoline. It is one of our most lukized snezlaus.

Now imagine that you have to respond to the following questions with the correct answer.

1. What is traxoline?

2. Where is it montilled?

3. How is it made?

4. Why is traxoline important?

On the basis of the reading, you can probably answer all of these questions correctly. For example, for

question 4, you would write, "Traxoline is important because it is one of our most lukized snezlaus." You would score 100 percent on the assignment. But what does it mean that all your answers are correct? How much will you remember tomorrow?

The above paragraph was developed by Judith Lanier at the University of Michigan as a useful metaphor for the way science is often taught and assessed. Of course, there are no such substances as traxoline and fevon, and Ceristanna is not a real place. But by reading the paragraph and answering the questions, you can see how little you gain by memorizing new terms and facts that have no meaning in your own mind.

Reprinted by permission.

of researchers, including Noddings (1990) and Brooks and Brooks (1999), have presented ways of looking at constructivism as a methodological tool. In fact, the constructivist learning theory has helped transform many classrooms into places where students are active participants in their own learning. That is one of the goals of this book: to help you translate the theory into practice in your own classroom.

Concrete Experiences   One common classroom technique is to have students use concrete activities or experiences. A *concrete experience* involves interacting with objects and materials in the student's real world. These concrete experiences are also called "hands-on experiences" because they typically engage students in exploring materials by physically manipulating them. For example, students studying electricity may work with batteries, bulbs, and wires to construct different types of electrical circuits. Or for a science unit on fossils and ancient life-forms students may take a trip to a museum to explore the remains of dinosaurs.

Making meaning from concrete experiences

From engaging in such activities, students develop ideas about the natural world and begin to construct their own ideas and meanings in the way described by Piaget and Bruner. So, when we think of "learning science," we can envision it as a process of making meaning from concrete experiences. Also, as Vygotsky pointed out, it stands to reason that this process of meaning making is influenced by children's social interactions. Therefore, when we think about students learning science, we should imagine them engaging in concrete experiences *along with* their peers and their teachers.

Hands-on activities have been common in science lessons for decades. However, three crucial elements are often left out:

Finding the "fit"

1. *Connections to the students' own lives.* Because, as learners, all of us try to fit new experiences into what we already know, it follows that we will learn most readily if we can find the proper fit. If students view a school science experience as being completely unrelated to their lives, they are not likely to learn from it. To help students see the connections, we need to begin by valuing their own prior experiences and their own thinking. After all, it is through their own thinking that they construct new ideas.

2. *Opportunities for the students to actively reflect on their experiences.* This is extremely important. The process of active engagement must include discussion and reflection in order for the meaning making to happen. When hands-on science became a prominent science teaching movement, many well-meaning teachers used the experiences but neglected to reflect on them with their students—and not much science learning took place. After all, the real learning is not situated in students' hands, but in their minds. Some people therefore prefer to speak of "hands-on/minds-on" science.

Hands-on versus minds-on

3. *Clearly defined conceptual goals for the students.* As the teacher, you must have an idea of where your students' active experiences will lead them.

Knowing where your students are going

There may be many ways for students to make meaning about a science concept, but you yourself need to be clear about where you are taking them. Then you can help the students use their initial ideas to progress toward new ideas. In this way, you can extend their thinking and help them to create new understandings of the natural world. You will see many examples of this process in later chapters.

Meaningful Experiences   With the basic notions of constructivism in mind, we can say that its most important implication for teaching practice is that the learner must be actively engaged in science activities in order to construct new ideas about the natural world. We often refer to such activities as **meaningful science experiences.** A science experience can be considered meaningful if it:

When is a science experience meaningful?

■ Relates to the students' everyday lived experiences.

■ Engages students in the key processes of science: observing and predicting, inferring and hypothesizing, manipulating objects, investigating, and imagining.

■ Stimulates the students to reflect on what they are exploring and to come up with their own ideas.

■ Reveals the students' thinking.

■ Leads to new understanding.

This book can help you to construct meaningful experiences in science for your students. It will also help you understand the role a teacher plays in this process. Teaching science has a lot to do with providing students with experiences and listening to their ideas, as the following science story shows.

 SCIENCE STORY

Listening to Students' Ideas

Darlene McKie's third-grade class is studying sound energy. Ms. McKie has carefully engaged the students in experiences that should lead them to understand that sound travels by means of vibrations through a substance. The substance can be a gas, such as air, or it can be a solid or a liquid. The children use instruments to tap the base of their desks while holding their ears to the desktop. They "hear" the sound made through the desk. They also tap rocks together under water in pails and hear the sound made by the rocks. They place vibrating tuning forks in shallow pans of water and watch as the water splashes. Terms like *sound* and *vibrations* are used often in this classroom.

Discussing the students' ideas

After these hands-on activities, Ms. McKie gathers the students around to discuss their ideas. She asks the class, "Why isn't there sound on the moon?" The children sit quietly, unsure what the teacher is "looking for." Ms. McKie then explains, "There is no air on the moon, so there is nothing to vibrate, and there is no sound on the moon."

One girl, Terri, raises her hand and says, "But the moon is a solid, right?"

"Yes," replies Ms. McKie.

A puzzling question

"So if sound travels through a solid like a desk," Terri continues, "why can't sound travel *through* the moon?"

Ms. McKie realizes that Terri is grappling with the abstract concepts of sound energy and what it means for sound to "travel." Wisely, Ms. McKie looks at the class and then opens Terri's question up for the group's consideration, even though the day is carefully scheduled and Ms. McKie is going over the allotted time for science.

Listening and Mediating   What do you think of Ms. McKie's decision to discuss Terri's question with the class?

In classrooms, scientific knowledge is often bundled into packets of information that are frequently focused on a manipulative activity or experience. Under constraints to meet local state requirements for time spent on standardized testing, teachers often experience pressure to "cover"

What does it weigh? Kindergarten children are engaged in weighing objects and recording their mass. Engaging children in inquiry means that they often seek answers to their questions by manipulating materials.

Elizabeth Crews/Stock Boston

curriculum and are forced to ignore the processes required for thoughtful consideration of a topic. Yet everything we know about how learners construct meaning flies in the face of rushing through activities and their related concepts. If Ms. McKie had cut off the discussion of Terri's question, she would have cut short the possibilities for building useful concepts. The role of the teacher in this scenario is one of an active *listener* and *learner.* As much as we know about a topic, we cannot know *everything.* We can, however, come to know our students' thinking and follow their ideas to a reasonable conclusion—even if the conclusion is that "sound may travel through the moon, but we are not sure." With this process, we validate the fact that the students have been grappling with a significant concept and that in their struggle to understand they have come up with a new idea.

Telling versus mediating

Instead of *telling* students what to think, therefore, you will listen closely to them and become a *mediator* of their thinking. You will help them to learn by reflecting their own ideas back to them and guiding them in sorting out the inconsistencies. The chapter "The Teacher as Mediator" will develop this idea further, and you will see many examples of the teacher as mediator throughout this book.

Teaching Science for Understanding   As we explore some of the models for science teaching, it is important to keep in mind that the twenty-first century demands novel ways of solving problems, critical thinking about issues and ideas, and an ability to take ideas apart and put them together again. Our methods for teaching science must respond to the complexities of our society by stressing what some science educators refer to as "meaning over memorizing, quality over quantity and understanding over awareness" (Mintzes, Wandersee, and Novak, 1998). But what does it mean to understand something, and how do students demonstrate understanding? As Perkins puts it, "Understanding goes beyond knowing. . . . Understanding a topic is a matter of being able to perform in a variety of thought-demanding ways with the topic, for instance to: explain, muster evidence, find examples, generalize, apply concepts, analogize, represent in a new way, and so on" (1993, pp. 28–29). Think about what "understanding" means as you read the next science story.

Stressing "meaning over memorizing"

 SCIENCE STORY

The Search for Understanding: A Toaster Story

Ken Bulman, a sixth-grade teacher in Australia, was working on a classroom unit about electricity with his students. As an extension of the unit, he brought in old toasters for the students to explore. The students were challenged to take the toasters apart and, by examining how they were made, determine how they worked. One group of students said, "Can we use the library?" "Yes," was Ken's response.

Students believe they have the answer.

About half an hour later, the students returned to the class and said, "We have the answer." "Great," Ken answered. "Can you tell us?"

"Well," said one student, "the toaster works because it has a thermostat." "What's a thermostat?" Ken asked.

The students checked their notes from the library. "It is a bimetallic strip that bends when it is heated," replied another member of the group. "Can you show me where it is in your toaster?" asked Ken.

The students explored their toaster and showed Ken what seemed to be the contact strips in the toaster—the point where the electricity made contact with the heating element. "How do you know this is the bimetallic strip?" asked Ken. The students were unsure. "Well, what does the strip do?" Ken questioned. "It bends when it is heated," replied one of the group members.

The "answer" does not square with evidence.

So, with Ken's help, the students heated this metal strip. They learned that it did *not* bend.

"You need to base your conclusions on evidence," Ken explained, and the students resumed their exploration of their toaster.

Notice that, for this group of students, getting an answer was paramount. They had "learned" that teachers want answers. Not until Ken probed their *understanding* did they realize that they were not sure how the toaster worked. Then they investigated further so they could answer the question "How does it work?" with more than just words from a book.

One fundamental question this textbook emphasizes involves your understanding of what you want for yourself and for your students. What is enough for you? What are you satisfied knowing? What is it that you want your students to understand?

The Learning Cycle   Teaching science for understanding has been facilitated by the **learning cycle** approach. This method has its roots in experimental science programs designed over fifty years ago, most notably the Science Curriculum Improvement Study (SCIS). The learning cycle approach is based on a series of five phases, although the first two are sometimes collapsed into a single phase. However many steps it employs, the learning cycle is a useful tool for teaching science and for designing your lessons. In its five-phase version, the learning cycle takes this form:

Phases of the science learning cycle

1. *Engagement Phase.* The first phase of the science learning cycle engages students in the topic at hand by inviting them to think about it, explore an opening demonstration, or come up with everything they may already know about the topic. This is the "hook": How can you get your students interested and on board with the topic?

2. *Exploration Phase.* This phase invites students to explore a problem by manipulating materials. Students interact both with each other and the materials as they work to find optimal solutions to the problem. The teacher facilitates the students' work and visits with them as they are handling the materials and performing tests.

3. *Explanation Phase.* The third phase involves the teacher interacting with the students as they share the ideas they derived from their explorations. This is the time when the teacher explores the students' thinking. In this book, I am talking largely about this phase when I refer to the teacher's role as a "mediator" of students' thinking.

4. *Elaboration Phase.* In the fourth phase of the science learning cycle, teachers take advantage of opportunities to make connections between the science concept, the students' lives, and the students' prior knowledge. During this phase, students may come up with their own ideas and may want to test them or discuss them—like the girl in Ms. McKie's class who asked about sound traveling through the moon.

5. *Evaluation Phase.* During this final phase, teachers explore what the students know and are able to do as a result of their experience. For this purpose, teachers can use various assessment techniques, as described in the chapter "What's the Big Idea?" Students are often encouraged to assess their own understanding of a topic.

Many of the ideas described by these five phases will be recognizable to you as you read the coming chapters. There are many ways to explore science ideas with students while valuing their beliefs and their ideas about the natural world. In this book, I stress creating meaningful science experiences that are designed with specific concepts in mind.

Students' "Misconceptions"   As you can imagine, sometimes children (and adults, too) use their experiences to develop scientific ideas that are misconceptions—inaccurate ways of understanding the natural world.

"Wrong" ideas?

For example, if you merely observed sunrise and sunset every day, you might think that the sun revolved around the Earth, instead of the Earth's moving around the sun. Some researchers in science education have called such ideas "prescientific conceptions," while other researchers refer to them as "alternative conceptions."

All the learner's ideas have value.

In fact, there is a strong movement away from referring to these ideas as "misconceptions" because that term implies that they are simply wrong, have no value, and should quickly be discarded. Therefore, *alternative conceptions* is the preferred term. Constructivist philosophy suggests that *all* of the learner's ideas—even the ones we think obviously wrong—have some value because they are part of a process that eventually can lead to a better understanding of the natural world. One science teacher remarked that alternative conceptions are like stepping-stones that students construct. With the teacher's help, these stepping-stones eventually lead to a full understanding of the scientifically accurate concept.

Again, it is important to value the ideas that learners offer. This is the first step in helping students construct new ways of seeing. Throughout this book, you will find illustrations of how this approach can work in the science classroom.

This Book's Approach   Drawing on the many teaching implications of constructivism, we can summarize this book's approach to science teaching as follows:

- Engage students in activities.

- Encourage them to think about the activities and reflect on what they found out.

- Pay attention to the prior knowledge and alternative conceptions that the students bring to each learning experience.

- Listen to the students' thinking and regularly engage them in conversation about their ideas.

As the constructivist model of teaching and learning science has evolved, science educators and classroom teachers alike have recognized the need to publish guidelines for educators at all levels. This impulse has contributed to the recent national standards movement, a movement that, as you will see in the next section, has an interesting background.

Standards for Science Education

STANDARDS ✔

In the early 1980s, several national reports expressed deep concern about the state of scientific literacy among students at various levels in their schooling, from kindergarten through twelfth grade. *A Nation at Risk* (1983) and *Educating Americans for the 21st Century* (1983) warned the American public that all students need to have a firm grounding in mathematics, science, and technology. The reports showed, for instance, that test scores of American students on international proficiency examinations in science lagged behind those of students in other countries. Fearful that our students were falling behind and that our country would lose its competitive edge, these reports and others sounded an alarm.

Scientific literacy, as defined by these reports, required students to be able to work with the "intellectual tools of the 21st Century" (National Science Board, 1983, p. v). Top priority was given to providing earlier, more intensive, and more effective instruction in science, mathematics, and technology in grades K–6. The scientifically literate person was described as an individual who could use the processes of science to make important life decisions. In particular, such a person should have the ability to explore a problem through careful reasoning.

One response to the alarms of the 1980s has been an attempt to establish **national standards,** first for mathematics, then for science, and, more

The Benchmarks

recently, for technology. One prominent example is *Benchmarks for Science Literacy* (AAAS, 1993), which provides guidelines not only for science, but for technology and mathematics as well. Published by the American Association for the Advancement of Science, *Benchmarks* addresses what students should know and be able to do in science, mathematics, and technology by the end of grades 2, 5, 8, and 12. It explains the value of the processes as well as the content of science. *Benchmarks* is part of a larger movement, Project 2061, named for the year Halley's comet returns to earth's orbit. This larger movement involves teachers, teacher educators, and scientists in science education reform.

The NSES

Less than three years after *Benchmarks,* an even more ambitious document was published. Designed to offer guidelines for teachers, teacher educators, curriculum developers, and school districts, the **National Science Education Standards** (NSES) were published in 1996. These standards make the case that acquiring scientific knowledge, understanding, and abilities should be a central aspect of education, just as science has become a central aspect of our world.

The NSESs are divided into separate sections that set forth standards in a variety of related areas, including the teaching of science, professional development of science teachers, and assessment of student understanding of scientific concepts. In the chapter "Science Content and Curriculum," we'll look at the specific areas of science content as we explore how to use these standards to construct a curriculum. That chapter will also discuss how the standards movement has led to the development of new local and state frameworks. For now, I want to emphasize five themes that are infused throughout the NSES—themes that this book will illustrate repeatedly:

Key themes from the NSES

1. *We learn science by doing science.* This theme relates to the need to engage students in meaningful science experiences.

2. *We learn science by inquiry.* The term *inquiry* refers to the importance of science as process; it implies an understanding of how scientists study the world.

3. *We learn science by collaboration.* This point emphasizes the importance of students' working with other students and with teachers to share ideas and meanings as they develop their own conclusions.

4. *We learn science over time.* It takes time for students to construct their own understandings from science experiences.

5. *We learn science by developing personal knowledge.* This is another way of saying that students construct their own understandings.

As the last of the five themes makes clear, principles of constructivism are deeply embedded in the National Science Education Standards.

Issues of Diversity

STANDARDS ☑

The emphasis that the NSESs place on personal knowledge and collaboration should remind us that learning occurs within each person's social and cultural context. In fact, the NSESs specifically appeal to teachers to "recognize and respond to student diversity and encourage all students to participate fully in science learning" (p. 32). Learners function within so many different social and cultural contexts that it makes sense to find out as much as we can about our students and their personal experiences to help them learn science.

Questions to Ask About Your Students

What does it mean for you as a future classroom teacher to "find out" about your students' personal experiences and recognize their diversity? Basically, as we become teachers, we need to ask ourselves several important questions about our students. Wherever you live, whatever the particular types of diversity you encounter, answering these questions will help you to become a better teacher:

Learning about your students

- *Who are my students?* This question refers to students' interests, concerns, hobbies, beliefs, and feelings about themselves and others.

- *What are their lives like?* This question encourages us to explore our students' family and home structure. For example, do they have siblings? Do both parents work outside the home? What do the students do after school? Do they have enough to eat? Who is at home with them in the evening?

- *Where do they live?* Is their home a room, an apartment, a private house? Is their block or neighborhood safe? Are there friends nearby to play with?

- *What interactions with nature are possible for them?* How does nature present itself in the neighborhood of your school and community? Are there trees and grass, mountains and plains, rivers and valleys, or is there only concrete and cement where, even so, a dandelion grows?

- *How do events that shape my students' lives become opportunities to learn science?* In other words, what things happen in your students' daily lives that you could explore through a meaningful science experience? For instance, if your students live near a shore, you could observe the tides coming in and out as part of a science lesson.

- *How are my students' beliefs about the nature of science informed by their cultural backgrounds and their gender?* The ways we think about science and scientists are often based on where we live, how we grow up, whether we are male or female, and what cultural group we belong to. In the next chapter, as you explore the socially constructed images of science and scientists, consider how students from different parts of the country, different cultural groups, and different nationalities might construct scientific images.

Connecting Science to All Students

As you can see, learning to teach science involves a lot of learning about the students you will teach. This is increasingly important because diverse classrooms are increasingly prevalent in the United States. Global migration has become commonplace, bringing more students from distant countries to our schools. As well, studies have shown that students with special needs, such as those with physical and/or learning disabilities, have a far greater chance to succeed academically and socially in the regular classroom than they do in a segregated classroom. Consequently, classes are intentionally organized to include students with broad ranges of learning and physical abilities as well as wide differences in cultural background. Typically, you can expect that your students may differ from one another by country of origin, native language, socioeconomic status, particular learning abilities, ethnicity, and gender, to name just a few characteristics.

Helping students make meaning on their own terms

Students can make meaning with whatever language and learning abilities they have available to them. As teachers who are engaging diverse groups of students in science experiences, we want to observe how they construct meaning *on their own terms*. It is our job to honor their processes and help them move forward to increase their understanding.

For example, a student who is not a native English speaker may completely understand the science experiences he or she is engaged in, but may have difficulty expressing that knowledge in appropriate English terms. By encouraging the student in any way possible to communicate his or her meaning, we are honoring that child's process. When we do that, we say, in essence, "Your thinking is valued and appreciated." This prepares the ground for future understanding to emerge in the student that is more scientifically sound. In this book you will learn how to build on your students' ideas in order to lead them to accurate understandings of the natural world. Helping students to develop their thinking in a structured way has been called *scaffolding.* We will see examples of that process later in the book. It is important to remember, however, that to build on students' ideas, you must learn what those ideas are. You begin by creating a learning environment in which all your students feel valued and able to make a contribution.

Accommodating students with special needs

Constructivist teaching, as noted earlier, has the potential to give students more control over what they are learning. That is, instead of telling students what and how to think, we invite them to create their own ideas in ways that are congruent with who they are. For students with physical, emotional, or learning disabilities—who often have been discouraged in traditional science classrooms—this approach is especially vital. And accommodating students with special needs is compatible with the methods of constructivism: providing concrete activities, emphasizing the importance of process rather than the memorization of facts, promoting cooperative group experiences, and allowing the big ideas to emerge from specific contexts. As you teach, you will learn what accommodations your students with special needs require. The important point is to abandon the idea that only a certain type of student can be a good science learner. Teaching science is an engaging and empowering experience for you and all your students. Students with special needs are not the only population that has not been encouraged to pursue traditional science. Often girls and people of color have been noticeably distanced from science; for many of them, the subject seems unrelated to their lives and disconnected from any contemporary meaning. Studies have shown that to encourage the science participation of girls and people of color, science teaching needs to be more connected, to make connections to students' lived experiences, to engage students in social collaboration, and to consider topics of contemporary interest (Sanders, Koch, & Urso, 1997; Kahle, 1994; Sadker & Sadker, 1994; Koch 2002). When we discuss scientific stereotypes in the next chapter, it will become clear why boys have been identified with doing science more than girls. That is changing as researchers reveal to teachers how important it is to include all students actively in scientific work.

Differentiating Instruction   When you ask yourself, "How can I be a really excellent science teacher?" part of the answer is holding out the expectation that all types of children can learn science. But the answer also involves finding ways to tailor your teaching to meet the needs of the different types of students in your class. Teachers regularly contend with the challenge of how to reach out to students who span the spectrum of learning readiness, personal interests, culturally shaped ways of seeing and speaking of the world, and experiences in that world. In Part Two of this textbook, you will read stories of teachers who, with varying resources available to them, are reaching out to students of different ages, backgrounds, and interests. In the chapter "Planning for Science," we will also examine specific steps that are helpful when doing science with students who have a range of learning and physical disabilities.

Different approaches for different students

Each time you do science a little differently to help a specific student or group of students in your class, you are **differentiating instruction.** Teachers who have differentiated classrooms are those "who strive to do whatever it takes to ensure that struggling and advanced learners, students with varied cultural heritages, and children with different background experiences all grow as much as they possibly can each day, each week, and throughout the year" (Tomlinson, 1999). You may think that such classrooms are not equitable because groups of students are receiving different types of experiences. However, the goal of equity does not mean equality of *treatment*; it is equality of *learning outcomes and achievement* that counts. To reach that goal, differentiating our instruction is a necessary and important technique.

Engaging Your Students   As you will see, the same interventions that encourage more diverse participation in science classrooms also provide a better overall quality of instruction. Not only are those who were formerly marginalized in science more encouraged, but other students become more interested in the science experience as well. Hence, the national standards—and this textbook—support the idea that good science teaching can encourage the participation of all students. In other words, teaching to encourage diverse groups means good science teaching.

Knowing your students helps you engage them.

The important point is to *know* your students and *engage* them in activities that relate to their world. Suppose you had a class in which there were one or more homeless children. You might soon realize that these children, who often go hungry, have a preoccupation with food (Barton, 1998). To engage them in science activities, you might do as one teacher did: choose science experiences that regularly use food, such as making an earth science model out of fruits and vegetables (see *Science Experiments You Can Eat* by Vicki Cobb).

As another example, consider a group of girls in one fourth-grade class who thought science was just for boys (Sanders, Koch, & Urso, 1997). The teacher invited a young scientist to discuss her work with the class. Then she helped the students celebrate Women's History Month by engaging them in research about American women scientists. Not surprisingly, the girls in the class began to develop a more positive attitude toward science.

For you as a teacher of science, engaging diverse groups of students in meaningful science learning experiences—and watching what happens as they each construct their own meanings from these activities—can be an exciting opportunity. It is reasonable to expect that, depending on their prior experiences, your students will come up with a wide range of ideas. Hence, the challenge is to mediate the differences and lead your students toward some accurate understandings of nature. This task, though not a simple one, can be exhilarating for you as well as your students.

The Role of Technology

When we think about making connections with our students, we need to explore the ever-changing role of technology in their lives. Because technology is advancing so quickly, your students' involvement with it may differ from your own experiences in school. For instance, even if you spent a lot of time with a computer, it may be difficult for you to imagine how much some of your fifth-graders are affected by instant messages or interactive games on the World Wide Web. And if you're not a computer-driven person, some of these activities may even be mysteries to you. You may need to spend some time experimenting with the types of computer experiences that are commonplace to your students.

No doubt you have been using computers for word processing and perhaps for electronic communication. As you prepare to become a teacher, you will also discover how to use a computer to facilitate your own and your students' understanding of science. Meaningful science experiences can often include the use of computer software, associated hardware tools such as data-gathering probes, and research on the Internet. Such technology can expose students to scientific investigations well beyond their own classroom. The Internet also offers you many opportunities to enhance your own science learning and to explore a wide array of science activities for students. New web sites come online continuously, and you will need to be able to assess them for their usefulness and accuracy. Later chapters of this book, especially "Science and Technology," offer guidance as well as examples for incorporating technology into the science classroom.

Need to know— the key to using technology

Technology in and of itself, however, cannot help students learn science. It is the students' need to use the computer that makes it part of the science experience. Suppose a class was exploring the causes of different weather conditions. To research the effect of low-pressure systems, the students might turn to the World Wide Web to gather some weather reports. In this case, the students would be using the computer to collect data, part of the process of doing science.

The key point here is that the use of technology derives from a need to know more. Students turn to the computer as a tool to help them actively construct their own knowledge. The technology is not foisted on the student for its own sake; rather, it acts as a needed and useful resource.

Technology Education Standards

STANDARDS ☑

Given technology's great potential in education, educators have begun to seek standards for using it appropriately. To that end, the International Society for Technology in Education (ISTE), in partnership with teachers, teacher educators, and others, has developed the **National Educational Technology Standards** (NETS), which offer both guidelines and resource materials for students and teachers (ISTE, 2000, 2002). It is a good idea to become familiar with these standards and ask yourself how you may be implementing some of them as you teach science.

The ISTE technology standards for teachers highlight six major ways in which teachers should be technologically proficient:

Major themes of the NETS for teachers

1. Teachers demonstrate a sound understanding of technology operations and concepts.

2. Teachers plan and design effective learning environments and experiences supported by technology.

3. Teachers implement curriculum plans that include methods and strategies for applying technology to maximize student learning.

4. Teachers apply technology to facilitate a variety of effective assessment and evaluation strategies.

5. Teachers use technology to enhance their productivity and professional practice.

6. Teachers understand the social, ethical, legal, and human issues surrounding the use of technology in . . . schools and apply that understanding in practice. (ISTE, 2002, p. 9)

What do these major points mean for the actual practice of teaching school science? The following section explores a few ways that technology is used in grades K–8. More uses are described in the chapter "Science and Technology."

Ways of Using Technology

When you ask yourself the question, "How can computers and other technology help engage my students in meaningful science activities?" you will find many answers, depending on the situation. Let's explore a few of the basic categories of technology use in today's science classrooms. You will notice that some of the technology standards described in the preceding section are reflected in these tasks.

A computer-linked heat probe

A Resource for Collecting Data   As shown in our example of weather research, computer technology can serve as an important resource for collecting needed data. The World Wide Web has become a major source of science information. Moreover, your classroom equipment may come with computer connections. In one fifth-grade class I visited recently, students were investigating the rate at which a glass of hot water cooled after an ice cube was placed in it. They used a heat probe to measure the temperature every two minutes. The data were automatically transmitted from the probe to the computer screen, where a software package charted them in the form of a line graph. You can imagine how much time was saved by collecting data in this way—time that students gave to analyzing and reflecting on the data.

Simulating a violin sound

Interactive Problem Solving and Simulations   Some software packages and web sites are designed to pose a problem and then engage students in interactive manipulation of a simulated natural event. For example, some science software programs allow students to set up a simulated experiment and draw conclusions from their observations. Thus, the students have the opportunity to engage in science processes by manipulating the keys on a computer keyboard. One software program, on the topic of sound, allows students to vary the length, tension, and thickness of a simulated violin string in order to explore the effects these three properties have on the pitch of the sound created when the string is plucked. Using this program, third-grade students have the opportunity to manipulate the three variables in any way they choose. Today, many professional scientists study natural phenomena by using computer simulations.

Tools for Expression   As we encourage students to write about their ideas and observations in science, computers also become useful tools for them to use in expressing themselves. Using standard word processing

Multimedia presentations

applications, students can save, change, and refine ideas and draft reports on computer disks with minimal effort. Computer technology also allows students to display their understanding of science ideas by making multimedia presentations, which can include sounds and images as well as words. In our example of the simulated violin string, the student might use a multimedia package to present graphic and audio illustrations of several strings producing different types of sounds depending on their length, thickness, and tension. The graphics and sounds would be accompanied by explanatory text created by the student.

Brainstorming by email

A Means of Collaboration   The most social part of making meaning in science—collaboration or person-to-person communication—is facilitated by electronic telecommunication. Email and other forms of telecommunication allow classes to share their ideas and brainstorm with other students in neighboring schools or across the world. Scientists themselves collaborate in this way, by comparing the results of their investigations, so students will naturally find such collaboration useful and instructive.

Throughout this book, you will find references to web sites and other useful computer sources. Instructional technology tools can also include camcorders, VCRs, video-microscopes, educational television, and overhead projectors. You should be prepared to use whatever is available—and whatever will help your students to develop their own understanding of science.

Issues of Technology Access

As you explore technological tools for science learning, remember to ask yourself about your students and their lives. You may teach in a community where computers are commonplace, both at home and at school. Or you may teach in a place where students rarely have access to computers at home. This type of information is important as you plan for meaningful science experiences.

Are boys monopolizing computers?

If your students do not have ready access to email and the World Wide Web, you may need to take them to a local library or government facility. Even when students have plenty of opportunities to use technology, there can be important differences among individuals and groups. Many studies have shown, for instance, that boys use computers in different ways than girls do; the boys tend to "mess around" more, to see what they can make the computer do. In the process, the boys acquire a lot of know-how (Chapman, 1997), and their experience helps them in science activities that require computer use. Clearly, teachers need to promote this risk taking among girls as well.

One fifth-grade teacher, observing the gender differences in technology use in his classroom, decided that some of the free time in his class would be "girls-only" time at the computer. He also opened up the question of girls and computers to class discussion. In doing so, he discovered that the girls' approach to computer use was more rule-bound and that they were less willing to explore openly. Moreover, in this particular class, the boys tended to "hog" the computers, and the girls did not want to fight for equal time. Having a special girls-only time therefore worked well for this class, and the teacher encouraged more open exploration on the part of the girls.

No matter where you live or how much computer technology has pervaded your own life, you will find the technology connections in this book useful. True to the spirit of constructivism, I invite you to explore these connections and to develop your own ideas about using technology for meaningful science.

Structure of This Book

This book is structured in a way that will lead you into the world of teachers and students doing science together.

Part One: The Scientist Within

You'll always teach who you are.

Part One, comprising this chapter and the next, introduces the world of elementary and middle school science and invites you to look inward to explore your own feelings about science. Approaching the teaching of science is a complicated task. Frequently, teachers ask me for a sure-fire technique that will enable them to be successful. I am sorry to say that there is none, but there is an important place to begin—with your own personal reflections. Whatever the subject you are teaching, you are always teaching *who you are!* How you feel about science and whether you believe it can make a valuable contribution to your students' lives influences how successful you will be as a teacher of science. It is for this reason that I devote the next chapter of this book to what I call "The Scientist Within."

Part Two: Doing Science with Students: Inquiry in Practice

What are science stories?

In Part Two, we look outward to see how teachers do science with students in their own classrooms. Woven throughout this book, but most especially in Part Two, you will find more *science stories* like the ones you have encountered in this chapter. These stories are narratives of experiences that I have had or observed as I worked with in-service and preservice teachers. The stories describe what it looks like when teachers and students engage in scientific activities in the school environment. I have selected these particular stories because they explore a range of science activities in different grade levels in the physical, life, and earth sciences.

From each of these stories, certain ideas emerge. Some of them are "science ideas," that is, concepts about the natural world that comprise part of the body of knowledge known as science. Others are "teaching ideas"—thoughts about teaching strategies, teaching styles, and different

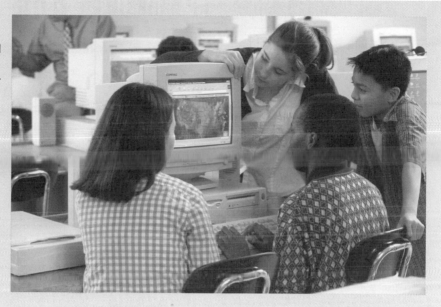

Students explore data on a computer. As noted by the ISTE standards, equal access to information technology is an important part of the learning experience. They should have as much access to technology as they do to a pencil.

Mugshots/Corbis

Using the Expanding Meanings sections

methodologies that the story illustrates. In later chapters, you will see that both of these types of ideas are incorporated in the *Expanding Meanings* section at the end of each story or sequence of stories. Also in the Expanding Meanings sections, you'll find connections between the science story and the national standards you have read about. Finally, be sure to look at the Questions for Further Exploration and Resources for Further Exploration. The questions invite you to consider other meanings that you may derive from your own interpretation of the story. The Resources include notes about science books and professional development books that can assist you, as well as web sites, children's literature, and software programs, where applicable.

Notice that in presenting stories, drawing out some ideas, and giving you vehicles to explore these ideas further, I become the "teacher as mediator" that I described earlier in this chapter. It's up to you to become the active learner, constructing your own meaning.

Part Three: Creating the Science Experience in Your Classroom

In Part Three, we investigate the nuts and bolts of doing science with students. We answer questions like these:

■ How do I plan? When and how should I modify my plans?

■ What should a science curriculum look like?

■ What science concepts should I study for my scientific self?

■ How do I assess the science experience?

■ How do I know I am doing it right?

Part Three also explores questioning strategies, the use of local and national standards, and the science "content" of the typical school curriculum.

Constructing your personal teaching model

Overall, Part Three pulls together the ideas from the two other parts of the text by considering all of the elements of a meaningful science learning experience and modeling the ways in which they can be developed to encourage your own and your students' success. Although all of the techniques and strategies discussed may be useful to you, the model you construct will be uniquely your own. Teaching is a highly personal activity. Not only do you have to make your own meaning from many well-meaning suggestions, but you also need to ask yourself frequently, "How am I doing?" In that spirit, the book closes back where we began, with a section on self-reflection, to help you answer the "How am I doing?" question for yourself.

Becoming a Science Teacher

Teaching science may seem daunting at first. Science is often the one area that was neglected in our own early schooling. When you chose your profession, it is doubtful that you pictured yourself planning "science lessons." Please know that you are not alone. Some future teachers are even shocked when they learn that, indeed, science is an integral part of the school experience in the earliest grades.

Becoming a learner yourself—and an explorer

Teaching gives you an extraordinary opportunity to be a lifelong learner. You will be constantly learning about your students, about yourself, and about new ideas. In particular, doing science with students enables you to become a special kind of explorer and meaning seeker. By that I mean that your own honest observations and experiences of nature are an important part of doing science with students. Although this is not a "how-to" book with step-by-step instructions on teaching science, I hope it is a how-to-think book—one that will help you to think about doing science in ways that bring both you and your students knowledge, pleasure, and confidence.

KEY TERMS

scientific method *(p. 3)*
process skills *(p. 5)*
constructivism *(p. 8)*
discovery learning *(p. 9)*
meaningful science experience *(p. 14)*
learning cycle *(p. 17)*

national standards *(p. 19)*
National Science Education Standards (p. 20)
differentiating instruction *(p. 23)*
National Educational Technology Standards *(p. 25)*

Resources for Further Exploration

Electronic Resources

American Association for the Advancement of Science: Project 2061. http://www/project2061.org/. Describes Project 2061 and includes an online version of *Benchmarks for Science Literacy.*

LDOnLine. http://www.ldonline.org/. A site with much useful information for teaching students who have learning disabilities.

National Educational Technology Standards. http://cnets.iste.org/. A site sponsored by the International Society for Technology in Education, where you can access the technology standards online.

National Science Education Standards. http://books.nap.edu/html/nses/. This web site includes an online version of the standards.

Teachnet.com. http://www.teachnet.com/. A World Wide Web site with tips, news, and lesson ideas. Although not exclusively devoted to science, it offers a number of resources for the science teacher.

Print Resources

AAAS. (1993). *Benchmarks for Science Literacy.* Washington, DC: American Association for the Advancement of Science.

Barton, 1998. Teaching science with homeless children: Pedagogy, representation, and identity. *Journal of Research in Science Teaching,* 35(4): 379–394.

Brooks, J., & Brooks, M. (1999). *In Search of Understanding: The Case for Constructivist Classrooms.* Alexandria, VA: Association for Supervision and Curriculum Development.

Bruner 1960 *The Process of Education.* Cambridge, MA: Harvard University Press.

Cobb, Vicki. *Science Experiments You Can Eat.* Philadelphia: Lippincott.

Driver R., Asoko, H., Leach, J., Mortimer, E., & Scott, P. (1994). Constructing scientific knowledge in the classroom. *Educational Researcher,* 23(7): 5–12.

Duckworth, E. (1996). *The Having of Wonderful Ideas and Other Essays on Teaching and Learning.* New York: Teachers College Press.

Ebenezer, J. V., & Lau, E. (1999). *Science in the Internet: A Resource for K–12 Teachers.* Upper Saddle River, NJ: Merrill.

Grabe, M., & Grabe, C. (2004). *Integrating Technology for Meaningful Learning.* (4th ed.). Boston: Houghton Mifflin.

International Society for Technology in Education (ISTE), 2000.

International Society for Technology in Education (ISTE), 2002.

Kahle, J. B., & Meece, J. (1994). Research on girls and science: Lessons and applications. In D. Gabel (Ed.), *Handbook of Research in Science Teaching and Learning*. Washington, DC: National Science Teachers Association.

Koch, J. (2002). Gender issues in the classroom. In W.R. Reynolds & G.E. Miller (Eds.), *Educational Psychology. Volume 7 of the Comprehensive Handbook of Psychology*, Editor-in-Chief: I. B. Weiner, New York: Wiley.

Lederman, N. G. (1992). Students' and teachers' conceptions of the nature of science: A review of the research. *Journal of Research in Science Teaching*, 29(4): 331–359.

Mintzes, J., Wandersee, J., & Novak, J. (1998). *Teaching Science for Understanding: A Human Constructivist View*. San Diego, CA: Academic Press.

National Research Council. (1996). *National Science Education Standards*. Washington, DC: National Academy Press.

National Science Board. (1983). *Educating Americans for the 21st Century*. Washington, DC: National Science Foundation.

Noddings, N. (1990). Constructivism in mathematics education. *Journal for Research in Mathematics Education*, no. 4.

Perkins, D. (1999). The many faces of constructivism. *Educational Leadership*, 57(3): 6–11.

Phillips, D. C. (1995). The good, the bad, and the ugly: The many faces of constructivism. *Educational Researcher*, 24(7): 5–12.

Reynolds, K., & Barba, R. (1996). *Technology for the Teaching and Learning of Science*. Boston: Allyn and Bacon.

Sadker, M., & Sadker, D. (1994). *Failing at Fairness: How America's Schools Cheat Girls*. New York: Charles Scribner's Sons.

Sanders, J., Koch, J., & Urso, J. (1997). *Gender Equity Right from the Start: Instructional Activities for Teacher Educators in Mathematics, Science and Technology*. Hillsdale, NJ: Lawrence Erlbaum Associates.

Locating Your Scientific Self

Many new teachers don't think of them- selves as scientists. They often regard science as a subject beyond their grasp. This un- easiness leads them to rely on external authorities in science rather than looking inside themselves and cultivating their own scientific approach. Yet, as I mentioned at the beginning of this book, there is a budding scientist in everyone, and the task for a new teacher is to rediscover his or her scientific instincts and develop them. Think about that as you read the following story about a school science workshop for new teachers.

FOCUSING QUESTIONS

▌ How do you normally react to the presence of a scientific expert?

▌ Do you believe you have scientific skills yourself?

▌ Why do your personal feelings and atti- tudes about science matter when you are teaching?

SCIENCE STORY

Why the Balloon Doesn't Pop: An Experience for New Teachers

The science workshop at the state school science conference was titled "Have Fun with Science." In parentheses the announcement said, "New teachers especially welcome." It was a well-attended workshop. There were fifty elementary schoolteachers gathered in a lab room at the local state college. In front of us stood Rose, a gray-haired woman who had placed bottles of different sizes, colored liquids, yellow balloons, and pins at the head lab table.

How are the two balloons the same?

To begin, Rose pulled two yellow balloons out of a bag and asked us to notice the ways in which they were the same. The teacher audience

33

chimed in with, "Same color, same shape, same size." "They are both de-flated," one participant shouted. Someone in the back approached the front table and asked if she could smell the balloons. "Hmm," she mused, "they smell rubbery." Someone in the front shouted, "If you blow them up, they will both be round." Everyone seemed quite engaged with these two ordinary yellow balloons.

Rose inflated both balloons so that they were just about the same size. On her worktable, she had a small bottle of a blue liquid and a box of straight pins. As she held a straight pin to the side of the first yellow bal-loon, she remarked, "Of course, we know what will happen when we strike the balloon with this pin." With that remark, she popped the balloon.

The mysterious blue liquid—what will it do?

Taking the next balloon, she dipped the same pin into her bottle of blue liquid and said, "Now, what do you think will happen if we stick this balloon with the pin that I have dipped in my blue liquid?" The audience was unsure, but the general feeling was that the balloon would pop as the first one did. Rose stuck the blue-liquid-coated pin into the end of the sec-ond yellow balloon, and there it sat. With the pin stuck halfway into the balloon, the balloon did not pop!

Why didn't the second balloon pop?

"Now," asked Rose, "why do you suppose *this* yellow balloon did not pop as the first one did?" Several teachers volunteered responses. "The blue liquid," one teacher offered, "sealed the hole the pin was making as it went into the balloon." Another said, "The blue liquid made the pin so slick that it just slid into the balloon without making a hole."

"You have made some interesting comments. Any other ideas?" Rose looked around the room.

Susan is observant.

One teacher, named Susan, sitting toward the back of the room, sheep-ishly raised her hand. "I thought, as I was watching you," Susan remarked, "that you placed the pin in a different part of the second yellow balloon. You placed the pin in the end of the balloon this time, but the first time you placed it in the side of the balloon."

"What about the blue liquid?" Rose asked.

"Well," Susan responded, "I don't think it has anything to do with it."

Before Rose could comment, I remember thinking how observant Su-san had been. I was impressed with her ability to offer an explanation that was so clearly unrelated to the blue liquid.

Rose asked, "How can we test this possibility—that it was where I placed the pin in the second balloon and that it had nothing to do with the blue liquid?" One teacher suggested that she take a pin, dip it in the blue liquid, and place it in the side of the balloon. Another participant sug-gested that she take a pin and, without dipping it in the blue liquid, place it in the end of the balloon.

What do the tests suggest?

Responding to these ideas, Rose inflated two more yellow balloons, identical to the first two. She placed a pin in the blue liquid and into the side of the first yellow balloon. *It popped!* Then she placed a pin without any blue liquid into the end of the second yellow balloon. It did *not* pop! Everyone sat back, apparently surprised yet again. Everyone, that is, except Susan.

Teachers as Scientists

Let's think about how the teachers in Rose's workshop behaved. Most of them were ordinary classroom teachers, and some were new to the profession. They were not scientific experts by any means. Nevertheless, they were behaving like scientists in a number of ways:

Observations

1. They made many observations of the yellow balloons. *Observations* include all our perceptions of an object or an event, using as many senses as we can.

Inferences

2. Next, the teachers offered possible explanations for why the second balloon did not pop. These possible explanations are called *inferences*. Inferences are based on our observations and sometimes lead us to set up further investigations. Each time the teachers came up with their own ideas and thought about the reasons for the events, they were behaving like scientists.

Challenging authority

3. While most of the teachers in the workshop were openly expressing their observations and inferences, one teacher, Susan, expressed a contradiction—a challenge—to Rose, the person directing the workshop and the one apparent "scientific authority" in the room. Rose made it appear that the blue liquid was the reason the balloon did not pop. In a way, she was tricking the teachers. Susan challenged this idea, and by doing so came up with the correct analysis of the situation—that it was where the pin was placed, not the blue liquid, that made the difference.

Susan's daring is especially important here. Many times, scientific investigations seem beyond our grasp, and for that reason scientific authority goes unchallenged. But once we begin to rely on our own perceptions, we may find that the science in question isn't as obscure as it first seemed. The balloon story demonstrates how important it is to trust your own observations and inferences in order to find out more about the world. In this way, you will get in touch with your scientific self and become *your own source* of scientific expertise.

Framing a hypothesis

4. By suggesting that the position of the pin had something to do with the balloon's not popping, Susan was creating a *hypothesis*. When an inference becomes a testable idea, it is called a hypothesis. Framed in more precise terms, Susan's hypothesis might sound like this: "The balloon will not pop when the pin is placed in a special spot at the top of the balloon."

Testing the hypothesis

5. After Susan offered the hypothesis, the teachers took the next step: testing it. Scientists extend their thinking beyond observations and inferences by reflecting on their ideas and determining how to test them. Rose, following the teachers' suggestions, tested Susan's hypothesis by planning a specific test procedure and then carrying it out. These steps distinguish science from other forms of creative human endeavor. Testing ideas by planning experiments and carrying out extended investigations is a critical part of the work of scientists.

Overall, then, the teachers in this workshop engaged in a variety of scientific activities. By observing, inferring, forming a hypothesis, testing it, and, most of all, *trusting their own judgment,* they behaved very much like scientists. Ultimately they came to understand that the balloon is thickest at its rounded end and therefore has the least tension there. A pin placed there will not pop the balloon. If you're doubtful, try the experiment yourself. Make your own observations and trust your judgment. This is part of developing a set of attitudes that help you do science. You can challenge authority and trust your own experience.

In the next section, we'll take the next step in locating your scientific self by exploring in more detail the kinds of ideas that teachers, and other people in our society, commonly hold about scientists. As you read, remember the story about the pin, the balloon, and the mysterious blue liquid. By the way, Rose finally admitted that the blue liquid was—did you guess?—just blue food coloring and water.

The secret revealed

Beliefs About Science: We Teach What We Think

You may be wondering, "Why all this fuss about the scientist within and locating your scientific self? If it's just a matter of trusting my own judgment, I can do that."

There is more to it than that, however. For one thing, looking inward helps you recognize your own feelings about science. Your feelings about the subject of science help to shape your attitudes toward it, and both your feelings and attitudes greatly affect the way you teach science in the classroom. A number of studies have demonstrated this point. One early study indicated that teachers' negative attitudes toward science made them reluctant to teach science or even avoid teaching it (Perkes, 1975). Additional research suggests that science attitude scores can be expected to correlate to the behavior of both teachers and students in the science classroom (see, for example, Shrigley, 1983, 1990; Koballa & Crawley, 1985). In various ways, both overt and subtle, teachers' attitudes toward science greatly influence their ability to be effective science teachers. Let's explore some reasons why this is true.

Students recognize how you feel

Your Feelings Show   It is almost impossible to mask negative feelings and attitudes about science when you are dealing with your students. Students have an uncanny ability to see below the surface and get to the heart of their teacher's reactions, even when the teacher is a terrific actor and believes he or she is hiding the truth.

Teachers who are enthusiastic, interested, and who speak of the power and beauty of scientific understanding instill in their students some of those same attitudes.
—National Science Education Standards

Teacher Attitudes Affect Students' Attitudes   Many studies indicate that teachers' feelings and attitudes about science affect their students' feelings and attitudes. For instance, one study that used personal narratives to explore students' attitudes concluded that the scientific experiences that students reported as positive were clearly influenced by teachers whose attitudes toward science had been very positive (Koch, 1990). In other words, teachers who have a positive outlook toward science tend to instill that outlook in their students. In fact, interviews with scientists often reveal that they had inspirational teachers whose love of science motivated them to pursue scientific careers (Koch, 1993). Unfortunately, the reverse is also true. Teachers with negative outlooks toward science often inadvertently discourage their students from pursuing scientific interests. As early as 1969, a study found that elementary school teachers' negative attitudes toward science were passed on to their students (Walberg, 1969). Overall, the literature reveals that the role of the teacher is vital in shaping students' attitudes and aptitudes in science (Jones & Lovin, 1994).

Teaching who you are   As we noted earlier in the book, whatever subject you teach, you are always, in a sense, teaching *who you are*. This means that your authentic self is visible and vulnerable in your classroom, and it has a great effect on your students.

The exercises in the rest of this chapter will help you acknowledge your innermost feelings about science. As you engage in these activities,

Scientists often work outside, in the field, collecting data and specimens for investigation. What do *you* think this scientist is investigating?

Laima Druskis/Stock Boston

you will learn more about your scientific self. If you were "turned off" to science in secondary school and college, this chapter should help you become more comfortable with it. The important thing is to acknowledge your feelings and consider "making friends" with science as one of the goals of locating your scientific self.

What Is a Scientist? Stereotype Versus Reality

What do you think a scientist is? What does a scientist look like? To begin discovering your scientific self, let's explore how you conceive of scientists.

Drawing a Scientist

We've reached the point in the chapter where you will need to close this book. But first get a piece of paper and a pencil and find a firm writing surface. Set this book aside, and sketch a picture of what you think a scientist might look like. When you have completed the drawing, open the book again to this spot.

What kind of scientist did you draw?

If you are like most people, your scientist drawing will show a white male with one or more of the following characteristics: wild hair, eyeglasses, a white lab coat, a pocket protector, and some bubbling flasks (see Figure 2.1). Studies reveal that both students and teachers frequently draw this popular image of the scientist (Fort & Varney, 1989; Barman, 1997). Of course, this image is a stereotype that exaggerates what real scientists look like. This stereotype is reinforced by the images of scientists that we see in cartoons, movies, magazines, and the popular press. Such stereotypes become part of our belief systems and influence our future behavior. All too often, they limit what we do and think.

Third Graders Draw Scientists   Not long ago, two third-grade teachers in a local elementary school were interested in exploring their students' beliefs about scientists. Distributing crayons and drawing paper, they asked each student to draw a picture of a scientist and describe what the scientist was doing. The thirty-nine students' drawings contained thirty-one men and eight women. Further, of the thirty-one male scientists, twenty-five had beards and messy hairstyles.

Students' ideas of scientists

One boy added a bubble quote for his scientist that said, "I'm crazy." Another third-grade boy described his scientist as follows: "He is inventing a monster. He painted his face green." Still another boy wrote, "My scientist makes all kinds of poisons. He is a weird person." Another caption on the bottom of a drawing said, "Dr. Strangemind," and on the back the student explained, "He does strange things like blow up things and other crazy stuff." Many of the children described their scientists as "blowing things up," "acting crazy" or "goofy," or working with "a lot of potions." (See the typical student drawings in Figure 2.2.)

FIGURE 2.1
Responses by two preservice teachers to the assignment "Draw a scientist."

Think about the stereotype

You can see that most of these third graders, young as they were, had already internalized the stereotyped image of the scientist. To understand why this is important, ask yourself the following questions:

■ Who is omitted in this stereotype?

■ Does the type of person represented in the stereotype reflect the makeup of any class you have recently seen?

■ If the students in a typical classroom were omitted by the stereotype, how would that make them feel about science?

You may suppose that stereotypes about scientists diminish as children mature. In fact, however, a study of over 1,500 students in grades K–8 revealed that students' drawings of scientists became more stereotypical as the students grew older. These students drew mostly white male scientists, suggesting that the stereotype persists despite recent changes in curriculum materials (Barman, 1997).

Effects of the stereotype

Stereotypes Can Be Discouraging   As you may suspect, the scientist stereotype can discourage individuals who are other than white and male from seeing themselves as truly scientific. Some of the consequences of this are obvious. For example, substantially fewer females enroll in advanced science courses than do males, beginning in high school and continuing

FIGURE 2.2
Responses by three
elementary school
children to the
assignment "Draw a
scientist." Compare
these to the teachers'
drawings in Figure 2.1.

FIGURE 2.2
Continued.

FIGURE 2.2
Continued.

through college (see, for example, U.S. Department of Education, 2000, 2001). This is most noticeable in the physical sciences, computer sciences, and engineering. The gender gap persists despite many types of interventions designed to encourage girls and young women to participate in science.

It is a complex issue, but the way in which we conceptualize "who does science" certainly contributes to the problem. One primary school teacher holds a gigantic mirror up to her students whenever the question of who can be a scientist emerges. This helps the students envisage themselves in the role of the scientist, ensuring that they will feel entitled to that role as they explore natural phenomena in their own classrooms.

Think about your own drawing

Reflecting on Your Drawing   With this discussion in mind, go back and look at your own sketch of a scientist. What exactly did you draw? Who is your scientist? Is the person you drew similar to yourself or very different? What does this tell you about your feelings and attitudes toward science?

Keep the draw-a-scientist activity in mind, not only while you read this book but when you teach science. For both students and adults, the activity can be useful in exploring the implications of the scientist stereotype. You may want to try it with your own students.

Naturally, if people had more contact with real scientists, they would observe much more diversity than the stereotype allows. In the next section, you will be asked to meet with a scientist and ask questions about his or her work.

Interviewing a Scientist

When it seems as if all the images of scientists that you encounter conform to the narrow stereotype, it is time to do your own research. Meeting and interviewing an actual scientist is one way to decide for yourself if the attributes of the dominant scientist stereotype are accurate.

Research scientists can be found at private or public colleges and universities, community medical centers, pharmaceutical companies, privately funded research institutions, and government agencies. Your local chamber of commerce can provide the locations of laboratories or corporations that are likely to employ scientists. At many of these institutions, the director of public relations can help you find a scientist who would be willing to be interviewed.

Preparing for the Interview   When contacting laboratories or other organizations that employ research scientists, explain that you are interested in interviewing a research scientist because you are preparing to teach science in the elementary or middle grades. Explain that you would not need more than one hour for the interview.

When you have the interview date, be prepared; arrive for your meeting with some interview questions prepared and a note pad. The following suggested questions may help you draw up your own list:

Sample questions to ask

What experiences with school science, if any, influenced you to pursue a career in science?

Are there any teachers who stand out in your mind as having encouraged you to explore a career in science?

What is the best part of the work you do—what gives you the most satisfaction? Conversely, what is the downside of your work?

In what ways is the scientific work you are pursuing similar or dissimilar to the science experiences you had in school?

What contemporary scientific issue are you most concerned about?

What would you say to a student who wanted to shape her or his future toward a career in science?

If you were to define science, how would you complete this sentence: "Science is . . ."?

You will have your own questions to add to this list, and the interview itself will probably generate further questions that you could not have anticipated in advance.

What you learn may surprise you.

When teachers conduct interviews of this sort, some of what they learn surprises them. For instance, they learn that many scientists actively pursue family life and religious and political interests. They also learn that sometimes a special teacher was a major influence in an individual's decision to pursue a scientific career. Interviewing a scientist is a way to change the culturally constructed "mad scientist" image that many adults and students hold.

Science and Curiosity: An Excerpt from an Interview with a Scientist

Connie (a preservice teacher): What would you do if someone came to you and said, "I hate science, I don't see how it relates to anything, I don't understand it, and I don't see how you can do it"? What would you say to that person to make her or him see that science is a significant field?

Dr. B.: Most people who hate science hate it because they were tortured by it in elementary school. There's a good way and a bad way to teach people science. The bad way is to present science as a set of known things, of facts and relationships that they have to know. Then it becomes a burden. The proper way to teach science is to get the students to understand that science is a way of explaining how the world around them works, and engaging their curiosity. Anyone who has curiosity can't help but find science interesting, if it's presented properly.

Helpful Hints for the Interview   The following hints should be helpful in your interview:

Tips for the interview

- Do not just ask questions. Engage your scientist in a conversation. Respond to his or her answers with points of your own.

- The scientist you interview may be eager to hear about your own preparations for becoming a teacher.

- Scientists who have young children may share stories about their children's experiences with school science.

- Honor the interview time frame. Do not exceed your allotted time, unless the scientist offers or chooses to do so.

- Some scientists may not be able to talk freely about their research because it may be classified or may lead to a patented product. If this is the case, ask her or him to talk about the general area of research they are engaged in—for example, biomedical research, geological research, theoretical physics research, and so on.

- You may also want to ask who funds her or his research.

- Send a thank-you note!

Becoming more aware of your tacitly held beliefs about scientists is part of the task of locating your own scientific self. The drawing-a-scientist and interviewing-a-scientist activities are tools to help you reflect on your beliefs about scientists. In the next sections, you are asked to construct other tools to help you locate your scientific self: the science autobiography and the science journal.

Reflective Practice I: Your Science Autobiography

As far back as the turn of the twentieth century, the philosopher John Dewey spoke of the need to educate future teachers in ways of thinking about teaching, not just in the technical aspects of teaching (Dewey, 1904). Since then, the image of the teacher has frequently shifted back and forth between two poles. On one hand, the teacher is seen as a technical expert who has acquired and can execute a series of specific skills related to teaching. On the other hand, the teacher is seen as Dewey's type of *reflective practitioner,* someone who has the capacity to think critically about her or his work. Actually, both facets of teaching are important. Certainly there are particular techniques for teaching and there are ways of thinking that help teachers decide which techniques are preferable in any given teaching situation.

What does it mean to be reflective?

The term *reflection,* when applied to teachers, generally refers to a process in which they explore their own teaching practice, asking themselves important questions about their interactions with students as well as the curriculum. **Reflective teachers** have the capacity to think about their roles as teachers from the standpoint of who they are, who their students are, and what they hope to accomplish. Reflective teachers are very conscious of their feelings about their school environment, their students, and their teaching situation. They are able to recognize potential and existing problems and explore multiple approaches to solutions. To put it another way, a reflective practitioner is always looking inward and asking, "How am I doing?"

Research shows that a deliberate, conscious, inward look at teaching and learning can promote your professional development as a teacher. For one thing, it helps you identify areas that you can research and explore. A foremost researcher in the field of reflective practice, Donald Schon (1983), remarks that the reflective teacher constructs her or his practice. What he means by this is that instead of following a list of rules, the reflective teacher explores the classroom environment and creates or modifies her or his own teaching methods to establish new and better contexts for learning.

Your future depends on your past—and how you deal with it.

Since so much of your professional life will involve personal reflection, this is a good time to begin to look inward. In this section, you are asked to reflect on your past science experiences. This type of personal reflection is very important since your ability to be a successful science teacher is influenced by your experiences as a science learner. Whether you know it or not, your own experiences with science in school helped to shape your beliefs about teaching and learning science. Your personal reflections hold the key to uncovering these tacitly held beliefs about science. They also provide the opportunity to begin to modify these beliefs if you feel that is necessary.

Writing Your Science Autobiography

Time to close this book again! First, follow these directions:

1. Take out a fresh piece of paper and a pen or turn on your computer.

2. Think back to your most vivid memories of being a science student, up to and including your college experiences.

3. Are you ready now? You're going to write your own science autobiography.

A personal account

This is a writing exercise in which you explore your feelings about science. Your science autobiography should be a *personal* description of your experience with science, in or out of school, through teachers, friends, family, museums, magazines, and other sources. The following questions can help you to think about this task:

■ When you look back at your science education, what do you see?

■ How much science did you study in school?

■ Did you like science? Hate it? Did you ever even think about it?

■ What personal experiences with school science, scientists, science in the media, and science teachers stand out for you?

Teachers who have written their science autobiographies often begin by saying that at first they could not remember anything. Then they took a few moments to look back and consider their science educations grade by grade, or year by year, and their stories were reclaimed. If you're having trouble getting started, it may help you to read the accompanying feature, "Excerpts from Preservice Teachers' Science Autobiographies."

Write freely!

Write candidly and freely about your evolving experiences with science and your beliefs about it. It does not matter how limited or extensive your experiences are, only that you describe them. There is no prescribed length or format for your science autobiography. It is your story and needs to reflect your experiences. When you have finished writing, go on to the next section.

Reflecting on Your Science Autobiography

The very process of writing a science autobiography helps us to examine our remembered experiences. But that is only the beginning. By reflecting on your story, you can gain a deeper understanding of how your experiences shaped your current thinking about science and your attitudes toward science. We know that teachers bring these beliefs—formed by their direct experiences with science in school, the people they meet who work in science, and the publicity science receives—to their teaching practice. Chances are that you will too. The challenge is to reflect on what you have written and make a conscious decision about how these remembered science experiences will influence your behavior as a teacher.

Reflective thought involves "active, persistent and careful consideration of any belief . . . in the light of the grounds that support it."
—John Dewey

Excerpts from Preservice Teachers' Science Autobiographies

The following passages, drawn from the science autobiographies of five preservice teachers, indicate some of the feelings that teachers have expressed about their experiences with science.

Albert Einstein I am not. Even as a young child, I was not enthusiastic about science. Although I was a very good student and I always excelled in my science classes, including honors chemistry and biology in high school, I was never excited about doing dissections or experiments. When I was given the option in senior year to take advanced placement science courses, or just drop science, I quickly stopped taking science altogether. . . .

When I reflect on my past experiences with science, two words come to mind: "Not interested." Then I entered fourth grade, and science came alive.

My outlook on science was much brighter, thanks to the efforts of Mrs. M, who helped me to feel confident by giving the class activities that we could make our own judgments about. . . .

When I think of science, I can only remember how much I dreaded it. It was boring, rote memorization that never seemed to end. I found it impersonal. Everything that was science came straight from the textbook. You were not expected to understand it, just to know it. . . .

When I was in college, I finally had a good science experience. It was in college biology. For the first time a teacher related the ideas we were learning about to events in the students' experiences. He also allowed the students the freedom to explore their own questions. . . .

Think about what you've written.

Begin your reflection now. You may want to start a new chapter in your science autobiography at this time. Ask yourself, "Why did I remember some stories and not others? How did these stories affect my current feelings about science and the prospect of teaching science?" You may already be starting to see science in a different light as you find your "scientist within" and consider teaching science in elementary or middle school. In the next section, you can try another method for locating your scientific self.

Reflective Practice II: Keeping a Science Journal

At this point in your preparation for teaching, you may already be familiar with reflective journals. These are usually personal journals, kept in a separate notebook, that record many of the feelings and events that have engaged you in your journey toward becoming a teacher.

Using a journal for reflection

Personal journals are nonthreatening vehicles that help you to explore your ideas and feelings about teaching and perhaps about classrooms in which you have been an observer or a participant. Teachers use personal journals as a way to reflect on their practice by writing about classroom situations that require careful consideration. Personal journals are important for developing your skills at looking inward. The activity of writing in your journal and reflecting on what you have written becomes your own process of meaning making, and this is an important tool for your professional development.

What Is a Science Journal?   A **science journal,** as we use the term here, is a personal journal in which the focus of your attention is nature and natural events you encounter in your daily experiences. Science can be thought of simply as a way of knowing your natural world. Therefore, a science journal contains your observations of and questions about nature. Often, as we charge through life in this fast-paced world, we are oblivious to the ways in which nature presents itself to us. Keeping a science journal forces us to take more notice of nature. For this reason, science journals are a way of contacting your scientific self.

Your own observations and questions

Science journals can also contain items about science in the news or science that you see in a classroom. You can write about a science show you saw on television or a newspaper story about a recent scientific breakthrough. If you have observed science in a school or classroom, write about it. What did you think of it?

How Do I Keep a Science Journal?   Keep your science journal in a separate notebook, and make entries in it on a fairly regular basis—about two or three times a week.

Remember that your science journal can encourage you to ask your own questions. If you observe something that you do not understand, write about it. A science journal may contain your mental wanderings and scientific wonderings. You may also think of a science journal as a "log," in which you record the natural events that capture your curiosity and take you by surprise.

You can be taken by surprise even in areas with which you are familiar. It is the surprises that hold the potential for further learning.
—ELEANOR DUCKWORTH AND COLLEAGUES

A Bird Story: Sample Entries from a Science Journal

The following excerpts from my own journal illustrate a type of story that sometimes emerges in science journals. This is the almost-daily log of a bird-watching experience I had in my own backyard. The experience took me by surprise, and I enjoyed writing about it. The geographic setting is a densely treed suburban area outside of New York City. Notice that I did not know how to explain everything I saw; I recorded my questions as well as my observations.

Tuesday: I never noticed the hollow in the middle of the trunk of the low-lying tree in the backyard. Imagine my surprise today when, as I glanced through the dining room window, I saw a bird fly right out of the tree! I wandered over to the tree trunk and peeked inside the hollowed-out area. I counted eight small white oval eggs. Each egg seemed to be about 4 cm long. The baby birds will soon be hatching, I think.

I'm wondering . . .

I wonder why the eggs are white. Wouldn't it be better if they were a dark color, for camouflage?

Tuesday [two weeks later]: Well, it has been two weeks, and the mother bird continues to fly into and out of the tree periodically. Sometimes when I glance into the hole, I can see her just sitting there. Yesterday, when I went to pay her my usual visit, she flew out just before I reached the tree. I leaned over to peek at the little eggs, but they were gone! In their place were several tiny birds, their necks extended upward and their beaks wide open. They made soft, small chirping noises that seemed clearly to say, "Feed me."

What type of bird?

Quietly I stared at them, and then, fearing that the mother bird would return at any moment, I walked away. Now I am wondering what type of bird this is. It's not one that I recognize.

Wednesday: This morning I ran out to the hollow in the tree. The sun was shining at just the right angle, into the hole in the tree trunk. The mother bird had just flown away, and when I peeked in, I counted at least eight pink baby birds, eyes closed, with no feathers. They really do look brand new and fragile. I wondered where the mother bird had gone and how long she would leave her hatchlings alone.

How long will she leave them?

An hour later, I returned for another glance, and as I looked down into the hole, the mother bird looked right back up at me. Was I surprised! I quickly walked away. But I've noticed that she has a pointed beak and brown feathers. When she flies off, I can see white feathers on her tail. She's a largish bird. I must find my bird book and identify her.

Sunday, late at night: I had to leave on Friday for a short trip, and I hated to miss the progress of the hatchlings. I've observed that the mother bird sits on the hatchlings often. Her frequent feeding trips take her into and out of the hollow in the tree many times a day.

Exploring at night

Tonight I arrived home at midnight, eager to see how the baby birds were doing. I took a flashlight and went outside. As I approached the tree, I noticed the mother bird perched inside, looking straight out of the hole, which is several inches above the nest. Her clawed feet must have been clinging to the inside of the tree. With my flashlight shining on her, I could see a black marking at her neck, as though she had on a collar. This black necklace seemed most distinctive. I have to get that bird book! I didn't see the hatchlings tonight—I decided to go back inside without disturbing the mother.

Found her!

Monday: The hatchlings are still there, a little bigger now. And I've found my field guide to the birds. Combing through the pictures, I spotted several birds that seem to look like the mother bird. She's a little like a catbird and a little like a mockingbird with her white feathers under her tail. But then I found her—and her black necklace. She's a northern flicker; I'm sure of it. I was so excited to identify her.

A mother flicker guarding her hatchlings at the hidden nest in the hollow of a backyard tree. Notice the black marking at her neck and the ever-hungry hatchlings!

Anthony Mercieca/Photo Researchers, Inc.

What happened to the mother?

Wednesday: It has been two days now since I last saw the mother bird. I look often for her, making her frequent runs into and out of the nest, and I'm getting worried. Last night I woke up in the middle of the night and went out to the tree with my flashlight, but there was no sign of her at her guard post in the hollow of the tree.

A rescue mission

Thursday night: This was the third night, and still no mother bird. I made my decision. The eight baby hatchlings would starve if I didn't do something! I prepared a deep, small cardboard box with wood chips and shreds of newspapers. I was nervous as I reached down into the hollow of the tree to lift the baby birds out, one at a time. Oh my, I thought, they're down much deeper than it appeared. It took almost the entire length of my arm to touch one. Slowly, I grabbed the bottom of one bird and then another, and after ten minutes, I had lifted all eight hatchlings from their nest. They felt very warm to the touch.

Feeding the baby birds

Earlier today, before finally deciding to remove the birds, I had contacted the owner of the local pet store to learn what he recommended for flicker hatchlings. I drove over there to buy some food and a small syringe for feeding them. Tonight when I put them in the box, I was ready. Using warm water, I mixed the food and filled the syringe. They were very hungry. They nestled together in a corner of the box on a table in my garage. I'm going to get up every two hours tonight to feed them.

Friday morning: It's not easy getting up every two hours to feed birds. But I'm glad I did it.

At 8 A.M. I called the local bird sanctuary and asked if I could bring the birds in for care. I got directions for finding the place. Mary, the director, turned out to be kind and caring. She immediately placed a small heating pad under the hatchlings inside their box. Using her fingers, she put solid, moist food down their throats with her fingers, and she showed me how their necks swell as the food goes down. The bulge in the neck shows which one has been fed. "My, what beautiful flickers we have here," she said. "Where is the mother?" I explained to her that I have not seen the mother bird for days. She said that if the mother was still around, I surely would have seen her as I was removing the babies from the tree. She said it was important to feed them often and that the mother bird would have fed them at least every two hours. So I guess my feeding them last night was the right thing to do.

Loneliness

As I left the bird sanctuary, glad to know that the birds were in good hands, Mary invited me back any time to visit with them. When I returned home, I was surprised to notice how lonely I felt after my days of observing the activity in the hollow of the tree. Now the tree is empty.

Friday evening: I've been realizing that the process of observing nature requires an investment of time and leads to an attachment to your objects of study. I really became *attached* to that bird family, and now that they're gone, I miss the activity as well as the birds themselves. I'm even slightly miffed that I won't have to get up every two hours tonight to feed birds!

Becoming emotionally invested

When you spend time making observations of nature, I suppose, you become invested in that experience. This afternoon I looked around for something else to study, but nothing caught my eye. I still wonder what has happened to the mother bird. Actually, I'm terrified that she'll return to the tree to find her hatchlings gone!

Monday: I returned to the bird sanctuary today to visit the hatchlings. They were still in the box I had prepared for them, and they seemed much bigger. Their feathers are appearing—black feathers emerging around their necks. I fed them with my fingers and chatted with Mary. In a week, she said, she'll place them in an indoor cage, so they can flut-

*Another question
answered*

ter around. Then they'll be removed to an outdoor cage, where they can practice their flying before being released into the wild.

Mary assured me that they are in very good shape and will be fine adult birds before long. I asked about something else that's been on my mind—why the eggs were white rather than colored for camouflage. She explained that since these birds lay eggs in hidden nests, they don't need camouflage.

Before I left the sanctuary, Mary told me that another flicker may choose to lay eggs in the same tree hollow. Funny—my heart soared! I'll welcome the chance to observe another bird family. I'm going to watch this tree (that I barely knew existed a few weeks ago), and I hope nature will give me another opportunity.

Learning from Your Science Journal

> *Our stories are the masks through which we can be seen, and with every telling we stop the flood and swirl of thought so someone can get a glimpse of us and maybe catch us if they can.*
> —MADELEINE GRUMET

As the bird story from my own journal illustrates, making careful observations of something in nature that engages you is one way to become your own authority on a given phenomenon. I never knew about northern flickers before that episode; I couldn't even identify one when I saw it. But after days of observing and writing in my journal, I certainly knew a lot about the birds in my backyard. In this way, the science journal helps bring forth the voice of scientific authority inside you.

It can also be helpful to share your journal with others. As my episode with the flickers unfolded, I was teaching one of my regular teacher education classes, and I took the opportunity to read my journal entries to my students, all of whom were preparing to become teachers. They all became nearly as wrapped up in the events as I was. Each time they saw me, they asked me anxiously, "How are the hatchlings doing?"

*Benefits of sharing
your journal*

Moreover, as I shared my science journal with these preservice teachers, they began to bring in books and articles about birds that they thought would interest me or that had piqued their own interest. It is not unusual for personal observations of nature to lead to some research, and that is what happened with us. We clipped a local newspaper article on bird watching that featured the northern flicker. We learned that our area has a rare-bird-alert hot line that provides a frequently updated report of what rare birds have been seen lately and where. Some class members contacted the local Audubon Society, which sponsors bird walks, lectures, and other opportunities to learn more about local and migratory birds.

By the end of the class, we had amassed a significant amount of information about local birds and northern flickers in particular. We all understood that this process had begun with my science journal and the entries I had shared with the group. Doing research about a science journal topic often happens when we personalize the experience of observing nature and invite others to share in the event.

As further illustration, the following excerpt explains how keeping a science journal helped one new teacher:

Linking personal observation to teaching

One of the things I am learning as I journal is that the more I look for things in nature to write about, the more I can pass on to my students. I have always appreciated nature, but I am even more attuned to it since I have been keeping this journal.

The greatest thing about observing nature is that I never know what to expect when I look out my window in the morning. Things are always new and changing and wonderful. All it takes is a little encouragement, and a little time, to take in all there is to observe. Hopefully, I will be able to pass that encouragement on to my own students one day.

It is snowing today. The first thing I will ask my students to do is to talk about the snow in their science journals: What are all the things they notice about the snow? What are their questions?

Some Guidelines for Your Own Science Journal

Keeping your own science journal means taking notice of your natural surroundings. It also invites you to develop a keen ear and eye for news stories that involve scientific matters. Anything can be grist for the mill. Keep the following reminders handy as you begin your journal:

Helpful hints

■ All of your observations are important. No observation is silly or too simple.

■ All of your questions have value; collect them in your journal.

■ Note the date and time of all your entries. This information can be helpful later if you want to go back and look for a pattern or connections.

■ Entries in your journal can be of any length.

■ Watch for interesting science shows on television.

■ Make use of any opportunities to find out what other people are thinking about natural events.

■ Have fun and write freely.

The Inner Scientist

The activities in this chapter have all been designed as tools to aid your self-exploration. They will help you to locate your scientific self through personal reflection and the exploration of science and scientists. From Rose's yellow balloons to your scientist drawing and science autobiography, they all concern the question, "What do *you* think about science, and how can you feel most comfortable with it?"

Opening doors

Remember, your "inner scientist" will ultimately be visible to your students. I hope that this book will help you to approach the teaching of science with pleasure and confidence. Science has the potential to help both you and your students open many doors to thinking about the natural world.

KEY TERMS

reflective teacher *(p. 44)*
science autobiography *(p. 45)*
science journal *(p. 47)*

RESOURCES FOR FURTHER EXPLORATION

Electronic Resources

Association for Women In Science. http://www.awis.org/. The World Wide Web site for this national organization has links to many resources. For example, the listing of local AWIS chapters can help you find a scientist to interview.

UT Science Bytes. http://pr.tennessee.edu/ut2kids/. Designed for both teachers and students, this web site has fascinating information about the current research interests of some University of Tennessee scientists.

Wonderwise: Women in Science Learning Series. http://net.unl.edu/wonderwise/. This site offers learning kits, including videos, activity books, and CD-ROMs, that are designed primarily for students in grades 4–6. All the kits feature the work of female scientists, and samples are available for free at the web site.

Print Resources

Barman, C. (1997). Students' views of scientists and science: Results from a national study. *Science and Children*, 35(1): 18–24.

Dewey, J. (1933; reissued 1998). *How We Think: A Restatement of the Relation of Reflective Thinking to the Educative Process*. Boston: Houghton Mifflin.

Fort, D., & Varney, H. (1989). How students see scientists: Mostly male, mostly white and mostly benevolent. *Science and Children*, 26: 8–13.

Koch, J. (1990). The science autobiography project. *Science and Children*, 28(3): 42–44.

Koch, J. (1993a). Face to face with science misconceptions. *Science and Children*, 31(3): 39–41.

Shepardson, D. P., & Britsch, S. (1997). Children's science journals. *Science and Children*, 35(2): 13ff.

Shrigley, R. (1983). The attitude concept and science teaching. *Science Education*, 67(2): 425–442.

Songer, N. B., & Linn, M. C. (1991). How do students' views of science influence knowledge integration? *Journal of Research in Science Teaching*, 28(9): 761–784.

Part Two

Doing Science with Students: Inquiry in Practice

In Part Two, we explore many types of science activities that help students to come up with their own ideas and seek answers to their own questions. We investigate these activities by means of *science stories,* narrative accounts of actual experiences that teachers, including myself, have had while doing science with students.

In the chapter "The Teacher as Mediator," we consider the teacher's role as mediator of the science experience. Next, we explore a classroom "science circus" that demonstrates what I mean by using process skills in science. In later chapters, we delve into other aspects of science teaching, such as making connections with students' daily lives, sustaining inquiry over time, and model making.

- In *life science,* students and teachers explore characteristics of living things and their interactions with the nonliving environment.

- In *physical science,* students and teachers look at properties of objects and materials, forms of energy, and motion of objects.

- In *earth science,* students and teachers investigate properties of earth materials, objects in the sky, and changes in the earth and sky.

The chapter on "Science Content and Curriculum" in Part Three will return to the subject of science content and how we organize it.

After each science story, look for the *Expanding Meanings* section. The subsections titled *The Teaching Ideas Behind This Story* and *The Science Ideas Behind This Story* will help you to think about the concepts illustrated by the story. The subsection called *The Standards Behind This Story* will help you to relate the classroom experience to the National Science Education Standards and the National Educational Technology Standards. *Questions for Further Exploration* can take you to the next level of thinking, and the section *Resources for Further Exploration* offers both print and electronic material to expand your knowledge base.

3 The Teacher as Mediator

FOCUSING QUESTIONS

- As a child, did you ever invent your own theories for why things happened— theories that were useful at the time but didn't necessarily match what the rest of the world believed?

- Can you remember some of these "alternative conceptions" you had as a child? Do they sound silly to you now, or do you see them as interesting, creative, and maybe even logical?

- Why do you think hands-on science is not enough to help students learn science concepts?

- What do you think of when you hear the word *mediator*? How might it apply to teaching?

The preceding chapter invited you to begin discovering your scientific self. As you did, you probably revisited your childhood wonderings and wanderings. One new teacher, who grew up in an urban area, remembered wondering why it was always cool in the summer in the basement of the apartment building where she and her family lived. When it got too hot, she and her friends would retreat to the basement.

Children have many questions like that, but too often schools do not make room for these questions, and the children grow up, as this teacher did, with their questions unanswered. This happens because teachers, no doubt meaning well, approach science teaching and learning from their own perspective only. They ask themselves, in effect, "What do I have to *transmit* or *deliver* to my students?" As you will see in this chapter, science education is much more about the exchanges that occur between teachers and students as they explore science together.

While you rediscover your scientific self, you will also notice the ways in which your students express their scientific selves when you engage them in meaningful science activities. As we mentioned earlier, students construct meanings from science experiences on the basis of who they are, where they have been, and their own prior understandings. In this chapter, you will see how you can act as a *mediator* in this process, helping your students to construct their own meanings by listening to their ideas and learning about how they think.

At times, you may engage all the students in a similar experience at the same time, or you may involve different groups in different activities that are centered on a similar theme. Sometimes you may show the students a natural event by way of a demonstration. That is what happens in the following science story.

SCIENCE STORY

The Bottle and the Balloon

I am visiting Ms. Hudson's third-grade class in a suburb of a major northeastern city. The twenty-four children come from many cultures— European American, Latino, African American, and Asian American— and a wide range of socioeconomic classes. I'm standing up front with the simple apparatus I've brought for this lesson.

A deflated balloon, an "empty" bottle

The children watch as I place a deflated red balloon over an apparently empty vinegar bottle. It hangs to the side like Santa's hat. I hold the bottle up to the class and ask, "What do you think is in this bottle?"

The children respond, "Air!"

I put this thick glass bottle into a pot of just-boiled water, holding the top to keep it upright. "Let's watch what happens here," I say. Slowly, the deflated balloon fills with air, until it stands erect at the top of the bottle.

The children are delighted. With only a little prodding from me, they carefully explain what they observe, and we record it: When we put the bottle in the hot water, the balloon filled up with air. "Where do you think the air has come from?" I ask. "What are some of your ideas?"

> *My thinking: At this point I am wondering if the children will grasp that making the bottle hot will heat the air inside the bottle and that the warm air expands and causes the balloon to inflate. I do not expect the children to have that level of knowledge, but I do hope they will make some connection between the heated air and the balloon's inflating. Instead, the children give me some creative but quite different explanations.*

The children's ideas

"The steam from the boiling water went through the glass and inflated the balloon," a boy named Mike offers.

"That is an interesting idea," I answer. "Have you ever seen steam go through glass before?" After thinking for a moment, he does not remember having seen steam go through glass.

A girl named Jamila agrees with Mike's focus on steam, but has a different idea about the mechanism: "The steam seeped into the balloon because the seal between the balloon and the bottle was not airtight." I respond, "That sounds as if you have really been thinking about this. Do you think that my placing the bottle in the hot water helped the steam to seep in?" Jamila says, "Yes, it helped steam get in."

Why does the teacher keep asking for students' ideas?

It's clear to me now that several students think that steam seeped into the balloon. I continue to question them about their thinking: "Do you think that if we made the seal between the bottle and balloon tighter, we could prevent the steam from seeping in?" The students believe this is true, so I ask them how we should do it. They decide to take several bottles and balloons and securely tape each new balloon onto its bottle before placing it in the pot of hot water. We try four different setups with bottles of different sizes and shapes as well as balloons of different sizes and shapes. In each case, the balloon still inflates.

More tries . . .

Though the results contradict their own ideas, the children enjoy watching the balloons inflate. Each time I repeat the experience, I invite the students (especially those who most firmly believe that the source of the air is *outside* the bottle) to stay close and observe. Jamila looks hard for steam seeping into the bottle. Mike holds the balloon tightly around the neck of the bottle to make sure it is airtight.

. . . and a new idea emerges

After the four additional tries, I ask the students what they are thinking now. At this point, they have mostly decided that the air inflating the balloon must be air that was already inside the bottle. We make connections between this experiment and hot-air balloons as well as to the places where we find the hottest room in our houses during the summer. Some students are coming, in their own way, to the science idea that I was hoping they would grasp, namely, that adding heat energy to the air changes the way the air behaves.

In these experiments, as the students have noticed, the balloon always fills gently and partially with air; it does not inflate completely. I ask them why they think the balloon did not blow up more than it did. Some students remark that it could fill up only with the air that was already in the bottle when we started. "Hooray!" I think. They really "get" it.

Another experiment

Finally, to help them build on their understanding, I ask myself what other demonstration I can do to show that there is air in the bottle. We proceed to take the balloon off the bottle and invert the "empty" bottle in a basin of water. The water does not rise in the bottle. Some students say that it must be the air in the bottle that keeps the water from entering.

EXPANDING MEANINGS

■ The Teaching Ideas Behind This Story

■ When students simply repeat answers they have heard, we cannot be sure that there is any deep meaning in this knowledge. The students in Ms. Hudson's class all agreed that the bottle contained air. Nevertheless, I could tell that many were not comfortable with this idea. For some, it was just a rote answer, something they had been told was true but hadn't fully incorporated into their own thinking. *Grasping terminology is not the same as understanding the concept or being able to apply it in a real-life context* (Yager, 1991; Brooks & Brooks, 1999).

- When I asked Mike if he had seen steam go through glass, I was not making fun of his idea. Instead, I was trying to draw out his prior experiences that might have contributed to it.

- Notice how I treated the children's "wrong" ideas with respect, inviting them to test whether those ideas were true. This is a vital technique that we will discuss further in the next section.

- Although the experiment began as a demonstration, it quickly became a participatory event as the students suggested their own variations.

● The Science Ideas Behind This Story

- Although air is all around us and seeps into everything, it is a difficult concept for young students to understand. They can blow air onto their hands, feel the force of a breeze—but, still, it is a tricky concept.

- Air that is warmed expands. Its particles move faster and become farther apart. Because its particles are farther apart, this warmed air is now less dense. In the experiment in Ms. Hudson's class, the colder air above—denser, with its particles closer together—dropped down, pushing the warm air upward.

- The method by which heat energy travels in liquids and gases is called *convection*. You can read more about convection in the chapter "Science Content and Curriculum." Ms. Hudson or I could have introduced this term and asked the students to memorize the definition. But even after learning the term, they might have been unable to relate it to the balloon and the bottle.

✔ The Science Standards Behind This Story

 STANDARDS The story of Ms. Hudson's class reflects the following portions of the National Science Education Standards (National Research Council, 1996):

- ✔ *Teaching Standard B:* "Teachers of science . . . encourage and model the skills of scientific inquiry, as well as the curiosity, openness to new ideas and data, and skepticism that characterize science" (p. 32).

- ✔ *Content Standard B, Grades K–4 (Physical Science):* "The children . . . have intuitive notions of energy. . . . Teachers can build on the intuitive notions of students without requiring them to memorize technical definitions" (p. 126).

Questions for Further Exploration

- How is *convection* of heat energy in the balloon experiment different from the *conduction* of heat that occurs when you touch a hot stove?

■ What stories do you know that involve hot-air balloons? What principle is behind the operation of these balloons?

■ How might you help young students discover that air has weight and takes up space?

Resources for Further Exploration

ELECTRONIC RESOURCES

Building an Understanding of Constructivism (1994). *Classroom Compass,* 1(3), http://www.sedl.org/scimath/compass/v01n03/2.html. This article from the third issue of the online journal *Classroom Compass* offers a fine overview of constructivism.

Crowther, David T. (1997). The constructivist zone. *The Electronic Journal of Science Education.* http://unr.edu/homepage/jcannon/ejse/ejse.html. Follow the links to volume 2, number 2, of this electronic journal. Crowther's editorial offers a historical perspective on constructivism and an overview of its impact on current practice. The issue as a whole is devoted to the "science wars"—the controversy over methods of teaching science.

PRINT RESOURCES

Duckworth, E. (1996). *The Having of Wonderful Ideas and Other Essays on Teaching and Learning,* 2d ed. New York: Teachers College Press.

Gallas, K. (1995). *Talking Their Way into Science.* New York: Teachers College Press.

Kaner, E. (1989). *Balloon Science.* Reading, MA: Addison-Wesley.

Logan, J. (1997). *Teaching Stories.* New York: Kodansha International.

Helping Students Construct Meaning

Let's reflect further on what happened in Ms. Hudson's class when I helped the students experiment with bottles and balloons. As we noted in the opening chapter, the view that learning is an active process of knowledge construction is part of a family of theories called *constructivism*. Basic to constructivism is the necessity for individuals to put together thoughts, interpretations, and explanations that are their own personal constructs (von Glasersfeld, 1995; Yager, 1991; Brooks & Brooks, 1999). This means that in order to understand a concept, individuals *must* be engaged in the active process of making sense of their experiences. They create and re-create ideas that give meaning to a specific concrete experience. This is an essential principle of constructivism: the belief that simply "knowing" something does not constitute understanding. Instead, we gradually come to understand ideas as we turn them over in our minds and reflect on our experiences.

An active process of making meaning

As you have already gathered, this theory has important implications for methods of science teaching. Understanding how the learner constructs meaning helps us to create environments that stimulate our science learners.

Prior Knowledge

The philosopher John Dewey said that concepts should be viewed as "known points of reference by which to get our bearings when we are plunged into the strange unknown" (1933, p. 153). That is, concepts don't just sit there in our minds; they help us interpret and deal with new situations. In turn, these new experiences help us refine our concepts. I like to think of our concepts as old friends—ideas we come to know as we grow and that we refine and revisit as we add new understandings to our repertoire. Our repertoire of such understandings is our **prior knowledge.**

Prior knowledge— our repertoire of familiar concepts

Did the students in Ms. Hudson's class have prior knowledge? To a casual observer, it may not seem that they knew very much about the matter at hand. Nevertheless, the prior knowledge they possessed was extremely important. They knew that boiling water gives off steam, for example, and they certainly understood some of the characteristics of steam.

As I conducted my experiments, I was really interested to learn that several students thought that the balloon inflated because of the steam from the just-boiled water. If I had merely told them something different, they might have nodded at me but failed to derive any real meaning from what I said. Instead, because my interest in their thinking was genuine, the students knew that I valued their ideas and respected their prior knowledge. This leads us to our next crucial point.

Valuing the Students' Thinking

Valuing the students' ideas is a way of communicating to them that they are important members of the class. That is important in itself, but there is more to it. When their ideas are genuinely valued, students begin to see themselves as *knowers.* Only as knowers can they construct new meanings by building on their prior beliefs and ideas.

Valuing students' ideas → students' reflection → new ideas

This is a vital principle to grasp. Creating an atmosphere in which there is a sense of trust makes it possible to help the students reflect on their new experiences and use those reflections to modify their prior knowledge. Without such trust, the students are not likely to do much serious thinking about the science experiences in which you engage them. They may memorize a "fact" or two, but their underlying conceptions may remain unaffected.

When you inquire about students' thinking, you need to be ready for many types of responses. *All* of their responses have value since they provide insight into the students' thinking. If you tell the students your thinking first, they will never feel comfortable sharing their own ideas. The students will immediately think the way you think, or at least they will

Avoiding the "teacher game"

say they do. This is called playing the "teacher game," and even young children are good at that.

If students have difficulty reaching a "correct" scientific understanding, that is okay. Listen to their ideas and reflect on them. Ask the students questions that help you understand the nature of their prior knowledge. Encourage them to:

- Write about and draw what they have observed.

- Create stories and poems about their science activities.

- Plan other similar experiments to test their personal ideas.

Such experiences will encourage them to come up with their own ideas and offer those ideas in the discourse of the classroom.

Science activities and experiments need to provide students with the freedom to say exactly what they think—even if that is the freedom to be wrong. In the rest of this book, you will find many examples of this teaching strategy.

Mediating the Students' Learning

What does it mean to "mediate"?

If our interest is helping students construct meaning, then we have to teach in ways that facilitate that process. The challenge is to help students delve deeply into their thoughts and expand their own thinking about an idea. Our role therefore becomes that of a **mediator.** In everyday terms, a mediator serves as a go-between of some sort, often by helping people resolve their differences by bridging the gaps between their points of view. A teacher who is a mediator helps students to bridge the gap between their initial understanding and the deeper knowledge they can build as a result of the lesson. The teacher can do this in a variety of ways, but the process usually begins by exposing students to new experiences and helping them to probe their own thinking. (In terms of the science learning cycle described earlier, the teacher's mediation takes place during the explanation and elaboration phases.)

In my entire life as a student, I remember only twice being given the opportunity to come up with my own ideas, a fact I consider typical and terrible.
—ELEANOR DUCKWORTH

In the bottle-and-balloon lesson, I was helping the students probe their thinking by inviting them to try the experiment again, in different ways. I facilitated that process by providing additional materials and becoming the mediator of their ideas. It wasn't easy. The students who believed that the air inflating the balloon came from outside the bottle had a hard time realizing that anything was already in the bottle when we started. Although they said "air" when asked what was in the bottle, they were merely being correct, not truly understanding the concept.

Students' theories

Hence, I encouraged them to test their own theories. By "theories" in this context, I mean their proposed explanations for a natural event. In science, we generally use the term *theory* to mean a belief about a science idea that has a lot of observable evidence to support it. By students' theories, we refer to their beliefs based on their own understandings at their partic-

One-Way Versus Two-Way Communication

The role of teacher as mediator is very different from the traditional concept of the teacher as simply a *provider* of knowledge. One way to understand this difference is to think of it in terms of communication.

In traditional science teaching, the process has been accomplished as one-way communication: the teacher talks, the students listen. But if we really believe that our students are knowers—that they bring their prior knowledge of the world to our classes—then we can never think of science teaching as a one-way process. Teaching becomes a *two-way* conversation, a dialogue in which the teacher explores a student's thinking and responds, and the student then explores the teacher's thinking and responds. Dialogue also happens between individual students; and when groups of students become involved, the conversation often involves three or four people or more. This is what is meant by the *social construction of meaning*, a phrase that is frequently used to emphasize the importance of social context in learning.

With this two-way style of communication, the teacher helps students flesh out their ideas and make meaning from them. In the end, this type of science teaching yields a deeper, more important, and more valid understanding of science ideas.

ular level of cognitive development. These may not be full-fledged theories in the scientific sense, but they can lead to genuine theory building as students construct further meaning.

Alternative conceptions—stages in a journey

As the bottle-and-balloon story demonstrates, different students construct meaning in different ways, and sometimes their ideas amount to **alternative conceptions**—ideas that are not scientifically accurate but represent a step toward full understanding of a concept. Alternative conceptions are like train stations. They are places the students pass through on their journey to fuller understanding. Obviously, teachers need a thorough grasp of the science concepts behind a given topic to know when the students' own ideas represent steps in the path toward fuller understanding. As a teacher, you achieve that grasp by exploring science experiences and science concepts one topic at a time—and by locating your inner scientist. (Do not worry; it is doable and very rewarding. The chapter "Science Content and Curriculum" contains some useful scientific information to jump-start your science content knowledge.)

Dealing with alternative conceptions

When students reveal alternative conceptions, teachers need to evaluate those ideas and take action. This "action" is what your role as mediator is all about. Valuing the students' ideas does not mean you must let them go unchallenged. Instead, you invite your students to examine their conceptions from multiple perspectives—making connections between the experience and something else in their memory, or trying the experiment again in a different way. Thus, I asked Mike if he had ever seen steam go through a bottle before. I asked the students, too, if they thought making the seal tighter would prevent the steam from seeping into the

The teacher is asking probing questions as a student shares her ideas about an investigation. Listening to students and having conversations with them about science is a necessary part of teaching science.

Annie Griffiths Belt/Corbis

balloon, and I guided them to explore that possibility. Through such means, we help them refine their ideas so their thinking matches their own enlarged experience.

Now let's look at another example of students constructing meaning with the teacher acting as a mediator.

SCIENCE STORY

Icicles

Mr. Wilson notices . . .

It is an icy-cold winter morning in the Northeast. It snowed two days ago, and the temperature has plummeted to well below the freezing point of water. Ice and snow cover everything.

On his way to school in this urban community, Mr. Wilson notices icicles hanging from the edges of roof lines. The icicles glisten in the sun. They are of varying lengths and thicknesses. He reaches up and breaks off some extra-long ones and brings them to his third-grade classroom, where he stores them temporarily on a ledge outside the window.

After the morning business, Mr. Wilson retrieves the icicles and shows them to the children. "Where do you think I found these?" he asks. The children call out all the places where they saw icicles this morning. Some of them noticed icicles hanging from tree branches; others saw icicles on roofs and awnings. Still others didn't seem to notice any icicles at all. As a group, the children are excited that Mr. Wilson has brought some icicles to class. He describes how he reached up to a low roof and gently pulled them off, trying not to break them.

The students notice . . .

"What are all the things you notice about these icicles?" Mr. Wilson asks.

The children respond in various ways: "They're long." "They're cold." "They're cloudy." "They're hard." "They're pointy." "They will start dripping when they melt." "You can hurt someone if you stick it into them!"

"Let's explore these things before they melt," says Mr. Wilson. "What are your questions? What do you want to find out about these icicles?"

Some children are interested in knowing how long it will take for them to melt. Others suggest different questions:

The children have questions.

"Will they weigh the same when they melt as they do now?"

"When they melt, will they be the same color?"

"Can we make them back into an icicle after we melt them?"

"Do they taste good?"

Why are the students' questions important?

Mr. Wilson's thinking: Notice that Mr. Wilson has asked the students to think about what they want to know about the icicles. He knows that what is really important is the students' questions—the ones they cannot answer yet, the ones that compel them to search for answers.

Mr. Wilson engages the children in a discussion of their questions. They talk about why it may not be a good idea to taste the icicles. (Some children think they may be dirty.) Most of the children want to make the icicles melt. Some children want to place the icicles on the classroom heater. Some want to light a candle (Mr. Wilson would do that for them) and hold the icicle over it. Some children want to place the icicles on the window ledge, where the sun is streaming in.

Why does Mr. Wilson let the children decide?

At this point, Mr. Wilson temporarily returns the icicles to the outside ledge. He asks the children to divide up into their usual science groups. Each group will get an icicle to work with, he says, and each group should decide in advance what to do with it before it melts. As a suggestion, Mr. Wilson repeats one of the ideas the students themselves proposed: "Let's do find out," he says, "if our icicles weigh the same when they melt."

As the children are deciding on their procedures, Mr. Wilson visits each group and coaches them. He points things out to them and asks them to explain what they have come up with. He prods them, leading them with his questions, coaxing and coaching their planning. "What should we do to find out if the icicles weigh the same after they melt as they do now?" he asks various groups.

"Weigh them, before and after," the children figure out.

Mr. Wilson's thinking: Although this is an impromptu lesson, Mr. Wilson has an objective in mind. He's hoping the students will begin to learn what melting really is. The question about an icicle's weight before

Being a coach

and after melting was an important one, so he stimulates their attention to it. He also guides them in framing their investigations so they will be able to explore the changes that occur when the icicle melts. He points things out and inquires about their plans. He is somewhat like a tour guide or a coach. Unlike a tour guide, however, he does not explain the details of all the sights. Instead, he listens to the students' impressions and asks for whatever meanings they may construct.

It turns out that one group cannot decide what to do. Mr. Wilson asks them what they have thought about so far. One student explains that "Jamie wants to make something that will keep the icicle from melting," while the rest of them (three other children) want to time how long it will take to melt.

Jamie's different idea

Mr. Wilson thinks about this dilemma and asks Jamie what question she has in mind. Her question is, "How long can I keep the icicle cold?" She wants to wrap the icicle up with materials from the classroom and put it in a shoebox. "Why are you interested in doing that?" asks Mr. Wilson. Jamie replies, "I want to see if I can keep it cold long enough to take it home."

"Okay," Mr. Wilson says, "why doesn't Jamie do that with one icicle? The rest of you can take another icicle and work on your plan to melt it."

Mr. Wilson's thinking: Although his main focus in this lesson is on melting, Mr. Wilson doesn't force all the children to work on that. He knows that Jamie is becoming invested in exploring her own question, so he allows this to happen.

Mass and Weight

In elementary and middle school science, students learn some basic ideas about matter. Matter can be defined as anything that has weight or mass and takes up space (as opposed to energy, for example, which has neither of those qualities).

Mass refers directly to how much matter is in an object. Often, the term *weight* is used interchangeably with *mass,* but in scientific usage, the two are different. *Weight* means the gravitational pull that the earth has on an object.

Since the gravitational pull of the earth is relatively constant, mass and weight are essentially the same on earth. But if you weigh an object on earth and then take it to the moon, it will weigh only about one-sixth as much because the moon's gravitational pull is about one-sixth as strong as the earth's. The object's mass, on the other hand, will be the same in both places.

Even on earth, the nearer a body is to the center of the earth, the greater the downward pull of gravity on the body and the more the body will weigh. The farther a body is from the center of the earth, the less the body will weigh.

When the groups have decided on their questions and procedures, Mr. Wilson takes out the scales—the double-pan balances commonly used for measuring mass in elementary grades. He distributes an icicle to each group, giving an extra one to Jamie. But before the students begin to weigh the icicles, he asks them, "How will you collect the water while your icicle is melting?" (Some of the icicles are already dripping.) The children have to consider the problem. He invites them over to the science supply table and asks for suggestions. They look at the plastic cups, aluminum foil pie pans, shoeboxes, and assorted plastic containers. Someone suggests that they allow the icicle to melt in an aluminum pie pan. Mr. Wilson encourages this idea since the pie pans are flat and can accommodate the icicles without tipping over.

Encouraging a good solution

Now he asks the children to weigh their icicles. As their standard masses, the children use teddy bear counters: thick plastic figures, about 5 centimeters long, shaped liked teddy bears. (Standard unit masses may be in gram units or in any other convenient units—for example, paper clips or pennies.)

In their small groups, the children take turns with the double-pan balance. Some children weigh the icicle and the pan together. Others weigh just the icicle. Mr. Wilson observes each group and does not give specific instructions. The children realize that the icicles have to be weighed quickly, before they melt.

No specific instructions

> *Mr. Wilson's thinking: Mr. Wilson does not want to direct the students in how to weigh their icicles. Instead, he gives them the freedom to experiment—the freedom to be wrong and then to explore further until they are right. He watches, he suggests, he leads a bit, and then he lets go—until (as we will see) he needs to intervene. He is mediating their experience.*

All of us learn through our experiments. Do we give ourselves the freedom to experiment, the freedom to be wrong, the freedom to be right . . . for a little while . . . until we turn out to be wrong again?
—Jacqueline Grennon Brooks and Martin Brooks

After the weighing, the children proceed with their different plans for melting their icicles. One group, which has weighed the icicle in the pan, places the pan on the sunny window sill and checks it every few minutes until the icicle melts. Then the group members weigh the melted icicle in the pan and compare the two measurements they have made:

A "right" answer

icicle + pan = 20 teddy bears
melted icicle + pan = 20 teddy bears

Other groups follow different methods of melting and come up with similar results in the weight test.

Predictably, however, the groups that have weighed an icicle by itself, outside the pie pan, run into trouble. For instance, one of these groups proceeds to melt the icicle in the pan on the heater and then weighs the resulting water in the pan. This group concludes that the melted icicle weighs more than the solid icicle. Now Mr. Wilson intervenes. "What about the pie pan that you have the water in?" he asks. "Doesn't it weigh something?"

A "wrong" answer

The children look at him. He explains, "You weighed your icicle on the balance scale all by itself, but you weighed the water in the pan. If you weighed the icicle all by itself, then you would have to weigh the water all by itself."

Thinking about this, the children come up with a new plan. They ask Mr. Wilson if they can try the experiment again with another icicle. "Yes," he says, and gives them a new one to work with. He has been keeping extra icicles outside the classroom window.

> *Mr. Wilson's thinking: Mr. Wilson intervenes when he realizes that the children have come up with an alternative, an idea that has been but is not scientifically accurate. He sets them on a path that will help them build a more accurate idea.*
>
> *It is interesting, though, that Mr. Wilson does not tell them to find the mass of the pie pan by itself and then subtract that from the total mass of the pie pan and water. The children have not thought of that option, and Mr. Wilson decides to allow them to redo their experiment rather than impose his procedure on them. This is an important decision: finding the right balance between guiding the procedure and allowing students to experiment for themselves. Here we see another facet of the teacher as mediator.*

The group that is redoing the experiment begins by weighing the icicle *in* the pan this time. They decide to let the new icicle melt in the pan on a table in the back of the room. This icicle takes longer to melt, so they weigh the resulting water after lunch. This is their result:

icicle + pan = 15 teddy bears
melted icicle + pan = 15 teddy bears

Once all the groups are finished, Mr. Wilson again engages the entire class in discussion. The students all agree now that you have to weigh the icicle in the pan at the beginning, and then you have to weigh the melted icicle in the pan at the end. They also agree that an icicle's weight does not change when it melts, though most of them are surprised by this conclusion.

"Well, what did you think would happen?" Mr. Wilson asks. The children say that the melted icicle looked so little compared to the original icicle that they thought it would weigh less.

"What other melting experiments can we do?" Mr. Wilson wonders aloud. The children suggest using ice cubes to see if the same thing will happen. Mr. Wilson promises to bring ice cubes to class the next day. Meanwhile, Jamie has wrapped her icicle tightly in aluminum foil and paper towels before placing it in a plastic bag and putting it in a shoebox to take home.

The Next Day: From Icicles to Ice Cubes

The following morning, the children in Mr. Wilson's class come to school ready to see if a pan of ice cubes will weigh the same before and after melting. This experiment was the children's own idea, and it generates curiosity and profound interest.

Jamie explains her results

Before addressing the ice cubes activity, however, Mr. Wilson gives Jamie a chance to present her experiment to the class. She explained to the class that her icicle in the shoebox did last, but it became a lot smaller. When she got home, she put it in the freezer.

Can they apply the concept?

Now Mr. Wilson brings out three trays of ice cubes from the school refrigerator. Weighing the tray of ice cubes before and after melting will be a repeated experience, another visit to the concept of masses remaining the same when the state of matter changes. It is an example of assessing how well the children can *apply a concept* they learned the day before. Once again, Mr. Wilson is engaging them in solving a problem, setting up an experiment, testing their own ideas, and drawing some conclusions.

The class wants to explore further.

But the students now are also interested in Jamie's type of experiment. They want to know if they can try different techniques to preserve the ice cubes. "Sure," replies Mr. Wilson. One ice cube tray can be used for melting, and the others can supply the cubes for the new experiments. Mr. Wilson sees that the class's further explorations can lead to ideas about the concept of insulation and the losing and gaining of heat energy. In this way, one student's question has become an entire class's experiment.

EXPANDING MEANINGS

■ The Teaching Ideas Behind This Story

- ■ The way Mr. Wilson used the icy weather to engage the students in a science activity reflects an important connection between the environment outside the classroom and the activity within it. Making this connection is a very important part of doing science with students. Nature is all around us, and frequently it presents itself through changes in the weather. These activities may be thought of as *informal science learning experiences*, as contrasted with the more formal, prescribed science curricula that we will explore later in this book.

- ■ Clearly, Mr. Wilson was engaging the children in a constructivist learning activity. Notice how he listened to their ideas about icicles, weighing, and melting, and then encouraged them to try out their notions. This method helps students recognize what they already know and build on it. For example, the students knew that the icicles would melt if kept indoors. They had their own ideas about places where the melting might happen quickly—the heater in the classroom and the sunny window ledge. Their prior knowledge also helped them choose an appropriate container in which to place each icicle before they melted it. Because Mr. Wilson acknowledged them as knowers, they could proceed to experiment with confidence.

■ Nevertheless, Mr. Wilson did not ignore what they were doing or let them experiment entirely without help. Instead, he *mediated* their experience by giving them suggestions and guiding their activities.

■ There are those who will think that Mr. Wilson should have told the children at the beginning that they needed to weigh the icicles in some kind of receptacle. Such an instruction may be time efficient, but it does not promote the development of the children's own ideas. He wanted the children to explore on their own so they could learn the best way to measure their icicles. For that reason, he created an atmosphere in which the children had the opportunity and *intellectual freedom* to investigate their notions. He also gave them the tacit message that it is okay to be "wrong."

■ When one team of students decided that the water weighed more than the original icicle, Mr. Wilson knew that this was an alternative conception that could become a stopping-off place en route to deeper meaning. It was, in effect, raw material for him to work with in helping the children construct deeper knowledge.

■ Mr. Wilson did not know in advance exactly where the icicle experience would lead. He did not impose a rigid procedure. He was intending that the students learn something about melting. But Jamie, the student who kept the icicle cold, would also learn something about insulation. He did make sure that each group explored the question of weight before and after melting—a question that the students themselves had raised in the beginning when he prompted them for ideas.

■ Do you see how the approach to learning Mr. Wilson took in his class parallels the scientific process itself? In professional science, one experiment often leads to another experiment because somebody in the research team has a new, but related question. In the same way, Mr. Wilson's students, stimulated in part by Jamie, follow their own questioning from one exploration to another.

● The Science Ideas Behind This Story

● The activity in this story addresses what happens when matter *changes state*, in this case from a solid to a liquid. The students observe that when a certain amount of matter changes state, its mass does not change. Changes in state are associated with different amounts of energy, but the amount of mass remains constant before and after the change of state.

This student is weighing a solid using washers as uniform masses. How many washers weigh the same as the solid object on the double-pan balance? In scientific activity, we are often seeking answers through measurement.

Tony Freeman/PhotoEdit

Each group of children added heat energy to its icicle so that it would melt. The icicle absorbed the heat energy. That caused its particles to move faster and spread farther apart, turning the solid into a liquid. But the additional energy did not affect the mass.

• This activity helped students understand that when you are weighing the same object in different forms, the method you use is very important. There is a key general principle here. In a science experiment we always ask, "What are we keeping the same? What are we changing?" Scientists call these **constants** and **variables,** respectively. The students were changing the state of matter; therefore, to make this a fair test of the effect on weight, the conditions under which the two states were weighed had to be the same. A **fair test** in science requires that we keep all of the experimental conditions the same (constant), except the one that we are testing for (the variable).

✔ The Science Standards Behind This Story

STANDARDS ✔

The story of Mr. Wilson's class reflects the following portions of the National Science Education Standards (National Research Council, 1996):

✔ *Teaching Standard B:* "Teachers of science . . . challenge students to accept and share responsibility for their own learning" (p. 32). You can see how Mr. Wilson models this idea.

✔ *Content Standard B, Grades K–4 (Physical Science):* "Materials can exist in different states—solid, liquid, and gas. Some common materials, such as water, can be changed from one state to another by heating or cooling" (p. 127). These science ideas are appropriate for Mr. Wilson's third graders.

Questions for Further Exploration

■ In what ways do you think the icicle activity stimulated the students' thinking process?

■ What prior experiences do you think the children were relying on to construct new meanings?

■ What science ideas did the teacher need to know before engaging children in this activity?

■ What connections could you make from this lesson to literature or social studies?

■ How might you integrate technology into this activity?

Resources for Further Exploration

ELECTRONIC RESOURCES

Just Think: Problem Solving Through Inquiry.   Videotape series available from the New York State Education Department, Office of Educational Television and Public Broadcasting, Cultural Education Center, Room 10A75, Albany, NY 12230. Offers an excellent view of teachers as mediators in real classrooms.

A Private Universe.   A 20-minute videocassette about basic science concepts and alternative conceptions. Available from the Annenberg/CPB Video Catalog, http://www.learner.org/, and from Pyramid Media, http://pyramidmedia.com/.

The Weather Unit.   http://faldo.atmos.uiuc.edu/WEATHER/weather.html. Lesson plans relating to weather, with projects in math, art, reading, and other fields, as well as science.

PRINT RESOURCES

Dyasi, H. (1995). Is there room for children's ideas in the elementary school curriculum? In William Ayers (ed.), *To Become a Teacher: Make a Difference in Children's Lives.* New York: Teachers College Press.

Hoover, E., & Mercier, S. (1990). "Melt an Ice Cube," an activity described in *Primarily Physics* (1990). Fresno, CA: AIMS (Activities Integrating Mathematics and Science) Education Foundation. Available at *http:www.aimsedu.org/.*

Museum of Science. (1992). *The Weather Kit.* Boston: Boston Museum of Science. This is a multidisciplinary curriculum kit from the Museum of

Science in Boston. Very student centered and interactive, it has great ideas for weather experiments.

Mediation and Alternative Conceptions

Situated cognition

Dewey (1933) talked about concrete experiences as the ground and generator of the thinking process. Remarking that experience would lead to the understanding of ideas and the capacity to conceptualize, he argued for hands-on learning fifty years before it became a catch phrase. This movement from objects to ideas is what rooting science learning in concrete experience is all about. Some researchers have used the term *situated cognition* or *situated learning* to refer to the notion that the situation or context of learning is critical and that real learning takes place only when it is situated in real-world activities (see, for example, Snowman & Biehler, 2003). In general, there is a strong theoretical foundation for rooting science teaching in meaningful, concrete activities.

Predetermined, predictable lessons

Unfortunately, many science teachers, unlike Mr. Wilson, offer students hands-on activities that are completely predetermined and predictable. Such lessons are often designed to control the outcomes; the teacher knows beforehand exactly where the students should end up. There are obvious attractions to this method. Certainly you do need specific learning goals for your students; but if you exercise too much control over the procedures and outcome of each activity, you are not honoring the multiple ways in which your students can construct the "right" answer.

The staying power of inaccurate ideas

The problem with imposing strict procedures on students when they are doing science is that the teacher does not learn what the students really think or how they construct meaning. Without learning what they think, it is extremely difficult to help them change or develop their thinking. Many years of research have revealed that most people have significant misconceptions about nature—that is, they believe that there are reasons for natural events that are actually not so. It appears that even many years of schooling do not help: people cling to their misconceptions. Even university science and engineering majors have many misconceptions about science. Often students will score well on standardized tests and yet be unable to change the experience-based interpretations of nature they acquired prior to instruction (Yager, 1991).

Alternative conceptions— a better term

Misconceptions are better characterized by the term we introduced earlier, alternative conceptions. This is because it is important to foster a tolerance for inaccurate ideas if we are to provide students with the experience necessary to change them. It is also important to recognize that alternative conceptions cut across age, ability, gender, and cultural boundaries. In a national study that collected data from more than 2,100 students in grades 3–5 (Barman et al., 1999, 2000), more than 13 percent of the students decided that an organism was not an animal if it didn't have fur. More than 9 percent of the students in the same age group explained

I think and think for months and years. Ninety-nine times, the conclusion is false. The hundredth time I am right.
—ALBERT EINSTEIN

Changing alternative conceptions

that something couldn't be an animal if it wasn't a pet. An award-winning videotape, *A Private Universe*, created by Project STAR (Science Teaching Through Its Astronomical Roots), shows that even Harvard graduates hold fundamental misunderstandings about the solar system. These examples point up the importance of using teaching strategies that are designed to reveal alternative conceptions and provide the repeated experiences that help change them.

Let's consider the icicles story again. Most of the children, seeing the small puddle of water left when the icicle melted, thought that it must weigh less than the original icicle. This is because, unlike other liquids, water expands when it freezes, taking up more space, and conversely it shrinks when it melts.

The idea that the water would weigh less than the icicle was contradicted by their experience. Without this experience, they might have memorized the fact that water expands when it freezes without really knowing in practice what that meant. It is only by becoming aware of students' embedded ideas about the natural world that we can begin to change their alternative conceptions. By providing opportunities for them to express their own ideas, talking about those ideas, and guiding them through tests of those ideas, we can mediate their development of more sophisticated and more accurate concepts. This role will take on deeper meaning for you once you experience it in your own classroom.

Now let's look at another illustration of how a teacher can mediate students' learning. In this case, the students are in middle school, but the teacher again helps them to explore their own questions and develop their own ideas. In the last section of the story, you will see how the teacher deals with an alternative conception that arises.

Some Strategies to Help Change Persistent Alternative Conceptions

- Listen to the students' ideas.
- Honor their thinking.
- Ask students to explain their thinking: "That's interesting—what makes you think that?"
- Alter experiments. For example, do the same experiment again with different materials.
- Ask students to devise a plan to demonstrate that their alternative conception works: "Could we plan an experiment to see if that works?"

SCIENCE STORY

The "Skin" of Water

The sixth-grade students in Ridgefield Middle School are mesmerized by the insects in the pond on the school grounds. On this warm winter day in the South, after many days of rain, the pond is quite full and the water very still. Ms. Parker has led the students outside to take some temperature readings of the pond, so they can compare them with the measurements they took a week earlier. But before the students are settled around the pond, Henry shouts, "Wow, look at those two bugs!!"

Marvelous bugs

Skipping over the water's surface are two insects known as water striders. "Oooh, gross," says Lanie. "How do they walk on water?" Shondra asks. "Yeah," adds Shana, "how can they walk on water?" Ms. Parker opens the question to the class. "Well, what do you think, everyone?"

> *Ms. Parker's thinking: Ms. Parker sees this question as a way to stimulate the students' thinking. For that reason, she doesn't leap to answer the question but instead asks the students for input.*

How can they walk on water?

Some students say the insects must be very light to stay on top of the water. Another offers that the bugs seem to have pads for feet. "Their feet are far apart," says yet another student. As soon as the temperature readings are taken—the water temperature has gone down after the rain—Ms. Parker accompanies the students back to class and says they will explore Shondra's question in science period the next day.

An Experiment to Explore Shondra's Question

> *Knowledge depends on questions, and the process of coming to "really know" something entails re-visiting the essential concept in new settings, under new conditions, and with new parameters— often enough to challenge one's own thinking.*
> —Jacqueline Grennon Brooks

The following day, I join Ms. Parker and her sixth graders as they perform a number of experiments with water. When I enter the room, the materials table is set up with cups of metal washers, basins, foil pie pans, index cards, and stacks of empty plastic cups. In Ms. Parker's class the students work in science teams and have assigned jobs. Each group has a materials manager, a director, a speaker, and a recorder, and these jobs are routinely rotated.

Ms. Parker asks the managers to collect a cup of washers, an empty cup, a basin, and a pouring cup filled with water for each group.

> *My thinking: I am impressed that in this class of twenty-eight students, only seven students come up for materials. Everyone seems to know her or his job. They have done this sort of work before.*

Ms. Parker explains that she would like each group of students to place their empty cup in a basin, fill the cup with water to the very top, and then carefully place the metal washers in the cup, one at a time. "How many washers do you predict can go into your full cup of water before the water spills over?"

As the groups make their predictions, Ms. Parker reminds the students to think about the constants and variables in this experiment. "What are you going to keep the same? What will you change?" The students discuss how important it is for the *same* person to put the washer in the water each time. "Why is that important?" Ms. Parker asks. The students respond that if the same person puts the washer in, it will be easier to keep the procedure identical. Ms. Parker then says, "How should we place the washers in?" One student describes a way of sliding these metal circles in on the edge of the filled cup. All other group members need to look carefully at the water level as the washer goes in each time. Ms. Parker says that keeping the procedure the same each time helps the experiment to be a fair test.

Shondra asks what this experiment has to do with her water strider question. Ms. Parker says that she hopes the class will be able to help Shondra answer her question when the activities are completed.

> *My thinking:* I appreciate the way Ms. Parker holds out the expectation for Shondra that her classmates— not Ms. Parker—will collaborate with Shondra on the water strider question.

After making their predictions, the students test them by sliding their metal washers into the cups. In every group, the students notice a difference between their predictions and their results. When the data are collected, the columns look like Table 3.1. One group asks Ms. Parker if they can try again. "Of course," Ms. Parker replies, and other groups follow suit. In their second try, the students adjust their predictions, but the results remain approximately the same.

Ms. Parker asks, "Why are the results slightly different from group to group and from one try to the next?" Students discuss how easy it is to start off with a little less or a little more water and so that is a variable.

> *My thinking:* By interrogating the data, Ms. Parker is reminding the students that there is a range of acceptable answers.

Now Ms. Parker asks the students about the observations they made as the washers went in. "What do you think is happening to the water?" One student responds, "The water level rises." Another offers, "The water looks like a dome." Another student says, "It looked like it was never going to spill over; it just kept getting higher and higher." Lanie says, "It's like the water has a skin." Henry blurts out, "I know what happened. It is *surface tension.*"

At this point Ms. Parker makes a circle on the whiteboard in the front of the room and writes the words "Surface Tension" inside. "Henry," she asks, "can you say more about surface tension? What do you mean by

Thinking about constants and variables

Students themselves will answer Shondra's question

Results do not match predictions.

What keeps the water from spilling over?

TABLE 3.1   Data from the Experiment in Ms. Parker's Class

| | Number of Washers | |
Group Number	Prediction	Actual Result
1	4	14
2	3	15
3	5	12
4	4	13
5	?	14
6	7	15
7	4	13

that?" Henry says that he is not exactly sure what it is, but "it's like when water sticks together." Ms. Parker then asks, "What were some of your observations when you placed the washers in the cup of water? What did you notice?"

Drawing a concept map

Ms. Parker records all the students' responses on the whiteboard. From the circle labeled "Surface Tension," she draws arrows out to other circles or ovals that contain all the comments the students have made about the water and the washers. As shown in Figure 3.1, Ms. Parker is making a **concept map** with Henry's phrase "Surface Tension" in the center. (This is just one use of a concept map; we can call this a "thinking map.")

Ms. Parker's thinking: Although there is a complex explanation for surface tension, Ms. Parker is confident that the students can grasp the concept with her guidance. The concept map will help represent and develop their thinking. It is a way of scaffolding the students' ideas.

As Ms. Parker creates the graphic, she steps back and asks the students to discuss the ideas they have offered within their groups and see if they can come up with further ideas about why the water behaves in this way at the surface. Suddenly Josh calls out, "It's like Henry says. It's surface tension." Ms. Parker responds, "But what does it mean for water to have surface tension?" The class is unsure. Shondra is beginning to get the idea that surface tension is behind the explanation for the water striders.

The answer is emerging.

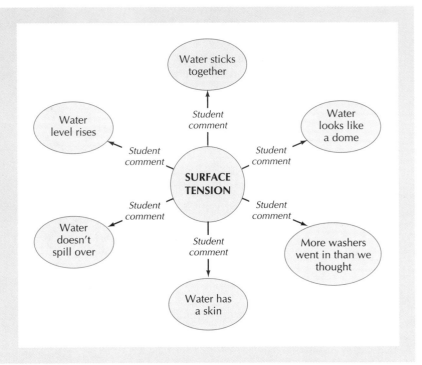

FIGURE 3.1
The Concept Map for "Surface Tension": Initial Stage

Ms. Parker now encourages the students to do some research about surface tension. She reminds them how to use search engines on the Internet.

Further Experiments and Discussion

Research and further tests

The next day, Ms. Parker asks the students to work within their science groups again and brainstorm ideas about surface tension. She also invites them to redo the water-and-washer activity, but using pennies in place of washers. One group places forty-two pennies in a cup of water before it overflows! Some groups draw pictures of water molecules; other groups retry the washer activity. Using both their research and their experience, they offer some ideas in discussion with Ms. Parker. These form a foundation for understanding what surface tension really is.

The speaker in each group then reports the group's thoughts about surface tension to the class. As the speakers do this, Ms. Parker places the ideas in another level of the concept map. Ms. Parker herself then offers a comment that reinforces the research that some groups have done: "Water," she notes, "is made of tiny particles called molecules." She places this comment on the board as well, connecting it with an arrow to Henry's idea that water sticks together. Shondra's group then says that "Water molecules attract one another." Next, Henry's group shares the idea that "Water molecules do not attract the air." Ms. Parker asks the students to think about how this affects the water at the surface. Lanie's group has drawn circles and arrows showing the molecules of water at the surface holding on to each other and to the ones below them. Ms. Parker writes this idea, too, in a bubble on the whiteboard and links it with a line to the related comments. Now the concept map looks like Figure 3.2.

Expanding the concept map

> *My thinking:* I admire the way the concept map expands through the negotiations that occur between Ms. Parker and the students and among the students themselves. It becomes a visual record of the scaffolding of their ideas as they approach understanding.

Shondra's answer

After the groups have all reported, Ms. Parker asks Shondra if she understands why the water strider can skip on the surface of the water. Smiling, Shondra says, "It's like the water molecules hold on tighter to each other at the surface of the water and that makes the water like it has a skin." Ms. Parker adds, "This helps the water strider skip across the water without falling under."

More Challenges

The following morning, students enter Ms. Parker's classroom and are challenged with another opportunity to explore properties of water. The

FIGURE 3.2

The Concept Map for "Surface Tension": A Later Stage

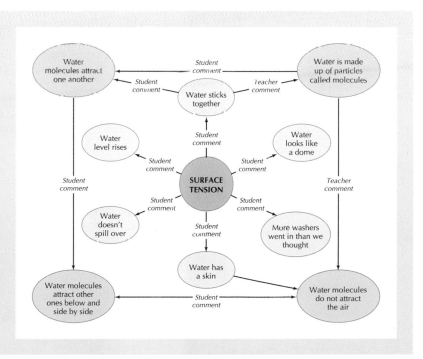

materials managers are asked to get plastic cups, basins, and square pieces of cardboard (about 3 inches on each side). Ms. Parker then asks each group of students to fill a cup of water to the top and cover it with a piece of cardboard. Holding the cardboard on the top of the cup with one hand, they are to invert the cup over the basin. The children gasp, "Won't it spill?" "If it does, that's OK," remarks Ms. Parker; "you have the basin under it." She then encourages the students to try this exploration and to experiment with different amounts of water in the cup.

Another surprise

Squeals of delight and frustration fill the room as students explore the inverted cup of water. Most of the time, the water remains in the cup, even with just the flimsy piece of cardboard on the bottom. (See Figure 3.3.) Ms. Parker asks each group of students, with the help of the student serving as their group director, to come up with a theory about why the water does not spill out of the cup when it is turned upside down.

Students discuss this question in their groups, and each speaker reports the group's ideas. The following three explanations emerge:

The students' theories

1. The water sucks the card to it.

2. The air is pushing the card up and holding it there.

3. The water molecules at the surface are attracted to the water molecules that seep onto the cardboard, and the surface tension of water keeps the card and the water in place.

The students look to Ms. Parker for the right answers. Instead, she invites them to do another activity.

The students gather foil pie pans (one for each group), a pepper shaker, and a small cup of liquid soap. In each pie pan they place about

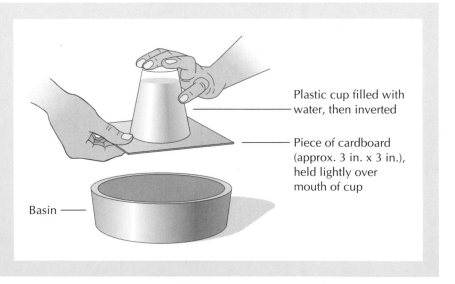

FIGURE 3.3
A Surface Tension Experiment

Plastic cup filled with water, then inverted

Piece of cardboard (approx. 3 in. x 3 in.), held lightly over mouth of cup

Basin

Adding soap—
dramatic changes

5 centimeters of water. They sprinkle the pepper on the surface of the water and observe as it clumps on top of the water. One student is instructed to dip her finger into the liquid soap and then place her finger in the pie pan. Suddenly, the pepper scatters—it appears to "run away" on the surface of the water to the edges of the pan. Then the pepper flakes begin to sink. Students are excited at this dramatic response.

Once again, Ms. Parker asks the students to discuss what happened and offer their own theories. This time the students have a plausible explanation. Each group says that the soap affects how the water acts at the surface. Two groups decide that the soap "breaks the surface tension of water."

Research supports the
students' findings

Ms. Parker sends the students to the Internet again to find out how this happens. Students find out that soap works by reducing surface tension. Soap molecules have two very different ends. One end likes to dissolve in water and the other in oil. When you add soap to oily water, it happily mixes with the oil because the oil-loving part of the soap is on the top of the water surface, facing out. Thus, grease will dissolve in soapy water and get rinsed away.

Ms. Parker asks, "How can we test our theories for why the inverted cup of water did not spill?" Students decide to test the surface tension theory by inverting a cup of *soapy* water that has a cardboard square over it. They find that the soapy water has less surface tension, and the cardboard square holds for a much shorter time.

Changing an
alternative conception

Ms. Parker informs the class that "Many people think the cardboard is held on by the air pushing up on the water. It is a common idea, but you have come up with a better one. You have shown how powerful the surface tension of water is and how that is responsible for holding the card."

Just before the class ends, Lanie says, "Can we do the washers in a cup of water again, with soapy water this time?" "That is a good idea; let's try that tomorrow," Ms. Parker responds.

EXPANDING MEANINGS

■ The Teaching Ideas Behind This Story

- When the class observes a new phenomenon, the water strider, and becomes fascinated by it, Ms. Parker honors the students' interests by creating a series of related science experiences. By helping students explore their own questions, she encourages them to go further in their investigations.

- Notice that Ms. Parker does not answer Shondra's original question but promises that the entire class will address it.

■ To help the students' group work go smoothly, Ms. Parker has set up clearly defined tasks for each group member. In this model, the *materials manager* collects and returns materials for the group; the *recorder* keeps track of data; the *speaker* reports on results and asks the teacher and other teams' speakers for help; and the *director* makes sure that the team understands the investigation and completes the tasks. You will read more about group structure in a later chapter.

■ While she honors Henry's "right answer" about surface tension, Ms. Parker knows that she has to negotiate the meaning of this term with the students.

■ In this context, concept mapping is a *mindtool* that can help students understand the *why* of something. It builds on the students' experience, helping to form a structure for discovering the underlying reasons for surface tension.

■ Notice that Ms. Parker gives simple, clear instructions and no handouts. She encourages students to use the Internet for research, and she also encourages them to test their own theories with direct experiments.

● The Science Ideas Behind This Story

● Water molecules have two hydrogen atoms and one oxygen atom, as indicated by the chemical notation H_2O. The extraordinary stickiness of water is caused by the two hydrogen atoms, which are arranged on one side of the molecule and are attracted to the oxygen atoms of nearby water molecules in a state known as "hydrogen bonding."

● Within the water, away from the surface, every molecule is engaged in a tug of war with its neighbors on every side. For every "up" pull there is a "down" pull, for every "left" pull there is a "right" pull, and so on. The result is that any given molecule feels no net force at all. At the surface, however, things are different. There is no up pull for every down pull since, of course, there is no liquid above the surface. Thus, the surface molecules tend to be pulled back into the liquid.

● If the surface is stretched, it becomes larger in area, and more molecules are dragged from within the liquid to become part of this increased area. This "stretchy skin" effect is called surface tension. Surface tension plays an important role in the way liquids behave. The surface tension of water is what gives the shape to raindrops.

● The water strider, also called a pond skater, is an insect that hunts its prey on the surface of still water. It has widely spaced feet rather like the pads of a lunar lander. The water strider's feet depress the skinlike surface of the water beneath them. But the insect is buoyed up by a combination of its water repellent hairs and the surface tension of the water. Water striders and their kin are relatively common insects.

✔ The Science Standards Behind This Story

STANDARDS

The story of Ms. Parker's class reflects the following portions of the National Science Education Standards (National Research Council, 1996):

✔ *Teaching Standard B:* "Teachers of science . . . orchestrate discourse among students about scientific ideas. . . . In successful science classrooms, teachers and students collaborate in the pursuit of ideas" (pp. 32, 33). You can see how Ms. Parker models these pedagogical strategies.

✔ *Content Standard B, Grades 5–8 (Physical Science):* "A substance has characteristic properties . . . which are independent of the amount of the sample. . . . There are more than 100 known elements that combine in a multitude of ways to produce compounds, which account for the living and nonliving substances that we encounter" (p. 154).

The students' Internet research in the story also reflects sections of the National Educational Technology Standards:

✔ Teachers "use technology to support learner-centered strategies that address the diverse needs of students" (International Society for Technology in Education, 2002, p. 9).

✔ "Students use technology to locate, evaluate, and collect information from a variety of sources" (International Society for Technology in Education, 2000, p. 15).

Questions for Further Exploration

■ How does the structure of a water strider help it move?

■ How does surface tension relate to a frozen skating pond?

■ Where should Ms. Parker go next with this lesson on surface tension?

■ Can you think of other ways to use concept maps? (In the chapter "What's the Big Idea?" you will find another illustration of concept maps.)

Resources for Further Exploration

Dabbagh, N.   Concept mapping as a mindtool for critical thinking. *Journal of Computing in Teacher Education,* 17(2): 16–24. Available online at http://www.iste.org/jcte/; look for the link to past issues of the journal and go to volume 17, number 2.

Exploratorium.   http://www.exploratorium.edu/   The web site of this San Francisco science museum offers a bundle of activities and other great resources.

The Physics Van.   http://van.hep.uiuc.edu/   Run by the University of Illinois Physics Department, this site features questions and answers about physical science.

Water Striders and Pond Skaters.   http://www.insect-world.com/gerromorpha.html.   This web site, part of a larger site on insects, provides anything you would ever want to know about water striders.

Students as Knowers

Being invested in seeking answers

This chapter has demonstrated that building scientific knowledge requires us to engage in an active process of meaning construction in which we explore our own questions and test our own ideas. For students, this means that they become invested in seeking their own answers. The answers they seek enable them to fit their new ideas into their already existing conceptual framework—their prior knowledge.

A shift in thinking

Constructivism as a theory of learning provokes us to find teaching strategies that honor students' ideas and create safe, open spaces in which they can create their own meanings. This is not the traditional notion of science teaching. For many people, it requires a shift in thinking. Rather than simply passing down or transmitting information through one-way communication, the teacher creates a forum for two-way or "multiway" exchanges, mediating the students' progress on the path to their own deeper understanding. The teacher's role as mediator includes the following:

Useful ways to mediate learning

- Engaging students in concrete experiences

- Encouraging them to express their ideas about what they observe

- Listening seriously to those ideas and considering how they are based on the students' prior knowledge

- Asking probing questions about the students' thinking—an important technique because students usually have alternative conceptions that ought to be modified

- Encouraging the students themselves to reflect on their ideas

- Offering additional possibilities, such as other possible avenues of thought for students to explore, further questions to consider, and new connections to make with their daily experience

- Suggesting new experiments and providing opportunities for students to carry them out

- Repeating this process as the students have further experiences, so they continually build new ideas and refine their old ones

The following poem in two voices helps to express the ideas we have developed in this chapter. The voice on the left side represents some traditional notions about science teaching. The right side represents the kind of approach that I hope this book will foster:

I teach science to students.   I do science with students.

I provide information.   I provide experiences.

I seek to control the lesson.	I watch the lesson unfold.
I like it when my students explore *my* thinking.	I like it when my students explore *their* thinking.
My students ask what they should be observing.	My students trust their own observations.
My students memorize facts from each lesson.	My students reflect on ideas from each lesson.
My students know the science ideas for the next test.	My students connect the science ideas to their lives.
My students know that science has all the answers.	My students know that science helps find some answers.
I teach science to students.	I do science with students.

KEY TERMS

prior knowledge *(p. 61)*
mediator *(p. 62)*
alternative conception *(p. 63)*
mass *(p. 66)*
constant *(p. 71)*
variable *(p. 71)*
fair test *(p. 71)*
concept map *(p. 77)*

4 The Science Circus: Using the Skills of Scientific Study

FOCUSING QUESTIONS

- Do you ever predict the day's weather from your early morning observations?
- Can you remember diagnosing a sick pet, a child, or a sibling on the basis of the symptoms you noticed?
- Did you ever vary just one ingredient in a recipe and come up with a new dish?
- Do you ever shop at the supermarket by arranging your grocery list according to the aisles in the store?

People who regularly engage in scientific activity use certain skills that help them gain information about nature and natural phenomena. As we noted at the beginning of this book, these skills, such as observing and classifying, are also important in our daily lives, though we often do not "code" them as scientific. Employing these skills on a planned and regular basis is what makes scientific activity different from ordinary activity. It is the essence of what we mean by the scientific process of **inquiry,** and these skills themselves are generally known as **inquiry skills** or **process skills.**

In this chapter, we explore a multistation classroom environment that provides students and teachers with science activities in which they must use certain process skills to resolve a question or solve a problem. By a "station" I mean simply a desk, a table, or any other special area in which an investigation is described and materials are provided. By examining this environment and thinking about how it works, you can become more familiar with the ways in which students develop process skills and use them to solve problems.

Multistation science activities are often developed around a content area theme, such as "states of matter" or "living things." In this chapter, however, we will look at an example in which the content areas of the stations are unrelated to one another. In other words, the context for each problem-solving activity is provided by the scenario created at that particular station. The organizing theme, in this case, is "using process skills to solve different problems."

The Science Circus

If you have ever been to a circus, you have noticed how many different things are going on at the same time. In three-ring circuses, entertainment acts of different varieties occupy the rings in the center, while jugglers, clowns, and people on stilts walk around the periphery. It is quite a busy place. One hardly knows what to look at first. For students, these events create a world of excitement that they want to explore.

Lots of activities— but not disorder

A colleague of mine introduced me to a multistation classroom activity that she labeled a "science circus" because many activities were occurring simultaneously. I said, "When I think of a circus, I think of disorder." "On the contrary," my colleague remarked. "It takes a great deal of organization to plan an activity where students are all at different places at the same time" (Abder, 1990).

A **science circus** is not quite as complicated as a real circus. Contained within a single room, the science circus consists of several stations at which the visitors are asked to perform certain tasks and record their results or reactions. It is circus-like because many different activities are going on simultaneously, but it is far from chaotic.

Providing personal context

Each time I set up a science circus, it looks different. I try to use materials common in daily life and to create a scenario that invites students to explore them and come up with their own ideas. Often, too, I situate the activities in a personal context that is related to my own experience—a context I hope the students will recognize and share. It is always important to provide a rich context for the science stations so you are not pacing the students through science activities just for their own sake. The experiences must be constructed in a way that makes a connection to a larger idea or a personal story.

Arousing a need to know

In the following story, I describe one typical science circus that I helped create, but keep in mind that the potential for different activities is practically infinite. Notice also that the stations try to arouse in the students a *need to know*, giving them a strong reason to use their science skills. As you explore these stations, you may be reminded of instances in which you have satisfied your own need to know by using the skills of science.

After seeing how the science circus works, we will explore the particular skills required by each of the activities. As you read, think about how *you* would describe the skills that the students are developing.

SCIENCE STORY

The Circus Comes to Mount Holly

I am visiting Ms. Markon, a new teacher at Mount Holly Elementary School. I have been her teaching supervisor, and today we are setting up a science circus in her fourth-grade class. We have used the students' lunch break to prepare the tables in the room. The students are aware that they will be returning from lunch to find that their room has been transformed.

A classroom transformed

When the students come in, they discover several tables, each with a different object or collection of objects and an index card with questions on it. They are delighted with the transformed classroom and eager to begin. Because it is important for students to share ideas with each other, Ms. Markon asks each to work with a buddy as they explore the stations in the science circus. Each pair of students is assigned to a different station to start. They are instructed to visit each of the stations, spending between five and ten minutes at each stop. As the students explore the stations, I have the opportunity to interact with them.

An Old Log

At one station, the table holds an old log from my backyard. It comes from a birch tree that was felled in a storm several years ago. The log is very dry,

What Is Inquiry?

The following passage from the National Science Education Standards *offers an important explanation of what scientists and educators mean when they speak of the process of "inquiry."*

Scientific inquiry refers to the diverse ways in which scientists study the natural world and propose explanations based on the evidence derived from their work. Inquiry also refers to the activities of students in which they develop knowledge and understanding of scientific ideas, as well as an understanding of how scientists study the natural world.

Inquiry is a multifaceted activity that involves making observations; posing questions; examining books and other sources of information to see what is already known; planning investigations; reviewing what is already known in light of experimental evidence; using tools to gather, analyze, and interpret data; proposing answers, explanations, and predictions; and communicating the results. Inquiry requires identification of assumptions, use of critical and logical thinking, and consideration of alternative explanations.

From National Research Council, *The National Science Education Standards.* Washington, DC: National Academy Press, 1996, p. 23.

but its thin, whitish bark is still intact. It is about 2 feet (60 cm) long and has a diameter of about 5 inches (12.5 cm). One end of the log is rough where it broke off from the rest of the trunk. The other end is smooth because the log was sawed for firewood. In the middle of one side of the log is a large, oval opening, probably made by the gradual pecking of a large-beaked bird.

Ms. Markon and I do not tell the students everything we know or surmise about the log. Instead, we refer the students to the index card on the table next to the log. It reads as follows:

> This is a piece of a tree trunk that I found in my backyard. Can you explore this piece of trunk and try to figure out what happened to it?
>
> What are all the things you observe about this tree trunk? What are some of your ideas about how it got to look this way?

The children handle the small log and record their ideas. Working in pairs, they talk about the log and how they think it got to be here in our science circus. One girl takes a marble from a neighboring shelf and drops it into the hole in the log. When I notice her doing that, I walk over to watch more closely.

Just playing around— or being creative?

"Oh!" she exclaims. "I'm sorry I took the marble!"

Surprised that she believes she has broken some rule, I reassure her that I think she has a great idea and that I'm just curious about what she wants to find out.

"I was just trying to see if the hole in the log went all the way through," she says. "It doesn't."

My thinking: The girl's reaction dramatically illustrated how rule-bound students become after only a few years in school. I reminded myself to rejoice in those moments when students use their creativity to explore.

The fascination of any search after truth lies not in the attainment but in the pursuit.
—FLORENCE BASCOM, FIRST WOMAN TO EARN A DOCTORATE IN GEOLOGY IN THE UNITED STATES

The students readily notice the differences between the two ends of the log. "Somebody sawed this," says one. "This looks like it broke off," another student suggests, looking at the other end of the log. "I bet a woodpecker did this," still another student offers, looking at the large hole inside which the marble has been rolling around. They draw pictures of the log in their science journal. They also record the title of the station and their observations and ideas about the log.

The Soda Can

On another table we have placed a soda can that was left in a car on a very hot summer day. The heated gas bubbles in the soda exploded the lid of the can at its seams and puffed out the bottom. The can is empty now, but it looks quite unusual. The lid is still attached at one point along the edge. The index card at that table reads:

> On a very hot summer day, I left my unopened soda can in the back of my car. Several hours later, when I returned to my car, the soda was all over the car seat and this is what the can looked like. What do you think happened?

Brainstorming

Listening to students brainstorm about this can is very interesting. "Once," says one child, "my mom left a soda can in the freezer by mistake, and this is what it looked like." Another child remarks, "It looks like it exploded." The students record their various ideas in their science journals.

My thinking: I am interested to learn whether the students make a connection between temperature and the behavior of liquids in a can. I'm us-

Effect of Temperature Liquids

At the soda-can station, students have the opportunity to learn what happens when we heat or freeze a liquid. When a carbonated liquid is kept in a very hot place, the carbon-dioxide gas dissolved in the soda water becomes less soluble as the temperature increases. Heat energy increases the speed at which the liquid and gas particles move. The faster the gas particles move, the more frequently they hit the sides of the container and the greater the pressure. This pressure can eventually burst the seams of the can.

As one of the students in the story realized, the same kind of thing can happen when a soda can is frozen. Even though most liquids contract when they are cooled, water-based liquids like soda water start forming crystals when they begin to freeze, and these ice crystals occupy more volume than the original water. As the carbonated liquid occupies more space, it can burst through the seams of the can. This usually does not occur when soda cans are left in the freezer or out in the icy cold weather because a little space is typically left in the can that the freezing soda expands into. But many containers of water-based liquid that are filled to the top and sealed do burst when frozen. Hence, if the students inferred that the can was left either in a freezer or in a very hot place, they were correct.

ing a real story from my experience, one that I hope they can relate to. Asking new questions about daily-life experiences is my way of engaging them in the task of problem solving.

Crazy Rocks

In a large plastic bowl on one table, Ms. Markon has arranged her rock collection, which consists of several different kinds of rocks. She has collected these rocks from many different places, and they are of various colors, textures, sizes, and shapes. The index card on the table reads:

> When astronauts brought rocks back from the moon, the first thing the scientists did was to group them according to similar characteristics. This is MY rock collection. You may have a rock collection too. I started collecting rocks when I was a small child.
>
> When you explore these rocks, what *do* you notice? In what ways are they the same? In what ways are they different? How many categories could you place the rocks into? Where do you think I found these rocks?

Making up categories

   The students love rummaging through these rocks. It is a fairly large collection, and they come up with categories like "bumpy," "smooth," "light colored," "dark colored," "shiny crystals," "no crystals," "stripes," and "no stripes." Some of these rocks may be ones the students have never seen before.

   My thinking: Although many students could not relate to some of the rocks in the collection, most could relate to the idea of having a collection—at least an informal group of rocks that they had picked up here and there because they liked them.

The Leaky Faucet

This station is at the classroom's sink, where water is dripping slowly from the faucet. (If your room has no sink, you can use a large jug of bottled water with its own spigot and a basin to collect the dripping water.) Nearby are a stopwatch, beakers, and graduated cylinders (see Figure 4.1). The card reads as follows:

These fourth graders are engaged in examining a collection of rocks. They are looking up ways to identify their rocks in a resource book.

Ed Lallo/IndexStockImagery/
PictureQuest

You may have seen a leaky faucet in your own home. Measure and write down the amount of water that drips from the tap in one minute. Work out how much water will drip in one hour. How would you find out how much water will drip in one whole day?

As I watch the pairs of students, I remind them to write their plan in their science journals before carrying it out. Then I continue to watch and listen as they solve the problem.

My thinking: I am interested in understanding how the students will fig-ure this out. What will they do? What units will they use? What will their decisions tell me about their prior experience and the ways they think?

*Surprise—and
understanding*

Many of the students are surprised to learn that as many as 7,200 mil-liliters of water can drip from a leaky faucet in one day if only 5 milliliters drip out in one minute. The next day, Ms. Markon brings in empty liter bottles, and the students help her stack seven of them up to see what 7,000

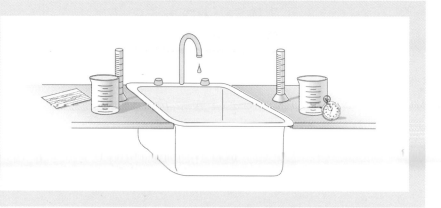

milliliters looks like. Several of them suddenly realize why their parents nag them to turn the water off.

The Penny in the Pie Pan

At this station there are some pencils and a few pennies on the table, plus an aluminum foil pie tin that is half filled with water. The students read the following:

> Many of us like to swim. Have you ever noticed that your hands and feet look different when they are under water?
>
> Today we are going to submerge a penny in the pie tin of water. Before doing that, take your pencil and trace the penny in your science journal. Now draw what you think the penny will look like when you put it in the water. Now place the penny in the water. What do you notice?

More surprise

The students trace their pennies with their pencils and sketch their predictions. When they see the pennies in the water, they are often surprised. "I didn't know it would look so big," one boy exclaims. They record their observations in their science journals.

My thinking: At this station, Ms. Markon and I want to engage the children in an activity that invites them to look at ordinary materials in a different way. Pennies, water, and pie pans are commonplace items. Making the connection to swimming is another way to provide a personal context for the activity.

Three Types of Soil

At this station there are no materials at all. This is a "thought experiment." The card reads as follows:

> Imagine you have three different types of soil. How would you determine which soil holds the most water? What will you keep the same? What will you change?

The students spend a long time at this station. They brainstorm a way (or several ways, sometimes) to figure out the problem. When they decide on a way to solve the problem, they write it in their science journals. Here is an example from two of the fourth graders:

Use three cups. Put three holes on the bottom of each cup and stand each cup in a pan—like a pie pan from the last station. Add each soil to a cup [one type of soil per cup] and then put the same amount of water in each cup. Wait 1 hour. Measure water that drips out the bottom. The cup that doesn't drip out too much water has the best soil.

Guiding with questions

I ask this pair of students, "How big is each cup?" I want them to understand that we need to keep the size of the cups the same. Then I ask, "How much soil do you put in each cup?" I want them to see that they should use exactly the same amount of each soil. They decide to use half a cup of each soil. Next I ask them, "How will you measure the water that drips out?" The two students explain that they will pour it from the pie pan into a measuring cup.

On my next visit, I bring in three types of soil, paper cups, and measuring cups, and these two students try their experiment. It works! We examine the soils for size of particles and color. We determine how the soils are the same and different.

A different plan

Another pair comes up with a different solution. They will also use paper cups, they decide, but they won't punch holes in the bottom. Instead, they will add the same amount of water to each type of soil and wait fifteen minutes. Then they will take three sheets of paper toweling, and on each sheet they will empty one of their cups, dumping out both the soil and the water. They have reasoned that whichever paper towel is the wettest will contain the soil that can hold the least amount of water.

"How much water will you add to each cup?" I ask.

They haven't thought about that—just that each cup would get the same amount of water. They think a little more about their plans. On my next visit, they carry out their experiment. They have decided to add one-half cup of water. But they find that their cups are too small for that amount, so they need to add less. They try again.

My thinking: I particularly like thought experiments, especially ones that involve experimenting with materials that the students can readily imagine. In this case I used soils because most children have had plenty of experience with dirt! Also, of course, it was easy for me to bring samples of three types of soil to the classroom on my next trip.

The Weather Station

This station has a computer set up to access an Internet weather site (**http://www.weather.com/**). This and other weather sites on the World Wide Web can provide statistics, photos, and explanations of unusual weather events. At this station the card reads:

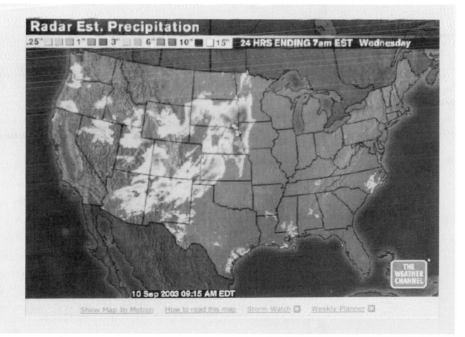

Accessing a weather map on the Internet allows students to collect authentic weather data in an instant.

Michael Newman/PhotoEdit

Online investigations

Compare the air temperature and weather conditions for San Francisco, California; Chicago, Illinois; and New York City. In what ways are they the same? In what ways are they different?

Which of these cities would you prefer to be in today? What city on the national weather map has your favorite weather today?

The students use the Internet site to gather data that they then record in their science journals. They need to manipulate the computer to obtain the information they are seeking.

My thinking: The relatively simple task of recording data from a web site is one way in which elementary school students can become familiar with using computers as a tool for scientific study. This same activity engages the children in map reading, which gives them experience with another significant tool. I like to personalize the activity by asking the students to choose a city that has their favorite weather.

EXPANDING MEANINGS

■ The Teaching Ideas Behind This Story

- The science circus stations provide opportunities for students to practice using scientific process skills. While doing this, they also gain practice with investigations that generate some original thinking. Scientific inquiry is not just about doing; it is also about critically thinking about what you do.

- Notice how curious the girl was at the station with the small log. When she acted on her curiosity by placing a marble in the hollow, she was momentarily unsure if she had done the right thing. Often youngsters are timid about trying out their ideas, fearing they will be "wrong." Teaching science depends on overcoming that fear.

- At the station with the thought experiment about three types of soil, there were at least several possible "right" answers. Challenging students to solve a "How would you find out?" problem invites multiple responses as students personalize the problem and critically explore potential solutions. Notice how, through my questions, I prodded them into setting up a fair test by pointing out how important it is to keep the experimental conditions the same. Notice, too, that at a later time I brought different soils to class. Thought experiments can be frustrating to students if the experiments cannot actually be tried.

■ The science circus engages students in using scientific process skills without necessarily naming the skills. In fact, this chapter itself has not yet named all the skills involved. (It will shortly.) But when, you may ask, should you name the skills for your students? Generally, naming and subsequent discussion of the science process skills are appropriate by the end of third grade and the beginning of fourth grade. At that point, both teacher and students should regularly use the names, like the process skills themselves, so their meanings become situated in the students' experiences.

● The Science Ideas Behind This Story

● The activities of the science circus are designed to develop particular science process skills. Though most of the stations involve more than one skill, the principal skills used at each station are highlighted next.

● At the station with the log, we are asking the students to use the skills of observation and inference. An **observation** is all of the information we can gain about an object or an event by using our senses. An **inference** is a reasonable statement about an object or an event that is based on an observation. We make observations with our senses and use our minds to make inferences—to really think about something. For instance, what happened to this tree trunk? Why does it look this way?

● An inference may or may not be provable. In science, if an inference or a guess is stated in a way that allows it to be tested, it is called a **hypothesis.** Typically scientists plan ways of testing their hypotheses to find out if they are true. In this way, a hypothesis may eventually become a **theory**—an idea that has been tested and (to some significant degree) corroborated. A theory is the best explanation we currently have for why something is so. Although theories can be strongly supported, they can never be absolutely "proved." As evidence for one theory grows, the credibility of others may be disputed.

● The same process skills apply to the soda-can station: observation and inference.

● When the students explored Ms. Markon's rock collection, we were asking them to observe in a particular way. This process skill is **classifying**—sorting objects or ideas into groups according to similar properties. Classifying is a basic way that human beings use to try to make meaning of the natural world and all its diversity. We use classifications in all of our thinking. For instance, by identifying the object in front of you as a book, you are classifying it—connecting it with a group of similar objects.

- The leaky faucet station involved **measuring,** another process skill. Here, the students had the opportunity to work with tools that help extend our abilities to observe. At this station, they used a stopwatch, graduated cylinders, and beakers, which are helpful for measuring time and volume. Other useful measuring instruments are balance scales, spring scales, thermometers, and meter sticks. Your students may also have the chance to use probe devices connected to a classroom computer. (We discuss these further in the chapter "Science and Technology.")

- When they wrote down their measurements, the students were **recording data.** In school science, data include many different types of information, and students can record them by using words, numbers, graphs, drawings, or a computer program.

- At the penny and pie-pan station, the students were asked to **predict** what they thought the penny would look like under water. Then, after they dropped it in the pie pan, they **compared and contrasted** their observations with their predictions.

- At the station without materials, which we called a thought experiment, the students were asked to **plan an investigation.** To do this, they had to recognize that testing ideas involves *controlling variables.* That is, they had to ask themselves, "What do I keep the same, and what do I change?" When we do science, we have to design experiments in which all variables but one are controlled. So if we want to find out which soil holds the most water, we need to keep the volume of the water, the amounts of the soil, and all other experimental conditions the same, changing only the type of soil.

- At the weather station, students were again recording data that they had gathered by accessing information on the Internet. Using computers as a tool to collect information is such an important skill that it may deserve to be called a "process" skill in its own right. This skill has become vital for scientists in many theoretical fields, especially when direct observation is not possible because the objects to be observed are too small or too far away. In these cases, computers make models of the objects of study, and data are generated as scientists manipulate the models.

- Educators differ in the exact way they list and define the process skills. But the ones highlighted in this section are included in virtually every list. These process skills are summarized in Table 4.1.

✔ The Science Standards Behind This Story

STANDARDS ☑ The science circus reflects the following portions of the National Science Education Standards (National Research Council, 1996):

✔ *Content Standard A, Grades K–4 (Science as Inquiry):* "Scientists use different kinds of investigations depending on the questions they are trying to answer. Types of investigations include describing objects, events, and organisms; classifying them; and doing a fair test (experimenting)"

TABLE 4.1	The Process Skills
Observation	Gaining information about an object or an event by using all of your senses
Inference	Making statements about an observation that provide a reasonable explanation
Classifying	Sorting objects or ideas into groups based on properties they share
Measuring	Determining quantities such as distance, volume, mass, or time by using instruments that measure these properties; instruments may range from simple ones like scales and stopwatches to more complex ones such as probes with a computer interface
Recording data	Writing down (in words, pictures, graphs, or numbers) the results of observations of an object or an event
Predicting	Guessing what the outcome of an event will be on the basis of observations and, usually, prior knowledge of similar events
Comparing and contrasting	Discovering similarities and differences between objects or events
Planning an investigation	Determining a reasonable procedure that could be followed to test an idea (listing the materials needed, writing out the procedure to be followed, and identifying which variables will be kept the same and which will be changed)

(p. 123). You can see how the science circus engages students in each of these types of investigation.

✔ *Content Standard A, Grades K–4 (Science as Inquiry):* "Simple instruments, such as magnifiers, thermometers, and rulers, provide more information than scientists obtain using only their senses" (p. 123). Notice how this content standard could include the use of balance beams, simple microscopes, graduated cylinders, a stopwatch, and, of course, a computer. These are instruments that extend our senses and refine our observations.

The students' use of the Internet at the weather station also relates to the National Educational Technology Standards, which specify that by the end of fifth grade students should "use telecommunications efficiently and effectively to access remote information" (International Society for Technology in Education, 2000, p. 20).

Questions for Further Exploration

Think about a science circus station that you would like to create—perhaps one very different from the stations described in this chapter. If possible, plan it for a particular class with which you have had some experience. Then ask yourself the following questions about your plans:

- What process skills will students need to complete the task?

- How engaged will the students be in their own thinking? Will your station provide opportunities for them to generate their own questions? How can you promote their thinking?

- When they see the materials at your station, what do you think your students will be most interested in learning about? (Sometimes I have an idea about what I think is important to explore in science, but the students have a different idea.)

- How can the station be relevant to your students' lives?

- What sorts of things do you expect to learn about the students from their questions? And how will this knowledge help you plan other science activities for them?

Resources for Further Exploration

ELECTRONIC RESOURCES

Excite: Weather. http://my.excite.com/weather/.   At this Internet weather site, students can look up local weather reports as well as explore the weather in other parts of the country.
SEGway: Science Education Gateway.   http://cse.ssl.berkeley.edu/SEGway/. This web site offers a variety of tools and lesson plans in earth and space science.
The Weather Channel.   http://www.weather.com/.   Another weather site, with easy access to maps.

PRINT RESOURCES

Bosak, Susan V. (2000). *Science Is . . . : A Source Book of Fascinating Facts, Projects and Activities*, 2d ed. Markham, Ontario, Canada: Scholastic Canada. A terrific sourcebook for elementary school teachers, this volume includes over 450 activities that can lead to exciting avenues of exploration with students.
Lowell, L., & Willard, C. (1999). *Sifting Through Science*. GEMS series. Berkeley, CA: Lawrence Hall of Science. This curriculum guide, designed specifically for early-childhood education, explains in detail how to set up learning stations in the primary grades.
Ostlund, K. (1992). *Science Process Skills: Assessing Hands-On Student Performance*. Menlo Park, CA: Addison-Wesley. Although its activities are

designed to be assessments of student process skills, the book also offers useful suggestions for a science circus.

Science in the Classroom and in Everyday Life

Process skills you use every day

The skills of scientific inquiry are also the skills we use to live thoughtfully throughout life. If you answered "yes" to any of the Focusing Questions at the beginning of this chapter, then you have been using process skills to make decisions that affect you every day. For instance, packing a suitcase for a trip requires lots of classifying: casual wear, dress wear, nightwear, toiletries, undergarments, shoes. Making decisions about products, the weather, our health, and the state of our nutrition requires careful observing, inferring, comparing, and contrasting.

When we exercise these skills in a particular way, our inferences can become hypotheses. Remember Rose in the chapter "Locating Your Scientific Self"? When Susan offered her the interesting explanation for why the balloon didn't pop, Rose said, "How can we test this possibility?" Susan's idea was framed as a hypothesis and subjected to a test. Testing ideas in such a planned and consistent fashion is the foundation of scientific inquiry.

Building process skills over time

Through activities like the ones in our science circus, young children begin to build their process skills, the foundations for their understanding of the natural world. They learn to observe closely, sort things into categories, and ask how things are the same and how they are different. Even very young children can make predictions—"what will happen if . . . ?" They come up with tentative explanations for their observations, and these inferences change as they get older. Children begin measuring by using string, centimeter sticks, and balance scales. They weigh objects using uniform masses like the teddy-bear counters in the icicles story from the chapter "The Teacher as Mediator." As they mature, they begin to use standard units of measurement for distance, mass, and volume. By third grade, many students can plan investigations, recognize variables, and control the experimental conditions. By middle school, students can design a greater variety of investigations, including experiments that involve more than two variables and require them to record detailed data. At all levels, students are recording data in some fashion, first through drawings and later through words, graphs, and numbers.

Engaging students' minds

Remember that the science circus experience, like all other science activities, succeeds only if it generates students' questions and promotes further thinking. Their minds as well as their hands have to be applied. They will not learn process skills merely by manipulating objects. The real learning occurs as a result of their brainstorming, discussion, and reflection.

Family Science Night

The concept of a science circus—several stations offering a wide variety of activities—can form the basis for an event that involves students' family members. Engaging adults in science experiences together with students is a way to not only bring families together, but also to encourage a deeper interest in science and science-related activities. Moreover, research tells us that parents' attitudes affect their children's attitudes, and some adults' fears of science have a negative impact on their children (Kober, 1993). By emphasizing the relevance of science *outside* school—in our students' everyday lives—we can help change those negative images of science.

Problem solving for families

A **family science night** can take many forms. At one school I observed, the event was spread over two nights so as many families as possible would have the opportunity to participate. As parents and students filed into the school cafeteria, they picked up red booklets titled, "My Family Science Journal." The teachers had designed seven stations that invited participants to manipulate materials and use trial-and-error problem solving. The activities were carefully planned to stress process skills like the ones described in this chapter.

Each of the stations offered complete directions, materials, and questions to encourage higher-order thinking and discussion. Each activity corresponded to a page in the journal on which the families could record or sketch what they were doing. The students were encouraged to act as the journal writers for the family. The journal also included questions to guide the students and follow-up activities to perform at home.

At one station, families investigated how many drops of water could fit on the head of a penny and how a water droplet can become a magnifier. At another station, students listened to their heartbeats with a stethoscope, counting the number of beats in a fixed period of time, before and after strenuous exercise. At a third station, families explored the movements of garden land snails. Four other stations touched on other aspects of life science, physical science, and earth science.

Using the science journals

All of the families' observations and inferences were recorded in their science journals, which contributed a great deal to the success of the evening. Families used their journals as a way to keep track of what they did and what they learned. Further, the journal became a symbol both of science and of family science night. At home, families could use their science journals to duplicate the science night activities.

Building a tradition

At this school I visited, family science night became an annual tradition. The teachers changed the design of the science stations each year. Letters sent home with the students asked community members what they would like to see at the next family science event, which established an ongoing science link with the students' homes.

This story illustrates just one successful format for a community science night. You can design your own format and your own stations. The key is to engage students and their families in a genuine process of inquiry that relates to their own lives and challenges them to construct their own ideas.

KEY TERMS

inquiry *(p. 86)*
process (inquiry) skills *(p. 86)*
science circus *(p. 87)*
observation *(p. 97)*
inference *(p. 97)*
hypothesis *(p. 97)*
theory *(p. 97)*
classifying *(p. 97)*
measuring *(p. 97)*
recording data *(p. 98)*
predicting *(p. 98)*
comparing and contrasting *(p. 98)*
planning an investigation *(p. 98)*
family science night *(p. 102)*

5 Making Connections

Science in the Students' Own Environment

FOCUSING QUESTIONS

- How can informal science-learning experiences shape your knowledge of science?
- What natural event has been making headlines recently?
- How does the area where you live adapt to changing climate conditions?
- What items do you tend to collect? Do they include anything from nature?

Many schools follow a **formal science curriculum** that has been developed at the state or local level or that has been commercially developed and purchased by the school district. We will examine some typical science curricula in the chapter, "What's the Big Idea?," later in this book. These formal curricula have primarily been put together with the guidance of the *National Science Education Standards*, the AAAS *Benchmarks*, or state and local frameworks.

Unfortunately, teachers often use *only* these formal guidelines when designing students' science experiences. They therefore limit the nature of the science experiences to those addressed in formal curricula. Although those experiences may be good—and may make some topical connections to students' lives—they do not include experiences that are *unique* to a particular class in a specific geographic locale.

Science experiences that are unique and very personal make up what I call the **informal science curriculum.** In this chapter, you will see that this informal curriculum can be extremely important. You can think of it as a way to integrate into the classroom spontaneous natural events from the school's locale and science experiences that the students bring from home. In the chapter "The Teacher as Mediator," you saw the informal science curriculum at work when Mr. Wilson brought icicles into class to teach students about changes in matter. Students can also study local objects from nature and even make collections of the plants they find outside the school.

This chapter explores a variety of informal science learning experiences and especially the ways you can develop them by using a classroom science corner and field trips. First, however, let's look at some reasons why it is so important to make these connections between science and your students' daily lives.

Diversity Within and Without

Look outside your classroom window.

Wherever your school is located, you will find enormous diversity in the nature around you. Often you can see some of it just by looking out your classroom window. You may find yourself amid the rich deciduous forests of the suburban or rural Northeast, close by the vast cornfields of the Midwest, or near the rocky shores of a coastal community. In the Southwest or Southeast, you may be surrounded by the dramatic flora and fauna of arid or tropical regions. Even at an inner-city school, you may find trees in the planting squares on sidewalks, or at least a dandelion breaking through the cracks.

How do different students respond to the surroundings?

You probably have a great deal of diversity among your students as well. They will notice different things in nature and respond to them in different ways. Consider the little dandelion in the sidewalk, for example. One student may see it as a sign of the stubborn persistence of plant life; a student with relatives in the suburbs may see it as a weed that ought to be exterminated. One student may come from a family that serves dandelion greens at meals; others probably have no idea that people would eat such a thing. One may think the dandelion flower is beautiful; another may think it ugly or not even recognize it as a flower. Whatever their particular reactions, your students' unique ways of experiencing nature will provide a rich tapestry of science experiences that can become part of the life of your classroom.

By taking advantage of this diversity inside and outside your class—seizing the opportunities to make interesting connections between students' lives and the natural world around them—you can make your classroom a dynamic, vital place. Moreover, building these links stimulates learning in two major ways:

1. It helps students see the larger picture.

2. It counteracts the traditional alienation of many people from science.

Seeing the Larger Picture: Content Plus Context

Problems of content without context

All students learn better if they can relate their school experiences to their daily lives. Recall what the opening chapter of this book said about the need to fit new concepts into our prior knowledge—a concept that many of this text's science stories have already demonstrated. Particularly in science education, however, many adults can recall learning the content without any context to which they could relate it. There was no larger picture, so to speak. As a result, these students "learned" science by memorizing decontextualized facts to pass tests and then forgetting them afterward (reported in science autobiographies; see Koch, 1990).

Today, even formal science curricula generally strive to find ways for students, especially young children, to relate science ideas to their lives. And the best curricula acknowledge that students' lives encompass a wide variety of activities, cultures, and home environments. By linking science to students' own, individual "larger pictures," we not only help them learn better, but we also help them use science ideas to understand events in their daily lives more fully. As we discussed at the beginning of this book, we are living in an increasingly complex world—one that requires its citizens to be observant, critical, and thoughtful about their immediate environment. Those who understand scientific ideas in the context of their daily lives have a head start in dealing with the issues that their lives present.

Linking science with a larger picture

Winter Laundry: The Excitement of Science in Everyday Life

The following event was recalled by a science educator who grew up in Nebraska. Notice how this ordinary moment in a young girl's life became a meaningful science experience.

As the oldest of ten children, I was expected to help with household chores, and on this occasion I drew "diaper duty." That usually meant taking a load of freshly washed cloth diapers out of the washing machine, tossing them into the electric clothes dryer, and then folding them when they were dry. But on this particularly cold and breezy winter day in northwestern Nebraska, the dryer was not working, and the clean, wet diapers were accumulating rapidly as the demand for dry ones was growing.

It is worth noting that the climate in northwestern Nebraska is semiarid, with extreme temperature differences from summer to winter. I was ordered to hang the soggy diapers on the clothesline outside the back door while my father dismantled the ailing dryer. I lugged the heaping basket of sodden cloth and the bag of clothespins up the basement steps. The task of hanging up wet diapers was challenging on that frosty day. Manipulating damp cloth and wooden clothespins with stiff wire springs was especially difficult with my hands encased in thick woolen mittens. By the time the first line was filled with the damp rectangles of loosely woven cotton cloth, I noticed that not only were my fingers stiff with cold, so were the diapers in the basket. When I went back to examine the first diapers on the line, they didn't look quite right, and they were making a racket. On closer inspection, I realized that they were swinging oddly in the wind. They were frozen stiff and clanking together like flat icicles!

I finished hanging out the rest of the diapers as quickly as I could. The rest of the diapers swung stiffly in the gentle breeze, just as the first ones had. As I finished, I went back to the first diapers. They were soft and pliable! What in the world had happened? They were frozen solid just a short time before. How could this be?

continued

I grabbed the dry, cold diapers and rushed excitedly back to the basement. Dad! Look, these diapers are dry! They were frozen solid, but now they are soft and dry! How could they go from wet to frozen to dry? What happened to the ice in the diapers? How did it disappear? Where did it go?

My father, a physicist, said just one word: *sublimation*. Was this, I wondered, the same as evaporation? He explained that the water didn't exactly evaporate. It sublimated. In this case, the water in the diapers froze, and then it transformed directly from the solid to the vapor or gaseous state.

Sublimation occurs when a solid is transformed directly into a gaseous state, skipping the liquid phase. The frozen diapers that dried in the cold air were an example of sublimation. A pile of snow that shrinks even though the temperature is too cold for it to melt is another example. Ice cubes that begin to shrink away from the edges of their tray after a long time in a freezer also show the effect of sublimation.

Since that time, I have encountered more examples of sublimation. It may be observed in dry ice (which must be handled with care), naphthalene (most commonly found in moth balls or moth flakes), or even crystalline iodine (which must be handled only in closely supervised laboratory settings by qualified personnel). I am constantly on the lookout for other examples. And the phenomenon still fascinates me to this day.

Sublimation. It was one of my earliest science moments, those vividly memorable encounters with natural phenomena followed by a new and satisfying sense of understanding how the world works. It was an unexpected encounter with nature by simply observing how laundry dries on a clothesline in cold, dry winter air.

—Kathy Ahern, science professor

Have you ever felt so excited yourself after discovering the reason for a natural phenomenon? What does this account suggest to you about the importance of linking science to the context of students' own lives?

From Alienation to Inclusion

Various researchers have investigated the reasons why science has often alienated students, especially females and members of minority groups. Studies have found that a major culprit is the absence of personal connections between science and students' everyday lives. For example, minorities and females often have a negative perception of the usefulness of science in "real life," and this attitude contributes to their lack of participation in science activities (Campbell & Clewell, 1999; Howe, 2002; Koch, 2002a, 2002b). Conversely, by relating science to these students' daily lives, we can create school science experiences that will invite their participation.

*Lack of connection →
lack of participation*

Do remember that all students come to school with a set of biases and beliefs about their world that are constructed from the social, cultural, and gendered contexts in which they live. These beliefs strongly influence students' tacitly held attitudes toward science and scientists. Part of your work as a science educator is to learn about your students' views of science and then use that knowledge to help them modify and enlarge their views.

Modifying biases

As we saw in the chapter "Locating Your Scientific Self," science is frequently perceived as a domain for white males, from which women and

The voice of the scientific authority is like the male voice-over in commercials, a disembodied knowledge that cannot be questioned, whose author is inaccessible.
—ELIZABETH FEE

all people of color are excluded. In addition, the mass media often portrays science as a relatively impersonal field. For example, many television documentaries show the results of scientific work—the content of science—rather than the process of science or its human side. Science then seems a dry collection of facts and principles. This absence of the human face helps to create in students a deep and abiding lack of interest in scientific study. Hence, it is imperative that teachers use science experiences to make connections with their students' daily, lived experiences.

In this chapter, you will read about several ways in which teachers in ordinary classrooms integrate science experiences into their students' daily lives. We will begin by discussing a technique that is particularly useful in elementary school classrooms: establishing a science corner. Later in the chapter, you will read about middle school teachers who follow similar principles.

Science Corners

One way to make science part of the daily life of the classroom is to reserve a table in a corner of the room and label it the "science corner" or the "science table." In some schools, this area is called the "science center" because it becomes the center of scientific activity in the classroom. Whatever name you choose for it, the science corner can reflect many possible activities in the life of an elementary school science class. Here are a few ideas:

Ideas for science corners

■ *Seasonal changes.* The science corner can reflect the cycle of ongoing changes in the seasons. For example, an autumn science corner might display acorns, pinecones, colorful leaves, chestnuts, and other tree parts that commonly fall to the ground at this time of year in many parts of the country.

■ *Materials related to the current science unit.* A science corner could reflect the science unit the class is engaged in at the moment. For example, a fifth-grade class studying ecosystems might create some small habitats in its science corner. A third-grade unit on sound energy might be reflected in the class's science corner by student-made instruments.

■ *A class nature collection.* A science corner can include a potpourri of items from nature that students brought in simply because they found them fascinating. An appropriate title for such a science corner might be "The Class Collection from Nature."

Making the Science Corner an Interactive Experience

In many classrooms you can find objects of nature on display in a science corner. Unfortunately, if it is just a display area, teachers and students often lose interest in it. These objects merely collect dust and serve no useful purpose.

*An invitation
to explore*

To connect science with students' lives, the science corner needs an invitation for students to explore, a reason for them to visit. For example, the science corner can be a place where students are challenged to consider some questions and then generate their own questions. After visiting the classroom science corner, students could be encouraged to write in their science journals or notebooks, reflecting on what they did and what questions the experience raised for them. Students should also generate their own ideas for materials that could be added to the science corner as well as questions that could be asked about these new objects.

The following sections offer some clues for turning the science corner into an interactive experience that engages students in thinking, in exploring, and in developing their science process skills.

Designing the Science Corner with Your Students   One way to interest students in the science corner is to involve them in designing it and supplying its contents. This participation will help ensure that the informal science curriculum reflects their interests.

In setting up a science corner with your students, here are some questions you can ask that will engage them in the process:

Questions to ask

What should we put in our science corner?

What can we *do* there?

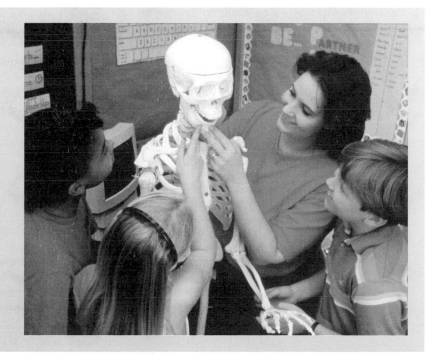

A teacher is examining the skeleton in her classroom's science corner with a group of students.

Charles Gupton/Corbis

Guidelines for Creating a Science Corner in Your Classroom

■ The classroom science corner should reflect the students' interests and, wherever possible, be set up by them. Its contents should change regularly, to keep stimulating students with new objects and questions they can investigate and ponder.

■ All the signs and cards at the science corner should be printed in large, bold lettering for students who have visual impairments. Similarly, the signs should not be placed too high or too low so students who have physical disabilities can read them easily.

■ No objects that could pose a danger to students should be kept in the science corner—for example, no heating devices or objects with sharp edges. See the section on safety tips in "More Resources for Teachers" at the end of this book.

■ The corner should include tools for measuring different properties of objects, such as a balance scale, uniform masses for weighing, centimeter sticks for measuring distance, and graduated cylinders for measuring liquid volume. The cen-ter can also include other common science tools, such as magnifying lenses, prisms, magnets, and mirrors. The questions and activities should give students reasons for using these tools.

■ If your classroom has a single computer, it should be in the science corner. It should be loaded with some meaningful software programs to engage students in problem solving, and the questions posed in the corner should often lead students to use the computer as a tool. If your classroom has more than one computer, then at least one of them should be in the science corner.

■ If the science corner reflects the theme of the current science unit, set out materials and experiences that extend the students' thinking. For example, for an electricity unit, set up the science corner so that it invites students to construct different kinds of circuits. The corner might feature books about electricity and perhaps have some small electrical appliances (unplugged!) for students to take apart and explore.

What materials will we need when we explore the objects in the corner?

Can we keep a small class pet there?

What rules do we need about how and when to use the science corner?

Science corner crews   In the upper elementary school grades, students can largely control the contents and activities of the science corner. Science corner "crews" can rotate monthly, taking the responsibility for changing some displays and maintaining others, as they see fit. This regular attention will help ensure a regular flow of materials into and out of the corner.

For very young students, the teacher can take a more active role in designing the exhibits. Even in these earlier grades, however, you can engage students in designing the science corner by offering possibilities and inviting them to share their own special objects from nature.

One first-grade teacher found that her class's science corner, which focused on the seashore, was getting *too* exciting, at least in terms of the way students behaved there, so she engaged her students in developing rules for the science corner. The teacher felt that any rules she could have imposed on them would have been burdensome rather than effective and helpful, so she let the students consider their own comfort level and come up with reminders that only they could have created. Here are the guidelines the students themselves made up:

The Science Center Reminders

1. No traffic jams, please. Three students at a time.

2. Wait your turn and say "please" and "thank you."

3. Share books.

4. Sit the right way.

5. Visit about ten minutes.

With their own rules in place, the students found the science corner to be an excellent place to investigate seashore topics independently. Often, during science discussions, these first graders would refer to books they had read in the science corner or to questions they had wondered about while exploring the resources there.

Questions and Activities   Like the science circus stations described earlier in the book, a classroom science corner should have cards (or displayed pieces of paper) that contain questions. For example, if the science corner has a collection of acorns, the card could read, "How would you classify these acorns? Why did you classify them this way instead of some other way?" Whenever possible, the teacher should have the students themselves construct the questions when they set up the displays. The students often answer the science corner questions in their science journals.

Encouraging students to experiment

The science corner questions should encourage the students to explore and experiment with the materials at hand. One second-grade science center displayed eyedroppers and a cup of water. Next to them were some pieces of an old newspaper. The card read, "Place a drop of water on the letters in the newsprint. What happens?"

Imagine a science corner or science table that changes every few weeks, contains an assortment of objects collected by the students and teacher, and challenges the students to find answers to questions. This is the sort of informal learning experience in which students can become deeply engaged.

Connections to Literature and Other Subjects

Books in the science corner

Science corners are perfect places to display the students' favorite science trade books or books of fiction that have some topical connection to the science objects on display. For example, one third-grade class I visited was studying local trees during the fall. Besides including many parts of trees for students to explore, the science corner also had a field guide to trees as well as Shel Silverstein's *The Giving Tree* and Dr. Seuss's *The Lorax*. (See Figure 5.1.) Although the latter two books are fiction, both connect important factual information about trees to their story lines.

When the science corner includes books of fiction, it is often useful for teachers to ask students to compare the story to what they know to be true about the subject. With *The Giving Tree*, for example, one of the cards at the science corner might ask, "In what ways is this story like what we know to be true about trees? In what ways is it different?" Even very young children will know—and enjoy explaining—that trees don't talk!

Integrating social studies and math

Besides literature, science corners can be readily linked with other elementary school subjects. The story of *The Lorax*, for instance, has important implications for the environment. Set in silly rhyme, it tells a powerful story about the results of constant logging. With this book in the science corner, you could connect a science unit on trees to social issues as well as to literature. Integrating mathematics into class lessons also becomes routine as we do science with students. In one third-grade class, the science corner displayed a cross-section of an old tree trunk and invited the children to count the tree rings and predict the age of the tree.

FIGURE 5.1
A science corner for third-grade students who are studying local trees. Notice the various materials to explore, the instruments for studying them, and the books for browsing

In later chapters of this book, you will see many possible links between science topics and other subjects. By taking advantage of these connections, you can strengthen the interdisciplinary nature of the learning experience, while at the same time developing your students' abilities to make their own connections.

Sample Science Corners from Around the Country

Looking at some science corners that teachers and students have set up in different areas of the country will help you think about ways to connect science concepts with your students' daily lives.

A Third-Grade Science Corner in the Northeast   This science corner contains a collection of seashells in a plastic container. An index card on the table next to the shells has the following message neatly printed on it:

> Can you classify these seashells? In what ways are they the same? In what ways are they different?

A Second-Grade Science Corner in the Northwest   One second-grade student has brought a very large pinecone to class. It becomes part of the science corner. The teacher asks the students what they want to find out about this pinecone. The children wonder how much it weighs, where it came from, and why it is so big. As the pinecone is placed on the science table, the teacher writes this on the accompanying question card:

> How many red chips weigh the same as the pinecone? How long is the pinecone? Where do you think it came from? Why is it so big?

The children who wander over to the science corner are free to explore any or all of the questions.

A First-Grade Science Corner in the Midwest   A stuffed, furry yellow chick sits on the science table. The index card asks a science question connected to literature:

> In what way is this baby chick like the real chick in the book we read in class? In what way is it different?

The book mentioned here is Ruth Heller's *Chickens Aren't the Only Ones* (1999).

A Third-Grade Science Corner in the Autumn   A group of leaves sits on the table. They have different shapes, sizes, and colors. An index card reads:

> What types of trees do you think these leaves came from? Are they from very large trees? Deciduous trees? Coniferous trees? Explain your thinking.

A Second-Grade Science Corner   A small basin of soapy water is surrounded by pipe cleaners shaped to look like bubble wands. Some are triangular, and some are square. The index card reads:

> What shape is a bubble?

In the same science corner, next to a prism, an index card reads:

> Hold this up to the light. What colors do you see?

A Third-Grade Science Corner   A basin of water invites the students to place different objects in the basin to see if they sink or float. The objects on the table are a marble, a paper clip, a wooden block, and a small ball. The children are allowed to try other objects as well (but dunking peanut butter sandwiches from their lunch boxes is discouraged). An index card asks:

> Which objects sink in water? What happens when they sink?

Field Trips

Another common way to link science to the world outside the classroom is to take the students outside, whether for a short stroll around the school grounds or a more extensive field trip.

I was visiting an elementary school in the Northeast one winter morning when a teacher I knew said, "Hi. The class and I are going to visit the Hall of Science today." This is a fine hands-on museum not far from the elementary school. I responded, "Great! How come you are going now?" She said that she had planned the trip weeks ago and thought that, at this time of year, it would be good to get the students out of the classroom.

Making field trips meaningful

It struck me that something was lacking in her definition of the trip's purpose. Certainly it is always a treat, if your school has the resources, to take students on class trips, but science field trips can be much more meaningful if they are directly connected to the unit or topic the class is studying. By linking the trips with class study, we reinforce the learning experience—and we demonstrate that science is more than a subject confined to the classroom.

Tips for Outdoor Science Experiences

- Careful planning is essential. For field trips, letters of consent are usually required from parents or guardians, and students should be guided to dress properly for the chosen site.

- Remember to prepare the materials you need to take so students can collect samples and record information. Resealable plastic bags, plastic collecting cups, student science journals and pencils, and magnifying lenses will always come in handy.

- Students should understand the reason for the outdoor trip and have some ideas about the problem they are exploring.

- The trip should lead to further investigations or research in class, as illustrated by the following science journal entry by a young student named Ana:

I went on a field trip with my class to the Duck Pond. We were looking for something new we had never seen before. When we came back to the room we all guessed what it was. Based on our past experience we all said it was either a beehive or a wasp's nest. We tried different experiments to find out what it was. After researching it we identified it as a praying mantis home. (Reprinted by permission.)

- Adult supervision is required. Depending on the type of excursion and the number of students you are taking, you may need to ask other adults to accompany you. These adults should also participate in the planning for the trip, if possible.

Exercising process skills

In addition to offering relevant science content, a field trip should provide students with the opportunity to exercise their science process skills. Invite your students to engage in some problem solving outdoors. For example, a fourth-grade trip to the seashore might involve taking notes, collecting articles of interest, and perhaps using a ball or two to explore the actions of the ocean waves. The teacher could engage students in recording their observations, drawing what they see, and solving one or more problems that they have previously brainstormed in class. On a similar field trip, an eighth-grade class might collect beach samples in Ziploc plastic bags to be examined later under a microscope. They might also collect some ocean water to determine density, turbidity, and salinity. Allowing the ocean water to evaporate is another exciting activity; what remains behind will include the various dissolved and undissolved substances contained in ocean water.

Whenever possible, share your rationale for venturing outdoors with the students. Involve them in planning both the excursion itself and the questions it will seek to answer. Ask them, for instance:

Questions when planning a trip

Why do you think we are going there?

What shall we bring?

What do you wonder about?

Students on a field trip are making observations and are ready to record their findings.

David Young-Wolff/Getty

Your students will have good ideas concerning the trip as well as their own stories to tell about related experiences.

In the following science stories, we will see some examples of informal science learning experiences both in and outside of the classroom.

SCIENCE STORY

Making Connections, Inside and Outside the Classroom

The Osage

When a fourth-grade student in southern New York State brings an interesting-looking fruit to class, neither the teacher nor the other students have ever seen anything like it. "This fell from a tree near my house, and I don't know what it is," the student says. "Can we put it in our science corner?"

"That's a very good idea," remarks the teacher. "What question can we put on our index card?"

"Let's ask, 'What do you think this is?'" the student replies.

What is this strange fruit?

Over the next few days, the class becomes intrigued by the strange-looking fruit. The students write in their science journals the qualities they notice about it. It is green, they observe, and has thick, bumpy skin like an orange. It also smells a little like an orange. They wonder why the skin is so thick.

After recording their observations and questions, the students explore the school library and finally ask for assistance. With the librarian's help, they find a picture and description of the fruit in a resource book. It is an osage, they learn. But their curiosity has been piqued, and they don't stop there.

Where is it from?

Now they read about where the tree grows, how it got its name, and much more. They learn that an osage is the fruit of the osage orange tree, which belongs to the mulberry family of trees. It was originally found in Texas, Oklahoma, and Arkansas and named after the Osage Indians of that region. It is an inedible fruit, and its tree has a short trunk and crooked branches. It is planted around the United States for hedges and ornamental purposes.

For the rest of the school year, everyone in that fourth-grade class looks for osage orange trees.

A Snow Story

One winter morning after a heavy snowfall, a fourth-grade teacher in Nebraska uses an empty coffee can as a scoop and fills it with snow. She asks the students what they can learn from it. She knows that they see snow every winter and probably have many unanswered questions about it. "What are your questions?" she asks. "What do you wonder about? How can you find out?"

Questions about snow

The students wonder if all snowflakes are really different. Why is it so quiet when it snows? Is snow a solid, liquid, gas, or all three? When the snow melts, will it still fill the can? What temperature is snow?

A surprising discovery

They take the can of snow to their science corner, where they measure its temperature with a thermometer. They examine small bits of the snow under a microscope and discuss what they see. They predict how high the water level in the can will be when the snow melts. They are shocked to see what a tiny amount of water the can full of snow melts into! They wonder what takes up all the space in the snowflakes.

On that day, the snow becomes the science curriculum. The formal curriculum waits for a while. The snow will not last forever, and the moment is there for the taking.

Two Seashores

With collection bags in hand, students in a sixth-grade science class on Long Island visit the south shore, the ocean side of the island. The sand forms smooth dunes here, and its fine grains glisten in the autumn sun. The students make drawings of the sparse plant life on the beach, and they study the shells that have washed up. They collect various artifacts to take

Exploring a Coastal Plain

As teachers, we often have fascinating natural phenomena right under our noses, but familiarity tends to breed indifference. The first step in bringing the local environment alive for our students is to pay attention to it ourselves.

In a small coastal fishing community in Maine, ten elementary school teachers accompanied me to a part of their coastline, an inlet where granitic mounds of rock dotted the landscape. This place was just down the road from the elementary school, and the teachers were discussing how to use their local environment as a living laboratory for their students. For me, it was a mysterious and interesting site, but for these local teachers it seemed quite ordinary because they had seen it countless times before. "What do you notice?" I asked them. "Tell me everything, anything." Thus prodded, they began to observe more than they had suspected they would. For example, it was low tide, and my companions pointed out that all the mounds of rock had water marks, which indicated the point to which high tide had risen that day. *Tides*, these teachers knew, are the rise and fall of the oceans caused mainly by the moon's gravitational pull on the earth. The waters on the side of the earth facing the moon bulge out toward the moon's gravitational pull, creating a **high tide.** The other side of the earth, facing away from the moon, has high tide simultaneously because the moon's gravitational pull has pulled on the solid earth as well, leaving the waters bulging on the opposite side of the earth. Meanwhile, as the waters bulge on two sides of the earth, the waters on the other two sides flatten, causing lower levels of water, or **low tides.** Because the earth rotates on its axis once every twenty-four hours, the tide rises for about six hours at a particular point, then falls for about six hours.

The teachers knew all this, but it hadn't occurred to them that they could use the inlet down the road from their school as a place for their students to investigate the concepts of tides, gravitation, and the movements of the earth and moon.

As we stood there, we noticed that some untidy seagulls had left the shells from the mussels they had eaten atop a large rock, which had served as the gulls' dining table. That observation sparked a discussion about food chains.

One teacher picked up a dried scallop shell in which a spider had spun its web. Talking about it, we brought up ideas about animal habitats, ecosystems, and more.

These teachers were so impressed with the natural phenomena under their noses that they took their students to the inlet the next day to collect materials for science corners

Why are seashores different?

back to their classroom. Back in the school, using reference books and web sites, they identify the marine invertebrates whose shells they have found.

On another trip, they visit the north side of the island, where the bay gently brushes against a craggy shore. They notice how very rocky and pebbly it is. Encouraged by their teacher, the students begin to wonder why this north shore looks so different from the south. They make more drawings and return with sand and rock samples to compare with the samples from the south shore.

In the next weeks, using books, CD-ROMs, and the Internet, they learn about the effects of the ocean and inlet bays on landform. They make inferences, come up with their own ideas, and research areas of personal interest. The students' comparison of the two shores yields some important science concepts.

Investigating a Natural Disaster

A major earthquake strikes California. News of the sudden destruction floods the television and print media nationwide. In Texas the next day, one fifth-grade teacher begins doing "earthquake science," despite the fact that it is not listed in the formal fifth-grade curriculum.

Making models to understand an earthquake

The students clip newspaper stories on the disaster and hang them around the room. Prompted by the teacher, they write down their earthquake questions and research them in library books and on web sites. In the science corner, some students make clay models of the earth's crust and use plastic knives to cut lines in the clay to represent faults. Others use layer cakes in cake pans that are precut before the cakes are baked. (When you bake a layer cake in a pan that has been cut slightly on the bottom, the layer comes out sporting a large crack, which resembles a fault in the earth's crust.) Using these models, the students learn that an earthquake is a sudden slippage of rock that sends enormous shock waves through the earth.

The students also write stories about the earthquake and take collections for the earthquake victims. Besides increasing their understanding of earthquakes in particular, these explorations help make the students aware of the impact of natural events on human lives.

Coconuts Outside the Door

Outside the door of his apartment complex in south Florida, Mr. Appleton, a seventh-grade teacher at the local middle school, finds a coconut that apparently has fallen from one of many palm trees that line the street opposite the beach. He looks up and under the spreading arms of the palm tree's large leaf stalks he sees bunches of coconuts, some already brown, that appear ready to detach themselves and fall.

Bringing the coconut into his science class, Mr. Appleton shows it to the students. "Look what I found outside my door," he says. "I was wondering what you think. Is this living or nonliving?" The students are amused; they know they are starting life science in seventh grade, but yesterday they looked at pond water and explored single-celled organisms with their microscopes. "What does this have to do with paramecium?" asks Dean.

"What makes you ask that question?" responds Mr. Appleton.

"Well," Dean says, "I thought we were doing life science now."

"We are," says Mr. Appleton, "so we are wondering: Is this coconut living or nonliving?"

New thoughts about a familiar object

All of the students have seen coconuts before. In their coastal neighborhood in tropical Florida, palm trees are everywhere. The students offer various ideas about the coconut. Most of them are reluctant to say it is not living, but they are unable to say why they think it is alive. The consensus in this class is that the coconut *will become* a living palm tree if planted in the ground, but for now it is "dormant." Mr. Appleton asks what they mean by dormant and invites them to do research on the coconut.

The students then proceed to explore, in research books and on web sites, what processes living things perform. As they do so, Mr Appleton raises more questions about the coconut: "Why do you think it has a hard outer shell?" "What about the texture of the nut inside the shell?" "What purpose does the liquid inside, called the milk, serve?" "Do you think the coconut would sink or float in water?"

Interrogating their own environment

In the days that follow, students come to class with additional data about the coconut. They place the coconut in a large basin and watch it float. Although they have seen coconuts every day, they have never before interrogated their own environment in this way, and they are surprised that some of the trees in their daily life have become the science topic for the class.

EXPANDING MEANINGS

■ The Teaching Ideas Behind These Stories

- ■ Science comes alive when you think of it as a way to explore nature in your own backyard. In four of our five stories, the students' scientific inquiry was connected directly to where they lived. In the earthquake story, the inquiry was linked to news reports the students had just heard and to their own collections to assist the victims.

- ■ We can say that these students followed a "both/and" curriculum (McIntosh, 1983). That is, they pursued both the prescribed, formal curriculum of the school and their own informal, self-constructed, experientially grounded curriculum. In effect, an informal curriculum constructs a new textbook—the textbook of our daily lives. ("Making textbooks of our lives" is a phrase first used by Emily Style, codirector of the National SEED [Seeking Educational Equity and Diversity] Project on inclusive curriculum, based at the Wellesley College Center for Research on Women in Wellesley, Massachusetts.)

- ■ Connecting science to students' own lives—in a way that encourages them to explore their own questions—both engages them in using science process skills and validates their sense of themselves as scientific thinkers. This is particularly important for students who might be discouraged or marginalized by traditional science teaching.

■ Since classroom science corners should reflect the lives of the students, it makes sense that they vary with the geographic location of the school and the interests and backgrounds of the students. For instance, classrooms in coastal regions may be rich in seashell collections, and inland regions may have rich rock collections. A school in the Southwest may have a marvelous display of different sands and sedimentary rocks on its science table.

■ In the coconut story, notice how Mr. Appleton was respectful of Dean's question about whether they were "doing" this subject now. Students see school science as separate from their world and almost resist broadening their point of view. Undaunted, Mr. Appleton continued with his coconut questions and hooked the students on a product of nature that is part of their everyday lives.

● The Science Ideas Behind These Stories

● Osage trees are distinctive because of the fruit's thick, pebbly skin. Like many other plants that originated in dry climates, the osage fruit has evolved an outer coating that protects it from dehydrating. They are not common in southern New York State, where the fourth grader in our story noticed one.

● Snow forms from water vapor that condenses when the temperature of the air is below freezing. The term *condenses* means that the particles of water vapor come close together, forming droplets of water. When the temperature is below the freezing point, the water vapor condenses into snow crystals rather than into rain. Snow, then, is frozen water vapor. There is a lot of space between snowflakes. The air fills the spaces between the snowflakes, and that is why snow takes up so much more space than the water it turns into when it melts. That is also why the environment seems so quiet after a snowstorm; sounds are absorbed by the air spaces.

● As the students in the Long Island story discovered, seashores have sand particles of different sizes, depending on how the shore was created. On the south shore of Long Island, the constant wave action of the Atlantic Ocean causes rocks to be worn down into tiny sand particles— a process called **weathering.** On the north shore, the water is from a bay, a smaller inland waterway. Here the water action is gentler, the process of weathering is much slower, and hence the rock particles are much larger and coarser than the fine-grained sand on the south shore.

● An earthquake is a sudden slippage of rock. Earthquakes occur because the outer layer of the earth (the part we live on), called the *crust,* is made up of huge chunks of rock called *plates.* Rock plates lying next to each other are pressed tightly together. Sometimes the pressure is so great that they need to slip past each other ever so slightly in order to settle in a new position that eases the pressure. This slippage is what we experience as an earthquake. Earthquakes are most common in areas where there are boundaries between the plates or huge cracks in plates. These boundaries and cracks are called **faults.**

- The coconut thrives on sandy shorelines in the tropics. As Mr. Appleton's class discovered, the fruit can float in water, and in fact coconuts can travel long distances by floating. When they wash up on a new shore, they can germinate to create new trees. Coconut oil is used in a wide variety of products, including soap, cosmetics, and cooking oils.

✔ The Science Standards Behind These Stories

STANDARDS These stories illustrate the following guidelines of the National Science Education Standards (National Research Council, 1996):

✔ *Content Standard F, Grades K–4 (Science in Personal and Social Perspectives):* "As a result of activities in grades K–4, all students should develop understanding of . . . types of resources, changes in environments, [and] science and technology in local challenges" (p. 138). By fifth and sixth grade, the Standards go on to say, "the study of science-related personal and societal challenges is an important endeavor" (p. 167).

✔ *Content Standard A, Grades K–4 (Science As Inquiry):* "In the early years of school, students can investigate earth materials, organisms, and properties of common objects. Although children develop concepts and vocabulary from such experiences, they also should develop inquiry skills" (p. 121).

✔ *Content Standard A, Grades 5–8 (Science As Inquiry):* "The students' questions [for inquiry] should be relevant and meaningful for them" (p. 144).

Questions for Further Exploration

- On what kind of landform do you live? For instance, is it a coastal plain, an interior plain, a plateau, a mountain? How can you investigate what it is called and how the land achieved its current configuration?

- How does nature present itself in your surroundings? Are you near a seashore, a desert, a grassy plain, or a park rich with conifers?

- How many distinct seasons are noticeable in your area?

- In what ways have people changed the natural landscape of your environment?

- What is the local plant and animal life like?

- How can aspects of your local landscape and plant and animal life inform your students' science experiences? How might they be linked to the formal science curriculum?

Resources for Further Exploration

ELECTRONIC RESOURCES

The Coconut Palm in Florida. http://edis.ifas.ufl.edu/MG043. This University of Florida web site offers a good deal of information about coconuts and their habitats throughout Florida.

Frank Potter's Science Gems—Earth Science II. http://www.sciencegems.com/earth2.html. This page of Frank Potter's Science Gems web site contains links to many resources for lessons on the atmosphere, weather, earthquakes, water, and more, grouped by approximate grade level.

Science Adventures. http://www.scienceadventures.org/. This online directory makes it easy to find locations near your home that offer hands-on experiences, exhibits, and teacher and public educational programs. Its search features allow you to search by location within a specified radius of by a zip code. The list includes zoos, parks, gardens, aquariums, nature centers, and planetariums.

Science Learning Network. http://www.sln.org/. This web site has important links to museum web sites all over the country as well as to other resources that make science connections to daily life.

USGS Earthquake Information. http://quake.wr.usgs.gov/. This government web site offers up-to-date information on earthquakes around the world, with maps.

PRINT RESOURCES

Brainard, A., & Wrubel, D. (1993). *Literature-Based Science Activities: An Integrated Approach*. New York: Scholastic Professional Books. Designed for students in kindergarten through grade 3, this volume highlights children's books for introducing, extending, or enriching the science content in twenty topic areas.

Gardner, R., & Webster, D. (1987). *Science in Your Backyard*. New York: Simon & Schuster. Encourages students in grades 4 through 6 to use their backyards, parks, and playgrounds as sites for scientific investigations.

Parker, S. (1989). *Seashore*. New York: Knopf. Using actual photographs (a characteristic of this book series), this book provides a wonderful seashell reference.

Roth, C., Cervoni, C., Wellnitz, T., & Arms, E. (1991). *Beyond the Classroom: Exploration of Schoolground and Backyard*. Lincoln, MA: Massachusetts Audubon Society. How to use your school's immediate environment to create a familiar laboratory for activities in kindergarten through grade 6.

Rylant, C. (1988). *Every Living Thing*. New York: Aladdin Library. A wonderful book of short stories about people and animals; an excellent way to connect science to literature for middle school.

Trolley, K. (1994). *The Art and Science Connection: Hands-on Activities for Intermediate Students* and *The Art and Science Connection: Hands-on Activi-*

ties for Primary Students. Menlo Park, CA: Addison-Wesley. Source-books for creative art activities that integrate art and science, for students in kindergarten through grade 6.

Zolotow, C. (1992). *The Seashore Book.* New York: HarperCollins. A fictional story in which a mother's words help a little boy to imagine the sights and sounds of the seashore even though he has never seen the ocean; appropriate for grades 2 through 6.

The Daily Life of the Classroom

We are all designers of our own life's big experiment. We can design the small experiments that comprise school life too. Schools can be places that encourage the unfolding of answers.
—JACQUELINE GRENNON BROOKS

When you enter an elementary school classroom, the life of the class is often reflected by the materials that adorn the room. I often look for a science corner. When I find it, I spend time exploring the materials on it. Sometimes they tell me only what science unit the students are studying; at other times, though, I learn about the students' own collections and interests. The tacit message I receive from classrooms that have student-generated science corners is, "Science is a regular, meaningful part of the life of this class."

Similarly, in a middle-school science classroom, I look for more than the typical scientific equipment and posters. What I want to see is some evidence that the students' own interests and lived experiences have informed their science activities. For instance, the displays may include student research reports that focus on areas of student interest.

Benefits of the informal curriculum

The same principles apply to field trips and other outdoor activities. By constructing an informal curriculum out of natural items and events in the students' own world, we make it possible for them to value themselves as scientists and to overcome the traditional factors that alienate many young people from science. We help them understand science content more deeply and more personally, as part of a larger picture. Finally, we raise their awareness of their natural environment and the issues it poses for their future life as adults.

KEY TERMS

formal science curriculum *(p. 104)*
informal science curriculum *(p. 104)*
high tide *(p. 119)*
low tide *(p. 119)*
weathering *(p. 122)*
faults *(p. 123)*

6 Science Is Not Neat
Explorations of Matter

FOCUSING QUESTIONS

▪ What is important about the process of classifying?

▪ What types of things do you classify in your daily life?

▪ What types of "messy" explorations do you do?

▪ What do you think is meant by the statement, "Science is not neat"?

One of my favorite definitions of *science* refers to it as a way of making sense of the world. To me, that suggests in part that science helps us deal with the enormous diversity of the materials—both living and nonliving—that exist in our environment. In this chapter, we are going to look at classrooms where students are exploring nonliving materials and trying to make sense of them. This sense making usually begins with the process of **classifying**—that is, grouping materials with similar properties into the same categories. As you read the stories in this chapter, look for these themes:

▪ Knowing *why* an object belongs in a particular category is as important as knowing *where* to place it.

▪ Choosing a category for an object or an idea isn't always simple.

▪ Science can be messy—in more than one way. Often you make a mess when exploring materials. Often, too, the ideas that are generated during the process of classifying are themselves complex and "messy."

This chapter will deal mostly with children in the early grades. In later chapters, you will see how older elementary and middle school students build on the knowledge and skills described here.

Classifying

As we discovered in the chapter about the science circus, classifying is one of the basic process skills. For children, classifying begins with the simple recognition of properties and matures into a grouping and sorting process. The categories that very young children employ are usually mutually exclusive

From simple categories to hierarchies

and not hierarchical (Siegler, 1998; National Research Council, 1996, p. 128). This means that the children are grouping and sorting materials into categories without thinking of a larger picture in which those categories themselves could be placed. The larger picture emerges as the students mature. By fourth grade, they are often able to classify an object into more than one category, and they are more and more able to arrange categories into hierarchies.

Using property words

In elementary school science, children often learn classifying skills by identifying the properties of materials through careful observation, and then comparing and contrasting those properties. The basic words we use to describe the material world are sometimes called **property words.** These are words that refer to the common properties of objects, such as size, shape, color, odor, texture, taste, composition, and hardness. *Big,* for example is a property word, as is *red.* In developing their classifying skills by using such property words, children are also learning language and communication skills.

In the following two science stories, we'll see how some students in the early grades identify certain properties as they attempt to classify objects according to their state of matter. The states of matter—solid, liquid, and gas—sound simple, but they are not always obvious or visible.

 SCIENCE STORY

Exploring Solids, Liquids, and Gases

Ms. Harrison's multiage class is in a rural setting, far from the action and resources of metropolitan areas. When I enter, I see that she has set up five stations around the room so the students can work simultaneously in groups. It is late in the school year, and the children have already learned the rules of their classroom setting. They seem comfortable and are functioning well independently. The class has nineteen students at different stages of development, in grades 2 and 3.

Ms. Harrison has prepared five identical sets of materials, one set for each group of students. Each set has three plastic bags, all the same size. In one bag she has placed a wooden block; another bag holds 8 ounces (1 cup) of water; and the third bag Ms. Harrison has blown full of air. All the bags are closed with twist ties. The only labels on the bags are as follows: All the bags with solid blocks in them are labeled "bag 1." All the bags of water are "bag 2," and all the bags of air are "bag 3."

Why such vague labels?

Ms. Harrison plans for the students, in groups of four, to explore these bags and describe their contents. To introduce the activity, she says, "We have the opportunity to explore some materials today. We are going to observe them in any way we can, and then we will try to classify them. In your science journals, write down all the things you can say about these materials."

Ms. Harrison's thinking: Although Ms. Harrison wants the students to recognize the differences among solids, liquids, and gases, she sees no reason to supply those labels up front. She wants the children to do their own thinking about the classifications, and the labels can be introduced later.

Ms. Harrison guides the students along: "What are all the things we can say about the materials in bags 1, 2, and 3? Remember to write your observations in your journal."

Alena supplies the names

Suddenly, Alena, one of the older students, calls out, "That's easy, Ms. Harrison. One is a solid, one's a liquid, and one's a gas!"

"Yes, Alena, that is one type of label we can give these materials, but I asked all of you to make observations. Let's talk about why one is called a solid, while another one is called a liquid and another one a gas. Your observations can help us with that."

Ms. Harrison's thinking: Okay, Ms. Harrison thinks, the labels are more obvious than she planned. Several students already know that these materials are examples of solids, liquids, and gases. But she is hoping for some discussion of the meaning behind the labels. She wonders whether the students will be able to determine what properties are usual for any solid, liquid, or gas.

An accident!

As the students examine the three bags and write their observations in their journals, Ms. Harrison visits each group. Suddenly, there is a scream. One of the water bags has spilled all over the table and Todd's leg. Another student gets paper towels, and the group cleans up the mess. Todd says, "Sorry!" It appears that the bag broke because he handled it a bit too much or too roughly.

After making sure that Todd does not mind a wet pant leg, Ms. Harrison says, "Sometimes science can get messy, but that's okay. Why don't you put some water in another bag, Todd. Tie it tightly, and go on with your observations."

My thinking: As I watch the class working, I am impressed with the calm way Ms. Harrison handles the spilled water. Certainly this is not the first time a spill has happened, and it won't be the last. I agree with what she told the class—that getting messy is sometimes a part of doing science.

The children's observations

When the students appear to be finished writing in their journals, Ms. Harrison gathers their observations and records them on a class chart. Table 6.1 lists some of the students' responses.

My thinking: I see that the distinctions among the different states of matter have begun to emerge in the students' minds. Now the lesson is really going beyond the labels.

TABLE 6.1   Observations by Students in Ms. Harrison's Class

The block	The water	The air
It is yellow.	It is white.	It is light.
It is hard.	It is wet.	I can see through it.
It's a rectangle.	It is drippy	I can grab it and make it fly.
It has eight corners.	It has no shape.	It has no shape.
It has six sides.	I can see through it.	It doesn't drip.
It can float in water.	I can pour it into a glass.	
I can bang it on the table. It makes a loud sound.	I can squeeze the bag.	
It doesn't change its shape.		
I can't squeeze it.		
It's smooth.		
It is medium-sized.		

Ms. Harrison begins to pull the lesson together by remarking, "Alena said, when we began, that these materials in our plastic bags were a solid, a liquid, and a gas. What do you think about that?" After discussing the question, the students conclude that the air is an example of a gas, the block of a solid, and the water of a liquid. Ms. Harrison tells them these are three states of matter. "Scientists say that matter is anything that has weight and takes up space," she goes on. She urges the students to see if their three samples meet those criteria. Do they all take up space and have weight?

Does air have weight?

The students agree that the block, the water, and the air take up space, but not everyone is convinced that the air has weight. "How many of you think that we can weigh the air that is in this bag?" Ms. Harrison asks. About half of the students raise their hands.

Ms. Harrison proceeds to blow air into another plastic bag and tie it. She rests a book on the bag of air and invites the children to observe how

Students are pouring liquids and examining their properties.

Cassy Cohen/PhotoEdit

the air takes up space and supports the weight of the book. She explains that blowing the air into the bag and tying the bag pushes the tiny air particles together. Then she asks, "How can we prove that this air weighs something?"

My thinking: As I know from other experiences—like the ones described in earlier chapters—the gaseous state of matter is least concrete for children and most difficult for them to grasp. I think that Ms. Harrison is wise to pursue the idea that compressed air can be weighed.

Asking for predictions

The students aren't sure how to weigh the air. Ms. Harrison takes a double-pan balance and places an inflated balloon on one side of the balance and a deflated balloon on the other side. Before she lets go of the balloons in the pans, she asks the students what they think. How will the scales tip? The students are divided about the outcome.

The inflated balloon tips the scale downward, indicating that the balloon filled with air weighs more than the balloon with no air. Then Ms. Harrison asks the children to blow on their hands, feeling their own exhaled air.

"It tickles," Julia says. "It feels warm," remarks Marika.

Ms. Harrison's thinking: Ms. Harrison hopes that all these little "air" experiences will help reinforce the idea that air is matter: in addition to taking up space, it has mass, you can feel it, and it can be warm or cold.

Ms. Harrison continues, "Let's look at the list of properties on our chart. Notice that we had more things to say about the solid than about the liquid or gas. Why do you think that is so?"

My thinking: I see that Ms. Harrison is beginning to generalize from the block, the air, and the water to solids, liquids, and gases. It is true: solids have more attributes for students to describe than do liquids and gases, and it is easier for children to come up with property words that apply to solids.

Understanding properties of solids

The students go over their list of the wooden block's properties. They begin to understand that solids have surfaces, shapes, and textures, and that they are easy to measure compared to objects with changeable shapes. Ms. Harrison invites the students to name the solids in their classroom. The students generate a long list of objects: tables, chairs, walls, posters, books, and so forth.

How can we weigh a liquid?

Ms. Harrison then asks, "What liquids do you drink or see every day?" The students generate a long list again. She says, "Let's look at our bags of water. How can we weigh the water?" The students ask her to put one bag on a scale, and she does so for them. She points out that the bag weighs something as well, but its weight will be too small to notice.

"What if we were weighing our water in a cup?" Ms. Harrison asks. Some of the older students remark that they would have to weigh the cup first, then weigh the cup and water together, and then subtract the weight of the cup.

My thinking: I notice how Ms. Harrison varies her tactics. She asks the students to find examples of solids in the classroom; but when she turns to liquids she realizes that the students will see few or no liquids in the room. So she changes the question into one about their everyday lives. I also like the way she asks them to think about weighing the water in the cup, wanting them to understand that weighing the liquid alone is not that easy. (I am reminded of the students in Mr. Wilson's class who weighed the melting icicles.)

Finding examples at home

For the next day's class, Ms. Harrison asks the students to write down all the solids, liquids, and gases they notice in their own homes. And for each item, they should write down why they think it is a solid, a liquid, or a gas.

SCIENCE STORY

Mysterious Matter

Ms. Hager, a first-grade teacher in a primary school in south Florida, is combining 2 cups of cornstarch with 1 cup of water in a large bowl. She is creating an activity that in some ways will be even more challenging than the one in Ms. Harrison's class. She is going to take advantage of the fact that it is sometimes difficult to decide what state of matter an object is in. Sometimes matter can have properties of more than one state.

Before mixing the ingredients, Ms. Hager has invited the students to explore the cornstarch and decide its state. This generates a lot of discussion. The children think it is a powder, and they have a hard time deciding if a powder is a solid or a liquid. Ms. Hager challenges them to think about it but does not tell them the answer.

"Where have you seen this white powder before?" Ms. Hager asks. One student says that her mother uses it to cook. Another student says that his parents use it to diaper his baby brother.

A peculiar green goo

Now Ms. Hager takes 1 cup of water and adds green food coloring to it. Then she adds the water to the cornstarch and stirs the two together. This produces a peculiar green goo. After the students help Ms. Hager cover all the tables in the classroom with newspaper, she distributes a piece of the green goo in an aluminum-foil pie pan to each pair of students. She encourages the students to explore the mixture, discuss it, and express all their possible observations.

Experimenting with the "gushy mess"

The students are delighted. As they quickly discover, the goo looks and feels like a liquid, but it can be shaped into a ball. It looks as if it should splash when they drop an object in it, but it does not. All in all, this "gushy mess," as one student describes it, provides them with a wonderfully tactile experience. As they get it all over the newspaper-protected tables, they come up with many observations about it. One student records in her journal that the mixture is "soft, smooth, and mushy." Another writes, "It was a little like a solid and a little like a liquid." Still another student observes, "We made green goo. If you hold it in your hand and squeeze, it drips!"

> *Ms. Hager's thinking: Ms. Hager knows that it is important, especially with young children, to provide opportunities for them to explore interesting materials and use language to describe what they are experiencing. And she knows that this mixture will provide a good workout for their skills of observation and description.*

"What happens when you add more water to it?" one girl asks.
"Let's try it!" replies Ms. Hager.

Changing the proportions of ingredients

The students observe that adding water makes the mixture more like a liquid. Ms. Hager says that the measurements of the two ingredients are important. Another student wants to add more cornstarch. Again, they try the experiment, and it makes the mixture seem more like a solid. It also turns it a paler shade of green.

Ms. Hager challenges the students to decide what state of matter the green goo is in. They cannot make up their minds. They decide to place it in a new category for their matter unit: "Not Sure."

The children's categories

The students already have a list on the board, and now they add their latest observation to it:

Solids	Liquids	Gases	Not Sure
wood	water	air	green goo
chalk	orange juice	soda bubbles	
blackboard	milk	helium	

They have learned that sometimes materials can fall into two categories—or none at all!

EXPANDING MEANINGS

The Teaching Ideas Behind These Stories

- In Ms. Harrison's class, the important distinctions between solids, liquids, and gases *emerged* as the students examined the contents of each bag. Ms. Harrison did not rush to label the materials. Even Alena, the student who called out the correct labels, was missing the point. The main question is, "What does it *mean* when we say something is a solid or a liquid or a gas?"

- When Todd broke the water bag, Ms. Harrison treated the mess as routine—a result of scientifically exploring water. It's important that students see exploration as nonthreatening. Honest explorations are impossible in an atmosphere where students are terrified to have an accident.

- Notice how Ms. Harrison used several techniques to demonstrate that air is matter. This provided multiple opportunities for students to grasp the concept and relate it to their own experiences.

- When Ms. Hager asked the students where they had seen cornstarch before, she was making connections between the science experience and their experience outside the classroom.

- Ms. Hager did not tell her first graders the answer to the state of matter of the cornstarch. She let their dilemma sit with them for a while. As they worked with the cornstarch, they recognized that it must be a solid.

- Inviting her students to explore the cornstarch and water mixture was a way for Ms. Hager to encourage them to use descriptive language.

- "Oobleck" is the name sometimes used for the cornstarch and water mixture. It comes from the Dr. Seuss book *Bartholomew and the Oobleck* (1949). Whether or not you call the mixture oobleck, the Seuss book offers a great way to connect the science lesson to literature. So does *Horrible Harry and the Green Slime* (1989), written by Suzy Kline.

The Science Ideas Behind These Stories

- There are three common **states of matter** that we can explore with students: solids, liquids, and gases.

- **Solids** have a definite shape and can hold that shape for an indefinite amount of time if outside conditions remain the same. Besides shape, children come to know that solids have a definite size, texture, and color and can be easily measured and weighed on a scale.

- **Liquids** have a definite size but no definite shape. Liquids take the shape of their container. The most commonly found liquid on Earth is water. Many foods have a large water content—as does the human body.

- **Gases** have neither a definite size nor a definite shape. Gases take the size and shape of their container.

- In addition to solids, liquids, and gases, scientists have identified two other states of matter: (1) *Plasma* is the random array of very hot matter— gases so hot that they no longer resemble any known gases because electrical particles have been stripped away from the central part of the molecules. Plasma is the stuff of which stars are made, and it is the most common state of matter in the universe, but not on Earth. A tiny bit of plasma can be found in a fluorescent light bulb. (2) The *Bose-Einstein condensate* is, in a way, the opposite of plasma because it occurs at ultralow temperatures, close to the point when atoms are not moving at all. Although its theoretical existence was predicted early in the twentieth century, the Bose-Einstein condensate was not actually created in a laboratory until 1995.

- Air is a mixture of gases. While to our bodies oxygen is the most important part of the air, only about 21 percent of the air is oxygen. Air is about 78 percent nitrogen.

- Cornstarch is a powdered solid. Even though it does not have rigid surfaces, a clump of cornstarch powder stays together on a surface, in its own small mound.

- The cornstarch and water mixture is actually a **suspension**; the solid particles are literally suspended between water particles.

- Just why the cornstarch and water mixture has such odd properties, acting sometimes like a liquid and sometimes like a solid, remains a mystery to scientists. There are several theories involving electrical charges and a theory about molecular size—but no conclusions.

● Frequently objects do not fall into neat categories. Understanding that the study of science does not always provide clear answers is an important way to make school science more like real science.

✔ The Science Standards Behind These Stories

 STANDARDS In the National Science Education Standards (National Research Council, 1996), *Content Standard B for Physical Science in Grades K–4* states that all stu-dents should develop an understanding of "properties of objects and materials" (p. 123). You can see how this standard relates to the activities in Ms. Hager's and Ms. Harrison's classes. More specifically, note some of the "fundamental concepts and principles" that underlie this standard (p. 127).

✔ "Objects have many observable properties, including size, weight, shape, color, temperature, and the ability to react with other substances."

✔ "Objects can be described by the properties of the materials of which they are made, and those properties can be used to separate or sort a group of objects or materials."

✔ "Materials can exist in different states—solid, liquid, and gas."

Questions for Further Exploration

■ For the experiment that Ms. Harrison's class performed, what other materials might you use in place of the block of wood, the water, and the air in the plastic bags?

■ Think about gelatin. What state of matter is it? What about mayonnaise? Oatmeal?

Resources for Further Exploration

ELECTRONIC RESOURCES

Exploratorium. http://www.exploratorium.edu/. This web site, sponsored by the Exploratorium science museum in San Francisco, is full of interesting articles and experiments to try.

Rader's Chem4Kids. http://www.chem4kids.com/. This site provides a nice explanation of many chemistry ideas, including the states of matter (though not the Bose-Einstein condensate).

PRINT RESOURCE

Sneider, C. (1988). *Oobleck: What Scientists Do*. GEMS series. Berkeley, CA: Lawrence Hall of Science. GEMS stands for Great Expectations in Mathematics and Science, a curriculum writing project from the Lawrence Hall of Science. For information on GEMS materials, see **http://www.lhs. berkeley.edu/GEMS/**.

Matter and Energy

The exploration of nonliving materials belongs to the branch of school science called **physical science.** The study of physical science encompasses the interactions between matter and energy.

As we saw in an earlier chapter, **matter** means anything that has weight and takes up space. If you can measure it and weigh it, it is usually matter. By **energy,** we mean the ability to produce a change in matter. Scientists define energy as the ability to do work, and work is defined as a force moving through a distance. So, for example, energy is needed in order to push a rock off the edge of a cliff. The amount of force that is used and how far the rock moves is a measure of how much energy is needed to move the rock.

Matter and energy are two very broad categories in which the diverse materials of the world can be placed. Matter can be further described by its different states—solid, liquid, gas, and plasma. By the upper elementary grades, students often begin to learn about chemical composition as well, distinguishing elements from compounds and mixtures. By middle school, students learn about atomic structure and its implications for the ways materials combine with one another.

An **element** is the building block of all matter. The simplest form of matter, an element is made up of only one type of material. Examples of elements are iron, nickel, gold, silver, oxygen, hydrogen, helium, carbon, and mercury. There are ninety-two naturally occurring elements in the universe, and fourteen others that have been produced by scientists in laboratories. The smallest part of an element that still has the properties of that element is called an **atom.**

A **compound** is a combination of two or more elements in a definite proportion. For example, water is H_2O—two parts hydrogen to one part oxygen. The smallest part of a compound that still has the properties of that compound is a **molecule.** Molecules are made up of atoms. Salt, carbon dioxide, and water are three common compounds. When compounds form, the elements that comprise them lose their original properties.

Finally, a **mixture** is any combination of elements, compounds, and other mixtures. Because there are only ninety-two naturally occurring elements, most matter that we encounter is either a compound or a mixture.

Similarly, there are many forms of energy, and by the later elementary grades, students commonly begin to distinguish them. For example, what do you think of when you think of energy? Well, you may think of the energy you exhibit when running or playing tennis. That type of energy is the energy of movement. Scientists call the energy that an object has because it is moving **kinetic energy.** A moving car, a falling rock, and a strong wind all have kinetic energy.

Objects can also have energy when they are not moving. The stored-up energy that your body has when you are sleeping the night before a big race is called **potential energy.** In most cases, potential energy derives from position in space. A rock about to fall off a very high cliff has greater potential energy than a rock about to fall off a low cliff. The first rock is higher, so it can move farther and therefore has a greater amount of this potential energy. Students can readily learn this idea, just as they learn about gravity, which will cause both rocks to gain speed as they fall.

Do remember, however, that it is less crucial that students memorize the definitions for matter and energy than it is that they understand *how to think* about making order out of the diverse materials we encounter in nature.

If It's So Messy, Can It Be Science?

Two kinds of messiness

In Ms. Harrison's and Ms. Hager's classes, the children were engaged in what we might call messy investigations. They were messy in a literal sense: the water spilled, the green goo got all over things. In fact, if you try the cornstarch experiment, it is a good idea to cover the tables or desks as Ms. Hager did. Luckily, the mixture will wash off readily with plain water.

Second, there was a metaphorical messiness. The green goo behaved like a liquid sometimes and like a solid at other times. You may think that classifying objects, including living things, is a neat and clear process. It is not. As you will see later in this book, there used to be two kingdoms of living things, and now we have five kingdoms. The more we know about things, the more categories we need; and sometimes, when our categories fail us, we end up with a puzzle, at least temporarily.

Let's look in more detail at these two types of messiness and examine their implications for doing science with children.

Messiness in the Classroom

Often new teachers find themselves making a mess with their students as they engage in science experiences, just as Ms. Hager and Ms. Harrison did. Should you worry about this?

Several years ago, while I was visiting a suburban elementary school in the Midwest, the principal said, "I can't wait to take you to our science room. We have a science teacher who is so wonderful that when you walk in her room, you can hear a pin drop."

"When the children are in there?" I asked.

"Oh, yes," the principal replied.

A class where neatness rules

I knew I was in trouble at that school. My science projects tend to make the children excited and rather noisy. When I saw the classroom, my fears were confirmed. Not only was the place too quiet, it was too neat. I thought that meaningful exploration could not possibly be taking place if the room was dead quiet and perfectly neat.

New teachers intimidated

Sometimes, new teachers who want to engage their students in a student-centered, activity-based science learning environment are intimidated by messy materials and by what appears to be disarray. It is true: when students are using materials, working in groups, and trying to solve their own problems, the classroom will look a bit messy and sound a little noisy. But those are good signs. They are indications that active learning is taking place and that the students are taking charge of their own experiences—with guidance and coaching from their teacher.

Think back to the chapter "The Teacher as Mediator," where you read about Mr. Wilson's students working in groups with icicles—weighing them, melting them, weighing them again, and so on—while Mr. Wilson walked around the room to make suggestions and ask questions. During this activity, do you think the room looked neat and perfectly arranged? I can tell you that it didn't. Some of the melted water spilled; shirt sleeves got wet; and for a while it seemed that pie pans and wadded-up paper towels were scattered everywhere. But these were signs of important activity.

Sometimes a messy room is just a part of doing science with children. So is a time for cleanup. When an activity is completed for the day, the teacher can assign students tasks that make the room cleanup easier to handle. Occasionally, if your class grows somewhat messy or noisy during a science activity, you may encounter criticism from an administrator or a parent. If so, be prepared to explain what the students are doing and why, and don't be intimidated.

Safety   You'll need to make certain, of course, that your students' activities and explorations are not dangerous in any way. (See the feature "Safety Is Elementary" later in this chapter.) Being safe, however, doesn't require perpetual neatness. The science education reform movement recommends that you use a variety of materials and activities to engage students in doing science. It is understood that this process will not always be tidy.

Messiness in the Categories

After reading about Ms. Hager's class, you may be wondering why she involved her students in an activity that did not result in a clear classification of the strange green matter they created from cornstarch and colored water. What is the point of having first graders investigate something that is a little like a liquid and a little like a solid?

First, remember that teaching science entails getting students excited about new materials and the ideas they provoke. We want students to be

Safety Is Elementary

Sometimes school teachers, particularly those in elementary school, are wary about doing science because they lack training in safety procedures. Safety is indeed a very important concern.

The National Science Education Standards are explicit about safety as a "fundamental concern" (National Research Council, 1996, p. 44), and there are plenty of resources available to help classroom teachers learn about safety. Your school and district should have guidelines for you to consult. Another good resource is the book *Safety Is Elementary: The New Standard for Safety in the Elementary Science Classroom*, available from:

The Laboratory Safety Institute
192 Worcester Road
Natick, MA 01760
Phone: (508) 647-1900
Web site: http://www.labsafety.org/

The same institute offers a variety of publications relevant to lab safety in higher grades, and you will also find a number of safety tips in the *More Resources for Teachers* section at the end of this book.

We sand away at the interesting edges of subject matter until it is so free from its natural complexities, so neat, that there is not a crevice left as an opening. All that is left is to hand it to [students], scrubbed and smooth, so that they can view it as outsiders.

—LISA SCHNEIER

Daring to keep it complex

engaged, eager to explore their own questions and create possible solutions, thus building their own meanings. However, engaging students in their own thinking often exposes the complexities of a subject matter. Students may come up with questions that they cannot answer, or that we as their teachers cannot answer. Sometimes they may even raise questions that the most accomplished scientists in the world have not been able to answer.

"Keep it simple" is a standard phrase of advice we often hear. Do we dare, then, as teachers to keep it complex (Duckworth, 1991)?

I think we can dare—and we ought to. Doing so is an exciting challenge for science teachers. We must not run away from complexities. We need to help students feel comfortable with the known and the unknown. We want them to understand that the process of scientific exploration does not always lead to a single right answer. If they become convinced that science is just a series of collected facts about the natural world—facts without ambiguities and uncertainties—they have missed the point, and our teaching has missed the mark. To sum it up neatly: in the real world, science sometimes offers answers that are *not* neat.

In the case of classification, what we know about children's development suggests that they gradually learn more complex classification systems as they mature (Siegler, 1998). How useful, then, to challenge them with green goo—a type of matter that can fit into two categories at the

Doing science sometimes means getting messy. Here, some younger students explore the properties of soapy water.

Elizabeth Crews/
The Image Works

same time! This type of classifying activity can help prepare them for more sophisticated classifying schemes as they continue their science experiences in later grades.

Implications for adult life

What students learn through "messy" science can have broad implications. After all, our own lives are not always neat, simple, and absolute, and the world we live in is complicated. If we can help students become genuine explorers and investigators, willing to confront complexity and try out their own ideas for making sense of it, we will have taken a big step in preparing them for adult life.

KEY TERMS

classifying *(p. 126)*
property words *(p. 127)*
states of matter *(p. 134)*
solid *(p. 134)*
liquid *(p. 134)*
gas *(p. 134)*
suspension *(p. 134)*
physical science *(p. 136)*
matter *(p. 136)*
energy *(p. 136)*
element *(p. 136)*
atom *(p. 136)*
compound *(p. 136)*
molecule *(p. 136)*
mixture *(p. 136)*
kinetic energy *(p. 136)*
potential energy *(p. 136)*

Sustained Inquiry

Explorations of Living Things

7

Y ou may remember the first time you planted a seed and watched it develop into a plant with a stem and leaves and sometimes even a flower, depending on the type of seed it was. You may still be planting seeds in a home garden or window box. Plants and their growth and development remain a fascination for many home gardeners. All living things, including we humans, share the common thread of growth and development over time. This change over time is particularly exciting for students to explore.

In this chapter, we first look at young children as they experiment with seeds and small living organisms. Then we examine how the activities can change as students reach higher grades. Notice from the stories in this chapter how the complex relationships between living things and their environment are explored more and more deeply as students mature.

Especially in the stories of students in the third grade and higher, you will see an emphasis on **sustained inquiry,** that is, the development of an extended investigation over a period of time. You'll see students working in pairs or small groups, collaborating with their teachers and with each other to exchange ideas and discoveries. Watch for evidence of three of the encompassing themes from the National Science Education Standards that we discussed at the beginning of the book:

FOCUSING QUESTIONS

- What experiences, if any, have you had with planting seeds, indoors or outside?
- What do you think it means to be "alive"?
- What is the point of a class science exploration that takes days or weeks to complete?
- How does working with a partner or small group affect your learning experience?

1. We learn science through inquiry.

2. We learn science by collaboration.

3. We learn science over time.

We begin this chapter with some brief stories about experiences I have had discussing with young children the basic science question "What does it mean to be alive?" These stories will set the stage for the more extended experiments described later in the chapter.

 SCIENCE STORY

What Does It Mean to Be Alive?

The science idea of "living" versus "nonliving" has its own special magic for children, and they often wonder on their own what it is that makes something alive. There are many ways you can draw on this natural curiosity to spark a class discussion. In the following two stories, we'll see how some first and second graders approach the subject.

What Makes a Rabbit Real?

A classic story

One day, I bring a velveteen rabbit to a class of first graders, along with the famous children's classic *The Velveteen Rabbit* by Margery Williams. In this book, a stuffed rabbit comes to life in the eyes of a little boy who loves him so much that for him, the rabbit is real. When the stuffed rabbit is old, a fairy makes him a *real* rabbit—"real to everyone." Released in the woods, the velveteen rabbit is a stuffed toy no more; he is at home with the other rabbits.

I read the book to the class. They are absorbed and attentive—it really is a good story. Afterward, I hold up my own stuffed, velveteen rabbit with both hands. It has a button nose and no hind legs.

Approaching a profound question

"In what ways is this rabbit like a real rabbit?" I ask.

Many of the first graders respond. "It is soft and brown like a real rabbit." "It has two ears." "It has two eyes." "It has a white tail." "It is furry."

"In what ways is it *different* from a real rabbit?" I ask.

Again they have many good ideas: "It doesn't move." "It doesn't breathe." "It has no hind legs." "Its nose is a button." "It doesn't eat or drink water."

"What wonderful observations," I remark. "Let's think about what a real rabbit needs to stay alive."

My thinking: The question of what is alive is a profound one. I want to establish a major science idea here without "talking" it to the students, so I use same-and-different comparisons to help them make sense of the properties of the stuffed animal and of a real animal. Besides exploring the science idea, I hope to build their process skills as they observe, reflect, and compare.

The students respond that a real rabbit would have to eat and drink and breathe. So they seem to know that food, water, and air are necessary for a real rabbit to stay alive.

Pondering the characteristics of life

"So what about this real rabbit?" I wonder out loud. "We know what it takes in. Does it give anything off?"

The students ponder this.

"Let's think about breathing," I say. "When we breathe in, does the air stay in?"

"No," one student calls out. "We breathe out too."

"And the rabbit?"

The students all agree that the rabbit breathes out just as they do. Two of the girls, who have petted real rabbits, remember that they could feel the rabbits' breath on their hands.

Then we discuss whether rabbits give off anything else. I'm looking for them to realize that if the rabbit takes in water and food, it must also give off wastes. One of the girls with prior rabbit experience suggests that a real rabbit would "go to the bathroom."

"Sure," I say, accepting this euphemism. "Why do you think it would have to?"

A "gross" inference

The children aren't sure. Then one student says that if a rabbit kept eating and eating without going to the bathroom, it would explode. Though others immediately label this idea as "gross," it seems that an important idea may be taking shape in their minds: when something is alive, it takes in things from the environment and gives off things to the environment.

Are Plants Alive?

On another day, in a second-grade class, I have a similar discussion, but this time I've brought in a silk plant and a real plant. With plants, it is often more difficult than with animals for young children to grasp what makes them "alive." (On the other hand, it is easier to have a real plant available in class than a real rabbit.)

I ask, "In what ways is the silk plant like the real plant? In what ways are they different?"

The children are quick to observe that we do not have to water the silk plant, and it cannot grow. It always remains the same size and color. Some children remark that the silk plant "won't die." That comment brings us to the idea that things that are not living cannot die.

How do we know if a plant is alive?

Some children also say that the silk plant looks so real that it is hard to tell it is a fake. I ask, "What could you do to tell if it were living or nonliving?" The children respond that they could feel the leaves and then would know whether it was fake.

"How do real leaves feel?" I ask. Now the responses are limited. The children are not sure how real leaves feel, although one student says "waxy." In general, they just know this plant does not feel real.

They persist in their comparisons: "The plant is not real because we don't have to water it." One students offers, "It is not in real soil." Still another suggests that "nothing will happen to it in the dark"—getting back to the idea that it cannot die.

> *My thinking:* The idea that living things grow and change develops with maturity. Many times the students hear the word *grow* used in the context of nonliving things, as in the phrase "growing crystals." I am hoping to nurture the idea that for something alive to grow, it needs resources—stuff from the environment around it. Hence, I am pleased that these students seem to get the idea that this silk plant requires no care—no "stuff."

An alternative conception of life

Sometimes young children think that even a real plant is not alive. "It is not moving," they may say. "It doesn't eat!" is another common response. This alternative conception is an understandable one that develops as young children apply ideas about animal life to plants. In such cases, it is useful to remind the children that since the real plant needs materials from the environment—like water and sunlight—in order to grow bigger, the chances are that it is alive.

EXPANDING MEANINGS

■ The Teaching Ideas Behind These Stories

- A stuffed animal or artificial plant makes an excellent prop for discussing the nature of living things. However, it is also helpful to have a real counterpart available to provide students with opportunities for observation and comparison.

- Students come to school with many ideas about what is living and what is not living. Often, though, some of these ideas are alternative conceptions. By allowing students to express their ideas, you can discover these alternative conceptions and help the students to change them.

- In addition to using props like stuffed animals, you may want to ask students to name and discuss living and nonliving things in their own environment.

● The Science Ideas Behind These Stories

- Living things are distinguished from nonliving things by their interactions with the environment. That is, they take in materials from the nonliving environment, and they give off materials to the environment.

● Using the materials they take in from the environment, living things carry on life processes that give them the energy for growth and development. Without these interactions with the environment, living things could not grow and change over time. (Human life processes are explored in the chapter "Science Content and Curriculum.")

✔ The Science Standards Behind These Stories

STANDARDS These stories illustrate the guidelines of *Content Standard C (Life Science) for Grades K–4* in the National Science Education Standards. This standard indicates that all students should develop understanding of "the characteristics of organisms," "life cycles of organisms," and "organisms and environments" (National Research Council, 1996, p. 127). The accompanying "fundamental concepts and principles" include the following (p. 129):

✔ "Organisms have basic needs. For example, animals need air, water, and food; plants require air, water, nutrients, and light. Organisms can survive only in environments in which their needs can be met."

✔ "Plants and animals have life cycles that include being born, developing into adults, reproducing, and eventually dying."

Questions for Further Exploration

■ If no rabbit is available in your school, what other animal(s) might you use?

■ What are the wastes given off by green plants?

Resources for Further Exploration

ELECTRONIC RESOURCES

Living Things. http://sln.fi.edu/tfi/units/life/. This web page, sponsored by the Franklin Institute in Philadelphia, provides numerous links to information about plants and animals and simple investigations.

Plants (1997). Chicago: Clearvue. Designed for children in grades 1 through 6, this CD-ROM explores plants in their natural environments as well as the interactions between plants and animals. It is available from CCV Software, Charleston, WV; **http://www.ccvsoftware.com/.**

PRINT RESOURCES

Brainard, A., & Wrubel, D. (1993). *Literature-Based Science Activities: An Integrated Approach.* New York: Scholastic Professional Books. This book offers ideas for using children's literature in science activities.

Carle, E. (2001). *The Tiny Seed.* New York: Aladdin. A reprint of a classic children's literature book about plants and seeds. The following two titles are also excellent literature resources.

Gibbons, G. (1993). *From Seed to Plant.* New York: Holiday House.

Heller, R. (1999). *The Reason for a Flower.* New York: Penguin.

Richter, B., & Nelson, P. (eds.). (1994). *Every Teacher's Science Booklist: An Annotated Bibliography of Science Literature for Children*. New York: Scholastic Professional Books. This book contains excellent listings for literature connections as well as science book titles in all areas of science, including the science of living things.

Plants and Animals in Your Science Corner

Practical animals for the classroom

Often, as with the velveteen rabbit and the silk plant, we can bring in objects or animals from outside the classroom to use in activities concerning the properties of living things. But it is also important to have living plants and animals in your classroom on a daily basis—as many as you are comfortable having and as local regulations allow.

Some localities have restrictions on animal use based on concerns about allergies or infections, not to mention the difficulties posed by caring for classroom pets. Even so, there are usually several options. For instance, you can legally keep fish of many varieties. Students often marvel at these vertebrate creatures that live so comfortably below the surface of the water. You can also have various types of invertebrates in your classroom. As you will discover in a story about snails later in this chapter, invertebrates tend to be easier to care for than vertebrates and are subject to fewer restrictions.

During the elementary grades, children build understanding of biological concepts through direct experience with living things, their life cycles, and their habitats.
—NATIONAL SCIENCE EDUCATION STANDARDS

Having plants and animals in your science corner makes them part of the daily life of your classroom, so students will be observing and caring for them regularly. These examples of living things can also help connect science to your students' environment outside the school, especially if you encourage the students themselves to bring in plants that interest them. (It is probably not a good idea to encourage them to bring in animals!)

Finally, keeping living things in the science corner can build students' enthusiasm and provide opportunities for more extended activities, such as those described in the following stories.

 SCIENCE STORY

From Seed to Plant: A Failed Experiment

Over the past week, Mr. Bauer, a first-grade teacher in a city environment in the Midwest, has kept some popcorn kernels in the class's science corner, with a card asking students to identify them and think about where they come from. Now he collects a wider assortment of edible seeds—pumpkin seeds, sunflower seeds, and pea seeds—for his students to explore and plant. He distributes cups of the seed mixture, and the children work in pairs to explore these objects.

*Observing
properties of seeds*

"What are all the things you can say about these things?" Mr. Bauer begins. The children respond mostly with property words: "Some are green." "They are small." "They are hard." "You can eat them." "You can cook them." "Some are white. Some are yellow."

One student, Bethanne, says, "They're seeds. You can plant them, and they will make a new plant." The students agree that seeds can grow new plants, though some are not sure that popcorn and peas belong in this category.

Mr. Bauer asks, "Where do you find these things?"

*Mystery of the
supermarket*

Some of the children answer, "The supermarket." Mr. Bauer then probes, "Well, where does the supermarket get them?" The children aren't sure. Some say that corn seeds come from corn plants and that pumpkin seeds come from pumpkins, but they are unsure how the seeds got to the supermarket.

Mr. Bauer asks the students to draw pictures of their seeds. Some label the drawings with the names of the seeds.

Mr. Bauer's thinking: Mr. Bauer is interested in having the students explore the seeds before they select one to plant in a cup of soil. He wants to encourage the children to notice things about seeds and to reflect on where they come from.

Mr. Bauer explains, "We are going to plant our seeds. What will we need?" The children say that they will need a pot of soil, plus water. Some say that they will need to place the pot in the sun. Their prior knowledge definitely includes some basic understanding of plants.

Planting the seeds

Mr. Bauer now invites each student to take one seed apiece and plant it in a paper cup filled with soil. The children do so. With Mr. Bauer's guidance, they place their seeds about 2 centimeters below the surface, moisten the soil with water, and place the cups on the window ledge of the classroom. In the following days, they check the cups to see what is happening.

*Success!—with
one exception*

The experiment meets with great success. All the cups sprout a new plant—except for one cup that belongs to a student named James.

Mr. Bauer's thinking: Concerned no—he was worried—that not all the seeds would germinate, Mr. Bauer has planned ahead by planting several cups at home. Early one morning, he makes a quick substitution, replacing James's empty cup with a cup that has a little seedling in it. He wants James to experience the same success as the other students.

James's astonishment

That morning, James appears amazed to find that his seed has finally grown. Mr. Bauer is delighted at James's reaction, but also puzzled at James's absolute astonishment. Nevertheless, later that afternoon, Mr. Bauer remarks to James that seed growth is often seen as a great miracle and he can understand James's joy.

"It really *is* a miracle," replies James. "I ate the seed!"

SCIENCE STORY

What's Inside a Seed?

I am visiting Ms. Fraser's third-grade class in a suburban area in the Southeast. I have been working with Ms. Fraser and other teachers at the school as they implement a series of science lessons they have developed.

Ms. Fraser's third graders have been exploring plants that grow in their community. Their science corner is full of examples. Today they are going to examine the seed of one such plant, inside and out.

Overnight, Ms. Fraser has soaked some lima beans (called "butter beans" in this southern community). She has provided paper towels, foil pie pans, and magnifying lenses for students to use. She also has a batch of beans that she has not soaked overnight. She holds these up to the class, and all the students recognize them as butter beans.

Students observe and infer

"Why do you suppose these butter beans are hard on the outside?" she asks.

One boy answers, "To protect the baby plant inside."

"How do we know there is a baby plant inside?" Ms. Fraser asks.

"Well, it's a seed," the same boy replies. "Seeds have baby plants inside."

The challenge

Ms. Fraser challenges him, "Okay, but we are doing science, and we need proof. What shall we do to prove your idea?" At this point a girl says, "Some seeds don't have a baby plant inside. They're empty."

Students marvel when a small seed germinates and produces a new plant. They compare their plants' growth as they explore life cycles.

Richard Hutchings/PhotoEdit

My thinking: Good point, I think. This reminds me of Mr. Bauer's problem when he worried that some seeds would not sprout.

Ms. Fraser asks the students how they can find a baby plant inside the bean, and they understand that they need to open the bean up. Now she shows the class the soaked batch of butter beans, and they notice how different these look from the unsoaked beans. (When a lima bean is soaked in water, the seed coat, which is a thin protective outer layer, peels away. The lima bean then is softer and its two halves are more obvious.)

Ms. Fraser divides the class into pairs of students and invites each pair to take two or three soaked beans, some paper towels, a pie pan, and a magnifying lens. Ms. Fraser asks them to draw pictures of the insides of their beans. Also, she points out some books about seeds that she has gathered from both the class library and the school library and invites the students to use them to label their drawings.

Ms. Fraser's thinking: To encourage the children's own research, she does not tell them which parts of the seeds to label or where exactly in the books to find the names they need.

As each pair of students examines the inside of a lima bean, they notice a tiny leaflike structure: the baby plant itself. Their magnifying lenses help them see the details of this baby plant. They draw it and label it "embryo," as it is called in the reference books. The embryo is embedded in the two thick halves of the bean seed. They label these thick halves **cotyledons,** again following the books. The science books have large, clear drawings of the inside of a lima bean seed, such as the one in Figure 7.1. The students look for these drawings to find the labels.

Mixing hands-on work with book research

The baby plant revealed

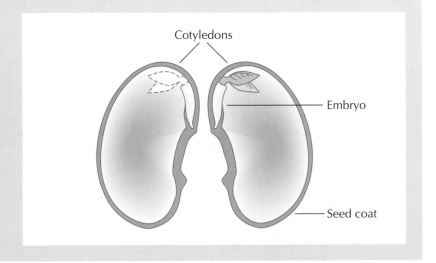

FIGURE 7.1
The parts of a seed, revealed by dissecting a soaked lima bean.

*Ms. Fraser's
questioning*

Ms. Fraser visits the students as they are working and asks questions. "What do you notice?" she asks. "Why do you suppose there are two halves to the seed?" One pair of students wants to know how the seed can produce a new plant. Ms. Fraser addresses this question to the class, explaining that they can have the opportunity to actually observe how the seed grows into a new plant right inside a plastic bag. The students are intrigued and excited.

The Following Days: Germination Bags

The next day, Ms. Fraser brings another batch of presoaked butter beans to class. She invites the students to join their partners and take a couple of presoaked beans, a small resealable plastic bag, and some paper toweling to their desks. The following instructions are written on a chart that is placed at the front of the classroom for all the students to see:

*Instructions for
germination bags*

Place a flat, moist paper towel in the bag, folded, like a lining for the bag. You may get some water from the sink in the classroom. Make sure the towel is not dripping wet. Place two presoaked butter beans inside the bag between the paper towel and one side of the bag. Put a staple on either side of the seed to hold it in place.

Ms. Fraser herself uses a large resealable plastic bag. In this one bag she places on the moist paper toweling a lima bean, a pumpkin seed, a

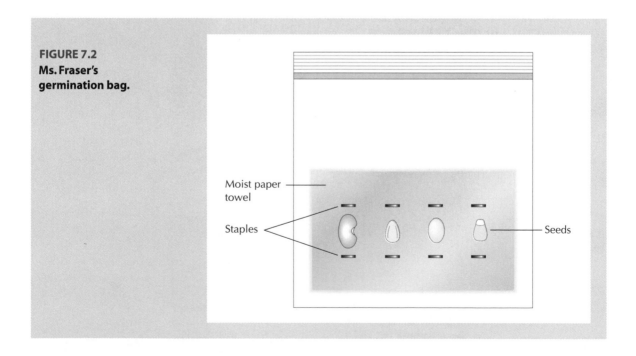

**FIGURE 7.2
Ms. Fraser's
germination bag.**

Moist paper towel

Staples

Seeds

bush bean, and a corn seed. She then staples the seeds in place so they will not shift in the bag (see Figure 7.2).

The teacher's modeling

Ms. Fraser's thinking: While the students are setting up their investigations with their lima beans, Ms. Fraser will model the germination of several seeds. Students will see that seed growth has certain common properties regardless of the type of seed.

Ms. Fraser asks the students to decide where they will hang their germination bags. **Germination,** she tells them, is what we call the process of seeds sprouting and beginning to grow. Do the students want their bags to hang in the well-lit classroom on the cork board — or in the dark, inside a closet? Should the plastic bag be laid down on a shelf? On the window sill? Somewhere else?

Choices for the students to make

My thinking: I notice that the only rule Ms. Fraser has given the students for the care of their bag and seed is that they should keep the paper towel moist. The other choices are for them to make, although she is helping them to see their options.

After placing name labels on their bags, the pairs of students engage in extended discussions about where to hang the bags. Some students insist that the seeds need light, while others believe the seeds will grow in the dark. One girl points out, "It is dark under the soil, and the seeds grow there." Some of the partners disagree with each other, but they work out compromises. In the end, some of the bags are hung with push pins on the cork board in the classroom, and others are placed behind closet doors where there is no light. Ms. Fraser suggests that all the students write down in their science journals exactly what they did and what they think will happen.

The students debate

Riddle: *I am very little. I can be different colors. I grow tall. I make plants. What am I?* Answer: *A seed.* —ANDREA P., THIRD GRADE

Ms. Fraser's thinking: Ms. Fraser wants the students to gather their observations about the seeds in the bags over the coming days and use them to reach some understanding about seed germination. She also wants the students to design their experiment any way they choose. She knows that the conditions that are needed for a seed to begin sprouting are often subject to alternative conceptions—the most common of these being that seeds need light to grow. Privately, she hangs her own germination bag in a dark closet, just in case no one else chooses to place a bag in the dark.

Sprouts growing in a bag

Each day the students observe evidence of germination. Like a miracle, the young sprouts appear, right inside the plastic bags. The roots grow downward, regardless of the position of the plastic bag. The young stem grows in the opposite direction from the roots. The students observe how thin and willowy the roots are in contrast to the thicker and stronger stem. The students come to learn that the paper towel should be kept moist, but the lighting conditions are unimportant.

The students continue to experiment with the amount of sunlight the baby plants need. In the following days, the plastic seed bags continue to hang all around the classroom. Each day the students monitor the seed growth. Each day the process of germination and growth is visible to them, no longer a well-kept mystery in the dark recesses of a pot of soil.

When the green leaves have emerged and the sprouting seeds can no longer be contained in the plastic bags, the students transfer each germinated seed to a cup of soil. They carefully place the roots in the soil and pack the baby plant in with their fingertips. They water their plants and observe the continuing growth.

Inferences about plants and sunlight

After about ten days, some differences are evident. Although the seeds germinated and the early seedlings grew regardless of the light conditions, the plants with leaves do well only in the light. In fact, the students begin to observe that their new green plants will *not* survive in a dark place. They do not understand why as yet.

On day eight of this seed-growth investigation, a student poses the question, "Why will the seedling grow in the dark, but the baby plant with sprouted leaves needs sunlight?" This becomes a research question for the class, and the students look up answers in their resource books and on the web about plants and seeds. They find out the following information:

The class's research findings

- The young plant, or seedling, gets its nutrition from the cotyledons and does not yet need sunlight.

- When the cotyledons are no longer needed, they emerge as seed leaves attached to the stem.

- When the plant begins to develop its first green leaf, it should be placed in a cup or small pot of soil to anchor the roots. At this time the green leaf should be exposed to the sun, because now the plant needs to make food. Green plants use sun, air, and water to make their own food.

> *My thinking: At this point, I believe the students still have a long way to go before they have a deep understanding of the science idea that green plants make their own food. What does it mean for a plant to make its own food? What does the food look like? Soon Ms. Fraser begins to address such questions.*

Introducing scientific terms

Ms. Fraser introduces the term **photosynthesis** to the group. This is the process, she explains, by which green plants use carbon dioxide from the air and water from the soil, in the presence of sunlight, to manufacture molecules of glucose. Glucose is a simple sugar that the cells of the plant use to make energy so the plant can carry on its functions, including growth. This chemical process, combining materials from the air and soil to produce new ones, takes place at a special site in the cells of the leaf called a *chloroplast*. The chloroplast contains the substance **chlorophyll,** which helps the process of photosynthesis to occur. Chlorophyll also gives the leaf its green color.

When the plants make their own food, Ms. Fraser continues, they give off extra water vapor and oxygen to their surroundings. This is something we can see, she tells the class. "How can we see it?" many of them want to know.

My thinking: Photosynthesis may be difficult for these students to understand, but by suggesting an observation the students themselves can make, Ms. Fraser helps to tie the idea to their own experience.

Making a complex process visible

Following her guidance, the students place a small green plant (somewhat larger and more robust than their brand-new plants) in a large glass

Taxonomy

By exploring seed plants, which scientists call **angiosperms**, Ms. Fraser's students are learning about one major category of plants. Angiosperms produce flowers that form fruits that have seeds. Garden and wild flowers, weeds, grasses, grains, plants that produce vegetables, and shrubs and trees that lose their leaves in autumn are all seed plants.

But why, you may wonder, do we bother to label plants with names like *angiosperm*? The answer is that classification schemes for living things help us understand and study the life on our planet. These schemes, which are human inventions, allow us to sort, group, and rank the types of life that share the earth with us (Margulis & Schwartz, 1982).

An entire classification system is called a **taxonomy.** The noted biologist and science writer Stephen Jay Gould (1981) remarked that "taxonomies are reflections of human thought; they express our most fundamental concepts about the objects of our universe. Each taxonomy is a theory about the creature that it classifies."

In other words, by creating a taxonomy in which pumpkins and lima beans fall into the same category called angiosperms, we are expressing ideas about those plants' relationships to one another and to other plants as well. Typically, the relationships expressed by today's taxonomies are based on ideas about evolution—how and when particular living things developed their current form.

No taxonomy is absolute. Consider the most basic grouping, the kingdom. In science, a **kingdom** is the largest, most inclusive level of classification of living things. When I was growing up, the living things we learned about were all placed into two kingdoms: the Animal Kingdom and the Plant Kingdom. Now, however, scientists classify living things into *five* kingdoms. The number changed because scientists have found out much more about what is alive than they knew a few decades ago.

The five kingdoms recognized today are:

Monera (monerans). Single-celled organisms including all types of bacteria.

Protista (protists). Single-celled organisms including algae, amoebas, paramecia, and others.

Fungi. Multicelled organisms such as slime molds, yeasts, and mushrooms.

Plantae (plants). Multicelled organisms that make all their own food through photosynthesis. Includes mosses, horsetails, ferns, trees, and all seed-bearing plants.

Animalia (animals). Multicelled organisms including plant eaters, meat eaters, and parasites. Animals range from sponges, jellyfish, and snails to fish, amphibians, reptiles, birds, and mammals.

jar. They cover the jar with its lid. After a day or two, they see water vapor droplets appear on the inside of the jar.

My thinking: I'm pleased that Ms. Fraser is introducing a very complex process at this early grade level. The students will now have some prior experience with this idea that they can build on as they mature.

EXPANDING MEANINGS

■ The Teaching Ideas Behind These Stories

- In the story of Mr. Bauer's class, we see how simple experiments with seeds can engage students in the mystery of growth and development.

- We also see that edible seeds can represent a challenge for young children. The fact that many foods come from the ground and start as part of a plant is not taken-for-granted knowledge.

- The activity through which Mr. Bauer guides his students has many fine points. It also shows us, however, that even with the best intentions, it is not a good idea to fool students. Instead of trying to sneak in a replacement for a seed that didn't grow, it would have been better for Mr. Bauer to avoid setting up an experience in which students might personalize the experiment's success or failure as their own. Mr. Bauer would have been better advised to use larger cups with two or three seeds. He was lucky that all the other students' seeds germinated.

- Science is about experimenting. Sometimes it works, and sometimes it does not work. There is often much to learn from failed experiments. They provide opportunities to change direction and explore other possibilities. For instance, if some seeds fail to grow, you can ask, "Why do some seeds germinate, while others do not?"

- Notice how, in her class, Ms. Fraser gives her students multiple opportunities for observation. For example, she demonstrates the importance of soaking the beans by asking the students to observe what has happened to the beans she soaked overnight. Hanging the germination bags in the classroom also allows the students many chances to make direct observations. By middle school, when these students begin to study plant cells under a microscope, their observational skills will be well developed, and they will have a good deal of prior knowledge about plants.

- Notice, too, how Ms. Fraser's third graders go beyond examining the seeds and move toward collaborating in the planning of their own investigations. She has structured the activity so they can discuss with their partners, and with other students in the class, the best way to germinate a seed. Each pair of students can make its own plans, carry them out, and determine the results.

- As her students develop questions that cannot be answered through direct observation and experimentation at this stage, notice how Ms. Fraser directs them to resources—in this case, books in the classroom or the Internet. Some schools use science textbooks, which can also serve as resources.

- The entire activity in Ms. Fraser's class, with its multiple spin-offs, takes place over two weeks or more—a significant allotment of time. Later in this chapter, we will see more examples of how science learning requires sustained inquiry over time.

- Even if a science idea is very complex, a demonstration or activity that presents part of it can be useful. By showing her students that a small green plant can release water vapor inside a closed glass jar, Ms. Fraser is leading them toward the beginnings of understanding, and she is helping to make an abstract concept more concrete.

● The Science Ideas Behind These Stories

- Seeds contain the baby plant or embryo and the food that the embryo needs to begin germinating. This food is contained within the part of the seed called a cotyledon.

- Some seeds do not develop properly, and some do not even have an embryo. Thus, it is always a good idea to plant more than one seed.

- Seeds do not need sunlight when they begin to grow. At first, they live off the stored food in their cotyledons. Once the new plant grows leaves, it needs sunlight to make its own food.

- When seeds sprout, the cotyledons become the first leaves of the baby plant, and they fall off as soon as the plant grows its first adult leaves. Some plants produce seeds with one cotyledon; these plants are called **monocots.** Plants that produce seeds with two cotyledons are called **dicots.** Grasses and grains are monocots. Flowers, flowering trees, beans, and vegetable-producing plants are usually dicots. For many seeds, soaking will begin the germination process.

- The soil must be firm and porous to support the roots of a **seed plant**. The soil supplies green plants with an anchor for their roots and space in which to grow.

- Dissolved minerals in the soil make their way to a plant through the water intake of its root system.

- Although the minerals from the soil are important, green plants do not get *food* from the soil. They make their own food through the complex process of photosynthesis. This is a chemical process in which the leaf, aided by its chlorophyll, uses water from the soil and a gas in the air called carbon dioxide to make a simple sugar called glucose and to release another gas, oxygen. The carbon dioxide enters the leaf through openings on its underside called *stomata*. The oxygen gets released into the air through these same stomata.

✔ The Science Standards Behind These Stories

STANDARDS ✔ Like the earlier science stories in this chapter, our seed stories relate to *Content Standard C for Grades K–4* in the National Science Education Standards, and particularly to the following underlying concepts and principles (National Research Council, 1996, p. 129):

✔ "Each plant or animal has different structures that serve different functions in growth, survival, and reproduction."

✔ "The behavior of individual organisms is influenced by internal cues (such as hunger) and by external cues (such as a change in the environment)." Notice how Ms. Fraser encouraged her students to think about the external cues that the seeds would need to germinate.

✔ "Plants and animals have life cycles that include being born, developing into adults, reproducing, and eventually dying." As the students continue to watch their growing bean plants, the mature plants may eventually produce new beans. This will allow the students to see a full life cycle in their classroom.

Questions for Further Exploration

■ Try planting citrus seeds such as grapefruit or orange seeds. How well do you think they will grow in your own home? Do they surprise you?

■ Buy wheat berries (typically found in health-food stores). Fill a shallow pie pan with soil. Sprinkle the wheat berries on the soil and water well. See what happens.

■ What do we mean by saying that green plants make their own food? How is this different from what animals do?

■ Since green plants make their own food, what is the plant "food" sold in stores?

Resources for Further Exploration

ELECTRONIC RESOURCES

Photosynthesis. (1997). Chatsworth, CA: AIMS Multimedia. This CD-ROM examines various aspects of photosynthesis in everyday life. It is available from CCV Software, Charleston, WV; **http://www.ccvsoftware.com/.**

Science Teacher Stuff: Photosynthesis. http://www.scienceteacherstuff.com/ photosynthesis.html. This site provides links to a large number of lessons as well as informational pages about photosynthesis.

PRINT RESOURCES

Kraus, R. (1945). *The Carrot Seed.* New York: Harper. This is a classic children's story, fine for grades K–2, about a tiny carrot seed and the plant it grows into.

Margulis, L., Schwartz, K. V., Dolan, M., & Delisle, K. (1999). *Diversity of Life: The Illustrated Guide to the Five Kingdoms.* 2d ed. Sudbury, MA: Jones & Bartlett. A detailed discussion of each of the five kingdoms of living things; a fine resource for teachers.

National Sciences Resources Center. (1991). *Plant Growth and Development.* Designed for grade 3, these experiments are useful for students learning how to plan and carry out controlled investigations. Available from Carolina Biological Supply Co., Burlington, NC; **http://www. carolina.com/.**

Olson, S., & Loucks-Horsley, S. (eds.) (2000). *Inquiry and the National Science Education Standards: A Guide for Teaching and Learning.* Washington, DC: National Academies Press. Developed by a committee of the National Research Council as a supplement to the National Science Education Standards, this book aims to provide a practical guide for inquiry-based teaching. It is available online at **http://www.nap.edu/.**

 SCIENCE STORY

Planting in a Vacant Lot

In one inner-city community, many of the students walk past an empty lot strewn with garbage on their way to school. Ms. Monteiro, a fifth-grade teacher, notices this, and she thinks about the possibility of planting seeds and nurturing plant growth as both a class activity and a means of community involvement. Recently she has read the book *Seedfolks* by Paul Fleischman, a delightful story of a community of diverse immigrants in Cleveland who contributed their time and energy to convert a vacant lot into a garden.

Inspired by this book, Ms. Monteiro and her class write letters to the local newspaper and to city officials in order to get the trash removed. It takes several months, but eventually the trash is indeed carted away. Now the students visit the lot and claim it for their own.

A transformation　　With the permission of the city, this fifth-grade class turns the vacant lot into a garden. Topsoil is donated by a garden supply store in a neighboring suburb, and the students get to work making the ground ready. They have already noticed how dandelions and crabgrasses grew in this lot despite the trash, so they have high hopes for their own plants. The students do a lot of work preparing the soil and researching the conditions under which their seeds will germinate.

Making their own decisions

The students have many decisions to make. Some want to plant vegetables; some want to plant flowers. Whenever possible, Ms. Monteiro allows them to make their own choices and select their own seeds. The final choices include lima beans, sunflowers, pumpkins, lentils, marigolds, and snapdragons. By early spring, the students begin sprouting the seeds in containers in the classroom. When the seeds have germinated and have well-formed roots, the students plant them in the ground.

Meanwhile, in their classroom, the students have examined the seeds and the leaves of their sprouting plants. They have studied germination and the role of the soil, water, and sun. They learn that outdoor plants have their own particular growing seasons but that they can simulate some outdoor conditions in the classroom.

Learning the effects of climate

Some students who have immigrated from the tropical climates of islands in the Caribbean are disappointed to learn that the harsh winters of their new home will not allow some of their favorite foods to grow. One boy originally wanted an avocado tree in the garden. Instead, he plants an avocado seed in a carefully controlled environment in the classroom (see Figure 7.3).

As the season progresses, the students make regular visits to their outdoor garden. In their eyes, nothing has ever been more beautiful than this formerly vacant lot. A sign identifying the class and the teacher stands proudly on the site.

The end of the school year—but not the project

The project is limited by the brevity of spring in this midwestern city. But before the end of the school year, arrangements are made for the garden to be cared for during the summer by students and community volunteers. In the autumn, when the students return, they plant crocus and tulip bulbs donated by local businesses.

SCIENCE STORY

When Is a Vegetable a Fruit?

Ms. Byrne's third-grade class is learning about parts of plants that we can eat. One day she brings in a number of such edible plant parts: apples, oranges, celery, pea pods, lettuce, spinach, tomatoes, red and green peppers, mango, papaya, collard greens, broccoli, carrots, avocado, persimmon, and fennel. (Ms. Byrne knows that her students come from several different cultures and that several students have arrived from Central America, so she makes sure to bring foods familiar to these students.)

Foods never seen before

After having the students divide into groups, Ms. Byrne invites them to use plastic knives to examine the specimens. "We don't know the names of all these fruits and vegetables," declares one student. "Yeah, I've never seen this before," another chimes in. Ms. Byrne explains that knowing the

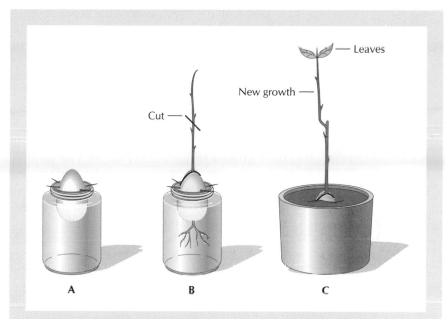

FIGURE 7.3
Steps in planting an avocado pit.

(1) After washing the avocado pit and peeling off the skin, place toothpicks in the seed and suspend it in a jar of water, pointed side up. Making sure the bottom of the seed is covered with water, place the jar in a dark place. (2) Wait until roots begin to grow and the stem is about 15 centimeters high. To thicken the roots, cut the stem about halfway up and return the plant to the dark for another few weeks. (3) Finally, when the stem has again grown to about 15 centimeters, place the seedling in a deep pot of soil so the roots are completely covered and the top 2 centimeters of the seed show above the soil. Water the plant well.

names wouldn't necessarily mean very much. "If all I knew about you," she says to one student, "was your name, then I wouldn't know very much, would I?"

To guide the students, she offers a suggestion: "We can begin by exploring which of our plant parts have seeds and which do not." The students begin to squeal with delight as they dissect their foods. John shouts, "This one is my favorite," as he holds up an avocado. "What's that?" inquires a classmate.

The students begin to share information about their favorite foods while creating two groups of plants: those with seeds and those without seeds. John holds up the pit of the avocado and explains how to plant it in a pot of soil in order to grow a new plant. Ms. Byrne makes a note to do this in class the next day.

The students then observe the seeds in one pile of foods and the absence of seeds in another pile. Holding up an apple and an orange, Ms. Byrne asks the students what we call these parts of the plant.

"They are fruits," declares Jessica, and everyone agrees.

"Yes, scientists refer to the parts of a plant that hold seeds as the fruit of a plant."

Puzzle: If a tomato is a fruit . . .

The students are stunned to notice, however, that the tomatoes, red and green peppers, pea pods, avocado, and persimmon are all in the pile with the fruits. "If a tomato is a fruit," asks Ruby, "then what are vegetables?"

Ms. Byrne responds, "What do you think?" She holds up the carrot and asks the students to think about what part of the plant it is. Someone knows it is a root. Others realize that celery is a stem; that broccoli florets are flowers; and that collard greens, lettuce, and spinach are all leaves of the plant.

Sharing information from different cultures

The students then take turns talking about the fruits or vegetables that they eat at home. Some take pleasure in describing the joys of eating mango or papaya or persimmon. Others explain how fennel or collard greens are prepared in their homes. This leads to a discussion of where the plant is grown, how it is eaten, and what significance, if any, the fruit or vegetable has in particular cultures.

EXPANDING MEANINGS

■ The Teaching Ideas Behind These Stories

- ■ In the vacant lot story, we see how nature can present itself in the most unlikely places. Plants break through wherever they can. These unlikely places can become precious resources to the urban teacher with a keen eye.

- ■ The vacant lot story also demonstrates one way to involve the students in the surrounding community and vice versa.

- ■ In the fruits and vegetables story, Ms. Byrne can create meaningful science experiences for her students because she knows who they are, what they eat, and where they come from. The experiences she provides help the students develop their personal knowledge of science.

- ■ The story of Ms. Byrne's class also reminds us of the gifts of diverse student populations and how excited students get when the class curriculum reflects their lived experiences.

- ■ In both stories, the students' ability to construct meaning is strengthened by their interactions as they collaborate with one another. They share knowledge, opinions, and observations.

■ In the vacant lot story, the activity takes place over a long period of time—most of the school year and on through the summer into the next school year. This sustained project allows students to develop a deeper, more personal knowledge of the science ideas behind plants.

● The Science Ideas Behind These Stories

- Fruits and vegetables are edible parts of plants.

- In everyday language, fruits are usually those plant parts that taste sweet, particularly those we get from trees, such as apples, pears, peaches, oranges, and bananas.

- In scientific classification, however, sweetness is not the important factor. A **vegetable** is a root, stem, leaf, or flower of a plant. The **fruit** is the part of the plant that is a container for the seeds. To be even more specific, a fruit is the ripened ovary of a flowering plant.

- Nuts, corn, wheat, tomatoes, peas, beans, cucumbers, pumpkins, and squash are really fruits.

✔ The Science Standards Behind These Stories

Again our stories relate to *Content Standard C for Grades K–4* in the National Science Education Standards, especially to the following fundamental concepts (National Research Council, 1996, p. 129):

✔ "Organisms can survive only in environments in which their needs can be met. The world has many different environments, and distinct environments support the life of different types of organisms." Ms. Monteiro's students learn, for example, that the cold winters of their local environment will not accommodate some plants from the Caribbean.

✔ "Each plant or animal has different structures that serve different functions in growth, survival, and reproduction." Ms. Byrne's third graders learn about several plant structures—fruits, seeds, roots, stems, leaves, flowers—and begin to understand their various functions in the life of the plant.

Questions for Further Exploration

■ What fruits and vegetables do you encounter in your daily life?

■ Are there any edible plant parts that you have difficulty labeling as fruit or vegetable? How can you find out the correct classification?

■ In a later chapter, we will learn about some students who use fruits and vegetables to make an edible model. What do you think it will be a model of?

Resources for Further Exploration

ELECTRONIC RESOURCES

Fast Plants. http://www.fastplants.org/intro.html.   This site offers a wealth of information about Wisconsin Fast Plants, a rapid-growing species useful for classroom investigations. Check the lesson plans and other teacher resources listed on this site.

Ontario Agri-Food Education. http://www.oafe.org/.   For various food-related classroom activities, click on "Resources" and follow the links.

PRINT RESOURCES

Fleischman, P. (1997). *Seedfolks*. New York: HarperCollins. This book describes a project to create a community garden.

National Sciences Resources Center. (1992). *Experiments with Plants*. Similar to the volume *Plant Growth and Development* cited earlier, but the experiments here are designed for grades 5 and 6. Available from Carolina Biological Supply Co., Burlington, NC;   http://www.carolina.com/.

A Classroom Invertebrate

Earlier in this chapter, we noticed young students experimenting with seeds. First graders planted them in cups, while third graders explored germination and some of the properties of green plants. Animal life is usually less accessible for classroom projects, and keeping an animal in the classroom often requires some kind of clearance from the school or the district.

Invertebrates vs. vertebrates

An exception to these constraints on using live animals with students is a small and lovely invertebrate animal called a land snail. **Invertebrate** animals have no internal backbone, and their skeleton is usually located on the exterior of the body rather than the interior. Insects, jellyfish, worms, crayfish, and crabs are all invertebrates. **Vertebrate** animals, in contrast, are those with internal backbones, including all fish, amphibians, birds, reptiles, and mammals.

The fascinating, commonplace snail

The land snail has many interesting features to observe. Between spring and fall, in many temperate climates throughout the United States, large numbers of land snails can be seen in gardens and wooded areas. They are quite common. They have beautiful, patterned shells, and they secrete a silver trail as they move slowly in moist, shady environments. Land snails may be ordered from biological supply companies (see *More Resources for Teachers* at the end of this book). They reproduce easily because they are hermaphroditic; this means they have both male and female reproductive structures.

Making a home for your snail

Land snails are easily kept in the classroom. Here are some guidelines for preparing a home for these snails:

1. Get a glass or plastic tank or terrarium. Alternatively, you can use a gallon jar or plastic container with a lid into which you have poked air holes.

2. Cover the bottom of the tank or container with 2 centimeters of gravel.

3. Add soil to a depth of approximately 5 centimeters. Keep the soil moist.

4. Add a rock, some moss, and some bark-covered twigs.

At varying stages of development and learning, students will delight in exploring these tiny creatures. For younger students, land snails may be fascinating objects to keep in the science corner for making observations. By fourth grade, students should be ready for the responsibility of handling these living organisms for more detailed study. At that stage, I like to have students work in pairs with its own snail to share their observations and inferences. First, though, it is important that you explore the snails yourself, with a colleague if possible, and record as many of your own observations as you can about these creatures.

Snail explorations

To prepare the students to observe the behavior of their snails, distribute magnifying lenses and paper toweling beforehand. Once they begin to explore, you will probably hear exclamations of delight fill the room. The land snails are adorable creatures. They are soft-bodied organisms that, when recoiled in their shells, can range from 3 to 5 centimeters in length. When fully extended outside their shells, they can reach a length of 10 centimeters. The snails have four frontal antennae. Upon examination, you will discover that they have eyes at the ends of two of these antennae. The students get quite excited when they discover the snails' eyes.

You may want to ask your students, "How can we compare the size of our land snails with our own size?" By fourth grade, many students can compare the sizes of two objects by using ratios. As your students explore, they will also come up with many fascinating questions of their own, as the following story demonstrates.

 SCIENCE STORY

A Book of Snails

Ms. Sigursky's fourth-grade class has twenty-four students and fourteen land snails. Ever since the snails arrived and the students helped set up the terrarium, they have been eager to take the snails out.

Before they begin to handle the animals, however, Ms. Sigursky points out that working with live specimens is a big responsibility. She invites the students to brainstorm about how they will interact with the creatures. They come up with a number of rules to write on a piece of poster board, including the following:

Rules that the class brainstorms

- Do not squeeze the snails too hard.

- Handle the snails gently.

- Do not hold them up too high.

- Keep the snails well fed.

- Keep the soil in their cage wet.

- Keep the tank clean.

- Do not disturb the snails unnecessarily.

"Those are good rules," Ms. Sigursky tells them. "I think we're ready to begin our explorations." She asks the students to pair up with their science partners, explaining that each team will get one snail to work with.

"That leaves two extra snails," Maria calculates.

"Those are for me," Ms. Sigursky replies. "I forgot to bring lunch."

"Ewww!" several class members cry. Ms. Sigursky's bad jokes have *One more rule* become a staple of classroom humor. Nevertheless, Maria adds one more item to the list on the poster board: "Do not let Ms. S. eat snails."

That day and the next, the students make their initial observations, writing notes in their science journals. Noticing the way the snails seem to move toward some things and away from others, they decide, with Ms. *What attracts a snail?* Sigursky's guidance, to conduct an investigation. The students carefully place their land snails on a flat surface, shine a flashlight in their direction, and watch the result. Then they place a piece of lettuce in the snails' path and observe the creatures' behavior. They do the same with drops of water. The students record these procedures and their observations, learning firsthand about the preferences of the land snails for the stimuli of light, food, and water.

In the next few days, these fourth graders generate many other snail questions. These are a small sample:

The students' questions

How do you tell the sex of a snail?

What is the shell made out of?

How do they grow?

How long do they live?

How do they reproduce?

How do they breathe? Digest food?

How are land snails different from water snails?

What happens if their shells break?

Do they lay eggs, or do they have live baby snails?

How do they hang upside down?

Observations of Snails

The left column below lists some observations of land snails that teachers made during an in-service workshop as they worked in pairs. The right column lists some observations made by fourth graders. How many similarities do you see? What are the key differences? On the basis of these comments, how do you think the teachers could mediate the learning experience for the fourth graders?

Teachers	Fourth Graders
"I love to watch the land snails. They really enjoy lettuce. When I place the lettuce near the snail, it stretches its antennae out. It eats very quickly. Their antennae look like little walking sticks."	"They're slimy."
	"They leave a trail when they move."
"All of the snails' movements seem so well planned. They have extremely flexible bodies. I saw one of the snails bend his head to reach up to the top of the container. It has such strong suction. It pulled itself onto the bottom of the roof of the container and stayed there—upside down."	"The green stuff is what they give off when they go to the bathroom."
	"They like to hang upside down."
	"They climb on each other."
"The snails like to be upside down."	"They're cute!"
"When they move, they seem to secrete a clear fluid that they leave behind them. This must help them slide along the surfaces they move on."	"They like the light."
	"They love lettuce."
"They follow hand movements."	
"The snails sleep a lot. They move slowly and they don't make noise."	
"When you touch the snails, they seem to shrink away."	
"They are really graceful."	
"They have different patterns on their shells."	
"They are slimy."	
"They excrete a green, slimy substance."	
"I love to watch their bodies moving as they glide across their container. It almost looks as if there are waves inside of them."	

Ms. Sigursky divides the students' questions into two groups: (1) questions they can answer through their own investigation and exploration, and (2) questions they can look up. (Which questions of those listed would you select for each category?)

The students remark that it will take a long time for them to answer some of their questions, and they wonder how long the class will have for snail observations. Ms. Sigursky responds that they can have as much time as they need.

A month-long investigation

The students turn to many resources to supplement their own observations: the Internet, resource books, CD-ROMs, and friends who have snails as house pets. By the end of a month, the class begins to produce its own book about snails, full of careful drawings, observations, and information drawn from their own research.

After some debate about the best title for their book, the students decide to call it, *Snails Are Too Cool to Eat*.

What is alive? When students explore the properties of the garden land snail, they begin to gain an understanding of what it means for living things to exchange material with their environment.

Frank Collins/Annette K. Goodman

EXPANDING MEANINGS

■ The Teaching Ideas Behind This Story

- ■ Inviting students to examine living things in detail provides them with a fuller understanding of the question, "What is alive?"

- ■ This sort of exploration can take many forms in the classroom. A wise teacher, like Ms. Sigursky in this story, creates an environment in which students' own ideas flourish.

STANDARDS

- ■ Exploring the snails in pairs encourages the students to collaborate and share ideas. This points again to one of the key themes from the National Science Education Standards: We learn science by collaboration. This is true because science is, among other things, a social process.

- ■ The theme that science takes time emerges here as well, as it did in both Ms. Fraser's and Ms. Monteiro's classes. Ms. Sigursky is generous in her promise of time for snail studies because she is confident that she can help the students make good use of the time they spend.

● The Science Ideas Behind This Story

- ● When you order land snails from biological supply companies, you are given complete instructions for their care and maintenance. Still, it is important to have the students themselves brainstorm about key aspects of snail care, as Ms. Sigursky's class did.

- ● In addition to lettuce, land snails like oatmeal flakes with a little milk and a raw carrot or potato. Moistened bran flakes or bread may also be offered. It is important to sprinkle the oatmeal flakes with calcium carbonate once a week so the snails get the calcium they need.

- ● Like many other invertebrates, snails are soft-bodied animals that have their hard parts on the outside as protection.

- ● Other examples of animals that have hard protective exteriors are crustaceans (such as lobsters, shrimp, and crabs) and arachnids (such as spiders and scorpions). The most numerous of such animals, however—in fact, the most numerous of all invertebrates—are insects. They have penetrated all environments on Earth. Insects, arachnids, and crustaceans are all called **arthropods.**

- ● Snails belong to a group of invertebrate animals called **univalve mollusks.** Other univalve mollusks are the slug, conch, and abalone. The land snails and slugs are the only univalve mollusks that live on land.

- ● The term *univalve* refers to the fact that snails have only one shell. Other mollusks, like clams, scallops, oysters, and mussels, have two shells and therefore belong to the group of invertebrates known as **bivalve mollusks.**

✔ The Science Standards Behind These Stories

STANDARDS ☑ The principles of collaboration and sustained inquiry, inherent throughout the National Science Education Standards, are developed particularly in *Teaching Standards B, D, and E,* which point out that science teachers should "orchestrate discourse among students," "nurture collaboration," and "structure the time available so that students are able to engage in extended investigations" (National Research Council, 1996, pp. 32, 43, 46). You can see all of these ideas at work in Ms. Sigursky's classroom.

In terms of science content, *Content Standard C for Grades K–4* is once more relevant, especially in its emphasis on learning about organisms' characteristics and environments. In examining the snails' reactions to the stimuli of light, food, and water, Ms. Sigursky's students are developing the following fundamental concepts underlying this standard (p. 129):

✔ "The behavior of individual organisms is influenced by internal cues (such as hunger) and by external cues (such as a change in the environment). Humans and other organisms have senses that help them detect internal and external cues."

✔ "An organism's patterns of behavior are related to the nature of that organism's environment, including the kinds and numbers of other organisms present, the availability of food and resources, and the physical characteristics of the environment."

Questions for Further Exploration

■ Could you find a land snail in your environment?

■ What other small invertebrates could you find where you live?

■ What other interesting snail studies can you think of?

Resources for Further Exploration

ELECTRONIC RESOURCES

Goodman, A. K. The Giant African Land Snail Site. http://www.geocities.com/Heartland/Valley/6210/. Offers photos and information about land snails, including interesting links, from a collector of giant African land snails.

Liu, K. Eye to Eye with Garden Snails. http://accessexcellence.org/AE/AEC/AEF/1994/liu_snails.html. A series of school snail lessons that includes many good ideas and lots of background information.

PRINT RESOURCES

Barrett, K. (1986). *Animals in Action.* Berkeley, CA: Lawrence Hall of Science. GEMS (Great Expectations in Mathematics and Science) inspired these activities designed for students in grade 6. They engage students in designing and evaluating their own animal behavior experiments, including experiments with land snails. Also in the GEMS series is *Mapping Animal Movements* (1987) by the same author.

Buholzer, T. (1987). *Life of the Snail.* Minneapolis: Carolrhoda Books. This is a wonderful resource book for any young person interested in collecting information about land snails. The photographs are wonderful too.

Hickman, P. (1993). *Wetlands.* Toronto, ON. Kids Can Press. A publication of the Federation of Ontario Naturalists, these reading selections and projects include the study of snails as wetland wildlife. Designed for grades 3–6, the book also explores environmental considerations for wetlands

Lionni, L. (1968). *The Biggest House in the World.* New York: Pantheon Books. A snail's father advises him to keep his house small and tells him what happened to a snail that grew a large and spectacular shell.

Ryder, J. (1982). *The Snail's Spell.* New York: F. Warne. The reader imagines how it feels to be a snail. A super story for all elementary grades.

Working Together to Conduct Investigations Over Time

In this chapter, we have visited several classrooms and noticed different types of explorations with seeds, plants, and small animals. One way in which these stories converge is that they all honor the students' ideas, a theme stressed throughout this book. In particular, the students in this chapter's stories were encouraged to research their own questions, even when that meant looking beyond the classroom to the Internet, in textbooks, in trade books, or down the block in a vacant lot. This is the basis of any true inquiry in science, and it is the way students can develop their own inquiry skills.

Encouraging students to pursue their questions

You also noticed, no doubt, that many of the experiences described in this chapter were time intensive; that is, the students were given plenty of time to explore their germinating seeds, their snails, and their fruits and vegetables. Plants and animals change over time, and in order to develop students' understanding of these living things, we need to encourage them to sustain their investigations over extended periods of time. In fact, you may often want to encourage your students to repeat experiments. This type of repetition is common to scientific research. Sometimes the students' second experience with the investigation helps them notice things they may have missed the first time around.

Sustaining investigations

Following through on science explorations over time is especially important for students in today's culture of "quick and easy." How, you may ask, can you maintain the students' interest in a single investigation that takes days, weeks, or longer? I believe you will find that when you ask your students to brainstorm answers to their questions about their own investigations, they become very interested in pursuing the answers. And as the stories in this chapter have illustrated, new questions often arise as

How do you keep students interested?

At all stages of inquiry, teachers guide, focus, challenge, and encourage student learning.
—NATIONAL SCIENCE EDUCATION STANDARDS

their investigation continues. Sometimes, in fact, students want to research more questions than there will ever be time for in your class.

Part of your role is to guide your students in their understanding of what can be explored through direct experimentation and what may require research from outside sources. You also take the responsibility to point things out and ask them to tell you what they have done so far. You guide and monitor and make suggestions. At the beginning of the school year, your students may need a good deal of structure, depending on how much experience they have had in working on their own. As the school year progresses and they get more practice in self-directed activities, they will become more able researchers.

Students—and their teachers—as collaborators

The stories in this chapter have also stressed the collaborative nature of investigations. The students worked in pairs or groups, sharing their ideas. The teachers, too, essentially collaborated in the experiments, providing the topics and the materials but then allowing the students to gain control over their own learning.

Collaboration works best when the exploration is arranged so that each group of students can participate in the efforts and work of *all* their classmates. Often a "reporting out" time becomes the best part of student collaboration. As we will see in Part Three, it is also a wonderful way to assess what students have learned. Remember that as you and your students engage in these collaborative explorations, you should keep asking yourself: "What are the science concepts behind this experience? What am I hoping the students will learn?"

As students mature, they are able to plan their own investigations in more detail and manipulate experimental conditions to gather new information. In the next chapter, we will see some fifth- and seventh-grade students exploring concepts related to density.

KEY TERMS

sustained inquiry *(p. 141)*
cotyledon *(p. 149)*
germination *(p. 151)*
photosynthesis *(p. 152)*
chlorophyll *(p. 152)*
angiosperm *(p. 153)*
taxonomy *(p. 153)*
kingdom *(p. 153)*
Monera *(p. 153)*
Protista *(p. 153)*
Fungi *(p. 153)*
Plantae *(p. 153)*
Animalia *(p. 153)*
monocot *(p. 155)*

dicot *(p. 155)*
seed plant *(p. 155)*
vegetable *(p. 161)*
fruit *(p. 161)*
invertebrate *(p. 162)*
vertebrate *(p. 162)*
arthropod *(p. 167)*
univalve mollusk *(p. 167)*
bivalve mollusk *(p. 167)*

8 Spiraling Curriculum
Explorations of Density

FOCUSING QUESTIONS

▪ Which weighs more: a can of Coke or a can of Diet Coke?

▪ Where do you float better: on a lake or on an ocean?

▪ Why are science teachers often on the lookout for unexpected discoveries?

▪ Why do science ideas from early grades keep popping up again in higher grades?

As students mature, their open-ended science investigations proceed in directions that we cannot always determine in advance. Sometimes the investigations lead to an unexpected exploration—and new science ideas.

As the teacher, you will always have specific learning goals in mind for your students. You will also consider the possible directions in which your students may take an exploration. Often, however, the students will surprise you, and the way you deal with the unexpected will have important implications for your students' learning.

In this chapter, we explore a story in which fifth-grade students examine the properties of liquids and pursue their own questions to higher levels of thinking and problem solving. The teacher is surprised that the students move toward inferences about the idea of density—it is not a topic she has planned to address—but she chooses to nurture their interests and help them expand their own thinking.

After seeing how the fifth graders proceed, we will look at a second-grade experience that seems much simpler in comparison. The second-grade activity addresses the basic ideas behind density by exposing students to objects that sink and float. You will see that such early experiences provide students with prior knowledge for their later, more sophisticated applications of the same science idea. The more varied and frequent students' manipulative science experiences are in the early grades, the richer will be the prior knowledge and preparation they bring to their investigations in later grades.

Finally, we revisit these concepts about density in a seventh-grade class, where the students investigate sinking and floating objects with an eye to testing their own theories and actually measuring density. As we explore these stories, think about your own role as a classroom teacher and how you will guide and facilitate experiences that allow students to move beyond the confines of a single experiment. Look for moments when the teachers do the following:

■ Acknowledge the students' ideas and reflect them back to the class.

■ Help pull one experience together before going on to the next.

■ Provoke students to look further and build on their insights.

■ Extend the lesson to pursue the new ideas and questions that arise.

 SCIENCE STORY

Looking at Liquids

A spirit of cooperation

M s. Drescher's fifth-grade class is in a small, urban community thirty-five miles north of a major metropolis. The students are from working-class and middle-class families with a diverse cross-section of ethnicities. Many of the students are immigrants and are struggling with English-language proficiency. Ms. Drescher arranges the students in heterogeneous groups, mixed by race, ability, gender, and ethnicity. A spirit of cooperation pervades her classroom, and all the students are willing to contribute to investigations because they know they will have the opportunity to explore their own ideas.

The students are working on a physical science unit, studying the properties of liquids. They have learned that many kinds of liquids have several properties in common. As the students have already seen, it is often possible to notice differences among liquids as well. Today, they are going to investigate the properties of yellow corn oil, clear corn syrup, and water to which blue food coloring has been added.

When the students return to their room after lunch, they find clear plastic cups and bottles containing the three liquids. The blue-colored water is labeled as such. The labels on the bottles of corn syrup and corn oil are also in full view, and Ms. Drescher asks the students, "Where do you usually find these items?"

Establishing connections

The students respond with their own experiences of using corn oil and corn syrup, or watching others use them, to cook. Most of these students have seen corn oil used in the preparation of fried foods or in salad dressings. One student's family prepares plantains with corn oil. Only a few students have seen corn syrup before. A couple of students know it is used to make candies, and one child's family uses it to make pecan pie. Some students have had experiences with food coloring for dyeing Easter eggs. Ms. Drescher shows the students how the blue food coloring mixes with water.

> *Ms. Drescher's thinking:* Ms. Drescher is eager to use materials that both work in the investigation and relate to the students' personal experiences. To establish the personal connections, she encourages a discussion of what the students already know about these liquids.

Working in groups of three, the students examine cups of the three liquids. They have been asked to measure 150 milliliters of each liquid by using a graduated cylinder. "What are we keeping the *same* about these liquids?" Ms. Drescher asks. Some children respond, "The same amount." Ms. Drescher looks at the class as a whole and says, "We know what scientists mean by 'the same amount.' Let's use the exact term." Several students then respond, "Volume."

Reinforcing terminology

> *Ms. Drescher's thinking:* Ms. Drescher is sure that the students know the meaning of volume, but she wants them to practice using the term.

She holds up equal volumes of the three liquids and asks, "In what ways are these liquids the same? In what ways are they different?" The students share observations about color, thickness, and transparency. Marisa offers, "You can see through the blue water and the corn oil, but it is harder to see through the corn syrup."

Another student notices that the cup of corn syrup feels heavier than the other cups. "Good observation," Ms. Drescher replies. "How can we prove that it is really heavier?" The students reply that they could use their balance scales. Taking out their double-pan balances, the students observe that 150 milliliters (ml) of corn syrup weighs more than 150 ml of blue water or 150 ml of corn oil.

How can we prove it?

Ms. Drescher invites the students to think about what would happen if they combined the three liquids in one container. The students spend some time writing their ideas in their science journals. "To make a fair test," she asks, "what must we keep the same?" "The volume," the students respond. "Yes," replies Ms. Drescher, and she explains how important it is to keep the volume the same when combining the liquids.

> *Ms. Drescher's thinking:* Ms. Drescher wants the students to see that "how much" you have of something can influence how it behaves with another substance. She knows that "doing science" means measuring and manipulating, but it also means planning investigations and thinking about procedures.

Ms. Drescher continues, "When we keep the amount or volume the same, we can honestly observe what happens when the liquids mix together. We can refer to the volume of the liquids as our *constant*, the property we keep the same. Then what is it that we are changing?"

The students respond that the liquids are different even though the volumes are the same. Ms. Drescher reminds the students that the things that change in an experiment are called the *variables*.

One student asks, "Which liquid should we pour first?" Ms. Drescher responds by saying, "That is your choice. Plan your investigation, and decide what volumes you will use."

Making plans and predictions

Working in their groups, the students think about what will happen when the three liquids combine. They have a total of 150 ml of each liquid and lots of empty plastic cups. Some students think the corn oil will form a middle layer and the corn syrup will sink to the bottom; other groups predict that the oil will sink to the bottom. Some think the liquids will change as they mix together. All the students become involved in sharing their ideas and planning their investigations.

> *Ms. Drescher's thinking: Because she wants the students to make choices about the plan of their experiment, Ms. Drescher does not provide lockstep directions. She is interested in seeing what variables they will use and which properties they will keep constant.*

Intriguing results

As it turns out, all the groups keep the volume of the three liquids the same by using the graduated cylinders. But the other procedures differ from group to group. Regardless of the methods they use, all of the students are surprised when they combine their three liquids. "Oohs" and "ahs" can be heard as the syrup falls to the bottom, the oil rises to the top, and the blue water becomes the center layer.

Many students are particularly surprised about the corn oil, and others are surprised that the results are the same regardless of the procedure. Ms. Drescher tells the students that they can spend the entire afternoon on their explorations. They write the results in their science journals. Some students also draw pictures of what they have observed.

> *Ms. Drescher's thinking: Ms. Drescher knew the students would need time to explore the liquids, so she planned the investigation on a day when she was certain that there would be no interruptions.*

The students' observations

After a time, Ms. Drescher asks the students to sum up what they have found out as a result of their explorations. The students offer ideas, such as, "Some liquids float or sink in water." On a large poster pad at the front of the room, Ms. Drescher records their ideas, including the following comments:

The liquids were different colors and different thicknesses.

The oil and water layers are clear, and the syrup layer is only partly clear.

The syrup layer poured more slowly than the other layers.

The oil layer feels greasy.

The syrup layer is the thickest and heaviest liquid.

"Well," Ms. Drescher continues, "let's reflect on what happened when you used the same amount of each liquid and weighed the liquids. Which was heaviest? Lightest?"

The students explain that the corn syrup was the heaviest and the corn oil the lightest. "Why do you think," she persists, the corn syrup is always the heaviest?" The students reason that the corn syrup must have more "stuff" in it than either the water or the corn oil.

A student's suggestion

One student asks, "Can we do this again, only this time keep the *weight* of the liquids the same?" Noticing that the class seems enthusiastic about weight being the new constant, Ms. Drescher says, "Sure." She reminds the students that now that weight is their constant, they need to use their balance scales carefully.

The children wonder . . .

As students begin to weigh their samples, they notice that the oil and water take up much more space than the syrup does for a given weight. That is because the corn syrup is so heavy; a little bit of it weighs the same as lots of corn oil or water. In other words, the students notice that the corn syrup has the smallest *volume* when the weights of the three liquids are the same. They wonder if it will still sink to the bottom even when there is so little of it.

. . . and experiment again

The students perform the investigation and—yes—the corn syrup always falls to the bottom, even though it has the smallest volume. They do not know why this has happened, and they turn to Ms. Drescher for help. "Remember, we said that the corn syrup sank to the bottom because it had more 'stuff'? Well," she says, "you have discovered another property of matter—the more 'stuff' in a substance, the *denser* it is."

Naming the new concept

"*Density*," she goes on, "is how closely packed together the particles are." Some students then reason that the oil floats on water because it is not as dense as water and the water floats on the syrup because it is not as dense as the syrup. They are catching on to the idea that densities remain the same regardless of mass or volume.

Ms. Drescher's thinking: The idea of density was not in Ms. Drescher's plans for this experiment; she would have been content for the students to observe differences in weight among the liquids, along with the other properties they have already noticed. But since the students wanted to explore the relationship between volume and weight, she decided to welcome this unexpected outcome of their curiosity and expand on it.

The Next Day: Building Science Toys to Illustrate Density

The next day Ms. Drescher brings a number of decorative liquid-display toys to class—items that use liquids of different densities and colors to create movement and attractive illusions. You have probably seen these objects in stores. The students are surprised to learn that the liquids in these toys resemble the ones they have been working with. "That one looks like corn syrup and water," one student remarks.

Ms. Drescher then gently heats some corn oil by placing it in a heat-resistant glass pot on a warmer plate. She adds several drops of red food coloring, and the red drops seem to dance around in the warmed oil. "That looks like a lava lamp," one student says. Suddenly the entire class begins to guess the types of liquids contained in the other decorative objects.

A new challenge

Ms. Drescher then sets out for them a variety of clear plastic cups, resealable plastic bags, glues, tapes, food coloring, and liquids. "Suppose you wanted to create your own science toy with these materials. What kinds of designs do you think you could make?" she asks. The students are excited at the possibilities, and Ms. Drescher asks them to work in their groups to develop their plans. "How will you create your own science toy?" she encourages them. "What liquids will you try? What volumes will you use? What do you want your toy to do?"

The groups discuss ideas . . .

Each group is given time to explore ideas and plan a procedure. The students discuss their ideas—both scientific and aesthetic—with enthusiasm. Before the groups can begin building their toys, however, Ms. Drescher must approve their designs.

Ms. Drescher's thinking: While giving the students the freedom to make their own plans, Ms. Drescher wants to be sure they are designing toys that can indeed be built with these materials and that the procedures will be safe.

. . . and invent their own toys

Using the plastic cups and bags, and working in their groups of three, the students create their own science toys. With their understanding of which liquids will sink or float in water, they can create their own designs. Using tape and glue to fasten cups and bags together, they even have liquids flowing from one container to another (see Figure 8.1 for an example).

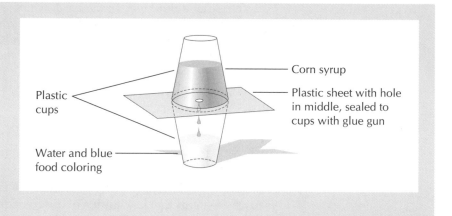

FIGURE 8.1
A simple science toy using clear corn syrup and water tinted with blue food coloring.
As the corn syrup drips into the blue water, it settles to the bottom. Turning the cups over begins the process again, so the syrup falls *through* the water to the bottom cup.

Corn syrup

Plastic sheet with hole in middle, sealed to cups with glue gun

Plastic cups

Water and blue food coloring

EXPANDING MEANINGS

■ The Teaching Ideas Behind This Story

■ Notice how Ms. Drescher prompts the students to make connections to their own lived experiences.

■ To honor their ideas and encourage their experimentation, Ms. Drescher allows the students to repeat the experiment using mass as their constant. When their exploration leads toward a new concept, she revises her plans and brings in new materials so they can extend their investigation.

■ The activities in which Ms. Drescher's students engage are pivotal to the science lesson, but they are not the entire lesson. She also provides students with opportunities to reflect on what they have discovered, talk about their ideas, and expand on their science experience.

● The Science Ideas Behind This Story

● In elementary school science, students explore materials within categories and classifications as well as between them. Remember our earlier stories about solids, liquids, and gases. In Ms. Drescher's class, the students are delving deeper into the category of liquids and realizing that substances in this category can be very different from one another.

● By fifth grade, the basic questions of what we keep the same and what we change become, "What are our constants; what are our variables?"

● A **graduated cylinder** is a scientific measuring cup. It is a glass or plastic cylinder that is calibrated in milliliters for liquid volume—a handy tool for the classroom.

- **Volume** is the amount of space an object takes up. Liquid volume is measured in milliliters and liters, and solid volume is measured in cubic centimeters (cm^3) and cubic meters (m^3). When we refer to the *size* of an object, we usually mean its volume.

- **Density** is mathematically defined as the mass of an object divided by its volume. It is expressed numerically in grams per cubic centimeter (g/cm^3). You can think of density as how closely packed together the particles are or how many particles can fit into a given amount of space.

- A substance's mass or volume may vary, but the density of that particular substance—the relationship or ratio between its mass and volume—is always constant. The densities of some common materials are listed in Table 8.1.

- The concept of density is complex because it relates to two factors in a given material: its weight *as compared to* its volume. Comparing two variables requires careful planning and frequent measurement.

TABLE 8.1   Densities of Some Common Materials

Material	Density (grams/cubic centimeter)
Cork	0.2
Wood (elm)	0.8
Alcohol	0.8
Olive oil	0.9
Water	1.0
Quartz	2.6
Aluminum	2.7
Iron	7.8
Nickel	8.9
Silver	10.5
Gold	19.3

✔ The Science Standards Behind This Story

STANDARDS ✔   This story illustrates two particular portions of the National Science Education Standards (National Research Council, 1996):

✔ *Content Standard B, Grades 5–8 (Physical Science):* "As a result of activities in grades 5–8, all students should develop an understanding of . . . properties and changes of properties in matter. . . . A substance has characteristic properties, such as density, a boiling point, and solubility, all of which are independent of the amount of the sample. A mixture of substances often can be separated into the original substances using one or more of the characteristic properties" (pp. 149, 154).

✔ *Content Standard E, Grades 5–8 (Science and Technology):* "As a result of activities in grades 5–8, all students should develop . . . abilities of technological design. . . . In the middle school years, students' work with scientific investigations can be complemented by activities in which the purpose is to . . . develop a product" (p. 161). By inviting the students to plan and construct their own liquid-display toys, Ms. Drescher engages them in this kind of technological design. We discuss the integration of design in science education further in later chapters.

Questions for Further Exploration

■ How does Ms. Drescher create an atmosphere of trust in her classroom?

■ Think about the densities of some other common liquids: for instance, dish soap, red wine, milk, engine oil, olive oil, and house paint. How would they compare in density to corn oil and corn syrup?

Resources for Further Exploration

ELECTRONIC RESOURCES

Chemistry Teaching Resources.   http://www.anachem.umu.se/eks/pointers. htm.   This site, sponsored by Umeå University in Sweden, includes links to various chemistry teaching resources, including curriculum material, software, and online journals. Though much of the material is for older grades, the site is also valuable for elementary and middle school science.

PRINT RESOURCES

National Science Resources Center. (1995). *Floating and Sinking.* Science and Technology for Children. Burlington, NC: Carolina Biological Supply. Designed for fifth grade, these materials introduce students to a series of investigations into fresh water and salt water and their effect on buoyancy. For information, call (800) 334-5551 or see   http://www.carolina. com/.

SCIENCE STORY

Delving Deeper into Density

Following up on the students' ideas

After observing her class pursue the idea of density, Ms. Drescher decides to carry the subject further. A few days later she brings in two soda cans, both unopened. One is Coca-Cola and the other is Diet Coke. She also has a large, deep, wide-mouthed jar, which is more than half filled with water. "We're going to see what happens when we place these soda cans in the deep jar of water," she tells the class. But before performing the experiment, she asks the students to make predictions.

"They'll both sink. Soda cans are heavy," says Tiffany.

"They'll float," offers Justin, "because they have air bubbles inside of them."

What do you think will happen?

Some students think the Diet Coke will sink and the regular Coke will float. Others believe the Diet Coke will float because it is "diet." They cannot tell just by holding the two cans of soda which one, if either, will float in water.

Results of the test

After everyone has had a chance to think and predict, Ms. Drescher sets the cans in the water. The Diet Coke floats, and the regular Coke sinks.

The students try the experiment several different ways—they place the soda cans in the water in different order, on their sides, and upside down—but always with the same results. Ms. Drescher asks them to make further observations about the cans. They weigh the cans on double-pan balances and examine the data on the can labels. Here are some of their observations and inferences:

The class's observations and inferences . . .

The cans have the same volume: 335 milliliters.

The Coke can weighs more than the Diet Coke can.

The Coke has greater *density* than the Diet Coke—that is why it sank.

The Coke has 39 grams of sugar in it. The Diet Coke has no sugar in it.

. . . and more questions!

The students want to know if the same thing would happen with other sugared and diet soft drinks. Ms. Drescher encourages them to bring in other soda cans and find out.

The Floating Egg

Another follow-up experiment

The following week, Ms. Drescher brings a number of hard-boiled eggs to school along with plastic spoons and containers of salt. She invites the students to explore what happens when they place a hard-boiled egg in a clear plastic cup that is three-quarters filled with water.

They try the procedure. "It sinks," one student quickly points out.

This school is not far from the Atlantic Ocean, and Ms. Drescher is confident that students have had experience with salt water. "Let's see

*Changing
one variable*

what happens to our egg," she says, "when we slowly add salt to the water and stir it to help it dissolve."

The students, working in pairs, slowly add the salt to their cups of water, first one teaspoon, then another. By the third teaspoon, the egg begins to rise; by the fifth teaspoon, it is floating on the water.

"Okay," Ms. Drescher says, "let's talk about this. What's going on here? What is our constant?"

The students respond, "The egg."

"What is our variable?"

They call out, "The amount of salt in the water."

Ms. Drescher continues, "Okay, what did you notice?" The students start talking at once. Ms. Drescher lists their comments on the poster pad in front of the room:

*More inferences and
connections emerge*

The more salt in the water, the better the egg floats.

The salt makes the water heavier.

Salt water helps you float better—that is why it is easier to float in the ocean than in a swimming pool.

The salt water is denser than the water from the tap.

The students reason that the salt dissolved in the tap water and gave the same amount of water many more particles. This made the water denser. The egg then was able to float on a liquid that was denser than the original tap water.

One student asks, "Could the egg float on the corn syrup?"

"What do you think?" Ms. Drescher responds.

"Let's try it!" the students exclaim.

And they do. What do you think they discover?

EXPANDING MEANINGS

■ The Teaching Ideas Behind This Story

- ■ Ms. Drescher keeps returning to the concept of density, offering the students different ways to conceptualize it and see what it means in practice.

- ■ The students are engaged with very familiar materials: soda, eggs, salt.

STANDARDS ✔   ■ All five of the major themes from the National Science Education Standards that we identified at the beginning of this book are embodied in this class's experience. Ms. Drescher's class had the opportunity to learn science by *doing*, by *inquiry*, by *collaboration*, over *time*, and by developing *personal knowledge*.

● The Science Ideas Behind This Story

- It takes fewer grams of artificial sweetener to produce the same taste as 39 grams of sugar. That is why the mass of the Coke is greater than the mass of the Diet Coke.

- When salt dissolves in water, the salt molecules separate or dissociate into charged atoms called *ions*. These ions fit between the molecules of water and make the same volume of water contain a larger number of particles. This increases the mass of the water but does not affect its volume. Salt water therefore has a greater density than fresh or tap water.

- Water exerts a lifting force on objects. This lifting force is called **buoyancy.** All objects appear to be lighter in water because of the buoyancy of water. Salt water exerts a greater lifting force than tap water does.

✔ The Science Standards Behind This Story

STANDARDS ☑ Again, the story illustrates *Content Standard B (Physical Science) for Grades 5–8* in the National Science Education Standards, especially the underlying idea that any substance "has characteristic properties, such as density, a boiling point, and solubility, all of which are independent of the amount of the sample" (National Research Council, 1996, p. 154). Ms. Drescher's repeated experiments related to the concept of density also illustrate Teaching Standard A, which states, "Teachers of science . . . select science content and adapt and design curricula to meet the interests, knowledge, understanding, abilities, and experiences of students. . . . Inquiry into authentic questions generated from student experiences is the central strategy for teaching science" (pp. 30–31).

Questions for Further Exploration

- ■ What do you think it would be like to learn science with Ms. Drescher?

- ■ What is the actual numerical density of pure water? Salt water?

- ■ What other foods or everyday materials would make good models of materials with different densities?

Resources for Further Exploration

ELECTRONIC RESOURCES

Air Travelers. http://www.omsi.edu/visit/physics/air/. This site, designed for upper elementary students, extends the concept of density to gases. It uses hot-air ballooning as an introduction to the basic principles of buoyancy, properties of gases, temperature, and the technology involved.

Buoyancy. http://www.billnye.com/. This site is designed for children and teachers exploring specific topics in physical science, planetary science, and life science. Click on "Episode Guides," followed by "Physical Science" and "Physics," before selecting "Buoyancy." The explanation of sinking and floating is excellent.

PRINT RESOURCES

Barber, J., Buegler, M., Lowell, L., & Willard, C. (2001). *Discovering Density.*
   GEMS series. Berkeley, CA: Lawrence Hall of Science. GEMS stands for
   Great Expectations in Mathematics and Science, a curriculum project
   from the Lawrence Hall of Science. Available at   **http://lhs.berkeley.
   edu/gems/.**

Extending Curriculum: Taking Advantage of Emerging Relevance

*Why did Ms. Drescher
carry on so long?*

You may be wondering what prompted Ms. Drescher to extend the unit
on liquids to such a degree. She not only seizes on the idea of density
when the students bring it up, she carries on with it for days afterward.
She offers students multiple ways of approaching the idea, repetitions
with variation, and new applications. We've seen this process in earlier
chapters, but Ms. Drescher is a particularly powerful example of it. She
has made an important pedagogical decision, electing to extend the unit in
a direction where the students' natural curiosities are leading them. Clearly,
Ms. Drescher works in a school environment that encourages curriculum
extension. As well, the students feel valued because their plans become
central to their science lessons for several days.

*Relevance
can emerge*

We know that when students work on a science problem that has
emerging relevance to them (Brooks & Brooks, 1999), they have a vested
interest in solving the problem and a personal commitment to making
sense of the solution. The term **emerging relevance** reminds us that relevance can *emerge* through teacher mediation, as it did in Ms. Drescher's
class. It does not have to be preexisting.

What is clear is that the *students* must see the problem as relevant. You
will know when questions or ideas of emerging relevance appear in your
own classroom. The key is to start with science problems that connect in
some way to the students' lived experiences. These problems then become
points of departure for other questions and other problems.

*Don't be frightened off
by complex questions.
Take them apart and
explore them.*
—ELEANOR
DUCKWORTH (1991)

Usually complex problems pose further questions to explore as students delve for deeper meaning. The layering of the three liquids that Ms.
Drescher used is a complex enough of an idea to promote further exploration. Remember, oversimplification is not in the students' best interests.
In fact, it often leaves them feeling more confused about solving complex
problems. So don't be intimidated by complex questions. Take them apart,
explore them with the students, and guide the students to consider possible experiments. If Ms. Drescher had not continued the class's explorations
of the three liquids, a complex concept like density would have been lost
to her fifth graders at a time when it was relevant to their explorations.

Your decision to pursue emerging problems should be based on several factors:

Factors to consider

■ The availability of materials.

■ The relevance of the emerging problem to the overall objectives of your science teaching.

■ The ways in which the students see the exploration as relevant to *them.*

■ What you have learned about your students' facility at pursuing independent investigations.

■ Your own belief that this extension will strengthen students' understanding of the natural world.

Allowing enough time

As a general rule, it is a good idea to allow more time for a science lesson than you may initially think it requires. The process of exploration takes time, and the follow-up experiences take time as well. Also, make sure that your science experiences involve relatively inexpensive materials that are easily accessible.

In the next story, we visit a second-grade class in the same school district as Ms. Drescher's class. Notice how early ideas about size and materials influence the class discussion. As you read, think about how an experience like this in a second-grade class relates to later activities, like the ones we saw in Ms. Drescher's fifth-grade class.

 SCIENCE STORY

Floating and Sinking Fruits

It is the week of Halloween, and Ms. Sacco's second-grade classroom is filled with items pertinent to the season, including pumpkins of varying sizes. The students are exploring the properties of pumpkins.

Measuring pumpkins

They measure the pumpkins with string, holding the string around the fattest part of each pumpkin and then marking the string to indicate this distance. Then they lay out the string against the calibrated centimeters of a meter stick. With this procedure, they find out how many centimeters around each pumpkin is at its bulging middle. They learn that this measurement is called the *circumference* of the pumpkin, and it may be compared to the equator of the Earth. Ms. Sacco holds up a globe and shows the students the equator.

Initial observations

The children are excited about the season. They know they are going to open their largest pumpkin and carve a face in it. First, however, Ms. Sacco asks them to make as many observations as possible about this pumpkin, and she lists them on a poster board:

It is large.   It has no smell.

It is round.   It has a stem.

It is orange.   It has lines on it.

It is hard.   Its circumference is 60 centimeters.

The children's prediction

Ms. Sacco asks, "What do you think will happen if we place our pumpkin in a basin of water?" The children laugh. "It will sink," they reply. "It will make a big splash."

Surprising results

Ms. Sacco takes the class to the large basin in the custodian's work area, and they hover around her as she fills the basin with water. As she places the pumpkin in the water, the children see that it bobs and floats! Squeals of surprise and chatter ring out as they walk back to their classroom.

Looking for a reason

The students do not know why the pumpkin floats. Ms. Sacco states, "Let's open the pumpkin, explore its insides, and do some more experiments to solve our mystery." She cuts out a lid around the stem of the pumpkin, and the children look inside. They see a large cavity and, within it, the pulp—the seeds and mushy, moist connecting threads. The pumpkin has a smell when it is opened.

"What else is in there?" Ms. Sacco asks.

"Nothing," the children reply.

The next day, Ms. Sacco brings grapes, oranges, apples, and a green pepper to class. "In what ways are these foods all the same?" Ms. Sacco asks. The second graders respond:

They are sort of round.

You can eat them.

They have skin.

They all come from plants.

Testing similar objects

Then the students use a large basin of water to explore whether these items will sink or float. They are shocked to find that only the grape sinks. All the other foods float. Michael wonders why a little grape sinks, but a great big pumpkin floats. It is time to do more investigating.

Ms. Sacco peels the orange and the grapefruit. Now they both sink!

An idea begins to develop

The children explore the skins of both these fruits with a magnifying lens. When they hold the skin up to the light, they notice spaces. "What do you think is in these spaces?" Ms. Sacco asks. Some students say "nothing"; others say "air." She asks them to study the apple fruit itself to see if they can notice spaces in the fleshy part of the apple.

Ms. Sacco invites them to look for what they think might be air spaces in the other fruits. The students find that the floating apples have spaces in the center cavities where the seeds rest. The green pepper and the pumpkin have large empty spaces inside them. The orange has the spaces in its peel. "The orange peel was the life jacket for the orange," Roselia says, and the other students laugh.

Ms. Sacco's thinking: In an earlier lesson on states of matter, the students explored plastic bags with air inside them. Still, Ms. Sacco has noticed many students are reluctant to acknowledge that air is inside the spaces in the foods. She is hoping to guide them to this idea. She also hopes that the students will notice that the size of the fruit cannot tell them whether it will sink or float in water. Size (or volume, as it is later called) is less important than what is inside the object.

The students reach their own conclusions

To pull the lesson together, Ms. Sacco invites the students to think about what makes some fruits float and others sink. She distributes grapes and magnifying lenses, and the children cut the grapes in half with plastic knives. They observe that there seem to be no open spaces inside a grape. That is why it sinks, they decide. They conclude that a fruit probably will float if there are open spaces inside it.

In an extended investigation students learn to take care of living things.

Elizabeth Crews/Stock Boston

EXPANDING MEANINGS

■ The Teaching Ideas Behind This Story

- To help the children make connections between science and their world, Ms. Sacco is using seasonally relevant materials to explore nature.

- Notice how she challenges the students to draw comparisons and consider properties of the various fruits.

- Ms. Sacco makes connections between the pumpkin and our planet, paving the way for the notion that different objects can be used as models for the Earth (see the chapter "Making Models").

- The students use mathematical skills when they measure the circumference of the pumpkin.

- When the students do not know why the pumpkin floats, Ms. Sacco does not tell them. She sanctions the question and gives the students confidence to believe that they will find the answer. She then provides additional experiences that help them do so.

- Ms. Sacco avoids emphasizing that "air" is inside the fruits that float.

● The Science Ideas Behind This Story

- Some fruits float in water because they have air inside them. The air decreases the overall density of the fruit, making it less dense than water. (However, as we will see in a later story in this chapter, apples can float even when the core with its air pockets is removed.)

- Objects with a density less than the average density of water will float on water. The average density of water is 1 gram per cubic centimeter. This means that 1 cubic centimeter of water (equal to a milliliter of water) has a mass of 1 gram.

✔ The Science Standards Behind This Story

 STANDARDS

Our story of Ms. Sacco's class illustrates the guidelines of *Content Standard A (Science as Inquiry), Grades K–4,* in the National Science Education Standards. This standard states: "As a result of activities in grades K–4, all students should develop abilities necessary to do scientific inquiry" (National Research Council, 1996, p. 121). The explanations of the standard include these points:

✔ "Full inquiry involves asking a simple question, completing an investigation, answering the question, and presenting the results to others" (p. 122). You can see how Ms. Sacco's students were engaged in this process.

✔ "Scientists develop explanations using observations (evidence) and what they already know about the world (scientific knowledge). Good explanations are based on evidence from investigations" (p. 123). In our story, Ms. Sacco's students found the evidence to support their tentative explanation for why some fruits float in water.

Questions for Further Exploration

- If iron has a density of 7.8 grams per cubic centimeter, why do steel ships float?

- What is the ratio between the grape's mass and volume? Greater than 1? Less than 1?

- What other common materials could children use to do the sink-or-float test?

Resources for Further Exploration

ELECTRONIC RESOURCES

Science and Mathematics Initiative for Learning Enhancement (SMILE). http://www.iit.edu/~smile/. This is a collection of elementary- and middle-grade lessons in chemistry, biology, physics, and earth science from teachers all over the country. Its chemistry link, **http://www.llt.edu/ ~smile/ cheminde.html,** provides several lessons on density, including density of liquids.

PRINT RESOURCES

National Science Resources Center. (1995). *Balancing and Weighing.* Science and Technology for Children. Burlington, NC: Carolina Biological Supply. This is a series of lessons designed to help students in the younger grades explore relationships involving balance, weight, and size. Students work with cupfuls of food. For information, call (800) 334-5551 or see **http://www.carolina.com/.**

Looking Back to Look Ahead

Constructing ideas—a complex, recursive process

You may be wondering why we visited Ms. Sacco's second-grade class after exploring Ms. Drescher's fifth graders at work with volume, mass, and density. The second graders were simply exploring sinking and floating fruits. Where's the connection?

Far from being a neat, linear process, the construction of new ideas is based on recursively visiting and revisiting prior conceptions, altering our views based on new experiences, reflecting on those views in peer groups, and then, sometimes, formulating a new idea. For this reason, what takes place in Ms. Sacco's class has important implications for what Ms. Drescher's students can learn from the experiences in their class. That is, if Ms. Drescher's students have had prior experiences like those provided by Ms. Sacco, they will be better prepared to understand concepts like volume and density. They can use that prior knowledge to build their new, more complicated ideas.

The more we help children to have their wonderful ideas and to feel good about themselves for having them, the more likely it is that they will some day happen upon wonderful ideas that no one else has happened upon before.
—ELEANOR DUCKWORTH (1996)

The children in Ms. Sacco's class believe that the large pumpkin will sink. They find out that that belief is not accurate, and they explore further. This work leads to a partial understanding that the materials inside an object determine one of its properties. They begin to understand that some objects have less "space" inside them than others, and this property can be more important, for some purposes, than the object's size. Ms. Sacco's students are approaching one conception of density—how closely packed the particles are. By the time they have a full-fledged lesson on density, in Ms. Drescher's class or elsewhere, they will be ready for it.

Most science curricula are constructed so that science topics, and the key ideas associated with them, pop up repeatedly in different grades. This **spiraling of curriculum,** as it has been called (Bruner, 1960), is one way to develop depth of understanding of a topic. Spiraling does not mean, of course, that students engage in the same activity over and over. Rather, as they mature, they build on earlier science experiences and develop a greater depth of understanding.

Spiraling of curriculum

Now let's skip ahead to seventh grade to see how the topic of density comes up again when students are old enough to conduct more sophisticated measurements and experiments.

 SCIENCE STORY

Apples, Potatoes, and Density

Students in Mr. Hutcheon's seventh-grade class in Lakeville Middle School in the Pacific Northwest address topics in life science, physical science, and earth science. In physical science, the local syllabus calls for the students to explore characteristic properties of matter, like density, boiling point, and solubility. Mr. Hutcheon decides to approach the idea of density through a sinking and floating exploration that engages students in testing some of their own theories about why objects sink or float. To prepare for this unit, Mr. Hutcheon has done extensive research on sinking and floating, and he asks me to visit and observe the process in which he is about to engage his students.

For the first exploration, Mr. Hutcheon gathers five sets of the following floaters and nonfloaters:

two different sizes of corks   a marble

a ball of Plasticine
    about 3 cm in diameter   a coin

a thick, waxy candle   an apple

a stick of chalk   a potato

a block of wood
    4 cm x 7 cm x 2 cm

Each set of materials sits inside a plastic basin. Also available for supervised use are plastic knives and vegetable peelers.

What happens when an object sinks?

Mr. Hutcheon introduces the unit to the class using a 4,000 ml beaker of water, a grapefruit, and a grape. As the students watch, he invites them to think about what happens when an object sinks and when an object floats. The students quickly respond that an object goes to the bottom when it sinks and stays on top when it floats. Class predictions about the grape and grapefruit are mixed; about half the students predict that the grapefruit will sink and the grape float. They are delighted to see that the reverse happens, and they want to know why. Mr. Hutcheon explains that "we are going to make observations of several objects in water and try to come to our own understandings about why some things float and others sink, but first, let's define what we mean by sinking and floating."

> *Mr. Hutcheon's thinking: Floating and sinking are commonly used terms, but scientists have their own meanings for them, and they are not quite as simple as the students have suggested.*

What do we mean by "floating"?

Mr. Hutcheon draws several diagrams of objects at different levels on and under the water. He then asks the students to comment on them. The first is a picture of an object sitting on top of the water, held up by surface tension, like a leaf or a water strider. Some students think it is "just sitting" on the water, but others declare that it is actually floating. Next is a drawing of an object that is partially on top and partially under the water. Some students say, "The top part is floating and the bottom part is sinking." "Actually," Mr. Hutcheon offers, "scientists would definitely call this floating." In the next drawing the object is immersed in the water but freely suspended, like a fish. Some students say, "No, it is under the water, so it is sinking." Mr. Hutcheon clarifies by saying, "This is another form of floating. Floating in a liquid refers to objects that are partly or wholly immersed in the liquid, as long as they are not touching the bottom. The object can be moving or stationary. Let's think about objects as floating or not floating."

The bells rings, and Mr. Hutcheon asks the students to think about whether an iceberg is floating and how they would define a "sinker." The students move on to the next class.

> *My thinking: I notice how engaged the students became in what, at first, seemed like a simple topic and how quickly the science period went by.*

The following day, Mr. Hutcheon has the class for two periods. The students are now prepared to discuss what it means for something to sink. They have found out that an iceberg floats. Now Mr. Hutcheon draws other objects on the board. The first is a ship, lower in the water than usual, and the students think it is sinking. "It may be," said Mr. Hutcheon, "but in this picture it is still floating. Try to remember," he adds, "that if the object is in any way supported by the water, it is floating." In the next picture, there is an object that is moving downward through the liquid and landing on the bottom, like a rock. "This object is sinking," all agree.

Group roles

"Okay," continues Mr. Hutcheon, "we are ready to explore materials," and the students form their science groups. Mr. Hutcheon's class uses the same types of groups as Ms. Parker's class in the chapter, "The Teacher as Mediator." Each group has jobs labeled *director, recorder, materials manager,* and *speaker.* This is an extension of a model developed by the educators at Biological Sciences Curriculum Study and revised by the Australian Academy of Sciences (1996).

The only directions that Mr. Hutcheon gives the students before they secure their materials are to fill their basins with water, make predictions about each of the objects, and then test whether they sink or float. Students need to keep a record of their science work in a personal science journal.

No worksheets

Mr. Hutcheon does not give out a worksheet, but for this unit the students are instructed to place the question "Why do objects sink or float" in their science journals.

> *My thinking:I am impressed that students are keeping their own science notes and not relying solely on worksheets. Often, in seventh grade, students see completing the worksheet as the goal of the exploration. This is clearly not the case here. Mr. Hutcheon is interested in fostering understanding.*

The class's consensus

Watching the students work is a treat; they are interested in all the objects and can relate to them. The speaker for each group goes up to the board to enter the group's data in a chart. The following list represents the consensus of the class.

Object	Sink or Float?
Corks	Float
Candle	Float
Marble	Sink
Chalk	Sink
Block of wood	Float
Coin	Sink
Apple	Float
Potato	Sink
Plasticine	Float and sink

"Let's look at our data," says Mr. Hutcheon. "Did anything surprise you?" he asks. Hands fly up. One student remarks that "I thought the chalk would float because it is so light, and I thought the candle would sink." "I didn't think we could get the Plasticine to float, because at first it sank straight down," says another student. "But then we spread it into a different shape, kind of like a boat, and it floated." "Yeah, and why do apples float but potatoes sink?" asks yet another. Mr. Hutcheon asks them to think about the following questions, which he lists on the board:

More questions

Do all light things float?

Why can a block of wood float, while a small piece of chalk sinks?

Can a log of the same type of wood float?

Will a piece of candle float or sink?

Why did the Plasticine float when it was reshaped?

Trying to define density

Students grapple with these questions. Mr. Hutcheon invites the class to consider one student's comment: "Katie says that the potato has greater density than the apple. Let's take this theory as a starting point and see if we can test it. What do you mean by density, Katie?" Katie is not sure exactly how to define the term, but says it has something to do with the particles the object is made of. Mr. Hutcheon records this observation on the board. Luke then suggests that the apple core has air spaces where the seeds are located, and the potato does not. Mr. Hutcheon writes this idea, too, on the board. Kara suggests that the skin of the apple is waxy and acts like a waterproof shield. Jenna suggests that maybe a small piece of potato would float.

> *My thinking: I presume that these students have had science experiences like the ones in Ms. Drescher's and Ms. Sacco's classes because they are quick to offer ideas. Clearly, the concept of density is not unfamiliar to them, but they have much to learn about it. I'm eager to see how Mr. Hutcheon can build on their prior knowledge.*

Students design investigations

Mr. Hutcheon asks the students to design investigations to test their ideas. He cautions them to be careful with the plastic knives, and he walks around the room assisting. I walk around the room, too. Students in one group decide to peel the apple and the potato. Another group of students is coring the apple. All the students are busy exploring their own questions.

One group of students is intent on finding a piece of apple that sinks. But the students discover that with or without the core and with or without the skin, apple slices will float! Other students peel and slice the potato but cannot get the potato slices to float, no matter how small they make the pieces.

> *Mr. Hutcheon's thinking: By having the students explore the many different ways to try the the apple and potato in water, he is hoping to get them to understand a qualitative way of describing density.*

Before time runs out, Mr. Hutcheon asks the materials managers to return the materials, and the class cleans up the mess left from the potato, apple peels, and water. Mr. Hutcheon then pulls the class together by asking

Students are exploring the effects of adding small amounts of one type of liquid to another liquid, with different density. Notice how carefully they are observing the process.

Bill Aron/PhotoEdit

Developing a definition

the students why they think the apple floated and the potato did not. Finally, Megan says, "The fibers in the potato are packed together more tightly than the fibers in the apple." Mr. Hutcheon asks the class to reflect on Megan's reasoning, and there is consensus that it is correct. Katie remarks that Megan's explanation means that the potato has greater density than the apple. Mr. Hutcheon writes this definition for density on the board: "How closely packed together the particles are."

My thinking: I notice how much this definition of density resembles the one that Ms. Drescher offered her fifth-grade students. These seventh-grade students, however, have developed the definition for themselves. They are taking their reasoning to a new level.

The Following Days: Further Tests and Measurements

For the following class, Mr. Hutcheon prepares circular cookie cutters along with peeled pieces of apple and potato. He asks the students, working in the same groups as the prior day, to use the cutters to make a piece of potato that is exactly the same size as a piece of apple. They should then compare the two pieces in any way they can. The students place the cut slices in their basins and then ask if they can weigh them. "Of course," Mr. Hutcheon replies, and the students use the scale to learn that the potato weighs more for its size than the apple.

For the next class, Mr. Hutcheon does a demonstration in a very large, clear plastic basin using four pieces of wood cut to exactly the same size. In mathematical terms, these wooden blocks are rectangular solids, and Mr. Hutcheon asks for student volunteers to help him measure their length, width, and height. Each block measures 7 cm long, 4 cm wide, and 2 cm high.

Computing volume — Using these measurements, the students compute the volume by multiplying length by width by height. Luke gives the answer as 56 cubic centimeters. The class agrees that each block of wood has this same volume.

> *My thinking: This is a more teacher-directed lesson than the earlier one, but it seems appropriate at this stage now that the students have done their own experiments with sinking and floating.*

Examining the samples . . . — Now the students examine other characteristics of the four blocks of wood. Collecting their observations, they note that one block has very little visible wood grain, whereas two other samples have more wood graining. The fourth sample is a black piece of wood, and one student asks if it is painted black. Mr. Hutcheon asks him to examine it to determine that it does not have paint on it. Each wood sample has a number, and this black block is number 4.

. . . and making predictions — Now Mr. Hutcheon asks the class how these four blocks will behave in water. All the students believe that all four blocks will float. After all, the wood floated in their earlier experiment. Mr. Hutcheon gently lowers each sample into the water. Number 1 appears to stay on the surface; number 2 floats but part of it is submerged; and number 3 floats with even more submerged. When number 4 goes into the basin, it sinks!

Using a digital scale, students now determine the mass of each of the four blocks of wood. Mr. Hutcheon lists the data in a chart on the board (see Table 8.2). He invites the students to study the table and draw some conclusions about the patterns they may see emerging. Rather quickly, they notice that the lower in the water the wood block floated, the more it weighed and that the black wood sample weighed the most for its size. Mr. Hutcheon then asks the students to divide the mass of each block of wood by its volume and compare the resulting numbers.

One student wants to know the identities of the four types of wood, and Mr. Hutcheon supplies the names: number 1 is balsa, number 2 is pine,

TABLE 8.2	Data for the Blocks of Wood in the Density Investigation by Mr. Hutcheon's Class	
Wood sample	Mass	Volume
1	6 g	56 cm^3
2	30 g	56 cm^3
3	43 g	56 cm^3
4	62 g	56 cm^3

Analyzing the results

Relating density to floating

number 3 is oak, and number 4 is ebony. "Is that the same type of ebony used for piano keys?" Katrina asks, and Mr. Hutcheon says, "Yes."

After dividing the mass by the volume for each sample, the students see that only ebony, at 1.10, has a number greater than 1. Mr. Hutcheon decides to help the students analyze that number by offering the idea that for every 1 cubic centimeter of ebony, there is a mass of 1.10 grams. He asks the students to think about this as another way of describing density—the amount of mass per unit volume of an object. Balsa's density is only .10 gram per cubic centimeter; pine's is .54 grams per cubic centimeter; and oak's is .76 grams per cubic centimeter.

"What about the density of water?" Mr. Hutcheon wonders. Katie remembers that water's density is 1 gram per cubic centimeter. So Mr. Hutcheon asks for a conclusion based on the class's observations and data. Luke offers that objects that have a density less than 1 will float on water, and those with a density greater than 1 will not float. Mr. Hutcheon remarks that they are off to a good start in understanding why some things float and some things do not float.

> *My thinking: How wonderful that Mr. Hutcheon calls this conclusion a "start"! The students have reached the "right" answer, but he knows that floating and sinking involve many complex variables, including the concept of buoyancy and the ways in which you can change the density of water.*

For homework, Mr. Hutcheon asks the class to consider why the ball of Plasticine did not float but a boatlike shape made from the *same* ball did float.

EXPANDING MEANINGS

■ The Teaching Ideas Behind This Story

- ■ Understanding takes time. The time that these seventh-grade students took to explore the many ways apples and potatoes can float or sink prepared them to consider a deeply complex concept—comparing an object's volume and weight. This is an essential concept that underlies density as well as sinking and floating, and it is appropriate for teachers to visit and revisit this concept in elementary and middle school science.

- ■ The students ultimately arrived at the mathematical definition of density: mass per unit volume. But first they defined density in a qualitative way, and this gave them a context for the mathematics. Often well-meaning teachers give numbers without providing prior meaning.

- ■ In Mr. Hutcheon's class, one further activity was to look at longer and shorter pieces of candle to see if a longer piece would float lower in the water. Another activity involved displacing water again (see Figure 8.2) to determine the volume of an irregularly shaped object. Students explored the Plasticine ball again and came to realize that altering its shape changed its volume. Keeping this topic complex led to many activities and opportunities for meaning making that would carry the students on to higher grades.

● The Science Ideas Behind This Story

- ● An object *floats* in water when it is supported by a buoyant force, even if no part of the object is above the surface of the water.

Measuring Water Displacement

Would you like to see how much water is displaced when a small object sinks or floats in water? Using three soft plastic cups and a graduated cylinder, you can perform your own test.

Take a plastic cup and cut a slit in it about 5 centimeters long and 2.5 centimeters wide. Fold this flap down like a spout. Then stand this cup on another cup that has been inverted, so its bottom is facing up. Place a smaller cup beneath the spout you have cut (see Figure 8.2).

Next, fill your cup with the flap until it overflows. Check that the overflow water is falling into the small cup; then discard this first bit of overflow water.

Your cup with the flap should now be perfectly full, up to the level of the spout. Gently place a small object in this cup. Take the displaced water that collects in your small cup and measure it with a graduated cylinder. Are you surprised by the amount?

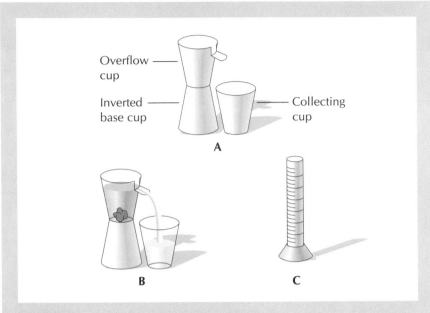

FIGURE 8.2
An experiment in measuring water displacement.
(A) Three plastic cups are arranged so that the one with a cut-out spout
overflows into a collecting cup. To begin the experiment, the overflow cup is
full and the collecting cup empty. (B) A small stone weighing 100 grams,
with a volume of 40 cubic centimeters, is placed gently in the overflow cup.
The stone sinks, causing water to overflow into the collecting cup. (C) The
water from the collecting cup is measured in a graduated cylinder, indicating
that 40 milliliters (cubic centimeters) of water were displaced. Thus, the
volume of displaced water equals the volume of the stone.

- Objects that float in water displace water. For a floating object, the mass
  of the water displaced is equal to the mass of the object.

- Objects that sink in water also displace water. For an object that sinks,
  the *volume* of water displaced is equal to the volume of the object, as
  shown in Figure 8.2.

✔ The Science Standards Behind This Story

STANDARDS ✔   Again the story relates to the National Science Education Standards (National Research Council, 1996). Notice how *Content Standard B for Physical Science* is revisited here for grade 7. Addressed in particular is the underlying idea that many substances have characteristic properties, such as density, or boiling point, or solubility, all of which are independent of the amount of the sample (p. 154).

The *Science as Inquiry Standard for Grades 5–8* includes the following ideas that were modeled by Mr. Hutcheon (p. 148):

✔ "Different kinds of questions suggest different kinds of scientific investigations. Some investigations involve observing and describing objects, organisms, or events; some involve collecting specimens; some involve experiments; some involve seeking more information; some involve discovery of new objects and phenomena; and some involve making models."

✔ "Mathematics is important in all aspects of scientific inquiry."

✔ "Scientific explanations emphasize evidence, have logically consistent arguments, and use scientific principles, models, and theories. The scientific community accepts and uses such explanations until displaced by better scientific ones. When such displacement occurs, science advances."

Questions for Further Exploration

■ Will an object float at different levels in different liquids?

■ Can you make a floater into a sinker?

■ Can you make a sinker into a floater?

■ Why do rotten eggs float and raw eggs sink? How about hard-boiled eggs?

Resources for Further Exploration

ELECTRONIC RESOURCES

Buoyancy. http://www.engineering.usu.edu/jrestate/workshop/buoyancy.htm. The Utah State University Junior Engineering site offers an online buoyancy workshop where you can learn more about buoyancy and Archimedes.

The Space Science Group. http://www.spacesciencegroup.nsula.edu/. This site is part of an outreach program of the *College of Science and Technology* at *Northwestern State University* in Natchitoches, Louisiana. Learn more about buoyancy and the origin of the buoyant force.

PRINT RESOURCE

Biddulph, F., & Osborne, R. (eds.). (1984). *Making Sense of Our World: An Interactive Teaching Approach.* The classic floating and sinking activities offered in this book are similar to those used by Mr. Hutcheon. They have been respected for more than twenty years as important ways for students to investigate this topic.

"Replacement" of Understandings

In our final density story, we visited the same basic science concepts in yet another grade. You should be able to see how this spiraling of curriculum gradually deepens the students' knowledge and leads them to ever more sophisticated levels of understanding.

As Jacqueline Grennon Brooks observes, "it is the constant replacement of present understandings with richer and deeper ones—rather than the constant addition of understandings—that characterizes the processes of learning" (Brooks, 2002, p. 95). Think about that for a moment. As learners grow, they do not simply stuff new science knowledge into their heads. Instead, certain science ideas get subsumed or altered by new, more complex ones. Since we know from the research on alternative conceptions that learners do not easily part with ideas, this frequent revisiting of embedded concepts is essential to help students reach a deep and meaningful level of understanding.

New ideas not simply added to old ones

In the next two chapters, we explore additional activities for the upper elementary grades and middle school years. As you read, think about the prior experiences that help students construct new ideas in these grades. Also consider how the middle years themselves offer prior knowledge that students will need to engage in more intense science study in high school and beyond.

KEY TERMS

graduated cylinder *(p. 178)*
volume *(p. 179)*
density *(p. 179)*
buoyancy *(p. 183)*
emerging relevance *(p. 184)*
spiraling of curriculum *(p. 190)*

Making Models

Explorations of the Solar System

9

W hen I was in fifth grade, I made a
model of a tooth for Dental Health
Week in my elementary school. In order to build
it, I needed to gather pictures of teeth and understand the various parts of a tooth. I had to decide which type of tooth to represent as well as
figure out the size and composition of the model.
I decided on a molar tooth (molars are the grind-
ing teeth toward the rear of your mouth) and plaster of Paris for the
model's material. I chose to make the model 8 inches tall, reasoning
that it would then be large enough to see and that I could draw
lines on it to represent the insides of the tooth.

What I remember most from making that tooth model—aside
from my struggle to create the plaster mold out of clay—was that,
to my surprise, the tooth is a complicated structure with lots of layers. In daily life we see only the crown, the visible part of a tooth.
My model, though, included markings to show where the root
canal, the nerve, and the pulp are.

Although not exact by any means, my model tooth remained on
display for all of Dental Health Week. Moreover, I never *forgot* the
structure of a tooth. Decades later, when I needed to have the contents of the pulp chamber of one of my molars removed because it
was infected, I pictured the root canal from my model.

This chapter explores what happens when we engage students
in making models of natural objects. I think you'll see that your students can have experiences that are as instructive and memorable
as mine was. We're going to look at models of the solar system.

FOCUSING QUESTIONS

- What models have you made? Did you ever build a model airplane? A clay model? An abstract model?
- What objects of nature can be explored only through a model?
- How can making models facilitate learning?

First, though, we need to answer the question: What is the point of making models?

The Usefulness of Models

The activities you have been reading about in earlier chapters invite students to become directly involved with their objects of study. Sometimes, however, it is not possible to explore the objects directly. They are too large or too small, too far away, or inaccessible for other reasons.

Physical models

When scientists are unable to work directly with materials, they construct models of them in an effort to gain a better understanding of their structure and function. A **model** may be a physical structure, either a smaller or a larger representation of a system or an object. My model tooth was one such structure. Scientists have long made physical models out of whatever materials are available to them. One of the most famous models involved the chemical structure of deoxyribonucleic acid, known as DNA—the material in our cells that passes genetic information from one generation to the next. The model—developed by scientists James Watson, Francis Crick, Rosalind Franklin, and Maurice Wilkins—marked one of the most important scientific revolutions of the twentieth century and was made out of materials resembling giant tinker toys.

Scientists construct models after they have gathered enough data about their objects of study to begin to make a reasonable facsimile. In the case of DNA, the scientists used data from an x-ray crystallography method employed at the time by Rosalind Franklin. Dr. Franklin was able to gather images of patterns made by the DNA molecule when it reflected x-rays. Her data became the basis for Watson and Crick's DNA model.

Mental models

A model does not have to be something you can touch. It may be a mental construct—a design that forms an image in your mind representing a concrete process or object. For example, I carry a mental model of an atom in my mind; it is the way I have conceptualized an atom on the basis of what I have learned.

Computer models

Models can also be computer programs or computer-generated images. Today, a great deal of scientific research is performed by using computer models. As just one example, meteorologists often explore potential weather events by using computer simulations based on actual satellite data. You see the results of these computer models on the television news each day when forecasters describe the possible tracks a storm system may take.

As you will discover from the following science stories, making models is a way of furthering your students' understandings of objects and events that they cannot manipulate directly. The nature of the scientific investigation changes somewhat when we need to gather data in order to construct models. In previous chapters, you saw students gathering the data while they manipulated their objects of study. In this chapter, however, students gather research data first, *then* construct the model, *then* look for deeper meanings.

Model making can take place at any level of science education. Here, we will see what happens when Mr. Johnston and his fifth-grade class build and explore a model of the solar system. In the next chapter, we will see eighth graders constructing models of atoms.

  SCIENCE STORY

An Edible Solar System

Mr. Johnston is a veteran elementary school teacher. He has a science room in a small, suburban elementary school, and students visit his room once a week with their classroom teacher. Together the students engage in science activities in Mr. Johnston's science room, which they then continue in their regular classroom. There are interesting materials on display and arranged in storage cabinets all around the room. Three hamsters, a rabbit, and numerous plants share the room with Mr. Johnston.

Familiar materials

This particular day, when fifth graders arrive for their morning visit, the only materials Mr. Johnston has set out are round fruits and vegetables of varying sizes: grapes, peas, cabbages, grapefruits, melons of different types, apples of varying sizes, oranges, apricots, and small tomatoes.

"Are we dissecting fruits and vegetables again?" the students ask.

Mr. Johnston laughs. "No," he says. "We are going to use these fruits and vegetables to make a model of the planets in our solar system."

The students have been exploring "objects in the sky," and they have just completed a huge poster-board model of the sun, so this project makes sense to them. They are excited to begin. "How do we do it?" they ask.

Mr. Johnston explains that they need to gather a lot of information before they can use these materials to make a model. "Remember all the research we did on the sun?" he asks. "What type of information do we need about the solar system in order to construct a reasonable classroom model?"

The students brainstorm various questions to answer, including the following:

The students' list of questions

What are all the objects in the solar system?

How far away from Earth are the rest of the planets?

How many moons does each planet have?

What are the planets made of?

How many planets have atmospheres?

How big are the planets?

How far away from the sun is each planet?

What colors are the planets?

Mr. Johnston records these questions on poster paper as the students record them in their science journals. He invites the students to work in groups of four and to decide on the particular questions they want to research. He explains that they are in the "data-gathering" phase of this model-making project, and they must select the questions they are most interested in exploring.

Why use these materials?

> *Mr. Johnston's thinking: Typically, solar-system models are constructed out of Styrofoam balls of varying sizes. The assumption people may make when observing this type of model is that all the planets are the same except for their size. That is not true. Planets differ from each other not only in size but also in composition and surface features. For that reason, Mr. Johnston thinks that fruits and vegetables will make a better representation, as well as a more interesting one.*

Gathering information

After selecting the questions they want to research, some students begin using the resource books available in their science room; others access the Internet on the networked computer in the science room; still others go to the school library, where other books and networked computers can be found. The students accumulate a good deal of information about the planets individually and the solar system as a whole.

All the students decide that one critical piece of information is the planets' distances from the sun. Here Mr. Johnston intervenes, explaining that the distances between the planets and from the planets to the sun are so huge that no classroom model can be truly accurate for distance. He

We construct models in order to make meaning of objects that are too remote and impossible to study through direct manipulation. Students created this model of Saturn to help conceptualize their information about the planet.

Anthony Freeman/PhotoEdit

Given a three meter sun at one end of the [school] building, the scale model planets we created wouldn't fit in the school. In fact, Pluto would be nearly 15 km away.
—David Whitney

tells the students that one fourth-grade teacher, in an effort to represent the distances accurately, spread out the model planets all over the local community (Whitney, 1995).

> *Mr. Johnston's thinking: Mr. Johnston knows that the fruit-and-vegetable model will not be completely accurate, but that is okay, especially if the students come to understand how it resembles the real solar system and how it differs. Later, he will ask them to make comparisons between the model and the real thing.*

To make the calculations more manageable, Mr. Johnston provides the students with distance dimensions in the form of astronomical units. One astronomical unit (AU) equals 93 million miles, the average distance from the sun to the Earth. All the other distances in AUs are relative to that distance. Table 9.1 lists these distances.

Exploring the data

Mr. Johnston distributes calculators to help the students explore the numbers while he uses an overhead projector calculator. Together, they multiply each of the planetary distances expressed in AUs by 93 million miles. The enormity of the numbers indicates to the class how huge the solar system really is.

TABLE 9.1   The Solar System Data Used by Mr. Johnston's Class

Planet	Average Distance from Sun (AUs)	Diameter (km)
Mercury	0.4	4,878
Venus	0.7	12,104
Earth	1.0	12,756
Mars	1.5	6,796
Jupiter	5.2	142,796
Saturn	9.5	120,300
Uranus	19.0	52,400
Neptune	30.0	48,600
Pluto	39.0	4,000

Now the students turn to the data they have collected on planet diameters, which is given in kilometers (see Table 9.1). They use many different web sites as their data source and using these data, the students order the planets from smallest to largest. Then they are ready to select the fruits and vegetables that will be most representative of the solar system.

For the sun, they choose a huge pumpkin brought in by Mr. Johnston. In reality, the sun's diameter is about 109 times that of Earth, and if the sun were a hollow ball, one million Earths would fit inside. Thus the students know that the pumpkin is not really big enough to accurately represent the sun in their model. As for the planets, different groups of students make different decisions. Here are the choices one group makes:

One group's choices for the model

Mercury: a small cherry tomato

Venus: an orange

Earth: an apple, slightly larger than the orange

Mars: an apricot, approximately half the size of the apple

Jupiter: a honeydew melon

Saturn: a cantaloupe

Uranus: a cabbage

Neptune: a grapefruit, slightly smaller than the cabbage

Pluto: a tiny pea

For many students, it becomes a challenge to remember which fruit is modeling which planet, so Mr. Johnston instructs each group to make a key.

Once the students have made their selections, it is time to go outside and place the model planets in such a way that they will also model the relative distances of the planets from each other and the sun. The class chooses the set of vegetables and fruits just listed as the ones to take outside. Mr. Johnston suggests using 1 meter to represent 1 AU. With this technique, the students observe that the first four planets occupy about 1.5 meters of space, while Pluto is 39 meters away from the pumpkin, the designated sun. The student carrying the little pea model of Pluto finds it *difficult to see* the student carrying the huge pumpkin model of the sun (see Figure 9.1).

Modeling distances

Model and reality: comparisons . . .

When the students discuss their model back inside in the classroom, Mr. Johnston asks, "In what ways is our model like the real solar system?" The students offer many responses, including these:

"All the planets are different, with different textures and insides."

"The relative sizes of the planets are the same, more or less."

"We set them up so the relative distances are similar."

"They're in the order of their distance from the sun."

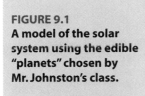

FIGURE 9.1
A model of the solar system using the edible "planets" chosen by Mr. Johnston's class.

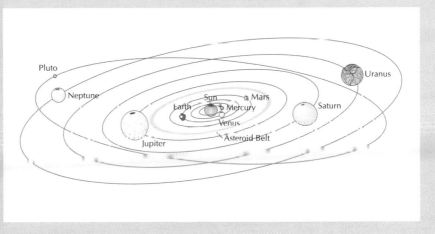

... and contrasts

"In what ways is the model *different* from the real solar system?" Mr. Johnston then asks.

"You can't eat the real planets!" the students point out. And they add other differences as well:

"The model is so much smaller than the real thing."

"The planets aren't moving."

"The distances are much much larger."

"Some planets have moons."

A crucial fact about models

> *Mr. Johnston's thinking:* The students are doing a good job of evaluating this particular model, and they are beginning to learn a crucial fact about models in general: you should always be aware of how your model differs from the reality it represents.

Extending the model

The remark about planets having moons leads to an interest in adding moons to the model. On another day, the class decides to use miniature marshmallows and toothpicks to represent the moons of the various planets. From their research, the students learn that Mercury and Venus have no moons, but Jupiter and Saturn have more than fifteen moons each, and scientists are still discovering new moons in the solar system. This activity generates further questions. For example, one group wonders if the mini-marshmallow moons are on a similar scale to the planets. They do some research on the Earth's moon and the moons of Jupiter, and they realize that a regular-size marshmallow would be a better model for our moon, which is about one-fifth the size of the apple Earth.

To conclude the lesson, Mr. Johnston asks the students to observe their models closely, think about what they have learned, and write their conclusions in their science journals. He asks them to be sure to answer these questions:

Mr. Johnston's questions

What planets seem similar in size to one another?

What planets are Earth's neighbors in the solar system?

What place in the solar system is the Earth in order of distance from the sun? In order of size?

The students finish the session by eating their favorite parts of the model.

EXPANDING MEANINGS

■ The Teaching Ideas Behind This Story

- ■ Inviting the students to generate their own questions about the solar system is a first step toward giving them ownership of the process of gathering the data.

- ■ Notice how Mr. Johnston encourages students to discover both the accuracies of their model and its limitations.

- ■ This experience of gathering data and creating an edible solar-system model is directed toward students in fourth grade and higher. You can adapt the activity for students in earlier grades. Instead of numerical data, you can use precut circles to represent the relative sizes of the planets. Students can select their fruits and vegetables using these circles as their data. In the younger grades, each astronomical unit becomes one "giant step."

- ■ It is the teacher's job to select a variety of fruits and vegetables that work as models. Using your data, choose carefully. Obviously fruits are not of uniform size, so your selections will be based on the season and the fruits that are available where you live.

- ■ You can think of model building as a step toward model manipulation, which itself leads to further research, more model building, and deeper understanding.

● The Science Ideas Behind This Story

- ● Our **solar system** is made up of a group of heavenly bodies that move around the sun. The main members of the solar system are the nine **planets.** If you cannot take your students outside as Mr. Johnston did, you can use Table 9.2 to construct a model of planetary distances inside the classroom.

TABLE 9.2	Relative Planetary Distances Expressed in Units Suitable for a Classroom Model
Planet	**Distance from the Point Representing the Sun**
Mercury	1.75 inches
Venus	3.25 inches
Earth	4.75 inches
Mars	7.0 inches
Jupiter	2 feet
Saturn	3 feet, 8 inches
Uranus	7 feet, 5 Inches
Neptune	11 feet, 8 inches
Pluto	15 feet, 3 inches

- Between Mars and Jupiter is a belt of several thousand **asteroids** of different sizes. These are like tiny chunks of planet, and they also move around the sun.

- The sun is the only member of the solar system that is a star.

- **Stars** shine by producing their own light.

- Planets shine by reflecting the light of the sun or of other stars.

- All planets travel in their own **orbits** (closed paths) around the sun, moving counterclockwise around the sun, from west to east.

- The solar system is an obvious example of materials that we cannot manipulate directly. While some objects in the sky may be directly observed, students will need to research most parts of the solar system in libraries or on the Internet. See the chapter "Science Content and Curriculum" for a more detailed description of the solar system and the motion of objects around the sun.

✔ The Science Standards Behind This Story

STANDARDS ☑   The story of Mr. Johnston's class illustrates the guidelines of *Content Standard D (Earth and Space Science) for Grades 5–8* in the National Science Education Standards. This standard states, in part, "As a result of their activities in grades 5–8, all students should develop an understanding of . . . Earth in the solar system" (National Research Council, 1996, p. 158). The fundamental concepts underlying the standard include the following:

> ✔ "The Earth is the third planet from the sun in a system that includes the moon, the sun, eight other planets and their moons, and smaller objects, such as asteroids and comets. The sun, an average star, is the central and largest body in the solar system" (p. 160).

By working with their edible solar-system model, Mr. Johnston's students learn this concept and much more.

Mr. Johnston's class also illustrates part of *Content Standard A (Science as Inquiry)*, which refers to "understandings about scientific inquiry" (p. 143). The underlying abilities for this standard include designing an investigation, gathering data, and making models (p. 145), all of which Mr. Johnston's students accomplish. The students are also developing the following fundamental understanding about the nature of scientific inquiry (p. 148):

> ✔ "Different kinds of questions suggest different kinds of scientific investigations. Some investigations involve . . . seeking more information . . . and some involve making models."

Questions for Further Exploration

■ What other round objects with diverse colors and textures could model the solar system?

■ Suppose you could not find a large pumpkin. What else could you use to model the sun?

■ What materials could represent the belt of asteroids?

■ How does the sun make its own light?

Resources for Further Exploration

ELECTRONIC RESOURCES

Arnett, Bill. *The Nine Planets: A Multimedia Tour of the Solar System.* http://seds.lpl.arizona.edu/nineplanets/nineplanets/.   Excellent for students, this site describes the current knowledge about each of the planets and moons in our solar system.

Ask Jeeves.   http://www.ask.com/.   This web site is an excellent search engine for many types of questions. If you ask, for instance, "What are the characteristics of the solar system?" many relevant web sites appear.

The Best of the Hubble Space Telescope.   http://www.seds.org/hst/.   This wonderful selection of images from the Hubble Space Telescope may inspire students to develop questions of their own.

PRINT RESOURCES

Council for Elementary Science International. (CESI). (1991). *Water Stones and Fossil Bones.* CESI Sourcebook VI. Washington, DC: National Science Teachers Association and CESI. This volume contains fifty-one illustrated science activities by many authors including a model solar system in clarity that is an extension of the edible model.

Sutter, D., Sneider, C., & Gould, A. (1993). *The Moons of Jupiter.* GEMS series. Berkeley, CA: Lawrence Hall of Science. Another fine series of suggested lessons from GEMS. In these, students are introduced to the work of Galileo and other astronomers. Students create a scale model of Jupiter using their schoolyard, and they explore photographs of Jupiter's moons taken by the *Voyager* spacecraft.

Models and Meaning

I have often built an edible solar system with elementary school students, and they tend to remember the project for years to come. The first time was in my daughter's third-grade class. At her high school graduation, a former third-grade classmate of hers greeted me and said, "I remember when you visited our class and the pumpkin was the sun."

From model to meaning

The fruits and vegetables make a very useful model for all students, especially for those who need to work with concrete objects to shape comparisons and interpret data. But remember that the construction of this model was not an end in itself. It was a step toward developing a meaningful understanding of the objects in the solar system. In Mr. Johnston's class, manipulating the materials generated further research, as when one group wondered about the sizes of moons and decided to research the topic.

Preparing for future learning

Making a model and interpreting data based on the model, exploring comparisons between the model and the real object, moving the model as though it were the real thing—these types of activities have important implications for future learning. Besides facilitating the understanding of abstract concepts, the use of models helps to prepare students for the science concepts they will encounter in later grades. For example, balancing chemical equations involves using chemical symbols and a mathematical process to model the actions of real atoms and molecules.

In the next science story, Mr. Johnston's fifth graders explore the properties of the planets' orbital paths around the sun. This lesson requires another type of model making.

SCIENCE STORY

A Model Orbit

The setup

On another day, Mr. Johnston distributes string, pencils, centimeter rulers, and pushpins to the class. He asks the students to work with a partner and explains that they are going to draw a shape that represents the path of planets around the sun.

First, he has each pair of students tie a loop with a string about 30 centimeters long. Then he invites them to insert two pushpins toward the middle of one of their journal pages, placing them about 8 centimeters apart and making sure the pins go through several pages. The pins should be anchored securely, Mr. Johnston explains. He goes around the room and supervises as each pair of students sets up the pushpins.

The experiment

Now the students are ready to proceed. They place the loop of string over the pushpins. Then, anchoring a pencil in the loop and keeping the loop taut, they trace a figure that resembles an oval (see Figure 9.2). Each team of students compares its shape with those drawn by others. Indeed, the shape is always oval, no matter who draws it.

New terms— why doesn't the teacher define them?

Mr. Johnston tells them that another word for this oval shape is **ellipse,** and he asks them to label the two points where they inserted their pushpins the **foci** of the ellipse. "In what way is this image different from a circle?" he then asks.

The students say that "you can draw a circle with just one pushpin." Also, they remark, a circle has a center, but the oval does not have one center. Mr. Johnston explains that the planets travel in an elliptical orbit around the sun. We can think of the sun, he says, as being located at one of the foci of the ellipse.

FIGURE 9.2

Drawing an ellipse (oval) with a pencil, string, and two pushpins.

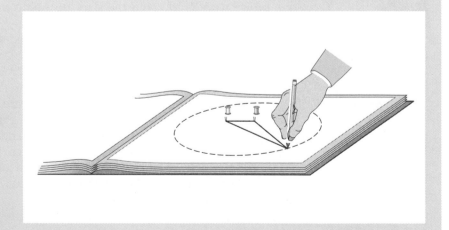

*Modifying
variables*

Mr. Johnston has also hung three large and thick pieces of white foam board from hooks at the top of the chalkboard. Each piece is about 1 meter square. He invites students to come up and place pushpins at different points on the foam board. Then he suggests that the students use string loops of varying lengths to determine in what ways the shape of the ellipse changes when the length of the string and the distance between the foci change. (For safety, Mr. Johnston distributes the pins only when the students come up to the board.)

"Be sure to measure the distance between the pins and the length of the string you use in centimeters," he reminds the students. "Record your data in your science journals." He watches as the students draw their different ellipses on the foam boards.

> *Mr. Johnston's thinking: Mr. Johnston knows that the students' new pencil tracings will change in shape as the length of the string and the distances between the pins increase. The challenge for the students will be to make the leap from these pencil images to the changes in the orbital path of a planet when its distance from the sun increases.*

*The students'
observations*

The students do notice how exaggerated the elliptical shape becomes as they increase the distance between the pins. Mr. Johnston suggests that they keep the distance between the two pushpins constant, changing only the length of the string, and they try the experiment in that way.

"Now, let's imagine that any one of these ellipses represents the orbital path of the Earth around the sun," Mr. Johnston suggests. He labels

*Exploring features
of the model*

one of the foci with an "*S*," for the sun. "Let's draw a line that represents the distance from the sun to the point on the ellipse where the Earth would be closest to the sun, and a line to the point on the ellipse where the Earth would be farthest from the sun." Mr. Johnston draws the lines with a ruler as the students watch.

> *Mr. Johnston's thinking: Since the orbital paths of the planets are ellipses, there must always be a point where a planet is closest to the sun and another point when it is farthest from the sun. Mr. Johnston is hoping that the students will see this.*

*Extending
the research*

Next, Mr. Johnston has the students observe pictures and drawings of the solar system from resource books and the Internet. Using these resources as well as their own drawings of the ellipses, the students make inferences about the time it takes for each planet to travel once around the sun. They reason that Pluto's journey must be the longest and Mercury's the shortest.

EXPANDING MEANINGS

■ The Teaching Ideas Behind This Story

- ■ Notice how Mr. Johnston engages the students in drawing first the ellipses of the same size and then ones of all different sizes.

- ■ Mr. Johnston offers labels for their images without precisely defining the terms *ellipse* and *foci*. The students will develop those definitions from their experience of drawing their figures.

- ■ Mr. Johnston uses each opportunity to extend the students' thinking about the solar system. The ellipse drawings become a springboard for further research about the time it takes for planets to complete each revolution around the sun.

● The Science Ideas Behind This Story

- ● A **satellite** is any heavenly body that travels around another heavenly body. The planets are satellites of the sun. The moon is a satellite of the earth.

- ● The planets' orbits around the sun are elliptical (oval shaped).

- ● An ellipse has no center. It has two foci or focus points. The sun is located in space at one focus of the planetary ellipses.

- ● The point in a planet's orbit when it is closest to the sun is called its **perihelion.**

- ● The point in a planet's orbit when it is farthest from the sun is called its **aphelion.**

- ● The time needed for a planet to make one complete turn or revolution around the sun is called its **year.**

✔ The Science Standards Behind This Story

STANDARDS As they investigate planetary orbits, Mr. Johnston's students continue to develop understandings that are related to *Content Standard D for Grades 5–8* in the National Science Education Standards. Now, though, another fundamental underlying concept comes into play:

- ✔ "Most objects in the solar system are in regular and predictable motion. Those motions explain such phenomena as the day, the year, phases of the moon, and eclipses" (National Research Council, 1996, p. 160).

- ✔ As the students draw their ellipses, they gain insight into the paths of the planets as they move around the sun.

Questions for Further Exploration

■ What is the difference between a center and a focus?

■ What are some implications of the planets' changing distances as they orbit the sun?

■ Do you think planets travel at uniform speed in their orbits?

■ If you were a Martian, how old would you be? That is, what is your age in Mars years?

Resources for Further Exploration

ELECTRONIC RESOURCES

NASA Quest.   http://quest.arc.nasa.gov/.   Sponsored by the National Aeronautics and Space Administration (NASA), this site provides links to online interactive projects, including opportunities for students to explore a multitude of topics and learn about the scientists and others who are involved in NASA's space missions.

NASA Spacelink.   http://www.spacelink.nasa.gov/.   This NASA site describes space-travel projects and more, with excellent graphics and links to instructional materials.

PRINT RESOURCES

VanCleave, J. P. (1991). *Astronomy for Every Kid*. New York: Wiley. The wonderful activities in this book address different properties of the planets, planetary motion, and the moon.

Whitney, D. (1995). The case of the misplaced planets. *Science and Children*, 32(5):12–14. Whitney, a fourth-grade teacher, tells of his discovery that, given a 3-meter sun, his students' scale model of the solar system required that some planets to be placed outside their town.

 SCIENCE STORY

Shapes of the Moon

In the early autumn, the students in a sixth-grade class in rural Maine have been exploring models of the solar system. They have shown an interest in learning how the moon, the Earth's satellite, appears different at different times of the month. One day their teacher, Ms. Hogan, tells them that each of them will begin keeping a *moon-phase journal*. It will give them an opportunity to observe part of the solar system directly, outside the classroom.

In this journal, she explains, they should record their observations of the moon over a period of six weeks. She gives them these general instructions:

■ Search the sky on a daily basis.

■ Keep daily records of your attempts to see the moon—whether you see it or not.

■ When you do see it, include the following things in your journal:

(a) A description or drawing of what you saw.

(b) The time and the date.

(c) What you were doing at the time.

(d) Anything else you want to write down.

■ Become more aware of when the moon is visible in the sky.

■ Watch for changes in the moon's apparent shape, and try to figure out the sequence of these changes.

> ***Ms. Hogan's thinking:*** *Ms. Hogan believes the students can best learn about the moon's phases through direct research. But she wants to leave the precise format of the moon-phase journal open for the students themselves to decide. This open format, she thinks, will be especially useful for students who express themselves better through drawing than they do verbally.*

Over the next six weeks, the students observe the sky and record their data in both words and pictures. Once a week, Ms. Hogan checks their progress and inquires about any difficulties they may be having. At the end of the six weeks, she asks them to bring their journals to class so they can share their observations.

Excited, they arrive in the morning to find large sheets of paper taped to the chalkboards in the room. On each sheet a heading reads, "WHAT WE FOUND OUT ABOUT THE MOON." The students take markers and begin filling in the sheets with their observations, discussing them as they do so.

> ***Ms. Hogan's thinking:*** *There are many ways to encourage the students to share their observations. Ms. Hogan thinks that this method will allow students who are not always comfortable speaking publicly to display their work.*

Here are some of the observations that the students write down for the class to see (reprinted by permission):

■ Sometimes, when the moon is rising or setting, it looks yellowish or even orange.

■ The moon looks bigger when it is rising or setting than when it is high in the sky.

- You can see the moon in the early morning and the late afternoon at some times of the month.

- You can't see the moon when the sky is very bright in the middle of the day.

- Sometimes you can see a very pale full moon in the sky early in the morning.

- Sometimes, when there is a crescent moon   appearing as a sliver in the sky—you can see the rest of the moon faintly lighted.

- As the crescent moon gets bigger, you can see a half-circle moon in the sky.

- The moon gets bigger as you watch it until it gets to a whole circle—a full moon.

- The moon gets smaller each night after the full moon.

- When the moon is almost full, it is bulging on one side. Then when it starts getting smaller, it is bulging on the other side.

- As the full moon keeps getting smaller, you can see a half-circle moon again in the sky.

- Soon, this half-circle moon looks like a crescent again.

- Sometimes you can only see the moon during the daytime.

Modeling the Moon Phases

In Ms. Hogan's class the moon-phase journals are not the end of the project. The next step is for the students to construct a model of the moon's phases. They use a volleyball to represent the moon, and they darken the room before they start.

Moving from observation to model

Ellen stands in the center of a large space, representing the planet Earth. Patrick, holding the volleyball, walks around Ellen, keeping the same side of the volleyball facing her at all times. Johanna, representing the sun, stands to one side of the moon-earth system with a strong flashlight, which she shines at the volleyball. As the volleyball reflects the light from the flashlight, these science ideas emerge:

Emerging ideas

- You can light only half the volleyball (moon) at one time because it is a sphere.

- As it moves around the Earth, only part of that lit half is visible from the Earth.

- The moon rotates once as it revolves once around the Earth.

- The same side of the moon is always facing the Earth.

- Different parts of that side of the moon receive light at different times in its journey.

- The shapes of the moon that we see in the sky are called *phases.*

- When we see the full moon, the entire side of the moon that faces the Earth is reflecting light.

New questions

By this time, the moon-phase journal and the following activity have led the students to formulate new questions. They wonder, for instance, about the yellow-orange color of a rising or setting moon; about the "halo" that sometimes appears around the moon; and why the moon appears bigger when it is low in the sky. These are complex issues, and the students explore them in resource books and on the Internet.

EXPANDING MEANINGS

■ The Teaching Ideas Behind This Story

- Giving students more than a month for the project allows them to observe the moon phases repeating themselves. Besides leading to better understanding of the moon, this process helps the students give meaning to the notion of cycles in other natural processes and in their own lives.

- Although Ms. Hogan hopes the students will understand that the moon's phases repeat and are predictable, she does not give them this information in advance.

- The information the students gain from keeping a moon-phase journal makes it possible to construct the volleyball model of moon phases in the classroom. Thus, like Mr. Johnston's edible solar system, the journal is not just an end in itself, but also the basis for further explorations.

● The Science Ideas Behind This Story

- Like the planets, the moon is visible because it reflects the sun's light. In other words, the light from the sun radiating outward in space in all directions bounces off the surface of the moon.

- The moon appears to have different shapes in the sky as it revolves around the Earth. These different shapes are called **phases of the moon** (see Figure 9.3).

- It takes twenty-nine days for the moon to progress from one full moon to the next. This is the time it takes the moon to make one revolution of the Earth, and it is the same as the time it takes the moon to spin (rotate) once on its axis. Because the moon rotates once as it revolves, we see only one side of the moon from Earth.

FIGURE 9.3
The phases of the moon in the northern hemisphere.
Beginning with a new moon, when the side of the moon facing the Earth is entirely dark and invisible, the moon waxes (appears to grow) until full moon, when we see it as a fully lit circle. Then the moon wanes (appears to diminish), passing through phases that are mirror images of the earlier ones.

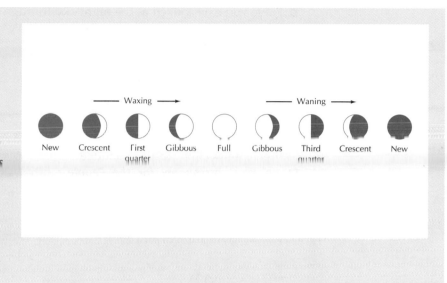

- As the moon moves around the Earth, different portions of its lighted side are visible on Earth because of the moon's position relative to the sun and the Earth.

- As the moon appears to get bigger in its progress toward a full moon, we say it is *waxing*. As it appears to get smaller after the full moon, we say it is *waning*.

✔ The Science Standards Behind These Stories

STANDARDS ✔ As in this chapter's earlier science stories, the students in Ms. Hogan's class are developing understandings related to the National Science Education Standards' *Content Standard D*, concerning the nature of the solar system (National Research Council, 1996, pp. 158–161). The students' moon-phase journals and subsequent activity in class are also good illustrations of *Content Standard A (Science as Inquiry) for Grades 5–8*. A fundamental ability that underlies the science-as-inquiry standard is expressed in this way:

✔ "[Students should be able to] develop descriptions, explanations, predictions, and models using evidence" (p. 145).

Questions for Further Exploration

■ What other types of objects could be used to model moon phases in the classroom?

■ What do you think is meant by "earthshine"?

■ Have you ever looked at the night sky through strong binoculars or a telescope? What kinds of details do you think you would see that are not observable with the naked eye?

Resources for Further Exploration

ELECTRONIC RESOURCES

Sky & Telescope. http://www.skyandtelescope.com/.   This site has current information on eclipses, comets, and other celestial events. Photos and timely news clips are also included.

Stone, Wes. *Astronomy for the People.*   http://skytour.homestead.com/. The wonderful "skytour" at this site offers pages devoted to the moon and its phases, including rich explanations of "earthshine," eclipses, and more. The site also has a section on planets that explores Mercury, Venus, Mars, Jupiter, and Saturn and their visibility in the night sky.

PRINT RESOURCE

Sneider, C. (1986). *Earth, Moon and Stars.* GEMS series. Berkeley, CA: Lawrence Hall of Science. This activity book was developed for grades 5 through 9 to explore astronomy models and simulations, including moon phases and eclipses.

Phases of the Moon: Another Perspective

I observe the moon wherever I go. What phase is it in, I wonder? When will it reach the full moon phase?

Now imagine what happened to me recently when I was teaching in Australia, 12,000 miles from home. Shortly after my arrival, seeing that the skies were cloudy, I checked the newspaper for a weather report. Typically, the weather page also gives times for sunrise and sunset as well as moonrise and moonset.

Picture my surprise when I discovered that the illustrations in the newspaper were, by my experience, wrong. The waxing moon appeared to be illuminated on the left side rather than the right side as I had always known it to be (see Figure 9.3). "I must call the newspaper," I thought. But I continued to study the images in the newspaper and then consulted a globe. When I imagined myself standing on a spot in the southern hemisphere, the answer came to me. Here, indeed, south of the equator, the waxing moon appears to be on the left. Try this in your imagination, and you will see it, too.

The point is that often we do not see things as they are. Instead, we see things as *we* are. That is why it is necessary in science to have many people making many observations of the same phenomenon. I am sure that to people in Australia, the moon in North America would seem strange as well.

Using Moon-Phase Journals

Keeping a moon-phase journal has many similarities with keeping a science journal. As we noticed earlier in this book, "journaling" invites students to observe nature in some way and then reflect on their observations. The moon-phase journal is most appropriate for students in fifth grade or higher, since this exercise requires that they be outside frequently at night. Although on some nights they may be able to see the moon through a window, it is important to alert families to this project and to licit their support and cooperation.

Recording both successful and unsuccessful experiences

During some parts of the month, the moon may not appear until after the students' bedtimes. Weather can also interfere with viewing. To keep the students from feeling frustrated, it helps to ask them, as Ms. Hogan did, to record all of their experiences, even the unsuccessful ones. And because the moon's period of revolution is about four weeks, it is important to define the project's time period as longer than four weeks; five or six weeks is a good idea so students can observe the repetition of the cycle.

It is my experience that students of all ages, from fifth grade up, take pride in their moon-phase journals. I have even used this project in my teacher education classes, where the preservice teachers become equally enthusiastic about the project. I explain that I hope the experience will enhance their confidence in their abilities to observe. I also make a point of giving them the freedom to express and present their observations in any way they choose. "Think of the task as an adventure," I tell my students. "What can you find out about the moon simply by observing it on a regular basis?" Many are astonished to realize that just by looking closely, they can discover a great deal about a natural object that they have seen all of their lives.

Think of the task as an adventure, I tell my students.
—Janice Koch

Sharing journals

When students bring their moon-phase journals to class, I find it useful to have them share the journals with each other before recording their observations. As they review and discuss all the information they have gathered after weeks of keeping a journal, the science ideas really begin to emerge.

Revealing hidden talents

If you start a moon journaling project with your students, you'll also find it offers one other advantage. It will allow you to learn about some of your students' hidden talents. The artists and the poets in particular will have an opportunity to show their creativity.

KEY TERMS

model *(p. 202)*
solar system *(p. 208)*
planet *(p. 208)*
asteroid *(p. 209)*
star *(p. 209)*
orbit *(p. 209)*

ellipse *(p. 212)*
focus (*plural* foci) *(p. 212)*
satellite *(p. 214)*
perihelion *(p. 214)*
aphelion *(p. 214)*
year *(p. 214)*
phases of the moon *(p. 218)*

Expanding the Science "Box"

Explorations of Electricity and Atoms

10

Energy is a fundamental concept in the study of science. People often use the word *energy* in daily conversation when they refer to not having enough energy or turning off the light to save energy. Yet, in spite of this ready connection to everyday life, energy remains an abstract concept for students because it is not a concrete substance with easily measurable properties, such as matter.

Energy exists in many forms, and comprehending that one form of energy may be transformed into another requires a high level of understanding. Elementary school students typically explore four forms of energy: sound, light, heat, and electricity. Their understanding deepens gradually as their exposure to these concepts increases, until by middle and secondary school students can deal with the fairly abstract concepts of energy measurement and transformation. Some of the scientific concepts that underlie the study of sound, light, heat, and electricity are discussed in the chapter "Science Content and Curriculum."

Since energy is such a complicated science idea, you probably think that many students develop alternative conceptions about it. You're right, as you'll see when you read the stories that follow. But this chapter also focuses on another type of alternative conception— one that exists in science education itself. It is found among teachers, administrators, creators of curriculum materials, and many others.

FOCUSING QUESTIONS

- Have you ever explored the inside of a flashlight?
- Does your home have fuses or circuit breakers?
- Why does faulty electrical wiring cause fires?
- How many atoms can fit on the period at the end of one of these sentences?

In the first two stories, we examine the ways in which two fourth-grade classes explore the beginning of a unit on electricity. Both teachers have been given a typical science "box," that is, a kit of materials to use with their students. The kit has arrived complete with specific instructions for the teacher and little booklets for the students. As you read, think about the nature of scientific activity in these two classes. Look for moments when true inquiry is taking place. Ask yourself what kind of alternative conception about science *education* is evident in one or both of these classrooms.

 SCIENCE STORY

Batteries, Bulbs, and Wires

L et's visit Ms. Stone's fourth-grade classroom in a midwestern suburb. The students are about to begin a unit on electricity, and Ms. Stone is excited. The school district has just received several electricity kits from a commercial manufacturer. Ms. Stone is pleased that she can use these new materials to teach the unit on electricity.

Ms. Stone's careful preparation

The night before the unit begins, she reads the kit's "Instructions to the Teacher" and prepares her lesson. When she examines the contents of the science kit, she finds packages of D-cell batteries, battery holders, small 1.5-volt bulbs that look like flashlight bulbs, holders for the bulbs, and spools of thin wire labeled "bell wire." The kit also includes several wire strippers and switches. Following the directions in the kit, Ms. Stone cuts 30-centimeter strips of bell wire and uses the wire strippers to remove the plastic insulation from the ends of each strip. With small self-sticking letters, she then labels one end of each wire strip "A" and the opposite end "B."

The next morning she explains to the students that they are going to begin the electricity unit. But first, they need some definitions. She has arrived early to write three definitions on the blackboard, which she now asks the students to copy into their notebooks:

Ms. Stone's definitions

An electric circuit is a continuous pathway for an electric charge or current to follow.

A *series circuit* is a simple circuit in which the flow of electricity has only one path.

A parallel circuit is a circuit where the flow of electricity has more than one path from the same power source.

Ms. Stone reads the definitions aloud and goes over the words. Quietly the students copy these terms into their notebooks.

Do you agree with Ms. Stone's thinking?

Ms. Stone's thinking: *Ms. Stone believes that the students need the vocabulary in order to carry out the investigation meaningfully. She* *believes in giving the meanings up front, before the students begin the exploration.*

Ms. Stone asks the students to divide into groups of four. Each group, she explains, will get four bulbs, two batteries, four bulb holders, and two battery holders. Also each group will receive seven stripped wires, each 30 centimeters long, with the ends labeled "A" and "B." One end of each battery holder is labeled "B," and the other end is labeled "A." She explains to the students that they are *not* to touch the materials until she gives them instructions.

Each group's materials

When all the materials are distributed, Ms. Stone begins. "Now, will one person in the group take the batteries and place them in the battery holders? Next, another person should gently screw each bulb into the bulb holders."

The students do as they are instructed. Then Ms. Stone continues, "Does everyone see that one end of the battery holder is marked A and one end of the wire is marked A? Okay, take turns as we follow the next steps. Attach the end of the wire marked A to the end of the battery holder marked A by putting the wire through the loop and twisting to make good contact. Now repeat what you just did with another wire, only this time take the end marked B and loop it through the end of the battery holder marked B.

Thorough instructions

"Now you should have one battery that has two wires coming from it, one from each end," says Ms. Stone as she holds up a sample of what she means. The students are fidgety, especially those who are not working directly with the materials at that moment.

Why are the students restless?

"The next thing we are going to do," Ms. Stone continues, "is to connect the end of the wire that has a B on it to one side of one of the bulb holders. . . . Then take another wire and connect the end marked A to the other end of that bulb holder. . . . Now take the end of that wire marked B and connect it to a second bulb holder. . . . Then take the A end of the other wire that is attached to the battery, and connect it to the other side of the second bulb holder."

Ms. Stone talks slowly and waits for the students to complete each step before proceeding with the next step. Finally, the bulbs light!

Success?

Ms. Stone's thinking: Ms. Stone is pleased that the students have followed the directions well. She notices that every group's bulbs worked.

"Okay," says Ms. Stone. "You have made a simple series circuit. Let's look at the definition on the board." The students listen as Ms. Stone reads the definition again. They are instructed to draw their series circuit and label it in their notebooks.

After Ms. Stone checks their drawings, she continues: "Now we are going to make a parallel circuit. This is a little more difficult, so you have to listen carefully." She proceeds in the same manner with direct, step-by-step

Different circuit,
similar procedure

instructions, which the students follow until the bulbs light. Once more, all the groups get the same result.

"This is called a parallel circuit," Ms. Stone explains. Together, she and the class read over the definition of a parallel circuit.

"Tomorrow," Ms. Stone tells the students, "we will use our series circuit to test for materials that carry electricity."

SCIENCE STORY

Batteries, Bulbs, and Wires Revisited

Extra materials

Ms. Travis is a fourth-grade teacher in another school in the same school district. She is working with the same materials as Ms. Stone—with one difference. She has requested funds from the fourth-grade science budget to purchase twelve flashlights and twenty-four C batteries, two per flashlight. She assembles all of the flashlights with their batteries. When the students enter the room the following morning, she invites them to form science groups of four.

A pound
of electricity?

Before starting the activity, however, Ms. Travis asks the students what they would purchase if she asked them to go to the supermarket and pick up a pound of electricity. The students call out different answers. One student says she would buy a pound of light bulbs. Another says he would buy a pound of batteries. Ms. Travis listens and asks them why they made those choices. "Is it the same to say that light bulbs *are* electricity," she wonders aloud, "as it is to say that light bulbs *work on* electricity?"

Bringing out
prior ideas

> *Ms. Travis's thinking:* Ms. Travis knows that students often think of the materials that produce or carry electricity as being the electricity itself. This alternative conception is common because electricity, a form of energy, does not have mass or volume like matter. Ms. Travis is trying to bring out prior ideas of this sort as the students begin the electricity unit.

The students listen carefully to Ms. Travis's question. One student remarks that you can't really buy a pound of electricity because it isn't a real thing. Ms. Travis prompts, "Can you say more about that?"

"Well," the student continues, "you can't really hold electricity in your hand, but it can give you a shock." Ms. Travis invites others to think about that.

She then shares the following idea: "We know that anything that has mass and takes up space is matter. So if electricity is not matter, what is it?" This class knows she means "energy" because they have spent weeks studying heat energy. But it is important to Ms. Travis to remind the students again that energy is more difficult to grasp than matter because we cannot hold it in our hands.

Beginning
an activity

Now they are ready to begin the activity. She explains that she would like them to explore some flashlights. "Take these flashlights apart; take out the inside parts," she requests as she distributes two flashlights to each group of four students. "It is better to work with one partner for this exploration," she adds. "How many of you have opened and explored flashlights before?" About half the students raise their hands.

"Girls and boys, you will notice that the top unscrews and then several pieces come out, including the bulb. Sometimes those pieces fall out, so be careful not to hold the flashlight too high. As you and your partner examine the insides of the flashlight, draw and label the parts in your science journal."

A challenge
to the students

The students take apart the flashlights and make rough drawings in their journals. Then Ms. Travis distributes strips of bell wire, one to each pair of students. "Let's see if you can use this wire, with one of the batteries and the bulb you have found, to get the bulb to light. Before you begin, let's look at these tools."

She holds up the wire strippers. "Where have you seen these before?" Some students recognize the wire strippers from tool kits they have at home. "Why are they important for our experiment?" Ms. Travis asks. Some students, who have prior knowledge about stripping wire, offer answers. Ms. Travis distributes the wire strippers and suggests that the students use them to bare the ends of their wires.

Suggestion—but
no instructions?

Ms. Travis's thinking: Ms. Travis wants her students to learn by doing. However, she knows that the battery, bulb, and strip of wire will be cumbersome to manipulate, and she doesn't want the students to get so frustrated by lack of success that they lose interest. Thus she suggests that they strip the ends of their wire, giving them a better opportunity to solve the problem.

Some efforts
succeed; others fail

The groups of students make several attempts before finding the ways that work. Most groups discover that the bulb will light if one end of the wire is wrapped around the bottom of the bulb and touching one end of the battery, while the other end of the wire is touching the other end of the battery. One group of students succeeds by stripping a portion of the center of the wire, wrapping that portion around the tiny bulb, and then touching either end of the battery with the free ends of the wire.

Students visit each other and try several ways to get the bulb to light. Ms. Travis asks them to draw the ways that work *and* the ways that do not work.

Another
proposal

She then proposes that the students use *both* flashlight batteries and the wire to light the bulb. Manipulating the two batteries and one wire is tricky. But when they finally manage to get the bulb to light, they notice it is much brighter than it was with only one battery.

Journal
writing

Opening the
kit at last

Some objects
familiar, others not

A problem
to solve

Ms. Travis asks the students to reassemble their flashlights, turn them on, and compare the light from the flashlight with the light that they have just created with the two batteries outside of the flashlight. The students notice that the brightness seems to be identical.

For homework, she asks them to write what they have done this morning in their science journals and to list some of the "rules" they have discovered for getting their bulb to light, first with one and then with two batteries.

The next morning, Ms. Travis empties the contents of the science electricity kit on the front table of the classroom. "Let's look at the materials we have to work with here. Can we identify some of them?"

The students recognize the bulbs as looking just like the bulbs in the flashlights. The wire, too, is identical to the wire they used the day before. Although the batteries are somewhat larger, the students have no trouble identifying them as batteries. But this kit also has battery holders and little bulb holders. Some students have seen these before, and others have not.

Ms. Travis says, "Each science group should take two bulbs, two bulb holders, a battery, a battery holder, and 60 centimeters of bell wire to start. You will also need a wire stripper. Our class's problem is this: How can we get both bulbs to light at the same time with as much brightness as possible? Start to explore your materials carefully. Notice how the battery holders and the bulb holders are constructed. Brainstorm with one another about where to attach your wires. Use the rules you developed from last night's homework. Then make a plan with all the members of your group. You will want to try out lots of ideas. Take your time!"

> *Ms. Travis's thinking:* *The students are excited about handling the materials, but Ms. Travis knows that connecting the wires to the bulb holders and the battery holders is sometimes tedious. Planning their procedure beforehand may save the students unnecessary labor. Also the discussions among themselves should help them learn.*

The students
make plans

Additional
suggestions

The students'
solutions

The students gather their materials and develop their plans. Some have a sense of where to go; some ask Ms. Travis where to begin. She offers responses such as, "You may want to screw the bulbs into the bulb holders."

The students start stripping the ends of the wires. The groups are busy and engaged. Walking around the room, Ms. Travis notices varying levels of comfort with the materials. She points things out and makes further suggestions. She reminds one group, "You may have to cut that strip of wire. You may need more than one wire." To the class, she announces that they can have more wire if they need it.

> *Ms. Travis's thinking:* *In walking around the room, Ms. Travis wants to see how the students are thinking. She is hoping that their experience the previous day will help them to construct their own electrical connections using these new materials.*

Most of the groups get the bulbs to light by using three pieces of wire and connecting the first wire from the battery holder to a bulb, the second wire from the first bulb to the second bulb, and the third wire from the sec-

These students are conducting their own investigation with batteries, bulbs, and wires. They are invested in solving their particular problem.

Ellen Senisi/The Image Works

ond bulb back to the battery. They notice that the lights are very dim—much dimmer than when they used one bulb and one battery the day before.

Collaborating on a label and a definition

After applauding their efforts, Ms. Travis begins to provide some labels for what they have created. "Can we label the pathways we have made with these batteries, bulbs, and wires?" she asks. "What do scientists call this type of path?" Some students shout out "circuit," and Ms. Travis writes the word on the chalkboard. Together, she and the students define a circuit as a complete pathway from one end of the battery through the wire and the bulbs to the other end of the battery and through the battery again.

This pathway, she tells them, is a continuous route for tiny charged particles called electrons. "These electrons carry the electric charge through the circuit. All these charged particles flowing along the wire is what is meant by an electric current." On the board, she draws a sketch of the circuit that the students have constructed (see Figure 10.1).

A new question— but no answer

At this point she slips in a new question: "I hope this helps to explain why our bell wire is *coated*. Let's think about that as we work."

> **Ms. Travis's thinking:** *At this point, Ms. Travis wants the students to associate the correct labels with the pathways they have created. She is not interested in brainstorming about the coating on the bell wire at this time; she just wants to plant the seed of this idea, to see if it will germinate as they work with the wire.*

A further challenge

Now Ms. Travis challenges the students to create a circuit that could enable the bulbs to be brighter while both are still lit at the same time. She

FIGURE 10.1
A series circuit with a battery in a battery holder, two bulbs in bulb holders, and three wires.

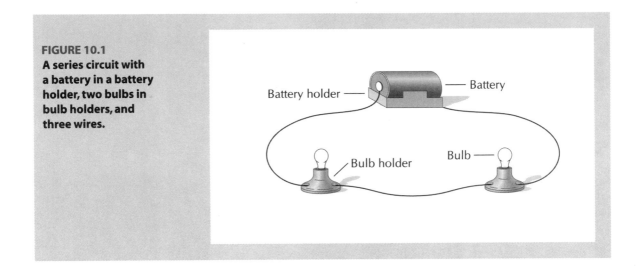

invites them to take more wire if needed. Once again, she circulates among the groups, directing and coaching, probing the students' thinking, and encouraging them when they get frustrated. "You may want to try one bulb at a time," she says to one struggling group. To another group she remarks, "Draw what you have done here. It really seems to work." With yet another group, she invites them to visit a group in the back of the room that has been more successful. All this time, students are trying to figure out how to light two bulbs at once with a single battery without making the bulbs so dim.

Sharing solutions

After a while, Ms. Travis asks one member of each group to come to the board and draw the circuits they have constructed. The solutions that work all involve using four wires and connecting each bulb to the battery independently of the other (see Figure 10.2). The difference in brightness is very noticeable. The two bulbs connected independently of each other are much brighter than the two bulbs that shared the same circuit.

Adding labels—after the circuits are built

"It is time to label the two types of circuits you have made," Ms. Travis tells the class. "In this one"—she points to the drawing she made of their first circuit (resembling Figure 10.1)—"the electric charges travel in a single path, through the battery, the wires, and both bulbs. This is called a *series circuit*. In the second type of circuit that you made"—now she points to their own drawings (resembling Figure 10.2)—"each bulb is connected in its own separate pathway. This is called a *parallel circuit*. Now, let's take some more batteries, bulbs, and wires and set up both of these types at the same time."

The students set up a series and a parallel circuit, with one battery and two bulbs in each. Ms. Travis asks them to find different ways of extinguishing one or both of the bulbs. She then asks the students to write about their findings in their journals.

FIGURE 10.2
A parallel circuit with a battery, two bulbs, and four wires.
Because the bulbs are connected to the battery independently of one another, they will shine brighter than the bulbs in Figure 10.1.

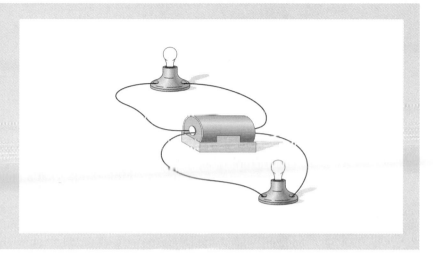

Varying the experiment

After some exploration, the students learn that, in the series circuit, any break in the pathway causes both bulbs to go out. In the parallel circuit, though, each bulb is affected independently, and for both bulbs to go out, there must be a break in each of the separate pathways. Further, in the series circuit, the children notice that when they unscrew one bulb, the other one goes out. In the parallel circuit, when they unscrew one bulb, the other bulb stays on.

Before the morning is over, Ms. Travis asks the students in each group to come up with other questions that they want to investigate. "What are you most dying to find out? List the questions that your experiments with batteries, bulbs, and wires can help you figure out. Make sure that you also list the materials you will need."

Here are some of the students' questions:

The students' own questions

Are the bulbs always brighter in a parallel circuit?

What happens with two batteries in a series circuit? In a parallel circuit?

What happens to the brightness in a series circuit that has three bulbs?

What is a light bulb made of?

What happens when we combine circuits with other groups?

Ms. Travis lists the questions and the name of the child posing it on poster paper in the front of the classroom. The children will be exploring their own questions for many days.

The Next Day: Lighting a Shoebox House

A simple household lighting model

The following day, Ms. Travis brings in a large shoebox that is set up like a room in a little dollhouse. It has cardboard chairs and a little sofa. On one inside wall is a picture of a fireplace. Through a hole in the top of the box, a miniature bulb (like the flashlight bulbs the students have been using) hangs as a ceiling light. On the outside of the box, the bulb holder is connected to two long wires attached to a battery. The light works! Unlike a normal household light, however, this light has no switch, and the students are given time to think about what a switch might look like.

The children love the shoebox room. Ms. Travis now brings out several switches for their circuits, and she invites each group to experiment with circuits and switches. (You may remember that switches were included in the kit of materials that all the fourth-grade teachers in this district received.) How, Ms. Travis asks the students, could they make her shoebox room brighter? They all suggest another bulb, but the question of how to connect the other bulb becomes a point of discussion.

A puzzle based on the model

Ms. Travis then demonstrates the effects of lighting the room with two bulbs in a parallel circuit versus lighting it with the same bulbs in a series circuit (see Figure 10.3). The students immediately notice that the parallel

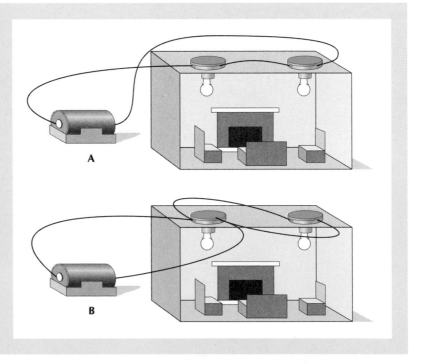

FIGURE 10.3
A shoebox room lighted with two bulbs, (a) in series and (b) in parallel. In which setup are the bulbs brighter?

A

B

circuit makes the room brighter, just as their two bulbs were brighter in the parallel circuit they made the day before.

As the class's electricity investigations continue, Ms. Travis offers a list of questions for the students to answer at home:

Questions to
explore at home

Is your home wired with fuses or with circuit breakers?

Can you ask a parent or guardian to show you the fuses or circuit breakers?

What types of things in your home work on electricity?

Do you have an idea about which appliances in your house may be connected in a series circuit and which ones in a parallel circuit? How could you find out?

In addition to answering these questions at home, the students pursue many interesting activities in the classroom during the following days. Although the groups do not all do the same things at the same times, each group reports its discoveries to the class at large. For example, one group discovers that the more parallel circuits they place on a battery, the faster the battery will burn out. Another group uses a series circuit to make a tester, and they test which materials conduct electricity (see Figure 10.4). Two groups create a series circuit around part of the room. It has four batteries and eight bulbs, and the students demonstrate how all eight bulbs go out when a single bulb is unscrewed. Ms. Travis also engages the students in building things with their circuits. Some students, following the model of the shoebox room, construct a lighted three-room shoebox house. Others make a model flashlight; still others build a blinking lighthouse and a quiz board that has secret circuits.

Whether working
with mandated content
and activities . . . or
creating original
activities, teachers
plan to meet the
particular interests,
knowledge, and skills
of their students and
build on their
questions and ideas.
—NATIONAL SCIENCE
EDUCATION STANDARDS

FIGURE 10.4
A simple
electrical tester.

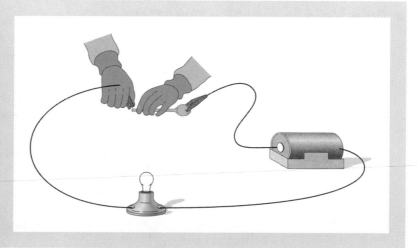

EXPANDING MEANINGS

■ The Teaching Ideas Behind These Stories

- Notice how Ms. Stone gives information at the beginning of the lesson, while Ms. Travis waits until the students have developed some understanding before providing new language.

- Ms. Stone engages students in the exploration of electrical circuits on *her* terms. She controls the activities, the time students spend on each step, and the outcomes they should achieve. Ms. Travis controls much of the experimental design and the initial problem posing, but then gives the students control over procedures and findings.

- Ms. Stone is concerned that everyone "get" all the science ideas from her, at the same time. Ms. Travis is certain that all the science ideas will emerge from the students, pieces at a time. She relies on the reports from the student groups to address ideas that do not emerge from the initial activities.

- Ms. Stone's procedures are lockstep and rigid. There is no room for students' own ideas about how to explore. Ms. Travis, in contrast, allows a diversity of procedures. She thinks such differences are important for learning.

- Ms. Stone does not provide personal connections or a personal context for the electricity unit. Ms. Travis provides such contexts by engaging the students with flashlights, a mock dollhouse room, and questions about their homes' wiring.

- All in all, Ms. Travis's students are likely to learn better and more deeply because they are conducting their own investigations and becoming invested in answering their own questions. They are doing more than just following directions and repeating the teacher's language.

● The Science Ideas Behind These Stories

- **Electricity** is a form of energy. In some respects scientists are still unsure of exactly what electricity is, but the word *electricity* is used to describe a flow of electrons.

- **Electrons** are negatively charged particles that are found in the atoms of all elements. Each tiny electron is thought to be a particle of negative electricity.

- An **electric current** is a flow or motion of electrons. Electric currents in wires are caused by electrons moving along the wire.

- An **electric circuit** is a pathway for a current. A circuit requires some source of electrical power, such as a battery or generator; a pathway for the electrons, such as copper wire; and some appliance that uses electricity, like a light bulb or a bell.

- In a simple electric circuit using a light bulb and a battery, the electrons flow from the negative (flat) end of the battery through the wire to the bottom of the bulb (or the side of a bulb holder), through the filament inside the bulb and out the bottom of the bulb (or the other side of the bulb holder), through the other piece of wire to the positive (bumpy) end of the battery. The current then passes through the interior of the battery to complete the circuit. There is a continuous flow of energy through these devices unless some part of the circuit is stopped or broken—for instance, if a bulb burns out, a wire gets loose, or a battery is used up.

- In a series circuit—the type of simple circuit just described—the electric current has only a single pathway through the circuit. This means that the current passing through each electrical device is the same. Each time an electrical device, like a bulb, is added to the series circuit, the total amount of electrical force must be shared among a greater number of devices. That is why each bulb becomes dimmer when a new bulb is added.

- In contrast, in a **parallel circuit** each device has a separate pathway—its own separate branch of the circuit. Thus, if one bulb goes out, the other bulbs or devices in a parallel circuit are unaffected.

- Each device in a circuit offers a certain amount of *resistance* to the current. In a series circuit, two bulbs present twice the resistance of one bulb. Since the current equals the force divided by the resistance, each bulb gets only half as much current. In a parallel circuit, on the other hand, there is only one bulb per path; therefore, there is less resistance on each path, the current supplied to each bulb is greater, and the bulbs glow more brightly. This also means that the battery will burn out twice as fast, because it is supplying twice as much current as in the series circuit. See the chapter "Science Content and Curriculum" for more information about electrical energy.

✔ The Science Standards Behind These Stories

STANDARDS ✔   Our stories of two fourth-grade classes experimenting with batteries and bulbs illustrate *Content Standard B (Physical Science) for Grades K–4* in the National Science Education Standards: "As a result of the activities in grades K–4, all students should develop an understanding of . . . light, heat, electricity, and magnetism" (National Research Council, 1996, p. 123). The fundamental concepts underlying this standard include the following:

✔ "Electricity in circuits can produce light, heat, sound, and magnetic effects. Electrical circuits require a complete loop [pathway] through which an electrical current can pass" (p. 127).

The activities in Ms. Travis's classroom also illustrate a fundamental concept for *Content Standard A (Science as Inquiry)*:

✔ "Scientific investigations involve asking and answering a question and comparing the answer with what scientists already know about the world" (p. 123).

Note how the students in Ms. Travis's class ask their own questions and seek their own answers.

Questions for Further Exploration

- Explore a small flashlight bulb to see how it lights.

- Why would a house be wired in parallel and not in series circuits?

- In the experiments described in our science stories, why is it important to use bell wire, which is copper wire coated with a plastic sheath?

Resources for Further Exploration

ELECTRONIC RESOURCES

How Do Christmas Lights Work? http://www.cvc.org/christmas/electric_xmas.htm. This site offers easy-to-understand explanations of electricity, the flow of energy, electrons, circuits, and generators.

Theater of Electricity. http://www.mos.org/sln/toe/. Sponsored by the Museum of Science in Boston, this highly electric site offers teacher resources, information about lightning, a safety quiz, and more.

PRINT RESOURCES

Markle, S. (1989). *Power Up: Experiments, Puzzles and Games Exploring Electricity.* New York: Atheneum. A book full of neat ideas to enhance any electricity unit.

National Science Resources Center. (1991). *Electric Circuits.* Science and Technology for Children. Burlington, NC: Carolina Biological Supply Co. Designed for grade 4, this series of activities explores electricity and circuits. The projects include how to wire a cardboard house to light each room. The teacher's guide is useful; the student activity books are not.

Parker, S. (2000). *Eyewitness: Electricity.* New York: DK Publishing. One in a series of books that explore science topics.

Taylor, B. (1998). *Exploring Energy with Toys: Complete Lessons for Grades 4–8.* Middletown, OH: Terrific Science Press. An excellent resource for background information as well as for lesson plans.

VanCleave, J. (1994). *Janice VanCleave's Electricity: Mind-Boggling Experiments You Can Turn into Science Fair Projects.* New York: John Wiley. Describes twenty experiments with electricity and discusses how to create a science fair project.

Thinking About Teaching and Learning

Let's think further about the two teachers whose classrooms we have visited so far in this chapter. Ms. Travis holds out the expectation that her students are knowers, that they have their own ideas, and that they are

*Ms. Travis's
belief system*

capable of constructing and carrying out investigations on their own. This is Ms. Travis's belief system, and it influences her teaching practice. Her teaching is a good example of the principles that this book advocates. She expands the science "box"—both in a literal sense, by letting her students use more materials and explore a wider range of activities than the school-supplied kit allowed, and in a metaphorical sense, by releasing herself and her students from the intellectual confinement of prepackaged instructions.

*Ms. Stone's
belief system*

But what about Ms. Stone? Clearly, Ms. Stone works hard, has respect for her students, and cares deeply about their instruction. She is, however, unwilling to trust that her students can come up on their own with the activities that are neatly laid out, step by step, in the student workbooks in the fourth-grade electricity kit. In Ms. Stone's personal model of teaching, she is the authority in the classroom. She believes that this is what the children require. She believes that they look to her for the right answers and that she is not doing her job unless she provides these answers.

This attitude is not uncommon, and it is not at all ill-intentioned. Well-meaning teachers all over the country believe that students learn only if the teacher tells them what and how to learn.

> *Does a teacher who guides and mediates do less than a teacher who "delivers" instruction?*
> —JANICE KOCH

You may be wondering, "Well, what is teaching if we don't tell students what and how to learn? What is left for us to do?" Think back to our earlier discussions of the teacher as mediator, and consider whether Ms. Travis is really doing *less* than Ms. Stone. And consider all the other science stories in this book that have shown teachers working very hard with their students. I think you'll find that the teacher who guides and mediates learning is doing lots of planning and active listening in ways that are not required of a teacher who merely "delivers" instruction. Also, even though Ms. Travis does not behave like an absolute science authority in the classroom, she is actually taking on a great deal of authority because she assumes the responsibility of constructing the science experiences for her students. It requires a lot of self-reliance—as well as thoughtful consideration—to take a package or kit of materials, discard the prescribed instructions, and ask yourself, "How can I use this kit to create a meaningful learning experience for *my* students?"

Now let's examine how an eighth-grade physical science teacher approaches the study of atoms—a subject that will lead students to consider other concepts related to electrical charges and energy. As you read the following story, ask yourself to what extent the teachers and students are breaking out of the "box." Are they following conventional routines, or are the students taking charge of their own learning?

Making Models of Atoms

Ms. Murray is an eighth-grade teacher in a middle school in a small suburban community. The students in eighth-grade science explore physical science, addressing topics in chemistry and physics. It is the beginning of the school year, and Ms. Murray is concerned because the topic of "atomic structure," which the students will tackle this term, involves very abstract concepts. After researching the best way to introduce concepts related to the structure of the atom, she has decided to explore the history of atomic theory, and then let students use their knowledge about atoms to design and construct models of an atom of a particular element.

Concepts Ms. Murray hopes the students will learn

I am going to be present as a visitor, but before the class begins, I have a chance to ask Ms. Murray what she hopes the students will get out of their unit on atomic structure. She mentions a number of basic concepts about atoms: that an atom is the smallest particle into which an element can be divided and still have all the properties of that element; that an atom is composed of a nucleus and electron clouds; that the atomic nucleus contains protons and neutrons; and so on. But she also hopes, she adds, that "the students will be able to understand the difficulty that scientists had developing the atomic theory, considering that they only had a mental model to work with. I hope they will understand that atomic theory may not be completely correct, and that is why there are always changes to atomic theory over time."

> *My thinking:* I am impressed that Ms. Murray views atomic theory as a fluid, constantly evolving collection of ideas.

As the atomic structure unit begins, Ms. Murray distributes newspaper photos and magnifying lenses. She asks students to make observations of the photos using the magnifiers and record their observations in their science notebooks. After a few minutes she says, "What did you notice?" A few students respond that they saw small dots. "Now try to see the dots without the magnifying lenses." Students say they cannot. Ms. Murray then asks if there are other examples of objects that are made up of small parts that can't be seen with the naked eye. Students' answers are varied. Brian says, "Molecules." Nat says, "Pigments," and another student says, "Atoms." Heather adds, "Cells are another example."

How many atoms in a period?

Ms. Murray now describes atoms as the building blocks of all matter. She explains that just like cells, which are the building blocks of living things, atoms cannot be seen with the naked eye. She then asks students to record the following question in their notebooks and think about an answer: "How many atoms can fit in a period at the end of a sentence?" Immediately, hands fly up. "What size period, one on the blackboard or one on a sheet of paper?" asks one student. Ms. Murray says that their questions are excellent, and she instructs them to think about a period at the end of a sentence printed in a twelve-point font. She suggests that they take out one of the prior handouts to examine the size of the periods.

After a few minutes, Ms. Murray asks for volunteers to offer their responses. Hands again fly up. The answers, which Ms. Murray writes on the board, range from 1 million to 100 trillion. All the students are eager to know the actual answer, so she informs them that there are roughly 1 trillion atoms in a twelve-point period. Wanting them to see the number, she writes it on the board. One student says, "Wow, a *penny* must have a lot of atoms." Ms. Murray gives the number of atoms in a penny in scientific notation by saying, "Yes, there are two times ten to the twenty-fourth power atoms in a penny." She then writes that number on the board as well: 2,000,000,000,000,000,000,000,000. For homework, Ms. Murray asks the students to come up with their own estimates for the number of atoms in other objects smaller than a penny, using the period and the penny as reference points.

Exploring the History of Atomic Theory

How atomic theory developed

The next class begins with six trays of materials set up around the room. Each tray contains information about a different scientist, including various books and cards that list addresses of web sites. Ms. Murray tells the class, "Since atomic theory has been around for over 2,500 years, it will be good to explore its history." The six scientists are Democritus, John Dalton, J. J. Thomson, Ernest Rutherford, Niels Bohr, and Maria Goeppert Mayer. She asks the students to work in research teams. Each team will use one tray of information to design and construct a poster illustrating the following information:

The time period in which the scientist lived

The major discovery the scientist made regarding the atom

Whether the scientist's theory is still accepted

Using its poster as a teaching tool, each group will teach the rest of the class about that scientist and that portion of history. Students get right to work on their projects, and they continue the next day. Ms. Murray visits each group to check its progress and make suggestions.

> *My thinking: It seems that each group of students will become knowledgeable about a specific atomic scientist on their own terms. They will decide what data to include. It will be interesting to see what the work reveals. I am also struck by how Ms. Murray has carefully constructed each group, mixing gender, ability, and ethnicity.*

When the posters are ready, Ms. Murray calls the groups in chronological order, from the earliest scientist to the most recent. As each group presents its scientist, a new piece of the history of atomic theory unfolds. The posters remain on the board in the order of the scientists' discoveries,

A timeline of discoveries

thus creating a colorful timeline of the history of atomic theory. Halfway through the presentations, one student blurts out, "Oh, I get it, the scientists build on each other." Ms. Murray also has the students describe the big ideas that emerged in each period. The students' comments are summarized in Table 10.1.

Ms. Murray then asks the students how many scientists they think actually contributed to the concept of the atom. Several students respond that hundreds did. "Why," says Ms. Murray, "aren't they up on the timeline?" One student answers, "Maybe their discoveries were small, but they made it possible for the big discoveries to be made." Finally, Ms. Murray asks if the atomic theory is 100 percent accurate. The class discusses how the theory has constantly been modified and probably will be modified

TABLE 10.1   Nuclear Theory Chronology as It Emerged in Ms. Murray's Class

Date	Scientist	Experiment or Theory	"Big Idea" of the Time Period
530 B.C.	Democritus	Material is made of atoms that cannot be split into smaller particles.	All matter is made up of atoms, too small to be seen.
1808	John Dalton	All atoms of any element are the same. Atoms of different elements are different.	Modern atomic theory: every element is made of atoms.
1897	J. J. Thomson	Cathode-ray experiments reveal existence of negatively charged particles.	Inside the atom are negatively charged particles called electrons.
1911	Ernest Rutherford	Alpha particle experiments show that atoms have a lot of empty space.	The atom has a positive nucleus, with electrons orbiting around it.
1922	Niels Bohr	Electrons emit energy only when they change energy levels.	Electrons travel in specific orbital "shells" around the nucleus. Each shell represents a discrete energy level.
1963	Maria Goeppert Mayer	"Magic numbers" of nuclear particles suggest a shell model of the nucleus.	Particles in the nucleus are also arranged in "shells." Protons and neutrons exist in pairs in the nucleus, and this arrangement gives different atomic nuclei different degrees of stability.

more in the future. The students are now ready to experiment on their own and create their own mental models.

Explicit talk about the nature of science

My thinking: I am struck by how explicit Ms. Murray is making the nature of science and scientific activity. She also illustrates that as one scientist's work was built on by the next, new ideas replaced older ones, and this took an exceedingly long time. Although many people feel it is important to teach these concepts in middle school, teachers do not always see their relevance. Ms. Murray manages to embed these notions in the discussion of atomic structure.

Mystery Boxes

The following day, students have a double period of science, and they are asked to perform experiments on "mystery boxes" to determine the contents of each box. Ms. Murray wants the students to develop a mental model of something that cannot be seen but can be known through evidence. This process, she hopes, will model the way in which scientists gather data about atomic particles they cannot see.

Identifying what they cannot see

Each pair of students receives a sealed box containing various items. They shake the box, listen, and use all their senses to try to determine the number of objects in the box and the identity of each. (The mystery objects include jacks, keys, marbles, small pencils, erasers, dice, and pennies.) Ms. Murray has the students record their procedures, their reasoning, and their answers. After the students present their results to the class, they open the boxes and are surprised at how many objects they inferred correctly. This success builds their confidence in their abilities to use their senses and their reasoning skills. Ms. Murray and the class then relate the mental models they have made of their boxes to the scientific models that evolved, and are still evolving, about the atom.

Discussing the Nucleus

The following day, Ms. Murray asks the students if they have ever heard the word *nuclear* before. They certainly have. The students mention nuclear fission, nuclear bombs, nuclear power, nuclear warheads, and nuclear power plants. Ms. Murray wonders, "Where do you think the word *nuclear* comes from?" A few students say it comes from the word *nucleus*. One student mentions that a nucleus is in a cell, while others say that it is part of an atom. Together the students review Rutherford's discovery of the nucleus of the atom and some of the other discoveries from their presentations. They talk about the nucleus being within the atom and posi-

Discussing the nucleus

tively charged, very dense, and made up of particles. The students recall that the nucleus is composed of protons and neutrons, and on the basis of the particles' names, they deduce that protons are positively charged and therefore neutrons must be negatively charged. At this point Ms. Murray helps them to explore other ways of interpreting the word *neutron,* and they realize that they can associate it with the word *neutral.* The students then arrive at the (correct) notion that a neutron has no charge.

An atomic puzzle

They go on to discuss what happens when two like charges are near each other. Using magnets as a reference, they conclude that two likes would repel, so Ms. Murray asks them, "What happens in the nucleus? If protons have like charges, wouldn't they repel each other and break apart the nucleus?" She gives the students time to think about this question and to come up with their own theories. Ms. Murray reassures them that she is not interested in the right or wrong answer but in their thoughts. She tells them, "Scientists always come up with theories that may be incorrect or partially true. It is okay if you are not sure." She lets them know that they can draw pictures to help them visualize their ideas, and she gives them ten minutes to prepare their answers.

When the ten minutes are up, Ms. Murray instructs the students to move their chairs into a large circle. She brings out a small beanbag frog and explains the rules of the discussion: you can talk only if you have the beanie frog, and you can throw the frog only to someone who has his or her hand up. In addition, if you can answer only part of the question, it is okay to pass the frog to someone else.

Students discuss their theories

The students toss the frog around and discuss their theories. Kate says that the attraction between the negative charges of the electrons and the positive charges of the protons causes the nucleus to stay together. Brian says that he too considered this idea, but "then I found a flaw with my theory. If the electrons were attracted to the protons," he says, "they would pull the protons away from the nucleus." Isaac has a totally different theory: that perhaps the neutrons prevent the protons from repelling. He imagines the nucleus as a sandwich: proton-neutron-proton. Jamie says that she can understand how the neutrons play that role because there is no other known reason for their existence in the nucleus.

> *My thinking:* Ms. Murray's use of the frog toss to engage students seated in a circle gives students the responsibility for managing their own participation. This is an effective way to get students talking about their theories.

The strong force

Ms. Murray compliments the students on their thinking and then tells them about what scientists call the *strong force,* a force that keeps the nucleus together. This force may derive from the neutrons, but scientists do not yet know exactly how it works. She then invites the students to create their own pictures of what the atom may look like. The students have enough evidence from their historical research to understand that protons and neutrons are in the nucleus and that the electrons move in different ways around the nucleus. When the students have made their drawings, Ms. Murray asks whether there is just one way to draw an atom. The students say no, because no one has ever seen the inside of an atom. She draws a diagram on the board, but explains that this is only one way to draw the atom.

The Periodic Table

Exploring the Periodic Table

The following week, Ms. Murray introduces the class to the Periodic Table of the elements. She shows how the atomic mass and atomic number are associated with each symbol in the table. After she models the element helium by indicating its two protons and two neutrons in the nucleus of the atom, Ms. Murray asks the students where to put the two electrons. The students all appear to understand that the electrons go outside the nucleus. After discussing the electric charge on the protons and the neutrons, Ms. Murray introduces the theory of electron clouds in the following way.

The class reviews what Bohr said about the way electrons move in orbits, and students discuss whether that theory is still accepted. They think not, because they remember hearing about electron "clouds." Ms. Murray then places a fan in front of the room and tells them to keep their eyes on one of the blades. The challenge is to follow that blade when the fan begins to move.

A demonstration to model electron "clouds"

Ms. Murray turns the fan on the low setting, and within a few seconds a voice calls out, "I lost it." I am assisting with the fan, so I ask students if they know roughly where their one blade is. "In that circle," Shana says. Ms. Murray asks, "Does anyone know *exactly* where the blade is?" The class answers, "NO!" She explains, "Just like you kind of know where the blade is, but not exactly, scientists kind of know where electrons are, but not exactly. That is why scientists talk about *electron clouds*." On the board diagram she draws a broad space around the electrons and shades it in. "Scientists think that electrons are somewhere in this area, but they don't know exactly where."

Ms. Murray then asks the students if they have peeled an onion before. Hands shoot up. She takes out an onion and asks whether it will be hard or easy to remove the top layer. "Easy," the class agrees, so she removes it. When she asks about the next layer, the students are a little unsure. She removes that layer, and a few students say the task was a little harder. When she goes on to ask about the third layer, the students say it will be harder to remove, and indeed it is.

Now Ms. Murray makes an analogy between the onion layers and electrons in the atom. The class spends a good deal of time discussing electron shells and electron clouds and trying to make sense of tiny particles moving very quickly at different distances from the nucleus of the atom. The onion proves a helpful tool. In the following days, the class examines the Periodic Table and the numbers in each of the table's boxes. Students then make a model of the table using fruits and vegetables. Their understanding of the atoms of each element is really beginning to grow.

The Atom Design Challenge

In week three, Ms. Murray poses a design challenge. She hands each student a booklet titled "Atom Design Portfolio." On the booklet's face is a page that states the challenge, as shown in Figure 10.5. In groups, students

A challenge:
Build your
own model

are supposed to build their own models to depict the atom of a particular element. The booklet contains various sections to guide students through the process: Selecting Your Element, Research, Resources, Brainstorming, Sketches of Possible Solutions, Selecting the Best Solution, Reflecting on the Process, and Evaluation. Ms. Murray explains each of the specifications listed in Figure 10.5 and addresses the importance of being creative and original. The students are excited and full of questions. Ms. Murray explains the materials she will bring (including balloons, markers, clay, rubber bands, and Popsicle sticks), and students generate a list of common materials they can bring from home (bubble wrap, string, felt, milk cartons, egg cartons, Styrofoam, and so on).

To begin the project, Ms. Murray has each student individually choose two possible elements to explore and list a reason why each would be interesting. Then the students meet as groups to discuss their choices, agree on a single element to use for the project, and begin to discuss the most important questions. The next class period is spent in the library, where the students research the answers to their questions about their element.

FIGURE 10.5
Cover Sheet for the
Atom Design Challenge

Atom Design Portfolio

Name: _____

Group Members: _____

Problem Statement: Your challenge is to build a model of an atom that creatively and accurately depicts an element.

Specifications:

- The element chosen must be between boron and argon on the periodic table.
- Your model needs to depict the atom of that element accurately, using the correct numbers of the three major subatomic particles.
- The model should be creative and original.

Constraints:

- The model can be no larger than 1 m x 1 m and no smaller than 15 cm x 15 cm.
- The model needs to stand on its own.
- The only materials that can be used are those found in class.

When selecting an element, explore one that you want to learn more about, remember that it must be between boron and argon on the Periodic Table.

Groups brainstorm

The following day, the students begin to brainstorm their designs for their atoms, incorporating a lot of the data from their research. For instance, the group designing an atom of sulfur wants to use yellow materials. After the day of brainstorming, Ms. Murray and the students together develop a *rubric* for evaluating their final solutions (Table 10.2). (You will

TABLE 10.2   Rubric for Design Project

Category	Score	Description
Success of the solution	4	The solution solves the problem statement. Detail and design are excellent. Hard work and planning are obvious.
	3	The solution solves the problem statement, and the constraints and specifications are met.
	2	The solution solves the problem, but not all constraints and specifications are met.
	1	The solution does not solve the problem; constraints and specifications are not met.
Creativity of the design	4	The solution is unique; never or seldom has this design been formulated.
	3	The solution is functional but not unique.
	2	The solution is similar to a number of others; it may be a modification or interpretation of another group's solution.
	1	The solution has been copied from another group's.
Accurate measurement and calculation	4	Rulers were used appropriately to measure material throughout the process of planning and implementing ideas.
	3	Rulers were used appropriately during the implementation of ideas.
	2	Measuring devices were rarely used. Some mathematical calculations are incorrect.
	1	Errors in measurement are evident.

read more about rubrics in the chapter "What's the Big Idea?") Many of the students want to know what they need to accomplish to receive a perfect score; they are not interested in receiving anything less.

Each group is required to draw three possible models for its design project, choose one, and then have the final sketch approved by Ms. Murray. She wants to make sure that when construction begins, the students will know where to start. Some groups come to agreement more readily than others. Ms. Murray actively participates in two of the groups that struggle to find consensus. Four of the groups need hardly any assistance from her at all.

My thinking: When I ask one group why they have chosen the element boron, they all say, "Because we didn't know anything about it." I am impressed by this group's willingness to take ownership of their learning.

Over four class periods, the students complete and decorate their models. Every day, the students come into class excited; the sense of pride they take in their work can be seen in their eyes and heard in their voices. A student in one of the groups says, "Ms. Murray, look at our project! Doesn't it look great?"

Ms. Murray's thinking: Ms. Murray now believes she has accomplished something bigger than teaching the students about atoms. Her students no longer need her to tell them their work is great. They have gained confidence in it, in each other, and in their knowledge. She is very proud of them.

When the students present their final design projects, they demonstrate their understanding of atomic structure as well as the specific uses of their elements. Overall, the class has built models of boron, carbon, aluminum, magnesium, phosphorus, and neon, and the models are quite different from one another. The neon group has used Popsicle sticks, beads, tape, paper towel rolls, and other materials to create a model of neon's ten protons, ten electrons, and ten neutrons. When they present this model, the students explain that neon is a colorless, odorless gas that is lighter than air and is used in neon lights. The students point out the two energy levels for neon's electrons and show how they twisted pipe cleaners around the sticks to represent electron clouds.

The boron group has used a white triangular Styrofoam base to hold a nucleus with five protons and six neutrons. Around the nucleus, fanlike blades represent boron's five electrons in two energy levels (see Figure 10.6). The students are especially proud of these electron clouds. They talk about the scientists who discovered boron and share the fact that boron is used in pyrotechnics and flares to produce a green color. It has also been used in some rockets as an ignition source.

My thinking: I find it wonderful that the electric fan lesson carried over to this group's stunning model of electron clouds.

Ms. Murray helps groups that need guidance

Students' confidence

Presenting the models

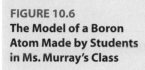

FIGURE 10.6
The Model of a Boron Atom Made by Students in Ms. Murray's Class

EXPANDING MEANINGS

■ The Teaching Ideas Behind This Story

- By examining historical scientific models, Ms. Murray gives the students insights into the nature of science and the role of historical, philosophical, and technological contexts in the development of scientific knowledge.

- Ms. Murray discards the rigid view of what an atom looks like in favor of a more open-ended (and more scientifically accurate) approach. By doing this, she allows her students to develop a much deeper knowledge of atomic structure than if they had merely studied the usual pictures and built conventional models.

- To make abstract concepts concrete, Ms. Murray uses her own everyday models—the electric fan and the onion.

- In a **design challenge,** students plan, research, design, and construct solutions that lead to a product or a process. Essentially, design is the technological counterpart of the science-as-inquiry process. We will talk more about design challenges in the next section.

● The Science Ideas Behind This Story

- As you saw in the chapter "Making Models," models are important in scientific research, both in formulating hypotheses to be tested and in describing scientific phenomena.

- Science in the twentieth century revealed a great deal about the structure of the atom. Scientists are now conducting experiments to explore the structure of the nucleus and the forces that hold it together.

- Atoms are so small that we cannot see them with an ordinary microscope. In 1981, though, a type of microscope called a *scanning tunneling microscope* (STM) was developed. The STM and its newer variations allow us to see atoms.

- Atoms of different elements have different properties and differ in size.

- All atoms are electrical in nature. They have positively charged particles called **protons** in their nuclei and have negatively charged particles called **electrons** surrounding the atomic nucleus. The number of protons in a given atom is equal to the number of electrons; hence, atoms are electrically neutral.

- In addition to protons, the atomic nucleus contains **neutrons,** particles without an electrical charge.

- The mass of a proton is equal to the mass of a neutron. Electrons have only about $1/1,800$ of the mass of a proton or neutron.

- Electrons revolve around the nucleus in distinct energy levels or "shells." Rather than call these paths *orbits*, scientists today prefer the term *orbital*, which refers to the wavelike function of the electron. Electrons exist both as particles and as waves. The various orbitals are at different distances from the nucleus of the atom.

- Since we can never know the exact position of an electron in its orbital, it is useful think of these particles as moving in **electron clouds,** general areas where they may be found. The densest part of the cloud is the area where the electron is most likely to be.

- Each electron cloud or energy level has a maximum number of electrons that it can hold. The first major energy level has a maximum of two electrons; the second, a maximum of eight electrons; and the third, a maximum of eighteen electrons.

- The farther away the electron is from the atomic nucleus, the more readily it can leave the atom.

✔ The Science Standards Behind This Story

STANDARDS The extended exploration of the atom in Ms. Murray's class illustrates the following parts of the National Science Education Standards (National Research Council, 1996):

✔ *Content Standard G, Grades 5–8 (History and Nature of Science):* "As a result of activities in grades 5–8, all students should develop understanding of science as a human endeavor, [the] nature of science, [and the] history of science. . . . The introduction of historical examples will help students see the scientific enterprise as more philosophical, social, and human. Middle-school students can thereby develop a better understanding of scientific inquiry and the interactions between science and society. . . . To develop understanding of the history and nature of science, teachers of science can use the actual experiences of student investigations, case studies, and historical vignettes" (p. 170).

✔ *Content Standard E, Grades 5–8 (Science and Technology):* "As a result of activities in grades 5–8, all students should develop abilities of technological design. . . . Students' work with scientific investigations can be complemented by activities in which the purpose is to meet a human need, solve a human problem, or develop a product. . . . Students should make and compare different proposals in the light of the criteria they have selected. They must consider constraints—such as cost, time, tradeoffs, and materials needed—and communicate ideas with drawings and simple models" (pp. 161, 165).

Questions for Further Exploration

■ How does Ms. Murray's atomic structure unit break open the science "box"?

■ How do the groups of students in Ms. Murray's class model constructivist inquiry?

■ What other middle school science topic lends itself to a design challenge?

Resources for Further Exploration

ELECTRONIC RESOURCES

Chem4Kids.com.   http://www.chem4kids.com/files/atom_intro.html. The pages on atoms on this web site are very informative and provide a friendly environment for students to do their own research.

How Atoms Work.   http://www.howstuffworks.com/atom.htm.   This section of the How Stuff Works site, prepared by C. C. Freudenrich, is excellent for both students and teachers, with information ranging from the history of atomic research to the structure of the atom.

The Periodic Table Online.   http://www.chemicalelements.com/.   This online periodic table gives a great deal of information about the table and each of the elements.

PRINT RESOURCES

Farinelli, Jill. (2002). *Simple Chemistry.* Monterey, CA: Evan-Moor Educational Publishers.

Harrison, A. G., & Treagust, D. F. (1996). Secondary students' mental models of atoms and molecules: Implications for teaching chemistry. *Science Education*, 80(5): 509–534.

Lloyd, M. (1996). A bonding experience. *Science and Children*, 34(3): 26–29.

Design Technology

The design challenge that Ms. Murray posed for her students leads us to the subject often known as **design technology** or *technology as design.* What does this mean exactly?

STANDARDS ✔

As you may have noticed in the "Science Standards Behind This Story" section you just read, the National Science Education Standards include the recommendation that students develop "abilities of technological design." The general explanation is as follows:

> As a complement to the abilities developed in the science as inquiry standards, these [Science and Technology] standards call for students to develop abilities to identify and state a problem, design a solution . . . implement a solution, and evaluate the solution.
>
> Science as inquiry is parallel to technology as design. Both standards emphasize student development of abilities and understanding. (National Research Council, 1996, pp. 106–107)

How design technology parallels scientific inquiry

Think of it this way: As part of scientific inquiry, students engage in the exploration and analysis of natural phenomena. They manipulate materials, plan experiments, make observations and inferences, and try to find answers to problems that they pose. As part of design technology, students plan, research, design, and construct solutions that lead to a product or a process. Like inquiry, design is a recursive and iterative process—trying one solution and, on the way to it, finding another.

When we add design technology to inquiry, we ask students to solve a problem—often called a design challenge—that requires them to use some of the scientific and/or mathematical ideas they are exploring through their inquiry. The solution typically involves constructing a product or process that meets stated specifications.

Design portfolios

As you saw in Ms. Murray's class, design projects often use a portfolio as a tool to assist students in the design process. Design portfolios include the problem statement, specifications and constraints, and several other sections.

From the sound of the term *design technology,* you may think it applies mostly to students in middle grades and high school. The National Science Standards, however, insist that abilities of technological design should be developed at all grade levels, beginning in kindergarten (National Research Council, 1996, p. 107). What might a design challenge for younger students look like?

A design challenge for younger students

As one example, the fourth graders who explored land snails in the chapter "Sustained Inquiry" might be challenged to design a "home" for their snails, given certain specifications and constraints. One specification might be that the snail's home be no taller that 16 centimeters and no wider than 20 centimeters. A constraint might be that the students could use only the shoeboxes provided in the classroom. The students would then design and construct their solutions using the materials present in their classroom and in their imaginations. They would then evaluate their solutions and redo their designs. In this iterative process, they most likely would learn a great deal about land snails as well as about larger themes of habitat and the structure of living systems.

In the chapter "Spiraling Curriculum," the liquid "toys" that the fifth graders construct are another example of design technology. Design challenges are one more way to expand the "box" of typical science teaching and learning.

KEY TERMS

electricity *(p. 234)*
electron *(p. 234)*
electric current *(p. 234)*
electric circuit *(p. 234)*
series circuit *(p. 235)*
parallel circuit *(p. 235)*
design challenge *(p. 247)*
proton *(p. 248)*
neutron *(p. 248)*
electron cloud *(p. 248)*
design technology *(p. 250)*

Part Three

Creating the Science Experience in Your Classroom

In this final part of the book, we will look at some practical matters that you need to think about as you prepare to teach science in an elementary or middle school classroom. Part Two showed you what school science "looks like." Part Three helps you to do it in your own classroom. It addresses lesson planning and questioning strategies; the use of technology in the classroom; science content in the physical, life, and earth sciences; selection of materials to match a curriculum; assessment; and self-evaluation techniques.

Many of the points I make in the following chapters refer to the stories you read in Part Two. Since all of these issues will become very pressing as you begin your teaching career, you may want to refer to this part of the book often. As you gain experience, you will increasingly be able to use the ideas and suggestions in Part Three to create your own personal style in the classroom.

11 Planning for Science
Lesson Plans and Instructional Strategies

FOCUSING QUESTIONS

▮ What is the difference between a science activity and a science lesson?

▮ Do you prefer to learn independently or in small groups?

▮ How do you plan for the unexpected?

▮ How can you set up your science lessons if you have only forty minutes in a period?

A friend of mine used to say, as each school year began, "Remember, Janice, teachers can never be over prepared." As I gained experience in teaching, I discovered what he meant.

Being prepared means, first and foremost, having done your planning. The role of planning for school science cannot be overstated. To develop a plan that guides your behavior and instructional strategies, you need to give serious consideration to the learning experiences you want to provide. Then you need to organize and structure those experiences in ways that make sense to you and to the students you are teaching.

In an early chapter of this book, I mentioned that we teach "who we are." That applies to planning as well as to your performance in class. When you come to school prepared, the students recognize it, and they develop an image of you as hard working and caring. This image helps you create a sense of community in the classroom.

This chapter looks at the plans you need to make for your science lessons, as well as at instructional strategies that are closely related to your lesson planning. In the chapter "Science Content and Curriculum," we will explore larger-scale planning for an entire science unit.

An Activity Is Not a Lesson

Planning the activity

A major part of planning is setting up the activity that your students will pursue. As earlier chapters have demonstrated, it is only by providing students with meaningful science activities—such as experimenting with liquids, exploring atomic structure, or investigating snails—that we can lead them toward critical exploration of their world. Planning therefore involves acquiring and organizing the appropriate materials and deciding how you will engage the class in the activity.

Planning for ideas and reflection

These steps, however, are just the beginning of the planning process. Although students may have a lot of fun experimenting with the materials you give them, *an activity is not a lesson.* You need to know what science ideas you expect your students to develop. Most important, it is not just the activity but the process of reflection that can lead to the construction of new ideas. Your responsibility is to facilitate the thought experience as well as the active experience. This involves helping to scaffold the students' ideas.

The process of performing the activity and reflecting on it may be considered the science **lesson.** This chapter will offer a general model for planning that can help you become a facilitator of your students' construction of meaning. In the sections that follow, we will begin with the lesson plan itself and then address the role of questioning, the use of cooperative learning groups, and some guidelines for reflecting on your teaching experience.

Planning to drop the plan

One more introductory point: Careful planning also includes the plan to drop the plan! This may sound like a contradiction, but when students are engaged in genuine inquiry, one question often leads to another. Your students' spontaneous curiosity will give you excellent opportunities to change your original plan and mediate their experience on *their own terms.* Remember to keep in mind the important science ideas that can emerge from a successful science experience.

Planning the Lesson

Let's imagine that you are planning a new science lesson for your class. What type of **lesson plan**—that is, a document that describes your plans for the lesson—will help you engage your students in a meaningful science activity *and* invite them to think about, reflect on, and construct ideas from this activity?

How to plan for flexibility?

There are many lesson plan templates or guides to help you get started. They are usually designed to predict the behavior of your students and of you as a teacher. But I have dedicated a great deal of this book to helping you understand that you *cannot* always predict where a meaningful science activity will lead. The goal, then, is to create a plan that allows for flexible procedures and critical thinking about the lesson.

The guide that follows is a useful model and can get you started in the planning process. Over the years, it has been modified by several science teachers as a result of their actual experiences doing science with students. As you begin working with other teachers and see different ways of planning, you too can modify the plan to meet your own personal needs.

A Planning Guide

The feature "A Guide for Making a Science Lesson Plan" lays out the steps of a basic model for lesson planning. Each step is a question that you ask yourself. Notice how the steps correlate with the five phases of the learning cycle that you read about early in this book: engagement, exploration, explanation, elaboration, and evaluation.

To illustrate how to use these steps, let's say that you are writing a lesson plan for a land snails experience like the one described in the chapter "Sustained Inquiry." The students will be exploring the snails' responses to the external stimuli of food, light, and water.

Stating your goals

Goals: What am I hoping the students will get out of this science experience? This part of your plan asks you to state the problem or phenomenon the students are exploring and what you are hoping they will discover. In the snails lesson, you might say:

> I am hoping that the students, through observing their land snails, will notice that the snails respond to external stimuli and that the snails' antennae assist them in sensing their environment.

Specifying the concepts

Science Ideas: What are the science ideas at the heart of this experience? What concepts am I hoping the students will understand as a result of this lesson? In this step, you state the science concepts—the underlying ideas about the natural world that you are hoping the students will construct as they engage in and reflect on the activity. For example, in the snails lesson, you could write:

> Snails are attracted to food and water, but tend to be repelled by light. Their behaviors are called "responses," and the lettuce, water, and light are called "stimuli."

Deciding how to engage students

The Hook: How will I command students' interest in the topic? This step refers to the engagement phase of the learning cycle. Also called "motivation," this part of the plan engages the students in the topic at hand by exposing them to a discrepant event or just by showing them the materials they will be exploring in a way that arouses their interest. For the snails lesson you might note the following:

> I will take a living land snail and place it on my hand. I will ask students to make some observations about this animal and let them know that they will be exploring it in groups of two.

Describing the activity

Science Activity: What will the students be examining and exploring on behalf of their own learning? This question relates to the exploration phase of the learning cycle. Here, you need to describe the activity briefly. For the snails lesson you might write:

A Guide for Making a Science Lesson Plan

Answer fully each of the questions listed below.

Goals	What am I hoping the students will get out of this science experience?
Science Ideas	What are the *science* ideas at the heart of this experience? What concepts am I hoping the students will understand as a result of this lesson?
ENGAGE:	
The Hook	How will I command students' interest in the topic?
EXPLORE:	
Science Activity	What will the students be examining and exploring on behalf of their own learning?
Materials	What materials do I need for the activity?
EXPLAIN:	
Reflection	What kind of meaning do students construct from this experience? How can I help students by scaffolding their ideas?
ELABORATE:	
Pulling It Together	How does the activity connect to what we have been doing in class? To the students' lives? How will I help the students organize their thinking and pull this lesson together?
EVALUATE:	
Evaluation	How will I know what the students have learned?

The students will work with three kinds of external stimuli—lettuce leaves, light, and water—to investigate the snails' responses to each stimulus. Each group will have magnifying lenses, lettuce leaves, water, and a light source. The students will test the three stimuli and record the results. The magnifying lenses will help them observe the snail's antennae.

Listing materials

Materials: What materials do I need for the activity? This section lists the materials that you need to organize before the lesson. In the snails lesson, the list is as follows:

garden snails	eyedroppers
lettuce leaves	water
magnifying lenses	flashlights

It is important, of course, to add quantities to your list so that you have enough materials for all the students to participate. How many flashlights and magnifying lenses? How much lettuce?

*Designing
your questions
and scaffolding*

Reflection: What kind of meaning do students construct from this experience? How can I help students by scaffolding their ideas? This part of the plan relates to the explanation phase of the learning cycle and to your own role in the classroom. It is here that you gather the students' own ideas and help them to make sense of their exploration. You may want to include key questions that you will ask the students during the lesson—for example, questions that will encourage them to use certain process skills. For the snails lesson, these questions could include:

What do you notice about the snails when the table is wet with drops of water?

How can you tell what the snails like?

Later in this chapter we will look more closely at the types of questions you might want to ask.

   As part of the planning process, you may also want to state that the students will be working in groups and that you will visit each group. Any advance thinking you do about your role as a guide and mediator belongs in this section of the lesson plan.

*Arranging to
pull together ideas*

Pulling It Together: How does the activity connect to what we have been doing in class? To the students' lives? How will I help the students organize their thinking and pull this lesson together? This question refers to the elaboration phase of the learning cycle. It is a closing part of the science lesson, when you give students the opportunity to formulate and express some of the science ideas they have developed from their experiences. For the snails lesson, you might write the following:

> Have students talk about their results with the lettuce, the flashlights, and the drops of water.
>
> Chart each group's responses on poster paper.

To connect the snails lesson to the students' lives, you might ask them about their own responses to food, water, and light. Or you might ask them how their household pets would react to these stimuli. Or you might invite them to think of other stimuli and their own responses.

*Planning
an assessment*

Evaluation: How will I know what the students have learned? This part of the planning relates to the evaluation phase of the learning cycle. Here you can plan an activity, a journal-writing exercise, or a formal assessment. You will want to see how the students' learning fulfills your original goals and any further goals that have evolved along the way. To evaluate the snails lesson, for example, you could ask your students to write a story about their snails, including their observations of the snails' responses. This assessment will help you to plan for future lessons.

If I Know It, Do I Have to Write It?

In the preceding section, you probably noticed the assumption that you would be *writing* your lesson plan. But you may have been thinking, "Is it really necessary to write the plan on paper or on my computer? Isn't thinking about it enough? After all, I'm not going to stop in the middle of the lesson and pull out a written plan."

Writing as part of reflection

Unfortunately, burdensome as it may sound, writing your lesson plan down is important, whether or not a written plan is required by your school. It is a way to collect and represent your thoughts, then save and modify them as you go along. Writing the plan down is another step toward becoming a reflective teacher. You should think of the document itself as part of your own teaching journal. It becomes a tool for you to reflect on, use again, and change over time.

I still have lesson plans that I wrote during my first year of teaching. The papers, now yellowing, remind me of how my thinking has changed in some ways and remained the same in others. I know that the process of writing these plans helped both me and my students, and it continues to do so.

Time Allotment

Your planning instrument becomes a tool for creating a science lesson in which the students have the opportunity to explore, reflect, and explore again. Sometimes one lesson plan will take you several days or more to implement.

You may wonder how to carry out such a plan in middle school, where you often have only forty minutes per day for the science period. Think back

---

A Planning Checklist

Before you complete your lesson plan for the science experience in your classroom, the following checklist can help you decide if you are fully prepared.

- Have I done enough research of my own? Do I understand the science ideas behind this topic?

- Do I need special arrangements for live materials?

- Do I need parental or administrative permission for any of the activities?

- Have I decided what types of student groupings I will construct? What will I ask each group

to do? How will the groups share information with each other?

- Do I understand how to guide the students from activity to reflection?

- Have I allowed enough time for the lesson—and extra time in case my estimate is wrong?

- Am I certain enough of the lesson's goals so I can tell when to modify my plan or let the students follow their own ideas?

to the chapter "Spiraling Curriculum," where Mr. Hutcheon created a sustained inquiry about floating and sinking by spreading it out, sometimes over only a single period of science, other times over a double period. Sometimes, in middle school, teachers take doable "pieces" of an activity and perform those in the allotted time, asking students to reflect on the experience for homework. It is important then to keep building on the prior day's activity with your students. Remember also that older students will require less time for distributing and cleaning up materials. In most cases you can plan thirty minutes for the activity itself, leaving only ten minutes for setup and cleanup. In elementary school, where you have more flexibility in your allotment of time, I suggest that you follow two principles:

Tips for allotting time

1. Allow at least one hour of class time for engaging students in any scientific activity, even a fairly simple one.

2. Always build in the flexibility to spend more time on an activity than you originally thought would be required.

After the Planning, the Letting Go!

Now that you have planned for the science lesson and organized the materials, how prepared are you to abandon your plan and respond to the students' interests, ideas, and questions? Remember the science story in the chapter "Spiraling Curriculum," when the students in Ms. Drescher's class explored liquids? In that case, a fairly simple lesson turned into several days' work on density, a concept that was not in Ms. Drescher's original plan.

Some teachers are so pleased with their lesson plans that the plan becomes an instruction manual for the lesson rather than a useful guide. This prevents the teacher from letting go of the plan even when the students' own ideas have taken the lesson to another level of awareness. As you have gathered from the stories in this book, you will often find that your students have questions of *emerging relevance*. You will even have students who ask you directly if they can try a certain experiment that was not in your original plan. More often than not, if appropriate materials are available, it is a good idea to encourage the students to explore these problems of emerging relevance.

Questions of emerging relevance

But how exactly will you know when to let go of your plan? Be assured that careful planning will give you the confidence to let go. This is because you will be able to evaluate the science ideas connected to each topic and consider the possibilities for students to expand their thinking through new activities. And the more experience you gain, the more comfortable you will be in thinking on your feet.

Here are some situations in which you can reasonably modify or abandon your original plan:

Times to modify your lesson plan

■ The science idea that you were hoping would emerge does not.

■ Students reveal alternative conceptions that are resistant to change. (Think about the bottle-and-balloon story in the chapter "The Teacher as Mediator," when the students needed to explore several different setups before they would abandon the idea that the air came from outside the bottle.)

The students want to explore a related investigation that you believe is a good idea. (Think about the liquids exploration with Ms. Drescher, when the students developed an interest in density.)

■ One or more students need to explore a phenomenon on their own terms. (Remember how Jamie in the chapter "The Teacher as Mediator" had a different question about icicles.)

It is impossible for you to predict where your students will take an activity that you have planned, but it is important that you listen actively to their queries and encourage creative explorations. Active listening requires that you probe your students' thinking as they develop new ideas. During the pulling-it-together time, the students can share the particular meanings that their explorations have had for them. The entire class will be enriched by the detours and alternative paths that your students will take.

The Role of Questioning

Importance of open-ended questions

Often you facilitate the science experience through the questions you ask your students. **Open-ended questions**—those that lead to multiple answers—are especially important because they help students think critically about the investigation. Frequently, too, the teacher's questions lead students toward their own new investigations. As you read earlier in this chapter, the nature of the questions you plan to ask can form part of your written lesson plan. Now let's take a closer look at the types of questions and the way they can help you guide students.

Types of Questions

Your questioning can be categorized in many different ways. For our purposes, we can divide questions into three main types: those that address process skills, those that help the students focus, and those that challenge the students.

Questions That Guide Students to Use Process Skills   Often you can use open-ended questions to encourage students to apply various process skills. The following list offers samples of questions that promote the use of certain skills. Of course there are many other questions you can use and many useful ways of phrasing each question.

	Question	Process Skill
Sample process-skills questions	What do you notice?	Observation
	Why do you think this is happening?	Inference
	In what ways are these things the same?	Comparing
	In what ways are these things different?	Contrasting
	How would you group these objects?	Classifying
	What do you think will happen?	Predicting
	How would you test this idea?	Planning an investigation
	How would you change this experiment if you repeated it?	Planning an investigation

Questions to Focus Students   Sometimes questioning techniques point students toward certain topics, much as the focusing questions at the beginning of the chapters do in this book. In other words, **focusing questions** invite students to come up with their own ideas about a specific topic or investigation. Teachers also use focusing questions to probe their students' understanding of a particular concept related to the investigation.

Here are some examples of focusing questions that relate to the snails investigation described in the sample lesson plan:

Sample focusing questions

■ How would you describe the effect of the light on the movement of your snails?

■ How would you test how far your snail moves in twenty seconds?

■ What evidence do you have for your statement that snails move toward water?

■ What type of investigation could you design to explore your snail's reaction to heat?

Three Keys to Good Questioning

1. Ask a question only if you are truly interested in knowing what the *students* are thinking.

2. Design questions to help students construct their own answers.

3. *Never* answer your own questions! It is better to leave a question unanswered for a while than to answer it yourself. The questions you ask the students are always more important than the answers you give them.

Questions to Challenge Students   Often the simplest question can challenge students to think deeply about an experiment or an exploration. My favorite example is, "So, what do you think is going on here?" I use this question to invite students to articulate the meaning they are making of an event.

Questions relating to daily life

We also challenge students when we ask them how the phenomenon they are exploring may relate to something they have seen in their daily lives. For example, with the snails lesson, you might ask your students, "What animals have you seen move like a snail? Are there ever times when people move like snails?"

Questions for critical thinking and expression

Another way to challenge students is to ask them simply, "What did you find out from this activity? Can you write it in your science journal?" Or you can ask your students what they liked about an exploration, what they didn't like, and, most important, "How would you change it?" Questions of this type encourage students to think critically. In addition, requiring students to commit their thoughts in writing helps them develop their skill in communicating about science and scientific processes. This process parallels the way scientists function as they carry out their research. They make tentative conclusions, try to connect their ideas to other ideas, and record their findings in their notebooks or journals.

For older students, it is fair to ask them to create their own theories about a phenomenon they have observed. Remember the chapter "Expanding the Science 'Box,'" when Ms. Murray asked her eighth graders to toss a beanbag frog to each other to prompt them to share some of their invented theories about how the particles in an atom's nucleus stay together.

Finally, challenging questions can give you windows into your students' thinking and let you know if they have developed alternative conceptions. Remember that unless you invite students to tell you what they are thinking, a true exchange of ideas cannot take place.

A Word About Wait Time

Whether you are asking students questions in their small groups or addressing the entire class, it is very important to allow them ample time to respond. **Wait time** refers to the time that elapses between the moment you ask a question and the moment when you select a student to respond, offer a clue, rephrase the question, or otherwise move ahead.

Research findings on wait time

A great deal of research documents the value of providing significant wait time. Studies conducted across grades kindergarten through 12 have compared longer average wait times (generally three to five seconds) with shorter ones (often one second or less). These studies indicate that the longer wait times raise the quality of the student-teacher interactions and the level of the discourse (Chuska, 1995; Rowe, 1974, 1987; Tobin, 1986).

Value of longer wait times

Wait time provides an opportunity for the students and the teacher to think about the exchange and process their ideas. In whole-class exchanges, researchers believe, longer wait time increases the number of students who participate, so more than just a few students respond. Similarly, in small-group exchanges, longer wait time helps engage all the members of the group.

The literature about wait time has been widely accepted in science education, and yet many teachers continue to rush to call on students. Often this occurs because we are not used to silence in the classroom. Sometimes teachers feel so uncomfortable when students do not respond after five seconds that they answer their own questions!

Science Learning Groups: Creating an Environment for Cooperative Learning

You may have wondered why so many of the science stories in this book feature classrooms in which students are learning in small groups. The teachers in our science stories created environments that nurtured collaboration among students. The basic reason is that scientific inquiry—the processes of investigation, reflection, and further investigation, whether undertaken by third graders or by adult scientists—benefits greatly from the collaboration of several people.

In this section, we address four important questions surrounding the small-group model of teacher and student interaction:

Questions about small-group learning

1. How do small-group investigations in science relate to what educators call cooperative learning?

2. In what ways is small-group learning consistent with constructivist views of learning?

3. In what ways is small-group learning consistent with the way science and scientists operate?

4. How can I set up small-group learning in my own classroom?

Cooperative Learning Groups

Research on cooperative learning

Extensive research has been done on **cooperative learning,** which can be defined as students working together in groups to accomplish shared learning goals. Studies have shown a variety of both social and educational benefits from cooperative learning. For example, cooperative learning helps students retain more conceptual knowledge. It also fosters a classroom climate in which students interact in ways that promote each other's learning (Johnson & Johnson, 1999; Slavin, 2003; Kagan, 1997).

It is important to recognize, though, that cooperative learning, as the researchers in this field define it, is not just any small-group instruction. It is a particular way of organizing the social interaction among students. If four students sit passively while a teacher talks at them, that may be small-group instruction, but it is not cooperative learning. A **cooperative learning group** is an arrangement in which a group of students, usually of mixed ability, gender, and ethnicity, work toward the common goal of pro-

Formal vs. informal groups

moting each other's and the group's success. In other words, in a cooperative learning group, each student is responsible for his or her own learning *and* the group's learning.

There are many ways to structure such learning groups. One basic distinction is between formal and informal groups. In *formal* cooperative learning groups, the group stays together until the task is done. In *informal* groups, the commitment is for a shorter term, as when each student checks with a neighbor to see if he or she understood (Johnson & Johnson, 1999, p. 15). The science stories in this book have involved formal learning groups, which stayed together until the problem was solved, the model was built, or the task was accomplished.

To be effective, cooperative learning must provide a good deal of structure for the group, and it must be supplemented with direct involvement by the teacher. You saw an example of this in the chapter "Expanding the Science 'Box,'" when Ms. Travis explained the meaning of the term *circuit* to the whole class. Another example is when teachers address the entire class to gather ideas from students before and after a science activity.

Working collaboratively fosters the practice of many of the skills, attitudes, and values that characterize science.
—NATIONAL SCIENCE EDUCATION STANDARDS

Constructivism and Small-Group Learning

Cooperative learning groups, such as the ones you have read about in this book, encourage the very constructivist learning processes that are at the heart of gaining conceptual knowledge in science. In such groups, students have the opportunity to discuss their ideas with others, discover differences

In cooperative learning groups, students exchange ideas with other students. Here one student holds a turtle while the others collect data.

Will Hart/PhotoEdit

As [students] interact, they acquire knowledge from each other, and they learn from the process of trying to put their ideas into words in order to allow someone else to understand them.
—MARK GRABE AND CINDY GRABE (2004)

between their own explanations and others', and defend their positions or alter their thinking as the group strives for consensus. Why is this interaction so important for learning? There are many reasons, but here we concentrate on three: reflection, the social context of learning, and the implications of cultural diversity and gender.

Cooperative Learning and Reflection Throughout this book, as we have explored the ways students best learn science, we have seen that science teaching and science learning rely on the active participation of students. But we have also seen that students must be mentally active as well as physically engaged with activities. In this chapter, by saying that an activity is not a lesson we have stressed the need for reflective mental processes to accompany the concrete activities.

Small groups foster reflection

Small-group, cooperative learning fosters these all-important processes of reflection. When students exchange and clarify ideas with their peers, plan an investigation, or refine their observations and conclusions, their minds are constantly engaged. Each student is prodded to more reflection by the inferences and opinions of others. The collaborative problem solver goes further in constructing new ideas and becomes better prepared for higher levels of thinking. The teacher is also a collaborator, visiting each group and helping it to focus.

Learning in a Social Context At the beginning of this book, I noted briefly how our understanding of the world is constructed in a social context. Even if you disagree fervently with your neighbor about, say, the value of exploring the moon, you both are working with many similar concepts, including understandings of what and where the moon is and what kinds of exploration are feasible. You are both also using similar language.

Shared concepts and language

In the same way, students' construction of new science explanations and theories is influenced by the social communication and language norms of our society. Peer communication in a small group helps the group's members find a common language with which to express their meaning, and this process promotes their learning. For example, in a lesson on density, the textbook might say, "Density is the mass divided by the volume." This type of decontextualized language can be baffling to many learners. But in a small-group conversation, the students may talk about how much 100 milliliters of corn syrup weighs and whether they think the corn syrup is denser than the corn oil. One student may then weigh 100 milliliters of corn oil and find out that it weighs less than the corn syrup. As this more contextualized meaning for density emerges from the common social discourse of the small learning group, each student can develop a more personalized, deeper understanding of the science idea.

Cultural Diversity and Gender in Cooperative Learning As shown in the chapter "Locating Your Scientific Self," images of scientists have traditionally excluded women and minorities. We know, too, that students who see themselves as marginal in a large group do not readily participate. Thus it is not surprising that girls and students of minority ethnic and cultural groups all too often distance themselves during science lessons, contributing little and learning little.

Encouraging diverse students to participate

Cooperative, small-group learning activities can help solve this problem. For girls and culturally diverse science learners, these activities attend to their academic needs far better than do individual learning activities (Barba, 1998). The climate of support created by cooperative learning groups encourages the participation of students who are less likely to volunteer and interact in a whole-class situation.

Benefits for all

We should not forget, too, that getting culturally diverse students involved benefits everyone else in the group. Remember the story of Ms. Byrne's third-grade class, which was investigating fruits and vegetables (in the chapter "Sustained Inquiry")? The students, who were from several cultures, shared information about foods that were familiar and unfamiliar to them. This type of interaction expands everyone's knowledge and often leads students to develop further questions to investigate.

As we will explore later in this chapter, students with physical or learning disabilities also contribute to the diversity of a cooperative learning group. They bring a way of seeing the world that enhances the science experience for all the group's members.

Scientific Investigation and Group Learning

In the adult world, scientific investigation is a social process. Scientific researchers collaborate with one another all the time. They work on teams; they share references to important articles; they access others' research through electronic communication and the Internet.

A real-life model

Classroom science learning groups are a real-life model of the collaboration necessary for true scientific inquiry to occur. They help eliminate the false stereotype of the lone scientist in a remote laboratory. They promote the kind of interchange and teamwork that are essential for scientific problem solving. Moreover, by fostering interactions among students who normally would not be relating to one another, they widen the range of students' observations and increase both the breadth and the depth of classroom investigations. The more diverse the perspectives on nature are, the greater is the likelihood of thorough explorations of natural phenomena. In addition, scientists agree that greater diversity in observations and inferences leads to a higher possibility that an accurate idea will emerge in the conversation.

Structuring Cooperative Learning Groups in Your Classroom

As we noted earlier, cooperative learning groups need structure. For the learning to be successful, the groups and their activities must be carefully selected. There are many different ways of structuring the groups, but some questions will always arise: Which students should be in which groups? What individual roles need to be assigned within a group? And how should I, as a teacher, mediate learning for the various groups in my class?

Assigning Students to Groups   Most small learning groups are created with two to four students. Sometimes groups of five are effective, but usually the smaller, the better. Keeping the group size small may limit the amount of diversity you can achieve within each group. Nevertheless, try to design the groups with as much heterogeneity as possible. Students of mixed ability, gender, and ethnicity should have the opportunity to work together toward common goals, learning about one another in the process.

Balancing group size and diversity

As a teacher, you should take the lead in designing the learning groups. When students are allowed to select their own collaborators, the groups are often homogeneous, with males working with males, white students working with other white students, and so on (Johnson & Johnson, 1999, p. 23). As a result, students do not interact with a wide variety of peers—one of the goals of cooperative learning.

You may want to gather information from the students before you design the groups. For example, you can ask each student to write down the names of three people he or she would like to work with. With this information, you can build groups that include at least one person of choice for each member. Groups should work together for as long as it takes for them to be successful, but at some point you will want to reshuffle the groups so that each student has the opportunity to work with as many other students as possible.

Seeking student input

Assigning Group Roles   In formal learning groups, each member is usually assigned a particular job or role. This is important not just to promote group efficiency but to make sure that every student participates fully. When everyone has a specific task that is essential to the problem solving at hand, each student will be a valued member of the group.

Importance of roles

You may remember that in some of the science stories in this book, the teachers used assigned jobs that included the roles of speaker, director, materials manager, and recorder. Another model for designing cooperative learning groups uses three prominent jobs for each group or team. The director makes sure that the team understands the investigation and completes each task in the directions. The manager collects and returns the materials that the team needs. The speaker asks the teacher and other teams when the team requires help. This model of three roles is popular in some school systems, and some schools even use printed badges that the students wear to designate their roles (Biological Science Curriculum Study, 1996). It is not necessary to use any of these particular labels for the group roles; you may design your own labels if you prefer. Whatever you call the roles, group work flows more smoothly when different students have different responsibilities.

Ways to structure roles

In the model of science learning groups that I often use, the teacher designs the groups, but the members of the group then select a leader, who is usually also the spokesperson responsible for reporting results to the entire class. The leader changes from week to week or project to project. The teacher also specifies the other roles to be filled, and the group then selects individuals to fill them.

As you can imagine, it is important for students to understand the responsibilities of each role. As a teacher, you will particularly appreciate the ways in which the group member responsible for getting and returning materials reduces the number of students wandering around the room at a given time. The more complex the investigation and the larger the group, the more roles may be involved. Whatever the assigned tasks for one investigation, the roles should change from project to project.

Mediating Group Learning   As the teacher, you manage and mediate the students' groups. You give directions for establishing the jobs and assigning the tasks, and then you facilitate the change of jobs when a new investigation begins. You can promote effective group work by monitoring how the group is functioning and making suggestions (Johnson & Johnson, 1999, pp. 42–45). Reminders to individual students like, "Did you check with your group?" or "What does your group think?" can help promote the value of the group.

Your role as mediator

One method for monitoring the group process involves a cooperative learning structure called "numbered heads together" (Kagan, 1997). The teacher has the students number off within groups. In four-person groups,

Helpful Hints for Planning a Science Lesson for Student Groups

■ Keep in mind that an activity is not a lesson. The lesson encompasses the thinking, reflection, and personal connections that occur because the students were engaged in the activity.

■ Be yourself, and be comfortable with what you and your class are doing.

■ Get yourself out of the way. That is, instead of delivering lockstep instruction, do the following:

Provide experiences.

Observe your students as they explore.

Gain insight into how they work together.

Listen to their ideas.

Offer suggestions, ask questions, prompt, and coach.

■ Prepare and plan as much as you can. Then be prepared to alter your original plan if the class's own ideas generate a new direction, one that you may not have thought of before.

■ Remember that your lesson plan should guide you, not limit you.

Monitoring group work

for example, each student would be number 1, 2, 3, or 4. The teacher can then pose a question and ask the groups to "put their heads together" to make sure everyone in the group agrees on the answer. After the group members have consulted among themselves, the teacher calls out a number— 3, for instance—and the students whose number is 3 raise their hands to offer their group's answer. Each time a new question arises, the teacher calls out a different number. This technique can be used to check that each student in each cooperative learning group is participating in the group's decision making.

Honoring differences

Different groups will make different decisions about how to proceed with scientific investigations, and it is important to honor and value these differences. Sometimes it will even be necessary to allow an individual to go off on an investigation by himself or herself, as Mr. Wilson did with Jamie in the chapter "The Teacher as Mediator." At the same time, however, you need to coach and prompt the groups as they struggle toward problem solving. When appropriate, offer ideas, provide focus, or give specific explanations of the problem at hand.

When the investigation is complete, invite the members of each group to discuss how well they collaborated with each other. Their comments will help you to evaluate the groups' effectiveness and plan for the next group science activity.

As you create this model in your own classroom, you will find that small-group cooperative learning is truly essential to doing science with students. You will see for yourself that the groups encourage the process of problem solving in ways that individual instruction cannot. You will also see the value of diversity in group problem solving.

Inclusive Science Education

Our goal as science teachers is to offer opportunities for all students to gain sufficient schooling in science in order to become better problem solvers, critical thinkers, and inquiring human beings. In the opening chapter, we discussed *differentiating instruction* so that all students can participate in a science education experience that maximizes the possibilities for their success. We also want all students, including women and ethnic minorities, to feel *entitled* to success in science.

Overcoming stereotypes

Feeling entitled to success in science is often based, as you have seen, on long-held stereotypes that persist in the media and in our minds. Every year in the United States, we celebrate Women's History Month and Black History Month to remind students that those who came before us made significant contributions to our lives today. Among those contributions are advances in science and technology. Each year, therefore, I would ask my sixth graders in middle school to research a woman and/or a person of color who had contributed to advancing knowledge in science and technology. Instead of writing a report, I would ask them to design and construct some artifact that represented their chosen scientist's life or work.

Students who researched the life and work of Nobel Prize–winner Barbara McClintock, for example, learned that McClintock worked extensively with corn plants in order to discover that genes can move from one place to another on their chromosomes, causing mutations. For their artifact, these students designed and constructed a three-foot model of an ear of corn. I strongly urge you to develop similar projects with your students, and not just during special months of the year.

People with physical disabilities and learning disabilities are another group that commonly receives little encouragement in science. Did you know, however, that one of the world's most eminent marine biologists is blind? A professor at the University of California, Davis, this scientist's work is with mollusks, those shelled invertebrates that inhabit marine waters. His extraordinary sense of touch enables him to study these creatures and make observations that elude other scientists. His name is Geerat J. Vermeij, and he has won several honors for his work.

In the following sections, we will discuss some of the differentiated instruction tasks that work best for students with physical and learning disabilities. There are many web sites available to assist you with instructional strategies, and some of the best ones are listed in the Resources for Further Exploration at the end of this chapter. Remember, our goal is to make it possible for *all* students to do science in the classroom.

Science and the Inclusion Model

The Individuals with Disabilities Education Act (IDEA) and the Americans with Disabilities Act (ADA) extend equal opportunity to those with disabilities so they can experience the same services that have always been

Geerat Vermeij Speaks About His Work

I study the history of life. I want to know when evolution occurred and when it did not. Although my research is concentrated on fossil and living shell-bearing animals like snails and clams, I apply the results to large scientific questions. I am especially interested in looking at the history of life on Earth from an economic point of view. This involves the study of technological innovations, the analysis of how workable ecosystems are constructed and maintained, and an understanding of how shifting availability of resources affects the everyday affairs of organisms in past and present ecosystems. The ultimate aim is to see what the economic history of life can tell us about how to construct human economies that are not dependent for their health on perpetual growth. On the way to these lofty goals, I am having a great time studying the classifications, architecture, and history of snails, whose beauty rivals that of any human artistic creation.

Source: "Geerat Vermeij Interview," Department of Geology, University of California, Davis, http://www.geology.ucdavis.edu/www/picnicday/interview/geerat.html.

The inclusion model

accessible to the general population. Under these laws, students with disabilities are not receiving something extra; they are merely gaining access to what the general population has taken for granted (Stefanich et al., 2003).

The laws lie behind the **inclusion model,** in which students with disabilities are placed in regular classrooms to the greatest extent possible. Findings in educational research support the inclusion model as a more desirable alternative than segregated instruction for students with disabilities. This is true regardless of gender, race, ethnicity, social class, or type of disability.

When "inclusion students," as they are often called, are placed in a regular education classroom, a special educator is usually available to offer support. What has sometimes happened, however, is that the regular classroom teacher has little to do with the development of the student's individualized education plan (IEP). Therefore, the regular teacher ends up presenting the science curriculum content without knowing much about the needs-specific pedagogy. At the same time, the special educator, who knows how to teach students with special needs, does not know enough about the regular content to relate it to the special pedagogy. Hence the student's science education gets lost in the gap between the teachers. To avoid this problem, it is important for the regular educator and the special educator to work as partners from the beginning.

Fortunately, the best science teaching practices—engaging students in using all their senses, in manipulating materials, and in asking questions—represent the type of multimodal approach that is also very successful for students with disabilities. While by no means comprehensive, the following section offers some strategies for helping special education students achieve success in learning science.

Before we begin, however, let's remember what all students need: They need to know that their teacher expects them to succeed and is working hard on their behalf. Holding out the expectation that your inclusion students will be successful in science is an important first step. Remember, you teach who you are.

Classroom Strategies for Doing Science with Students with Disabilities

Several general strategies are useful for students with any type of disability:

Methods for all students with disabilities

■ Allow more time for students with disabilities to complete the task at hand. This is an important step, and it should become routine in your classroom.

■ Get feedback from your students with disabilities. Ask, "How am I doing?" "Are you having a particular difficulty with this science experience?" "What are you most pleased about?"

■ Explore technologies that can help. Computer software programs can benefit students with many kinds of disabilities. In addition, there are science tools and materials that help students complete scientific tasks: for example, beakers with special holders, pouring spouts, and larger numbers for calibration.

The following subsections offer a number of suggestions (adapted from Stefanich, 2001) for teaching students who have particular kinds of disabilities.

Motor/Orthopedic Disabilities   The term *motor/orthopedic disability* encompasses a large number of impairments involving functional or structural aspects of one or more body systems. Examples include cerebral palsy, polio, muscular dystrophy, multiple sclerosis, and spinal cord disorders. Experts find the following instructional approaches useful:

Methods for students with motor/ orthopedic disabilities

- ■ Review work areas for appropriate height and accessibility of supplies.

- ■ Examine the classroom environment and make sure the student has appropriate access to other students.

- ■ Examine the students' movement patterns and needs. If necessary, rearrange classroom furniture and other objects so the student can move around as needed during a lesson.

- ■ Provide accessible means for reviewing drawings, charts, or graphs.

- ■ Look for adaptive computer software and other special equipment. Contact assistive technology agencies directly, and become familiar with the specialized equipment.

Visual Impairments   People with visual impairment are often characterized as having either "low vision" or "blindness." If they have low vision, they may be able to read with the help of large print or magnifiers (Irvine Belson, 2003). People with blindness may be unable to gather any visual information. Here are some ways to differentiate instruction for students with visual impairments:

Methods for students with visual impairments

- ■ Use tactile or auditory signals when appropriate.

- ■ Provide a magnifier if the student wants one.

- ■ Clearly label all items and equipment involved in a lesson.

- ■ Allow for direct manipulation of materials when appropriate.

- ■ Provide enlarged handouts.

- ■ Get thermoform sheets. (Thermoform is a plastic sheet material used for duplicating in Braille.)

- ■ Provide a supportive peer assistant to work with the student.

- ■ Allow the student and his or her peers to continue with science activities outside of the school day or at home.

Classroom Survey: How Accessible Is Your Classroom?

The following survey was developed to help you assess your classroom in terms of its accessibility for students with disabilities. You will notice, though, that many of the items refer to excellent science learning experiences for all students.

What is the average width of the aisles?

_____

(Aisles should average 42–48 inches minimum. This allows access for students in wheelchairs and those using other assistive devices.)

Describe the work surfaces, lab tables, etc.

_____

_____

_____

(Spaces under work surfaces should be 29 inches high, 36 inches wide, and at least 20 inches deep. The work surface should be no more than 32 inches off the floor. This allows access for students in wheelchairs and those using other assistive devices.)

Is safety equipment (fire extinguishers, eyewash, fire blanket, first-aid kit, and so on) easily accessible?

_____

(This is important for all science classrooms.)

What types of projection devices are used in the class? Overhead projectors? Data projectors used with computers?

_____

(Projectors are a useful visual aid for all students.)

What are the light conditions in the room?

_____

_____

_____

(The quality of lighting has implications for all students' learning.)

How are the acoustics in the classroom?

_____

_____

_____

(Again, your answer has implications for all students' learning.)

How are things stored in the room? Consider both the accessibility of desirable materials for doing science and the importance of keeping more dangerous materials, like hot plates and matches, in a locked facility.

_____

_____

_____

Source: Adapted from "Making Science Accessible and Inclusive: Strategies for Teachers in Science Education," a preconference workshop presented by Greg Stefanich, Marcia Fetters, Eric Pyle, Dawn Pickard, and Jim Ellis at the Association for the Education of Teachers of Science International Conference, St. Louis, Missouri, January 2003.

Hearing Impairments   People with hearing impairments can be described by two main categories—those who are hard of hearing and those who are deaf. Individuals who are hard of hearing still have some degree of hearing, which may or may not be enough for them to use auditory information in communication. Deaf persons have no ability to hear.

For your students with hearing impairments, try the following techniques:

Methods for students with hearing impairments

- In your classroom seating plan, locate the student where he or she can see your eyes and your lips. Be sure that the background, from the student's point of view, has sufficient contrast.

- Print activity cards in large type so the student can easily read them from a distance.

- Provide a supportive peer assistant to assist during games and construction activities.

- Allow the student and his or her peers to continue with science activities outside of the school day or at home.

Learning Disabilities   People who are described as having learning disabilities can suffer from one or more of a number of diverse conditions, ranging from dyslexia and attention deficiencies to identifiable brain injuries. The definition of *learning disability* varies between states, and it remains a contentious subject among researchers. Common to most definitions of learning disabilities is the idea of a significantly diminished capability for using and understanding language in spoken and written forms. While students with learning disabilities are of average or above average intelligence, the disability creates a gap between their inherent ability and their actual performance.

The following suggestions can help you improve your instruction of students who have learning disabilities:

Methods for students with learning disabilities

- Eliminate distractions and background noises as much as possible.

- Review directions with students in advance of a lesson or assignment.

- When you interact with a student who has a learning disability, give him or her your undivided attention. Focus on what the student says and listen carefully.

- Be straightforward in your approach. Don't pretend to understand if you do not.

- Allow for noncompetitive participation in classroom activities and games.

- Provide a reader when appropriate.

- Allow for direct manipulation of materials when appropriate.

- Engage students in design and construction activities.

- Maximize the availability of visual materials.

Attention-Deficit/Hyperactivity Disorder (ADHD)   Students with ADHD are easily distracted and have trouble concentrating on tasks for any length of time. Some are restless and fidgety, with excessive movements that appear aimless. Some people with ADHD, though—typically females—are quite underactive, and their problem may go unnoticed.

The following techniques are recommended:

Methods for students with ADHD

- Position the student with ADHD so that you can visually monitor him or her and exercise proximity control when needed.

- Seek out visual media and models to keep the student engaged.

- Slow down the pace of activities, and allow adequate time for student participation.

- Preview an activity sequence in advance and, when appropriate, write a contract with the student specifying what behavior is expected.

- Be straightforward and direct with the student.

- Allow for interaction with materials when appropriate.

- Allow for time out if a student needs it.

Questions for Your Own Reflection

When the science experience you have planned for your students is over, you may want to document what went on. If you use a constructivist approach, there is always a lot to write about because you really do not know beforehand where the lesson will go or what the students will say or do. It is the students' thinking that propels you forward. Besides actively listening to the students during the lesson, it is useful to take some time afterward to record their ideas and your own reactions to the way the lesson developed.

Here are some sample questions to ask yourself as you reflect on the lesson and write about it in your science journal:

Questions to reflect on after the lesson

- What did the students find out in this experience? Were there any surprises?

- How did the students in each group work together? Were there any problems?

- Was the activity open-ended enough, or did each group do more or less the same thing?

■ How did the students extend the investigation?

■ How did the students connect this experience to their daily lives?

■ How did I accommodate students with learning and physical differences?

■ Overall, what do I think the students got out of this experience?

■ What do I remember most about this science activity?

■ Would I do it again?

■ How would I plan differently the next time?

*Save your
plans and notes!*

Sometimes it is useful to record comments and reflections directly on the lesson plan itself. Keeping your plans together in a notebook is a good idea too. Your comments and notes have important implications for how you will address the topic the next time.

If you are comfortable using a computer, it can help you not only to create your lesson plans, but also to save them and add comments later. In the next chapter, we explore other ways in which computers and technological aids can facilitate your planning, your research, and your students' activities.

KEY TERMS

lesson *(p. 255)*
lesson plan *(p. 255)*
open-ended questions *(p. 261)*
focusing questions *(p. 262)*
wait time *(p. 263)*
cooperative learning *(p. 264)*
cooperative learning group *(p. 264)*
inclusion model *(p. 272)*

RESOURCES FOR FURTHER EXPLORATION

Electronic Resources

ADDvance. http://www.addvance.com/.   A resource for women and girls who have attention deficit disorders.

All Kinds of Minds. http://www.allkindsofminds.org/.   An organization that offers various products for students with learning disabilities.

American Speech-Language-Hearing Association. http://www.asha.org/. This site offers a wealth of information about communication disorders, including hearing impairments.

Council for Learning Disabilities. http://www.cldinternational.org/.   A key source of information on all types of learning disabilities.

ERIC Clearinghouse on Disabilities and Gifted Education. http://www. ericec.org/.   A federally funded clearinghouse of information about students with special needs.

IMSEnet: Instructional Materials for Science Education.   http://www. ncsu. edu/imse.   From the Network of Instructional Materials for Science Educators, this web site offers invaluable hypertext links to lesson plans and activities.

Inclusion in Science Education for Students with Disabilities.   http://www. as. wvu.edu/~scidis/.   This site includes a useful section of teaching strategies.

Inclusive Education.   http://www.uni.edu/coe/inclusion/.   The University of Northern Iowa's College of Education offers inclusion resources for both teachers and parents.

Intervention Techniques.   http://www.curry.edschool.virginia.edu/go/ specialed/information/interventions.html.   This site provides effective teaching techniques for exceptional learners.

Kagan Publishing and Professional Development.   http://www.kaganonline. com/.   Spencer Kagan is the originator of a structural approach to cooperative learning. This web site introduces some popular cooperative learning structures and resources that can help teachers become more proficient with cooperative learning groups.

National Association for Multicultural Education.   http://www.nameorg.org/.   As its name suggests, this organization is dedicated to cultural diversity in education.

Pitsco Lesson Plans.   http://www.pitsco.com/welcome.html.   Click on "Resources" and then on "Lesson Plans" for links to a multitude of lesson plans, many of them relevant to elementary and middle school science.

Schwab Learning.   http://www.schwablearning.org/.   Resources for teachers and parents of students with learning disabilities.

Print Resources

Cohen, E. G. (1994). *Designing Groupwork Strategies for the Heterogeneous Classroom.* New York: Teachers College Press.

Eltgeest, J. (1985). The right question at the right time. In W. Harlen (Ed.), *Primary Science: Taking the Plunge.* Portsmouth, NH: Heinemann.

Freedman, R. L. H. (1994). *Open-Ended Questioning: A Handbook for Educators.* Menlo Park, CA: Addison-Wesley.

Irvine Belson, Sarah. *Technology for Exceptional Learners: Choosing Instructional Tools to Meet Students' Needs.* Boston: Houghton Mifflin, 2003.

Johnson, D. W., & Johnson, R. T. (1999). *Learning Together and Alone: Cooperative, Competitive, and Individualistic Learning.* 5th ed. Boston: Allyn and Bacon.

Kagan, S. (1997). *Cooperative Learning.* San Clemente, CA: Kagan Cooperative Books.

Slavin, R. E. (1995). *Cooperative Learning: Theory, Research and Practice.* 2d ed. Boston: Allyn and Bacon.

Slavin, R. E. (2003). *Educational Psychology: Theory and Practice.* 7th ed. Boston: Allyn and Bacon.

Stefanich, G. (2001). *Science Teaching in Inclusive Classrooms: Models and Applications.* Cedar Falls, IA: Wolverton Printing Co.

Wilen, W. W. (1991). *Questioning Skills for Teachers.* 3d ed. Washington, DC: National Education Association.

12 Science and Technology
A Seamless Connection

FOCUSING QUESTIONS

▮ What types of experiences have you had with computers and computer applications?

▮ How do you use the Internet? For personal use? Professional use?

▮ What are your favorite web sites?

▮ What do you know about WebQuests?

Recently, when I was visiting with Kayley, my almost-five-year-old granddaughter, she asked, "Grandma, do you want to see my favorite web sites?" "Sure," I responded, and pulled up a chair next to hers at the computer. Deftly, she used the mouse to point to all her favorite web sites that were saved as "shortcut" icons on her personalized desktop, adorned with butterflies. As quick as a double-click, we were visiting **http://pbskids.org/**, a cleverly constructed web site sponsored by public television. Here, Kayley clicked on the icon for "games," and we were off to a seemingly limitless collection of clever matching and puzzle games that sang and spoke to her and required her to move playing pieces on the screen. When she made the correct move, the computer rewarded her by shouting "hooray" or "bravo." She played with several different games for almost forty-five minutes.

I think of my granddaughter as one of the high-tech "Internet babies" who are being born every day and getting ready for school in environments rich with computers and Internet access, often hooked into high-speed connections. These children are the offspring of parents who came of age with the information technology revolution. These parents have been using computers for more than ten years (often much longer), and having access to the Internet is an essential part of their daily life experience. They shop, make dinner and entertainment reservations, and schedule their vacations via the Internet.

These Internet babies will be your students. This fact has important implications for your use of technology in the classroom. Conversely, in socioeconomic areas where home computers are not commonplace, students will come to school with very different prior experiences. The school may be the most significant source of their technology education. You need to be prepared for students with both of these backgrounds, and everything in between. In each case, one central question can guide you: How can a technology-rich classroom environment enhance students' ability to see themselves as knowledge-seekers and information-builders?

In this chapter, we explore many different possibilities for using technology for teaching and learning science. You may remember that earlier in this book I talked about "locating your scientific self." You will not be surprised to learn that the same type of advice holds true for technology as well. Getting comfortable, in any way that is personally relevant to you, is a first step toward integrating the use of technology in your classroom.

The Meanings and Uses of Technology

Comparing technology to science

Many people assert that human beings were technologists long before they were scientists. The first person who fashioned a spear from the slender branch of a tree was modifying the world to meet a set of needs for him- or herself. That, according to some definitions, is the essence of technology. It is broadly thought that the goal of science is to *understand* the natural world, while the goal of technology is to *modify* the world to meet human needs (National Research Council, 1996, p. 24). Or we could phrase the distinction in this way: science usually explores that which has always been there, while technology creates that which has never been before.

Over the course of time, though, science and technology have become deeply intertwined. As humans explored the natural world, they became increasingly dependent on the technological tools that they developed to assist them. Eventually the tools of scientific inquiry—the microscope and telescope, for example—provided a great deal of data about the natural world, and that in turn helped technologists design even more sophisticated tools.

A reciprocal relationship

Today, science and technology are closely related. In fact, they have a reciprocal connection. The need to know more about the natural world prompts new technological developments, and new technology then drives scientific research. This research promotes new understandings about the natural world and new questions, which then demand new technology to provide answers. A good example of this reciprocal connection is the 1969 lunar landing. Scientific knowledge of the moon and its orbital relationship to Earth, coupled with a deep desire to explore the moon, spurred development of the Apollo rocket and the Lunar Exploration Module. That technology, which allowed human beings to step on another celestial surface for the first time, brought back new data about the moon that stimulated further scientific research and further advances in technology.

This chapter will explore some of the **instructional technology tools**—both tools for instruction and tools for learning—that have emerged from modern technology. It will focus on how these tools apply to science experiences. First, however, we should look at the goals for both teachers and students set by the National Educational Technology Standards.

The National Educational Technology Standards

STANDARDS ✔

Earlier chapters have mentioned the National Educational Technology Standards (NETS), which set technology-related goals for both students and teachers. Developed by the International Society for Technology in Education (ISTE), the NETS suggest that students should be prepared to:

General goals of the NETS

- Communicate using a variety of media and formats

- Access and exchange information in a variety of ways

- Compile, organize, analyze, and synthesize information

- Draw conclusions and make generalizations based on information gathered

- Know content and be able to locate additional information as needed

- Become self-directed learners

- Collaborate and cooperate in team efforts

- Interact with others in ethical and appropriate ways (International Society for Technology in Education, 2000, p. 5)

When you examine these basic statements that inform the NETS, you can see that they mesh well with the science learning experiences we have described throughout this book. Technology is particularly useful in providing students with means of obtaining data (for instance, Internet research) and with vehicles for communication (such as multimedia presentations).

Performance indicators

From these general principles, the NETS develop "technology foundation standards for students," which are then translated into specific "performance indicators" for various grade levels. For example, by the end of grade 5, students should be able to "use telecommunications efficiently and effectively to access remote information, communicate with others in support of direct and independent learning, and pursue personal interests" (International Society for Technology in Education, 2000, p. 20). You can review the full set of guidelines online at the NETS web site, **http://cnets.iste.org/**.

Professional standards

The NETS also elucidate professional standards for teachers, suggesting that they "demonstrate a sound understanding of technology operations and concepts" as well as "continual growth in technology knowledge and skills to stay abreast of current and emerging technologies" (International Society for Technology in Education, 2002, p. 9). Hence, as with science, using technology effectively requires that you establish your own level of comfort with basic technological functions. You need to be comfortable enough with technology to support both your own learning and your students' learning.

The feature "A Checklist for Your Computer Use" offers a handy list of questions to ask yourself. If your answers to these questions are mostly "No," you may want to become a self-directed learner and teach yourself some new technologies. For instance, you could seek answers to some of your burning science questions by using search engines on the Internet. (Be sure to "bookmark" your favorite web sites for easy-to understand scientific explanations.)

Also explore your own data collection process. Imagine that you are planning a vacation to several European cities. How can you collect data about those cities for the time of year when you are planning to visit? What web sites can you access? Where can you find weather data? Do you want the temperature in degrees Celsius or Fahrenheit?

Imagine, too, that you are planning to teach a unit on simple machines. What web-based resources will you use to enhance your own scientific understanding of simple machines? Where will you seek lesson plan ideas?

As you continue exploring this chapter, helpful hints will guide your way.

Integrating Technology with Instruction and Learning

Central to this chapter is the belief that technology should be fully integrated into the experience of learning and teaching science, so that the connection between the two becomes seamless. This is true in our private lives, where technology has become so pervasive that we scarcely notice

A Checklist for Your Computer Use

How would you rate your technology-use skill level? Beginner? Intermediate? Advanced? Innovator? The following checklist may be useful as you think about your own experience with computer technology:

■ Do you seek scientific information through reliable web sites?

■ Do you exchange science teaching ideas through email with other students of education or other teachers?

■ Have you explored the various uses of Power-Point?

■ Do you keep student grades on an electronic spreadsheet, such as Excel?

■ Have you ever explored WebQuest activities?

■ Do you get news online?

■ Do you "burn" your own CDs?

it. When you place a telephone call, send a fax, or type an email message, you spend little or no time pondering the technology itself; you just use it. Unfortunately, technology does not always play the same natural role in classrooms (Grabe & Grabe, 2004). Much remains to be done to integrate technology into our schools.

Why make the connection "seamless"?

But why, you may wonder, should the use of technology in classrooms be "seamless" and "natural"? Why doesn't technology, quite exciting in its own right, provide its own science lesson to students? The reason relates to the goals of the science lesson that we discussed in the chapter on lesson plans, "Planning for Science." Remember the question, "What am I hoping the students will get out of this science experience?" The response to this question is the fuller understanding of one or more science ideas and the use of several process skills. So if you want your students to learn about the solar system, for example, and to practice using their skills of observation and inference, you do not want them to become preoccupied with accessing a web site that has wonderful pictures of the planets. Rather, you hope they will use all available resources, including the computer, to support their investigation. When we aim for a seamless connection between school science and technology, we are asking ourselves this fundamental question: In what ways can technology help my students and me satisfy our goals for meaningful science instruction?

The Need to Know

At the heart of the process of scientific inquiry is the *need to know*. Whether the students are figuring out how to light a light bulb, wondering if their garden snails are ever going to move, or noticing the tiny green leaf that finally emerges from a seed, they are invested in the outcomes. In order to continue the investigation or confirm some findings, they need to know some bit of information, and this need creates its own momentum.

Technology as a resource for building meaning

It is in this context that technology can help the learner. It can make the search for information easier, supply another example, connect a student to others who are doing the same investigation, provide data, or help to begin a new inquiry. Computer technology and its related resources—the Internet, software packages, interfacing laboratory instruments, and multimedia presentation packages—help learners construct their own meaning. Many computer technologies make possible independent, learner-directed uses that fit comfortably into the learner-directed nature of inquiry-based science activities.

The need to think critically

In the sections that follow, we will examine several ways that technology can support meaningful science instruction and help satisfy the need to know. As you read, I invite you to think critically and to reflect on how you and your students can best use instructional technology tools. As teachers, our goal is to increase the possibilities for students to construct meaning and enhance their abilities to be active participants in their own learning. Often technology can help us to achieve this goal. At other times, though, we can best serve our instructional purposes with a minimum of technology. If technology merely gets students running faster and faster, it is not necessarily helping them to learn.

Assessing future developments

In the future, as new technology enters your classroom, keep assessing its usefulness and appropriateness in education. Personal computers, the Internet, and cellular telephones are three revolutionary developments that now symbolize the last decade of the second millennium. Today, wireless technology is appearing everywhere; many teachers and students can access the Internet without being tethered by wires and cords. Such broad, easy access to information is a boon for instruction and learning. Yet many educators and researchers caution us against using such technology just because it is there. Instead, as they remind us, we should always ask, "Is the technology use cloaked in understanding?" (Healy, 1998).

Making Observations and Gathering Data

This section explores ideas for using computer and video technology to enhance the scientific processes of observing and collecting data. In doing so, technology can also support the processes of making inferences, creating models, and planning investigations. Every day, new technologies improve the computer's ability to act as a "lab assistant" for scientific investigation. The applications described in the following sections are examples of the ever-increasing possibilities.

Obtaining Information from the Web

In one of the science stations in the chapter "The Science Circus," the students were asked to access a weather site on the Internet in order to obtain and compare real-time weather data in three cities. Clearly, this exploration would be impossible without computer technology. There are many other cases, too, in which school science data can be obtained from World Wide Web sites.

Real-time data

Another example might involve a fifth-grade unit on volcanoes and earthquakes. Real-time updates on volcanic activity are available on specific web sites. In one class I observed, the students were exploring volcanic activity in their own state and three neighboring states over the past 100 years. They learned that even areas not known for volcanic eruptions sometimes have considerable tectonic activity deep below the surface.

Scientific agencies on the web

Often students' spontaneous curiosities propel them to seek data from the web. (Later in this chapter, we will examine criteria for evaluating the reliability of web sites.) Most scientific agencies and public information systems, including the U.S. Fish and Wildlife Service, the U.S. Geological Survey, and many other reputable institutions, publicize on their web sites the data they collect as they track birds and wildlife, earthquakes, and volcanoes. These data become excellent resources for students collecting information for their own investigations. See the Resources for Further Exploration at the end of this chapter for some useful web addresses.

Data for Making Models   As we observed in the chapter "Making Models," building models often requires gathering data about the object or process we want to represent. The fifth-grade students in that chapter, who were making a model of the solar system, used the Internet as one of their resources.

One of my favorite models, you may remember, was my own model of the tooth. I've since done a web search for "teeth." What an extraordinary number of images and explanations were available for my tooth model! If I were building my model today, I would surely want to use some of that Internet information.

Online information for creating models

In a fourth-grade class I observed, the students were asked to create a project that would demonstrate their understanding of photosynthesis. One student made a "talking leaf" as her project. Karen brought in a cardboard model of a green maple tree leaf with a tape recorder attached to the lower surface. When she played the tape recorder, it gave an explanation of the process of photosynthesis using the first-person voice, as if the leaf itself were speaking. It turned out that she had done her research on the Internet. When I asked her why, she said that she had convenient access to it and there were lots of sites to choose from.

Information from Working Scientists   A number of web sites offer contact with scientists who will answer questions about specific topics in a variety of disciplines. Often, too, these sites contain archives of past questions and answers. Several such web sites are listed in Table 12.1. In addition to supplying information, these sites give students the sense of interacting with an actual scientist, even if only in cyberspace.

Direct connection with a scientist

Sometimes students and teachers can use the web or email to establish more personal connections with scientists. When one fifth-grade class in the East was studying invertebrates, the teacher dug up twenty worms from her backyard garden. With a collection of large jars and potting soil, each group of students constructed a home, or wormery, for these invertebrates. As the students examined their earthworms, each group came up with a different set of questions to explore. One group was concerned about whether their observations would be true for all types of earthworms. How did their worms compare to other earthworms in different parts of the country? Their teacher encouraged them to explore the World Wide Web to find out. Doing so, the students located a professor in Utah who had been studying earthworms of a different variety. From the professor's web site, the students found out how their worms compared to the Utah worms, and then they emailed the professor their own data about worms.

Evaluating Information from the Web   The ability to evaluate the information that you and your students discover on the Internet is critical. You can find material on the World Wide Web that you cannot find in any other medium—partly because any computer-savvy individual can post content on the Web. The upside of this situation is the remarkable access we

TABLE 12.1	Web Sites for Asking Questions of a Scientist	
Name of Site	**URL Address**	**Description**
AllExperts.com	http://www.allexperts.com/	Allexperts.com is a question-and-answer web site that links you with experts in specific areas of knowledge. If you have a science question, for example, you indicate the topic and the web site will show and describe a list of scientists to whom you can address your question. Answers are emailed to you within one to three days unless otherwise indicated.
Ask a Scientist	http://scorescience.humboldt.k12.ca.us/fast/ask.htm	Allows users to ask questions of scientists working within a variety of disciplines (e.g., geologists, physicists).
MadSci Network	http://www.madsci.org/	More than 250 scientists from around the world answer questions. The site also allows students to perform online activities and research.
Space Science Questions	http://spacescience.nasa.gov/questions/	Provides links to a number of ask-a-scientist sites related to space science.
WhaleNet	http://whale.wheelock.edu/	Research scientists with the Whale Conservation Institute of Wheelock College, Boston, will answer questions about whales. Hundreds of questions from other users have been archived on this site.
Windows to the Universe	http://www.windows.ucar.edu/	Allows students and teachers to communicate with astronomers.

now have to original and creative data. The downside is that there is no gatekeeping for the material that makes its way onto this infinite communication network.

The following points can help as a general guide in evaluating web sites:

Guidelines for evaluating web sites

1. If you find a web page that has information you want to use, learn who the author or organization is.

2. Enter the author or organization on a search engine, and see what you find. If nothing shows up, watch out! That often means the source is not reliable.

Computers are excellent resources for scientific data. Here, a student is exploring the Internet for data about tropical rain forests.

Mary Kate Denny/PhotoEdit

3. Check out the hypertext links on a web page. These links should point to other, external sites for your exploration. If all the links point back to internal pages, you may have unreliable data.

4. Communicate with the author of the web site by email if you cannot verify the source's information. Reliable web page authors will respond and give you additional information. If the authors do not respond, that could be a sign that the information is suspect.

Instruments with Computer Interfaces

Interfacing instruments are laboratory instruments that come with a means for connecting them to the personal computer. The most common are probes, which come with related software. The software package is usually on a disk that can be inserted in the computer disk drive, and the probe itself usually has a connecting plug or computer card that fits into a slot on your computer. In computer terminology, the probe "interfaces" with the computer.

Extending the ability to collect and record data

You may be wondering, "Why bother with such additional, fancy equipment?" The reason is that a computer probe can measure properties that are difficult to measure using conventional devices in the classroom. In one third-grade classroom, the students were exploring whether heat is produced during seed germination (see also Reynolds & Barba, 1996, p. 58). They were germinating seeds in plastic bags with wet paper towels and had inserted a temperature probe into one of the bags. This probe took the temperature of the air inside the bag every two hours over the course of five days. Collecting the data every two hours in a conventional way would have been impossible, since no one was around at night. Moreover, the probe stored the readings on the computer disk, making the data easily accessible and manipulable. Using this equipment, the students collected data that indicated a steady temperature rise as the seeds germinated.

Other students in the same class became further involved with the temperature probes and seed germination. Before they left one Friday afternoon, they set up four temperature probes—three in three different seed bags and one in the open air of the classroom—so they could compare the air temperature outside the bags with the temperature inside. On Monday morning, the students were waiting eagerly at the classroom door to see the results.

Video Cameras: Extending Our Senses

Science teachers are finding that a video camera and a tripod are useful technologies for improving and extending the process of observation. One science room teacher set up a video camera and a slow-running videotape the night the class hamster was having babies. Another teacher used a video camera on a tripod to tape the popping of a water balloon. Watching the videotape in slow motion, the students saw things they could not have seen with the unaided eye. Their videotape helped them answer the question, "What really happens when a balloon bursts?" (With a water balloon, from which the water is expelled as the balloon pops, the bursting process is slow enough for the details to be revealed in a video.)

Learning from teacher-made videos

Another excellent use of the video camera is the *video-microscope*, which reveals a microscopic world on a classroom television set. Using this technology, one sixth-grade class observed the single-celled organisms in a small sample of water from a nearby pond. The water was set up on a slide of a microscope connected to a video camera, which displayed its images on a television screen. Because the technology allowed all the students to view the slide at the same time, the teacher was able to facilitate a conversation about the microorganisms with the entire class.

Microscope images on a video screen

Internet Projects and Collaboration

Besides serving as a source of information, the Internet provides a tremendous resource for extending the projects your students undertake and their opportunities for interaction. Let's look at a few of the possibilities.

Web-Based Projects

Imagine that a third-grade class undertakes a project to track the path of monarch butterflies as they migrate in early fall. This annual migration is recorded on databases available on the web, and the data are public information, as are many types of earth and space science data. But the web can do more for the third graders than provide information. For monarch butterflies, the third graders could find a web site where they could contribute their own data and read other people's reactions to viewing the migration. This type of experience—a community of scientists and casual observers alike sharing data via a central site—is unique to the Internet.

WebQuests

Many teachers have begun using projects of this sort in which the web plays a central role in supplying resources, offering the potential for interaction, and extending collaboration. One well-known model of web-based projects is **WebQuest,** an inquiry-oriented activity in which most of all of the resources used by learners come from the World Wide Web. Learners explore these resources in order to perform a task or solve a problem, and often the tasks are designed specifically for teams of students. The student teams can work independently to gather data and complete the projects that the WebQuest defines. WebQuests are especially useful for investigating topics that do not readily lend themselves to concrete in-class manipulation.

WebQuests may be short or long in duration, depending on your goals and what you are hoping the students will learn from the lesson or unit. A good place to begin learning about the potential of WebQuests is the web site of Bernie Dodge, one of the educators responsible for developing the concept. A visit to his site (**http://webquest.sdsu.edu/**) will alert you to the idea that engaging students in a WebQuest requires doing more than simply pointing the students to a few convenient web resources. You need to provide a setting and an introduction to a topic, and you should gather the students' burning questions about that topic. For example, a WebQuest about earthquakes may involve questions ranging from simple ("Where are earthquakes most often found?") to fairly complex ("What causes earthquakes?"). The following science story provides one example of how a WebQuest can be structured.

A WebQuest on Marine Organisms

A group of seventh-grade science teachers wanted to design an inquiry unit on the complex topic of marine organisms. Unable to purchase actual underwater wildlife for their classrooms, they did the next best thing and found the creatures on the Internet. They designed the WebQuest to engage students visually and to motivate them to conduct their own explorations of marine organisms.

A series of
web pages

To present the WebQuest, the teachers created a set of web pages for students to access. The content of those pages is reproduced in the following paragraphs; underlines indicate links to related pages. Notice the structure of the activity: an introduction in the form of a greetings page, a set of tasks in the form of a "mission," a list of resources where students can find relevant websites, an evaluation section in the form of a rubric, and a conclusion. This WebQuest employs a fictitious scenario, in which students are invited to play the role of junior oceanographers.

Underwater Adventure

As members of the graduating class of the Junior Oceanographer Training Center (JOTC), your final mission is as follows:

This morning, upon arriving at the JOTC, we noticed a large cooler outside the main entrance. Inside the cooler, we found crustaceans, mollusks, mammals, fish, and invertebrates. We need your assistance in understanding these creatures. Luckily, they left us riddles—one for each creature, as our first clue.

A mission
for students

Your mission, should you choose to accept it, is to help the staff at JOTC identify and research one species of these marine organisms. Upon completion of this mission, you will be promoted to Senior Oceanographers. Good luck!

Mission

Before you begin, you must solve the riddle on the next page. This will tell you what type of species you are looking for in the cooler by the JOTC entrance. When you know your species, you may pick one organism within the species and then complete a series of tasks.

Task 1: Solve the riddle. It may be tricky, but you can do it! After solving the riddle, check with a teacher to make sure you're right.

Group research

Task 2: Each group of four will divide into two groups of two. Each group of two will then research a particular specimen. Find out where this creature lives (which ocean), what it eats, what level of the ocean it lives in,

TABLE 12.2   **The Assessment Rubric for the Underwater Adventure WebQuest**

	Excellent (20 points)	Good (15 points)	Fair (10 points)	Poor (5 points)
Riddle	The riddle was solved on the first try.	The riddle was solved in two tries.	The riddle was solved in three tries.	The riddle was solved in four or more tries.
Oral Presentation (Science)	Students correctly identify the level of the ocean where the specimen lives, as well as where in the world the organism is commonly found. At least three different foods of the organism are named. At least two of the creature's underwater neighbors are correctly named.	Students correctly identify the level of the ocean where the specimen lives, as well as where in the world the organism is commonly found. At least two different foods of the organism are named. At least two of the creature's underwater neighbors are correctly named.	Students correctly identify either the level of the ocean where the specimen lives *or* where in the world the organism is commonly found. At least one food of the organism is named. At least one of the creature's underwater neighbors is correctly named.	Students do not identify either the level of the ocean where the specimen lives or where in the world the organism is commonly found. Students omit either the organism's food or its underwater neighbors.
Oral Presentation (Language Arts)	The oral presentation is detailed. It begins with a hook sentence and ends with an effective closing. It is given in the first person.	The oral presentation is detailed. It is missing either a hook sentence or an effective closing. It is mostly given in the first person, with a few exceptions.	The oral presentation is not detailed (only general information is given). It is missing either a hook sentence or an effective closing. For the most part, it is not given in the first person.	The oral presentation is not detailed (only general information is given). It is missing both a hook sentence and an effective closing. For the most part, it is not given in the first person.

(continued)

TABLE 12.2   **Continued**

	Excellent (20 points)	Good (15 points)	Fair (10 points)	Poor (5 points)
Scale of Model	The papier-mâché model includes all mathematical work. The scale is correct.	The papier-mâché model includes most mathematical work. The scale is correct, with only minor exceptions.	The papier-mâché model includes some mathematical work. The scale is only partially correct.	The papier-mâché model either does not include mathematical work or includes work that does not correspond to the model. The scale is largely incorrect.
Creativity	The model is colorful and includes all of the organism's features.	The model is colorful and includes most of the organism's features.	The model is either not colorful or does not include many of the organism's features.	The model is not colorful. It is missing many important features of the organism.

and which other creatures might be its underwater neighbors. Prepare an oral presentation about the creature to give to the class. You are to deliver the information in first-person form as if you were the organism. Remember, the presentation will be graded according to both the scientific knowledge expressed and the quality of the language.

Creating models   *Task 3:* As a group, create a papier-mâché model of your organism to display with your oral presentation. Be careful with the details; use appropriate colors and include all the features found on your organism. As we have recently learned in math, your model must be built to scale; you may choose whatever scale you decide is appropriate. All mathematical work must be handed in to show proof that your model has the correct scale. (Be prepared to answer questions about this in your oral report.)

To see the assessment rubric, click here.

Resources

Looking for a resource? Look no further. Just click on one of the links below:

Crustaceans   Mollusks   Fish   Mammals

Conclusion

Congratulations! You have successfully completed your mission to identify and research the marine organisms that were dropped off at the JOTC. Thanks to your efforts, all of the marine animals are now safe at home with their families and friends. Your efforts will be recognized at your promotion ceremony, where you be given the title of Senior Oceanographer. Thank you for all of your help! This mission could not have been accomplished without you.

Extending Student Collaboration Through Email

In everyday life, electronic mail (email) has become a common means of communication. It also offers great potential for extending student collaboration. As discussed in earlier chapters, the communication of ideas is an integral part of doing science. It is a way to deepen and refine one's understanding of a science concept. Email enlarges and facilitates this communication and crosses geographic boundaries in the process.

Email buddies

In one application of email collaboration, students have email "buddies" located in another class across the country. Typically, the buddies' exchanges are related to a common unit or theme. For example, monarch butterflies have different migration patterns on the East Coast and the West Coast. Students tracking these patterns on opposite sides of the country can communicate with each other about what they have learned. In this way, the students get a new perspective on the science topic from their buddies' points of view. In addition, the contact with people from other regions and other cultures often leads to greater understanding of diverse lifestyles.

Students and teachers continue to invent new ways of using email. Here are some of the possibilities (Grabe & Grabe, 2004, p. 200):

Other possible uses of email

- *Global classrooms*, in which several classes study a common topic and exchange accounts of what they have learned.

- *Electronic appearances*, in which a scientist can respond through email to students' questions, as if the scientist were making a guest appearance in the classroom.

- *Electronic mentoring*, in which students in younger grades may be paired with mentors in older grades for email tutoring and the exchange of ideas.

Using Commercial Software for Science Instruction

Many different types of instructional software have science applications. As with the exploration of the World Wide Web, using computer software in the classroom should arise from students' need to know as reflected by their questions and investigations.

Interactive, problem-solving software

The software packages that best lend themselves to inquiry-based activities are those that pose a problem and engage students in interactive manipulation of a simulated natural event. You may wonder why you should use a computer simulation instead of a regular, hands-on experiment in the classroom. The reason is similar to that for using models: computer-simulated investigations often focus on phenomena that cannot be studied directly in the classroom.

Software dissection

As an example, the use of live animals for dissection has become a highly controversial issue. For this reason, among others, it is rarely attempted before high school. However, software simulations of dissections are very useful. They are designed to be interactive—the student acts, and the simulated environment reacts. As the student conducts the electronic procedure, more and more of the inner organs are revealed.

Other simulations allow students to learn in a controlled way about the motions of the planets in the solar system and how electrons flow though an electrical circuit. Many other science subjects also lend themselves to the use of interactive software. Besides permitting students to observe phenomena that are not readily available in schools, simulations often allow manipulations of the environment in ways that would not be possible in the real world. The Electronic Resources listed at the end of this chapter can lead you to some excellent simulations.

Evaluating Software

For any simulation or other software to be useful in creating personal meaning, it has to be interactive with the students in ways that foster their own problem solving. How will you know if a software package can help students build their own meanings? Consider these criteria for evaluating computer software:

Criteria for evaluating software

■ Does the software engage the students in a problem-solving activity?

■ Does it guide students to think about one or more new science ideas?

■ Are there opportunities for the student to personalize the experience presented by the software?

■ Does the software portray gender or ethnic stereotypes?

■ Is the language engaging and at the students' learning level?

■ Are the instructions clear?

■ Are the graphics and design clear and uncluttered?

■ Is there a high degree of student involvement as a result of using this software application?

■ Does the program encourage further discovery learning when it is over?

Where to find
software reviews

Grabe and Grabe (2004) recommend looking up reviews of commercial software products in magazines for educators. For science software, the *Journal of Computers in Mathematics and Science Teaching* and *Computers in the Schools* carry software reviews. The National Science Teachers Association, based in Arlington, Virginia, publishes its own software reviews, as does its science magazine, *Science and Children.* There are also web sites devoted to software reviews, such as the ones named in Table 12.3.

Internet Resources for Teachers

Not only does technology offer rich resources for students' investigations, it also offers many aids for the teacher. In this section we will look at information and curriculum resources that you can find on the Internet. The chapter "What's the Big Idea?" will discuss how to use technology to assess students.

Gateway Sites

There are so many online educational resources available now that teachers can become overwhelmed by the sheer volume of material. For that reason, it is often useful to start at a *gateway site*—that is, a World Wide Web site that provides and attempts to organize links to the wealth of information useful for teachers (Valenza, 2000). When I am interested in learning

TABLE 12.3   Web Sites Offering Reviews of Educational Software

Name of Site	URL Address
California Learning Resource Network	http://www.clrn.org/
Education World: Technology in the Classroom	http://www.educationworld.com/a_tech/
Learning & Leading with Technology	http://www.iste.org/L&L/
SuperKids Educational Software Review	http://www.superkids.com/
Technology & Learning	http://www.techlearning.com/

*A national
clearinghouse*

more about a topic, I often access two gateway sites in particular, ones I find especially useful for my scientific self and for my teacher self.

The first of these is the site for the Eisenhower National Clearinghouse for Mathematics and Science Education. Simply go to **http://www.enc.org/** and find the section on curriculum resources. With the site's search engine, you can define the types of information or curriculum materials you are seeking. (There is also an "Advanced Search" available if you need it.) You may even locate pedagogically appropriate software for use with a given topic at your grade level. In this case, you will be supplied with title, grade, cost, publisher, ordering information, and an abstract. Through this web site, abundant information is available on standards, professional development resources, and other recommended sites to enhance your own understanding of a given science topic.

Another useful gateway site is the Gateway to Educational Materials (**http://www.thegateway.org/**), sponsored by the U.S. Department of Education. At this site, you can specify any combination of topic and grade level, and the resulting web sites should be both useful and informative, offering lesson plans as well as other teaching ideas.

If you begin a search with a qualified gateway site such as these two, you will find material that has been selected for its integrity and relevance to the topic. This method is highly efficient as the number of web sites continues to expand at a phenomenal rate.

*Inspiration is out
there, on the internet,
free for the taking.*
—JOYCE KASMAN
VALENZA

Lesson Plans on the Web

Beyond the gateway sites just mentioned, many other web sites provide a wealth of science lesson plans. These range from the simple to the extremely ambitious, from small-group and single-class projects to multiclass collaborative efforts. The more you explore these sites, the more ideas you can garner for your own use.

*A wealth of
lesson plans*

You can find lesson plans on some of the web sites listed in the Expanding Meanings sections throughout Part Two of this book. In addition, Table 12.4 lists a number of sites that I have found useful, for both general information and lesson plans. I am not suggesting that you should adopt a lesson plan exactly the way you find it at a web site. Rather, you can examine various plans, and then pick and choose among their ideas or modify them for your own classroom.

Evaluating Lesson Plans   For any lesson plan or suggested student activity you find on the web, you may want to apply the general guidelines for web site evaluation listed earlier in this chapter. If the source looks unreliable, be skeptical of using its ideas for students.

Beyond that, here are some specific guidelines for evaluating lesson plans:

*Guidelines for
evaluating online
lesson plans*

■ Does the lesson plan articulate clear learning goals for the students?

■ Does it explain the science ideas behind the lesson?

TABLE 12.4   Some Resources on the World Wide Web for Science Educators

BrainPOP	http://www.brainpop.com/	An interactive site with hundreds of animated movies in science, math, and other areas, made for students in grades K–8. Multiple-choice online quizzes, activity pages, experiments, and comic strips accompany each movie. Two movies can be viewed for free each day.
Earth & Sky Online	http://www.earthsky.com/	An interactive site with excellent links and access to scientific communication, based on a daily science radio series.
Enchanted Learning	http://www.enchantedlearning.com/	Educational activities, games, information pages, diagrams, and label-me printouts for various topics in biology and physical science. A teacher-and-student-friendly site.
Exploratorium: Educate	http://www.exploratorium.edu/educate/	Activities and other features from San Francisco's Exploratorium museum.
Global SchoolNet Foundation	http://www.gsn.org/	Emphasis on global collaborative learning projects.
The GLOBE Program	http://www.globe.gov/	A collaborative, Internet-based environmental education project.
Hands-on Science Centers Worldwide	http://www-2.cs.cmu.edu/afs/cs/usr/mwm/www/sci.html	Links to public museums that emphasize interactive science education.
The Learning Web	http://www.usgs.gov/education/	Activities and teaching resources in earth science, from the U.S. Geological Survey.
NASA Quest	http://quest.arc.nasa.gov/	A NASA site that offers links to many resources related to space exploration.
PBS Science and Technology	http://www.pbs.org/neighborhoods/science/	Educational activities and resources associated with PBS television programs.

(continued)

TABLE 12.4	**Continued**		
Frank Potter's Science Gems	http://www.sciencegems.com/	Links to science activities arranged by topic and grade level.
Scholastic Teachers	http://teacher.scholastic.com/	A teacher resource center and online activities.
The Smithsonian Institution Field Trips and Lesson Resources	http://educate.si.edu/	Offers lesson plans keyed to the Smithsonian's exhibitions.

■ Is the plan written for a specific age or grade level?

■ Does the lesson plan indicate materials and where to get them? (Note this especially for live specimens.)

■ Does the lesson plan give lockstep instructions for the student to follow, or does it provide for flexibility in a constructivist learning environment?

■ Does the plan make connections to the students' lived experiences?

■ Does the plan indicate related sources, literature, or activity books?

Technology and Learning: Some Concluding Thoughts

If computers are destined to play an increasingly important role in education over the next 20 years, it is natural to ask what roles will be played by human beings.
—President's Committee of Advisors on Science and Technology (1997)

This chapter has only scratched the surface of the topic of instructional technology and its uses. Most of what you learn about technology will come—and should come—from your own experiences with it as you begin to teach. Remember that technological applications and lesson plans found on the Internet can never substitute for the exchange of ideas between students and teachers or between students themselves. It is in the process of manipulating ideas that we begin to understand our own thinking and make meaning for ourselves.

How much can technology contribute to learning? I believe it can contribute a great deal as long as certain conditions are met. We can express these conditions as a list of questions (adapted from Healy, 1998, pp. 245–247). Reflect on these as you think about your own experiences integrating technology with science:

Questions to ask about technology

■ Is the technology a substitute for some investigation or science experience? (It shouldn't be.)

■ Are you expecting the technology to teach the concept? (It won't.)

- Were you careful in selecting software and lesson plans? (You must be!)

- Were you seduced by flashy graphics and other technological "bells and whistles"? (Please don't be.)

- Is the activity meaningfully linked to the technology? (Do make the connection meaningful.)

- Did you include a classroom-based interactive activity? For example, did you help the students practice face-to-face interviewing before interviewing a scientist online? Did you engage the students in building a model of the rain forest while you were participating in a computer-simulated adventure in Central America? (This is a very creative use of computer technology and design technology!)

As you become more familiar with ways in which technology supports your own learning, it will be clearer to you how to implement its seamless use in the classroom.

KEY TERMS

instructional technology tools *(p. 282)*
interfacing instruments *(p. 288)*
WebQuest *(p. 290)*

RESOURCES FOR FURTHER EXPLORATION

Electronic Resources

Discovery.com. http://www.discovery.com/.   This web site, based on the Discovery Channel on cable television, provides current and standard information on a range of scientific topics that teachers and students will find valuable.

Eisenhower National Clearinghouse for Mathematics and Science Education. http://www.enc.org/.   An extremely useful gateway site that offers links to a huge variety of science resources.

eSchool News Online. http://www.eschoolnews.com/.   Offers a variety of online news about education topics.

Gateway to Educational Materials. http://www.thegateway.org/.   Another highly recommended gateway site.

Learn the Net. http://www.learnthenet.com/.   A useful site for learning how the Internet and the World Wide Web work.

National Educational Technology Standards. http://cnets.iste.org/   A site that offers the complete set of technology standards discussed in this chapter.

Net Frog. http://curry.edschool.virginia.edu/go/frog.   This site offers a pair of fascinating frog-dissection simulations.

U.S. Fish and Wildlife Service. http://www.fws.gov/. Provides a vast amount of information about wildlife in the United States, including data that students can use in their investigations.

U.S. Geological Survey. http://www.usgs.gov/. Do you want students to map earthquake regions? Track floods and droughts? The USGS site offers an abundance of data on all matters geological.

The WebQuest Page. http://webquest.sdsu.edu/. An excellent introduction to WebQuests.

Print Resources

Ebenezer, J., & Lau, E. (2003). *Science on the Internet: A Resource for K–12 Teachers*, 2d ed. Upper Saddle River, NJ: Prentice Hall. This guide helps teachers create and facilitate constructivist learning experiences for students by using the Internet as a tool for constructing meaning and furthering critical thinking.

Ertmer, P., Hruskocy, C., & Woods, D. (2003). *Education on the Internet: The Worldwide Classroom*. Upper Saddle River, NJ: Prentice Hall. This easy-to-use handbook is designed to guide the teacher in using the Internet. It explains how to access people, curriculum materials, and resources for personal professional development.

Gilster, P. (1998). *Digital Literacy*. New York: Wiley. This book's title refers to the ability to understand and evaluate the myriad of information, offered in a multitude of formats, that we get through computers. A fine discussion of the need for digital literacy in contemporary society.

Grabe, M., & Grabe, C. (2004). *Integrating Technology for Meaningful Learning*. 4th ed. Boston: Houghton Mifflin. A detailed and helpful guide to using technology in an integrated manner.

Reynolds, K., & Barba, R. (1997). *Technology for Teaching and Learning of Science*. Needham Heights, MA: Allyn and Bacon. This book speaks directly about the unique attributes of science teaching that are congruent with technology applications.

13 Science Content and Curriculum
The Big Ideas and Your Scientific Self

FOCUSING QUESTIONS

▮ What science concepts should you explore?

▮ How do you personalize science content and make it your own?

▮ When you think of a system, what comes to mind?

▮ What is the difference between a book of science standards and a curriculum?

▮ How can you use the National Science Education Standards in your own science teaching?

As a child, I was always highly curious about things, especially things related to nature, but there was very little available at my reading level that presented answers to my questions in ways I could readily understand. Today, many teachers I meet feel the same way. You may feel this way, too. You may want to gain more information about a scientific topic, but often find that the available resources provide excessive detail or technical jargon that obscures the underlying main idea or concept.

This gap in science literature presents a serious problem for teachers. As you should have noticed in the science stories throughout this book, effective teachers guide students as they make sense of new ideas. Teachers listen and reflect back the students' understandings of the ideas, and these conversations help to further the students' understandings. A teacher's ability to do this is often related to his or her own level of comfort with the scientific material.

As a teacher, then, you'll want to continue developing your own understanding of science concepts. In this chapter, I hope to give you a jump-start by offering a guide to some of the science content your students will be exploring. The chapter cannot discuss all of the topics you will delve into, but the ideas and understandings described here will help you frame many of your learning goals for your students. They will help you define what your students can come to understand about the natural world from the investigations in which you engage them. In the chapter's Resources for Further Exploration, you'll find suggestions for additional reading that can help you continue expanding your scientific understandings.

Our role is not just to "cover" a curriculum, but rather to help students uncover ideas and meanings.

After discussing some of the major science topics that elementary and middle school students investigate, this chapter will go on to explore how these topics are organized into a curriculum that meets local, state, and national standards. Wherever you teach, you will probably be given a textbook or a set of materials that represents the curriculum you are supposed to "cover." As you've seen throughout this book's *Science Stories*, however, our role as teachers is not just to "cover" a curriculum but to help students *uncover* the ideas and meanings that emerge through their own experiences. This chapter will help you understand how to approach a science curriculum so that this learning can truly take place.

Making Big Ideas Your Own Ideas

The major governing concepts in science are known as its "big ideas." The ones presented in this chapter have emerged from repeated experimentation and investigation, and they form part of scientists' "taken for granted" way of seeing things (Driver et al., 1994).

These scientific concepts were not magically revealed to people. Rather, they were arrived at by lots of intellectual struggle among scientists who have engaged with each other and individually in making meaning of their observations and experience. These ideas were created through the same sort of knowledge construction and conversation that you have seen in classrooms.

Understanding this, it is important to recognize that just by reading the following science ideas or concepts, you will not make them your own. You need to interrogate these ideas in the ways you know your own students will have to do. To construct your own meaning for the science concepts in this chapter, ask yourself the following questions as you read about each one:

Questions to ask

■ Have I had any experience with this idea?

■ Does it make sense to me?

■ How can I find out more about this topic?

■ How does this concept fit in with what I already believe about nature?

Having this conversation with yourself will help you to develop your scientific self and make these ideas your own. As you have noticed throughout *Science Stories*, it is even more helpful to discuss science concepts with others who may have different interpretations and prior experiences. Having such conversations helps you to clarify your own understandings.

Ways of Thinking About Science Topics

STANDARDS ☑

As noted in earlier chapters, students' scientific explorations will address a wide variety of topics, from classroom pets to electric circuits to the solar system. A traditional way of organizing this multitude of topics is to divide them into the three areas of life science, physical science, and earth science. The National Science Education Standards (NSES) specify topics for each of these three areas, as shown in Table 13.1 (National Research Council, 1996). The NSES also include five other "content standards":

NSES content standards

■ Unifying concepts and processes

■ Science as inquiry

■ Science and technology

■ Science in personal and social perspectives

■ History and nature of science

In this chapter, however, I also offer an alternative organization of science topics using just two conceptual categories:

TABLE 13.1	**National Science Education Standards for Physical Science, Life Science, and Earth and Space Science** STANDARDS ☑		
	Physical Science	**Life Science**	**Earth and Space Science**
Grades K–4	Properties of objects and materials Position and motion of objects Light, heat, electricity, and magnetism	Characteristics of organisms Life cycles of organisms Organisms and environments	Properties of earth materials Objects in the sky Changes in earth and sky
Grades 5–8	Properties and changes of properties in matter Motions and forces Transfer of energy	Structure and function in living systems Reproduction and heredity Regulation and behavior Populations and ecosystems Diversity and adaptations of organisms	Structure of the earth system Earth's history Earth in the solar system

Excerpted from Tables 6.8 and 6.9 in National Research Council, *National Science Education Standards.* Washington, DC: National Academy Press, 1996, pp. 109–110.

Two conceptual categories

- Systems

- Interactions and patterns of change

One of the essential components of higher order thinking is the ability to think about a whole in terms of its parts and about the parts in terms of how they relate to one another and to the whole.
—BENCHMARKS FOR SCIENCE LITERACY (*AAAS, 1993*)

I believe that these categories, adapted from the New York State *Learning Standards for Mathematics, Science, and Technology* (1996), can help you gain a better grasp of science content and understand how all the areas of elementary and middle school science relate to one another. This approach to science content is also consistent with the notion of "unifying concepts and processes" advanced in the NSES.

Figure 13.1 illustrates the way a number of science topics fit into the two conceptual categories. For reference, the figure also identifies the topics according to the three traditional science areas. In practice, you'll find that some schools and districts present science units strictly according to the divisions of life, physical, and earth science, whereas other schools organize the material according to unifying concepts. Some schools make explicit reference to the categories in the NSES. Whatever way the material

FIGURE 13.1
Basic science topics
Here the topics are organized in two ways: by conceptual category and by the traditional areas of life science, physical science, and earth science. Some topics, such as properties of matter, might fall in either conceptual category.

	Systems	Interactions and Patterns of Change
Life science	Ourselves Human body systems Plants Animals Habitats	The five senses Life cycles Tropisms Food chains
Physical science	Properties of matter: ■ Solids, liquids, gases ■ Sinking and floating ■ Solutions and suspensions Simple machines	Matter and its changes: ■ Chemical and physical change ■ Heat energy Electricity and magnetism Light energy and color Sound energy
Earth science	Solar system Dinosaurs	Weather and seasonal change Earth motions Rocks, soil, erosion Earthquakes and volcanoes Environmental science: ■ Oil spills ■ Conservation and recycling ■ Air and water pollution Moon phases

may be organized in your own school's curriculum, you can make it come alive by challenging yourself—and your students—to see what apparently different topics have in common.

Systems

Understanding how systems operate requires that you identify how the parts of a system interrelate and combine to perform specific functions. You also need to recognize the commonalities that exist among all systems.

As you read and think about systems, the useful questions you can ask yourself include these:

Questions about systems

- Is this system open or closed or both?

- Is it a naturally occurring system?

- Do human beings impact this system? How?

- How do the parts of the system contribute to the functioning of the whole?

In the school science curriculum, students are often asked to observe and describe interactions among components of simple systems. As examples, I have selected three topics commonly taught in elementary and middle school that relate to systems: the solar system, the systems of the human body, and simple machines.

The Solar System

The solar system is made up of a group of objects, sometimes called heavenly or celestial bodies, that move around the sun. These celestial bodies are also called *satellites*. Satellites can move around the sun or around other celestial bodies. Hence, the moon is a satellite of the Earth. The Earth itself is a satellite of the sun; or we could say that the Earth-moon system is a satellite of the sun. When one heavenly body moves around another, we call that movement *revolution*.

The Sun and the Planets   The sun is a *star*—one of billions of stars in the universe. Unlike the Earth, the sun is not a solid body; rather, it is a huge ball of extremely hot gases. It is much larger than the Earth. In fact, the diameter of the sun at its equator is 109 times greater than the diameter of the Earth. As we saw in an earlier chapter, if the sun were a hollow ball, we could fit over a million Earths inside it. Nevertheless, compared to other stars in the universe, the sun is not a particularly large star. It appears larger to us than other stars because it is so much closer to Earth. We often refer to it as *our star*.

There are nine planets that travel around the sun. (Recently, though, there has been debate about Pluto's planetary status. Many astronomers

A student explores a model of planetary motion as he tries to make meaning.

Stephen Frisch/Stock Boston

Planetary orbits

feel it is too small and remote to be a true planet in our solar system.) Along with the sun, these planets are considered the major members of the solar system. Planets are much smaller than the sun and do not make their own light. They shine in the night sky by *reflecting* the light of the sun.

The nine planets travel around the sun in specific paths called *orbits*. Since these orbits are slightly elliptical, all nine planets move closer to and farther from the sun at different points in their orbits. As you saw in the chapter "Making Models," the average distances of the planets from the sun place them in the following order: Mercury, Venus, Earth, Mars, Jupiter, Saturn, Uranus, Neptune, and Pluto. (However, Pluto's orbit sometimes takes it closer to the sun than Neptune.)

Most planets *rotate*—that is, spin like a top—as they travel around the sun. Hence, we say that they are rotating as they are revolving. They rotate around an imaginary axis, which runs though the north and south poles of each planet. The time needed for each planet to make one complete rotation is called the planets' *day*, and the time needed for the planet to make one complete revolution around the sun is called the planet's *year*. All the planets revolve in a counterclockwise direction around the sun; however, their periods of rotation and revolution differ quite a bit from each other. Obviously, the farthest planets have the longest periods of revolution, while the closest planets revolve in the shortest amount of time. Mercury's 88 days of revolution makes its year much shorter than the 365-day Earth year.

Most of the planets have satellites of their own. Like Earth's satellite, these are called moons. Astronomers have discovered more than sixty moons in the solar system.

Asteroids   **Smaller Objects in the Solar System**   Other celestial objects in the solar system include *asteroids*, which are also called planetoids. There are many theories about how these chunks of rocklike materials formed, but they travel together in what is referred to as the *belt of asteroids*. This belt contains more than 25,000 asteroids orbiting the sun between Mars and Jupiter.

The asteroids are much smaller than planets. They reflect light like planets do, and they differ in size and brightness. They are really like little planets, which is why they are also called planetoids.

Meteors   Other rocks, called *meteors*, are found in the space through which the Earth travels as it orbits the sun. When meteors encounter the Earth's atmosphere, the force of friction between the meteor and the atmosphere causes the meteor to heat up and begin to burn. As they burn up, they look like stars shooting across the sky, and for that reason they are often called "shooting stars," a term that confuses them with real stars. Meteors that fall to Earth without burning up are called *meteorites*. Sometimes meteorites form craters when they crash into the ground.

Comets   *Comets* are celestial bodies that revolve around the sun in long, oval-shaped orbits that sometimes cut across the orbits of the planets. Comets are made up of small rocks and dust, mixed with frozen gases. As a comet nears the sun in its orbit, it appears to form a "tail," which is really the changing of the frozen gases into vapor. A comet's tail may be millions of miles long; but as its orbit takes it away from the sun's proximity, the comet "loses" its tail. Some comets make regular appearances. For instance, Halley's comet orbits the sun every seventy-six years; it was last visible from the Earth in 1986. Other comets are seen once and never return, appearing to waste away. No one is quite sure how comets form.

Gravity and Inertia: Governing Principles of the Solar System   Think about all these planets, moons, and other celestial objects moving together in much the same way over billions of years. What makes these components into a system? Here we have a traditional earth science unit, but to understand it, we need to call on two important principles of physical science: (1) the law of gravitation and (2) inertia.

1. **The Law of Gravitation.** You may ask yourself: What causes planets' paths to bend into orbits around the sun?

Newton's law of gravitation

The scientist Isaac Newton (1642–1727) helped to explain the underlying reasons why the planets, their moons, and other objects in the solar system move in the way they do. The most important and significant understanding is called Newton's law of **gravitation,** which states that every body in the universe attracts or pulls on every other body with a gravitational force that increases when the masses of the objects increase and decreases as the objects move farther away from each other.

In the solar system, each of the objects exerts a gravitational pull on each of the other objects. Because the sun is enormous in comparison to the planets and other objects, it has a much greater pull of gravity than any other body in the solar system. The continual, mutual gravitational attraction between the sun and the planets keeps the planets revolving in their orbits around the sun. The sun tends to pull the planets toward itself, but the distance of the planets from the sun and their mutual gravitational attraction for each other serve to keep them in defined paths.

2. **Inertia.** A body in motion tends to continue in the same motion at the same speed unless it is acted upon by an outside force. Similarly, an object at rest tends to stay at rest unless it is acted upon by an outside force that gets it moving. These ideas were also constructed by Isaac Newton after repeated experiments and investigations. They are known as Newton's first law of motion.

Why planets keep going

The tendency of a body to continue with the same motion at the same speed or to remain at rest is called inertia. This principle is responsible for the fact that the planets, once they are moving in a certain path, remain in that motion unless some outside force changes it.

You can see that the solar system is indeed a working *system*, like an enormous, complex mechanism with many diverse components. The sun is at the helm, so to speak. It drives the orbits of the smaller parts with its enormous gravitational pull, relying on inertia and gravitational attractions to maintain the smaller objects' constant motion in their paths so that nothing comes crashing into the sun.

Thinking About   **SYSTEMS**

The Interconnection of Parts

Frequently, students are immersed in learning about the parts of a system without studying the larger picture: How do the parts connect? In the case of the solar system, each planet and each planetary system (those with one or more moons) affects and is affected by the gravitational attraction between objects in the universe. It is their cumulative *effect on each other* that maintains the entire solar system in its continual pattern of orbital motion.

The human body is another complex system—in fact, it is a system composed of a number of smaller systems. In a typical life science unit in elementary or middle school, students explore in depth the body's digestive, circulatory, respiratory, and nervous systems. Therefore, in the following section, I have chosen to expand on these four body systems. It is important to stress, however, that all these systems function together to maintain the lives of human beings. Hence, as we explore four of the major body systems, we will also be thinking about how interconnected they are.

Human Body Systems

In the science story "What Does It Mean to Be Alive?" (in the chapter "Sustained Inquiry"), you saw young children beginning to understand the most important aspect of living things: their ability to exchange materials with their environment, taking in what they need and getting rid of what they do not need. Our body systems perform these functions for us.

A *body system* is a group of organs that work together on a specific bodily activity. There are a number of large systems in the human body. Working all together, they produce this smoothly running machine called the human body.

One typical way of thinking about body systems is to divide them into ten different but connected systems:

Body systems

1. The *skin system* that covers the body and includes our nails, hair, and skin. The skin is thought of as the largest organ in the body.

2. The *skeletal system* of bones that support us.

3. The *muscular system* that makes it possible for the body and its parts to move; this system includes our muscles, ligaments, and tendons.

4. The *digestive system,* including mouth, stomach, intestines, and liver, which breaks down foods so that all parts of the body may use the nutrients they need to produce energy and grow.

5. The *circulatory system* that uses our blood vessels and capillaries to transport nutrients and get rid of some wastes.

6. The *respiratory system* that allows us to breathe in and out by using the nose, windpipe, lungs, and diaphragm.

7. The *excretory system,* including kidneys and bladder, that gets rid of the waste products formed in the body.

8. The *reproductive system* that produces offspring and includes organs that affect sex characteristics.

9. The *endocrine system,* a system of glands that secrete chemical messengers, called hormones, which control and regulate the actions of the body.

10. The *nervous system,* including the brain, neurons (nerves), and the spinal cord.

The following sections describe four body systems that students frequently examine in their school science units. As you read, think about interconnections among body systems. Notice how often, in describing one system, we make reference to another related system.

The Digestive System   The body needs food in order to live and grow. The foods we eat contain materials that give the body energy and enable it to build and repair tissues and regulate other activities. The **digestive system** breaks food down into particles so tiny that blood can take nourishment to all parts of the body. The food undergoes a process of physical change as it goes from larger pieces to smaller pieces. It also undergoes a process of chemical change as it is transformed into soluble nutrients that can pass through the membranes of organs and blood vessels and into the body cells. We will explore other aspects of physical and chemical changes later in this chapter.

The digestive system's main part is a 30-foot (9-meter) tube from mouth to rectum called the *alimentary canal*. Muscles in this food tube force food along. This muscular action, called peristalsis, is strong enough to allow a person standing on his head to chew something and have it go "down" (really up) to the stomach.

The digestive process

In the mouth, food is physically changed when it is chewed by our teeth; it is also chemically changed by the chemicals in our saliva. The food then travels from the mouth to the stomach by way of the part of the food tube known as the *esophagus*. For two to three hours, food stays in the stomach, where digestive juices further change it.

After the stomach churns and liquefies the food, it passes through the very convoluted small intestine, which is 23 feet (7 meters) long. In the small intestine, digestive juices from the gall bladder, the small intestine itself, and the pancreas break down food particles. Many of these broken-down particles filter out through tiny, fingerlike structures on the inside of the small intestine called villi. Food that cannot be digested or used by the body passes from the small intestine into the large intestine as waste material. There, this undigested food forms feces and leaves the body through the anus. This process is referred to as elimination.

The parts of the digestive system all work together to ensure that food is broken down and absorbed and unwanted food is eliminated. For the system to be effective, it must complete all three of these main tasks. As we explore the circulatory system, you will see that digesting the food would be useless if our blood could not transport the digested nutrients to the body cells.

The Circulatory System   The **circulatory system** is made up of the heart and blood vessels, which together maintain a continuous flow of blood around the body. The circulatory system has three main functions:

■ To carry digested nutrients to the cells in the body.

■ To bring oxygen to the cells so it can be combined with the nutrients to release energy.

■ To take away soluble waste materials and carry them to organs that remove them from the body.

Types of blood vessels

The heart pumps oxygen-rich blood from the lungs to all parts of the body through a network of tubes or blood vessels called *arteries* and smaller branches called *arterioles.* Blood returns to the heart through small vessels called *venules,* which lead in turn into larger vessels called *veins.* Notice that arteries carry blood away from the heart, while veins carry blood back to the heart.

A network of tiny blood vessels called *capillaries* links arterioles and venules. Capillaries reach all parts of the body, and they are the sites where the blood deposits oxygen and picks up carbon dioxide. This ongoing exchange between the blood and the body cells is regulated by the circulatory system.

The heart pumps the blood to every part of the body and back again in about thirty seconds. The blood, a liquid organ, has four main parts:

Components of blood

■ *Red blood cells* pick up oxygen from the lungs and carry it to the cells in the body. The cells use the oxygen to burn food, and the waste material is produced as carbon dioxide. Red blood cells pick up the carbon dioxide and carry it to the lungs where it is given off.

■ *White blood cells* are much less numerous than red blood cells (ratio of 1 to 600) and their purpose is to destroy bacteria and other disease germs.

■ *Platelets* are tiny cells, even smaller than the red blood cells, and their function is to help the blood clot when the body is injured and bleeds. The clot prevents the blood from flowing out of the body.

■ *Plasma* is the liquid portion of the blood.

How does circulation work?

The heart is a strong muscle, about the size of your fist, located to the left of the middle of the chest. It contracts and relaxes, acting like a pump. When it contracts, it pushes blood into the arteries; when it relaxes, blood flows into it from the veins. The human heart has four chambers: two upper chambers, called the right atrium and left atrium, and two lower chambers, called the right ventricle and left ventricle. The two sides of the heart are completely separated by a wall called a septum; hence, blood in the two sides of the heart does not mix.

The atria receive blood from the veins and pump it down to the ventricles. (Valves on both sides of the heart prevent blood from flowing back into the atria.) The ventricles then pump blood into the arteries. The right ventricle pumps blood to the lungs via the pulmonary artery, and the left ventricle pumps blood to the other organs of the body via the artery named the aorta. The steps look something like this:

1. The blood is pumped out of the right ventricle to the lungs, where it picks up oxygen and deposits carbon dioxide. The reasons for this exchange will become apparent as you read about the respiratory system in the next section.

2. The oxygen-rich blood then leaves the lungs and goes to the left atrium, where it is pumped to the left ventricle and then to the entire rest of the body, depositing oxygen to the body cells.

3. The blood returns to the right atrium of the heart, filled with carbon dioxide from the body cells and needing oxygen. It then is pumped to the right ventricle and starts the cycle all over again.

The *circulating* of the blood from the heart to the lungs and back again, and from the heart to the entire rest of the body and back again, is what gives this system its name. Figure 13.2 shows a simplified, schematic diagram of the system.

The Respiratory System   The **respiratory system** supplies the oxygen needed by body cells and carries off their carbon dioxide waste. Inhaled air passes via the trachea (windpipe), through two narrower tubes called bronchi, into the lungs. Each lung is made up of many fine branching tubes called bronchioles, which end in tiny clustered chambers or air sacs called alveoli.

FIGURE 13.2
The circulatory system
The right side of the heart pumps blood to the lungs, where it picks up oxygen and gives up carbon dioxide. This oxygen-rich blood then goes to the left side of the heart, which pumps it to the rest of the body. The cells of the body use the oxygen and give off carbon dioxide, which the blood then carries back to the right side of the heart, where the cycle begins again.

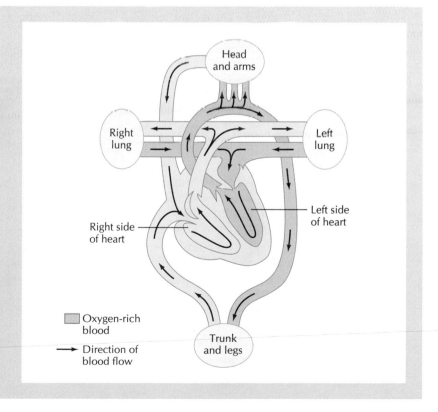

Structure of the lungs

The alveoli look like tiny clusters of grapes, and each lung is one great mass of these air sacs. Gases in the air pass through the thin walls of the alveoli to and from a network of capillaries. Thus, the oxygen in the air enters the blood through these air sacs. The capillaries send the oxygen-rich blood to the left side of the heart, where it is then pumped to the rest of the body.

The cells in the body use the oxygen to combine with digested food, producing energy and giving off carbon dioxide. The red blood cells then pick up the carbon dioxide, and this blood is pumped back to the right side of the heart, where it travels to the lungs via the pulmonary artery. Now the carbon dioxide leaves the blood, diffusing through the thin walls of the capillaries and of the alveoli. The air containing the carbon dioxide is then forced out of the lungs, and the fresh air containing oxygen is forced into the lungs.

The term **respiration** refers to this exchange of gases. Think again about the students in the chapter "Sustained Inquiry" who discussed the exchange of materials in which living things are engaged. Respiration and digestion are two of the body processes that implement this exchange.

Respiration vs. breathing: what's the difference?

Respiration should not be confused with breathing. When we talk about *breathing*, we are referring to the mechanical process of getting oxygen-rich air into the lungs and getting carbon dioxide–rich air out of the body. *Respiration* refers to the metabolic process by which cells take in the oxygen they need and give back carbon dioxide as a waste product.

How Do We Breathe?

A common alternative conception is that when we inhale, the lungs draw in air and the chest therefore expands. This is not true.

What actually happens is that air outside the body is forced into the lungs when the air pressure inside the body becomes lower than the air pressure outside. How can that occur?

When you begin to take a breath, a sheet of muscle in the bottom of your chest cavity, the *diaphragm*, contracts and moves downward. Simultaneously, your rib muscles contract and move upward and outward. These movements increase the size of your chest cavity, thus reducing the pressure of the air already in your lungs. (When you expand the space that a gas occupies, the pressure drops.) Air then rushes in from outside. When you exhale, the reverse occurs: the muscles in your diaphragm relax and your ribs move downward and inward, forcing air out of your lungs and out of your body.

The nose and nasal passages, the throat (pharynx), the windpipe (trachea), and the voice box (larynx) are all part of this system. They are passages through which the air passes. In the nasal passages, the air is warmed and moistened and tiny dirt particles are trapped. The back of the throat has a flap over the trachea called the epiglottis, which closes when food and water enter the throat, thus preventing the food and water from entering the windpipe.

The Nervous System   The **nervous system** is the body's internal, electro-chemical communications network. Its main parts are the brain, spinal cord, and nerves. The nervous system has many functions, including controlling the actions of the organs, muscles, and other tissues; controlling sensations such as smell, taste, sight, hearing, touch, pressure, heat, cold, and pain; and controlling thinking, learning, and memory.

The brain and spinal cord form the *central nervous system*, the body's chief controlling and coordinating mechanism. The brain is located in the skull, and the spinal cord lies along almost the entire length of the back. The spinal cord connects with the brain stem through a large hole in the base of the skull. The brain is the major organ of the nervous system and the control center for the body's voluntary and involuntary activities. It is also responsible for the complexities of thought, memory, emotion, and language. In adults, the brain weighs a mere 3 pounds (1.4 kilograms) but contains more than ten thousand million nerve cells.

Structure of the brain

The brain has three distinct regions, the brain stem, the cerebellum, and the cerebrum, each responsible for controlling different types of bodily functions. The *brain stem* controls vital bodily functions, such as breathing and respiration, circulation, and digestion. The *cerebellum*'s main functions are the maintenance of posture and the coordination of body movements. The *cerebrum*, the largest region, consists of the right and left cerebral hemispheres, and it is the site of most conscious and intelligent activities.

Nerves spread out from the brain and spinal cord to every part of the body. There are three main types of nerve cells, or *neurons*:

Types of neurons

■ *Sensory neurons* are the nerve cells that allow us to experience sensations. The cell bodies of these neurons are located in the brain and spinal cord, but they have long fibers that spread out to sense organs all over the body.

■ *Motor neurons* have to do with producing motion in the body. Their cell bodies are also located in the brain and spinal cord, and their fibers spread out to muscles, tissues, and organs of the body.

■ *Associative* or *central neurons,* located between the cell bodies of the sensory and motor neurons, transfer nerve impulses from the sensory neurons to the motor neurons. That is, the associative neurons act as go-betweens for receiving and sending messages in the nervous system.

The brain, the spinal cord, and the system of billions of long neurons control the operations of all other systems in the human body.

Thinking About   **SYSTEMS**

Noticing Similarities and Differences

Some systems are *open,* meaning that materials enter them and leave them. Other systems tend to be *closed,* so they do not receive external material or discharge material. Still other systems are open and closed at different times.

The digestive and respiratory systems are obviously open systems. What about the circulatory and nervous systems—are they open or closed?

The circulatory system is closed in the sense that the blood vessels and organs are contained within the body. When we bleed, however, the system is open. More important, when we exchange gases through the respiratory system, the circulatory system receives and releases those gases. In that sense, too, it is open.

The nervous system may be thought of as open in that it responds to external as well as internal stimuli. It is also closed in the sense that nothing tangible enters or leaves it.

You can see how complex and interrelated the body systems are. Think about these further questions:

■ Is the solar system an open or closed system?

■ What do the sun, the alimentary canal, the diaphragm, the heart, and the brain have in common?

■ In what ways is the circulatory system like a transportation system?

■ What do you think is meant by the often-used term "brain-dead?" How could a person be alive if his or her brain were dead?

■ How would *you* define a system on the basis of what you have just read and thought about?

We use the word *system* to mean many different things. We talk about political systems, for example, or school systems or transportation systems. The *Benchmarks for Science Literacy* (AAAS, 1993) remind us that most people see systems as a collection of things and processes (and often people) that interact to perform some function. The scientific idea of a system implies detailed attention to inputs and outputs as well as to interactions among the system components. In the next section, as you explore simple machines—a traditional physical science unit—think about what connections might be drawn among these devices, the solar system, and the human body. What links and similarities do you see yourself? What ideas might your students explore? In what ways is the functioning of the human body like a system of machines?

Simple Machines

Frequently, students learn about simple machines as discrete topics. Each type of machine discussed is not connected to other simple machines or to more complex machines. In this section, you'll read about several kinds of simple machines. As you read, consider how they relate to each other. Ask yourself questions like these:

Questions about machines

■ Where do I use this machine?

■ How does it make work easier?

■ Where does it appear as part of a more complicated device?

■ What makes it a system?

Remember, reflecting on the concepts that you read, having conversations about them, and making your own meaning from them will enable you to claim these ideas as your own.

Work and Force   A *machine* is any device that helps make people's work easier. But what exactly do we mean by work?

Defining work

In science, the term **work** is defined in this way: Work is done when a force is applied to move something. It is the act of applying a force to move an object through a distance. We change an object's position when we do work.

A **force** is a push or a pull. You encountered the term *force* earlier in this chapter in the discussion of gravity and inertia. Gravity is a force—an attraction, a pull of any object in the universe on any other. You can think of the sun as doing work as it exerts its gravitational pull and helps to keep the planets and other objects in orbit around it. Of course, forces are also produced by people when they use their muscles. When you pull this book toward you and change its position, you are doing work.

Machines help us do work in several different ways:

How do machines help do work?

1. By transferring force from one place to another.

2. By increasing the amount of force applied.

3. By changing the direction of a force: for instance, when you pull *down* on a rope to raise a flag *up* a flagpole.

4. By increasing the speed of a force so that things can move farther and faster.

One way to study simple machines is to divide them into different types. Let's look at six types that are commonly explored in school science: the lever, the wheel and axle, the pulley, the inclined plane, the wedge, and the screw. These simple machines receive their force mainly from human muscles, like yours. They are devices that are used to get specific tasks done. Although these simple machines are different, remember to look for commonalities among them.

Lever   A *lever* is a rigid bar that rests or moves around a fixed point, called a *fulcrum*. The seesaw is an example of a lever. So are a crowbar, scissors, and pliers. These types of levers, called *first-class levers*, change the direction of the force. As you apply force in one direction, the object you are lifting or moving goes in the other direction.

The seesaw as a lever

Think about being on a seesaw or teeter-totter (Figure 13.3a.). As you move down, your partner moves up. To understand why the seesaw is helping you perform work, think about how difficult it would be to lift your partner the same distance without the seesaw.

The seesaw example also helps show how force and distance are related. Your force on the seesaw depends on your weight. Let's say that your partner weighs more than you do. When you first sit on the seesaw, your weight isn't enough to move your partner up. What will you do? You will move to the very end of the seesaw, increasing your distance from the fulcrum; by doing so, you decrease the force needed to lift your partner.

A *second-class lever* also reduces the force you need to apply, but the force and the object you are moving go in the same direction. The wheelbarrow, a bottle opener, and an oar for a rowboat are examples of these simple systems.

A *third-class lever* supplies a gain in speed and distance. Examples of such levers are a broom, a shovel, and a fishing pole. To achieve greater speed and distance, the third-class lever actually causes a loss in force: as you sweep with a broom, the broom head moves faster and farther than your hands do, but with less force.

Wheel and Axle   A *wheel and axle* is like a spinning lever. A large wheel is connected to a smaller circular device, called the axle or shaft. The fulcrum is in the center of the axle and the wheel. Once the wheel turns, the axle

FIGURE 13.3
Simple machines
(a) A seesaw as a first-class lever. Notice how the lighter person can lift the heavier person by sitting farther from the fulcrum.
(b) A wheel and axle.
(c) A pulley.

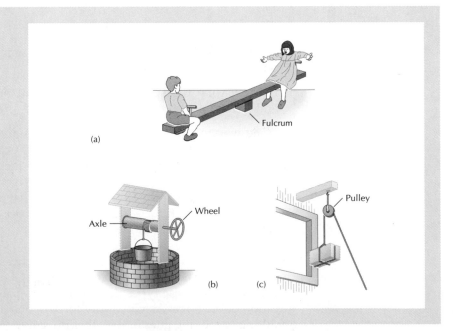

turns (see Figure 13.3b). A wheel and axle can change the direction of a force and also amplify the force.

Common wheel-and-axle machines

Examples of wheel-and-axle machines that contain complete wheels include the steering wheel in a car, the gear wheels of a bicycle, a doorknob, and a screwdriver. The steering wheel revolves around an axle called the steering column; the bicycle gears revolve around an axle called a shaft; and a doorknob revolves around an axle called a rod. The handle of a screwdriver does more than enable you to hold it. It amplifies the force you use to turn it to drive the screw home! Its axle is the screwdriver blade.

With a wheel and axle, as the wheel rotates it moves a greater distance than the axle but turns with less force. That is, when you turn the wheel, the axle turns with a greater force than the wheel. In this way, a small rotary motion can open a locked door!

Sometimes a crank instead of a wheel is attached to the axle. Wheel-and-axle machines with a crank include a manual eggbeater and a pencil sharpener.

Pulley   A *pulley* (Figure 13.3c) is a wheel that turns around a stationary axle. When the pulley wheel turns, the axle does not turn. Usually there is a groove in the pulley wheel so that a rope around the pulley will stay in place. Sometimes there are two or more pulley wheels side by side on the same axle. If the pulley wheel is attached to a stationary point, it is called a fixed pulley.

What does a pulley do?

You use a pulley to change the direction of a force and make work easier. Fixed pulleys are used when raising flags along flagpoles and when pulling curtains or Venetian blinds open or closed. A fixed pulley is like a spinning first-class lever. The fulcrum is at the center of the axle. An elevator is a single-pulley lifting machine. The elevator car is raised or lowered by a cable running over a pulley at the top of the elevator shaft.

Inclined Plane   An *inclined plane* is a slanting surface that connects one level to another level. A hill, a wheelchair ramp, a sloping floor, an escalator, and a stairway are all examples of inclined planes. Moving an object up an inclined plane requires less force than lifting it straight up to a higher position. The longer the inclined plane, the less steep the slope and the less force required. The tradeoff is that, to reduce the force needed, the inclined plane increases the distance traveled.

A tradeoff: less force, greater distance

Wedge   A *wedge* is a simple machine used to spread an object apart or to raise an object. The wedge is like a moving inclined plane. It has a sloping side, but it is moved under an object or into an object. A typical doorstop is a single wedge. Examples of double-sided wedges are the blade of an ax, a scissors blade, and a plow blade; each of these is sloped on two sides.

Common wedges

A nail is a type of wedge, and so is a pin. Shovel blades can be examples of wedges. A chisel is a perfect example of a wedge. The longer or thinner a wedge is, the greater the advantage in using it.

The screw as a winding plane

Screw   A *screw* is an inclined plane that winds around and around in a spiral. The spiral ridge of the screw is called the thread. An ordinary wood screw or bolt are examples. Other examples include the caps of jars and bottles, the base of an electric light bulb, and the part of a vise that opens and closes the jaws. Usually another simple machine, such as a lever or a wheel and axle, is used with a screw to reduce the force needed. With a wood screw, for instance, you use a screwdriver; with a vise, you use a handle.

Thinking About   SYSTEMS

Simple Machines As Systems

All machines make work easier for people. Each of the machines discussed in this chapter represents a system—parts working together to perform a function.

A single wedge, for example, is a movable inclined plane. Combine it with a simple lever and you have a shovel! Can you see why these are systems? The lever needs a bar and a fulcrum, working together. The wedge needs a flat slope and an inclined slope. Putting them together, you can clear the snow from your front walk or tend to your garden.

To expand your understanding of machines as systems, ponder these questions:

■ Are *you* part of the machine systems described here? If so, how?

■ Are there parts of your body that can act as simple machines? Which parts?

■ Earlier in this chapter, you saw that the solar system and human body systems have forces that make them work, just as simple machines do. What principles from physical science, life science, and earth science can be applied to *all* of these systems?

Compound Machines and Gears   Many of the machines we encounter, like the snow shovel, are *compound machines*. That is, they are made up of two or more simple machines. Consider an ax: its handle is a lever; its blade is a wedge. Here are some other examples:

■ A pair of scissors has two levers with wedges for blades.

■ The handle of a manual pencil sharpener is a wheel-and-axle system that turns two screws with sharp edges shaped as wedges. The edges act as blades to sharpen a pencil.

■ A manual rotary can opener is part wheel and axle and part circular wedge.

As you can see, these are simple systems that combine to form more complex systems, just as our planet-moon system forms part of a larger, more complex solar system and the respiratory system is part of a larger, more complex body system.

A commonly found compound machine is the bicycle. It is a wheel-and-axle machine that uses a system of gears. A *gear* consists of one wheel that is used to turn another wheel. These wheels have sawlike "teeth" on their circumferences that allow the wheels to interact with each other. A chain around both wheels connects them. The chain usually has notches, which fit into the teeth of the wheels.

The bicycle pedal turns a crank that turns a large gear. The chain then turns the smaller gear, and the smaller gear turns the rear wheel, which drives the bicycle forward. Each time the pedals turn the larger gear around once, the smaller gear turns the rear wheel around many times.

Exploring gears

It is fun to explore the relationship between the diameter of the gear wheels and the number of rotations. If you can obtain plastic lids from one- and two-pound cans of coffee, you can use corrugated border paper, a piece of foam board, and a couple of pushpins to make your own model gear system, as shown in Figure 13.4. Glue the border paper trim around the edges of the plastic lids. Place the lids on the foam board so that the border paper "teeth" interface with each other. Press the pushpins through the center of each lid to secure your "gears" to the foam board. Turn the larger gear once and count the number of times the smaller gear turns. Then repeat the experiment by turning the smaller gear once. Measure the diameters of both lids and create your own gear-ratio theory!

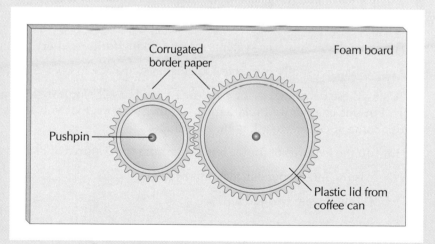

FIGURE 13.4
A simple gear experiment using two sizes of coffee-can lids. Using a setup like this, count the number of times the smaller gear turns for each turn of the large gear. Measure the diameters of both lids. Now can you devise a mathematical way of relating the difference in turns to the difference in diameters?

Corrugated border paper

Foam board

Pushpin

Plastic lid from coffee can

Thinking About **SYSTEMS**

The *Benchmarks for Science Literacy*

The *Benchmarks for Science Literacy* (AAAP, 1993, p. 262) point out that children tend to think of the properties of a system as belonging to individual parts of the system rather than as arising from the interactions of the parts. Think about the bicycle: the final system is quite different as a working vehicle than the properties of the individual parts. The same is true of the solar system and of the human body.

Sometimes, we think if students know the vocabulary, they understand how the system works. That is misleading, since vocabulary memorization can give the illusion of understanding. The *Benchmarks* assert that by the end of second grade, students should know that:

- Most things are made up of parts.

- Something may not work if some of its parts are missing.

- When parts are put together, they can do things that they couldn't do by themselves.

By the end of fifth grade, students should know that:

- In something that consists of many parts, the parts usually influence each other.

- Something may not work as well (or at all) if a part of it is missing, broken, worn out, mismatched, or misconnected.

And by the end of eighth grade, students should understand that:

- A system can include processes as well as things.

- Thinking about things as systems means looking for how every part relates to others.

- Any system is usually connected to other systems.

Using these benchmarks for your own scientific self, you can think about the systems described in this chapter and relate them to other systems that you know about in the natural world. Some questions to ask yourself include:

- How do the features of the system differ from the features of its parts?

- Where is the interdependence in this system?

- How is this system maintained?

Interactions and Patterns of Change

Many of the phenomena that we observe on Earth involve interactions among components of the air, land, and water, and forms of energy such as heat, light, sound, and electricity. We use the term **interaction** to mean a change in matter and energy. Interactions contribute to many patterns of change on the planet, such as the water cycle and weather; earthquakes and volcanoes; and the rock cycle, weathering, and erosion. As you read about interactions between matter and energy, you may want to ask yourself: What is changing? What is remaining the same?

One of the basic beliefs in science stems from the work of the scientist Albert Einstein (1879–1955). In 1905 he proposed a theory relating matter and energy to each other, a theory that many other scientists have tested through their studies of the atom. When such a statement about principles or patterns in nature endures over time and survives consistent tests, we call it a **scientific law**. Earlier, in the section on systems, you read about the law of gravitation. Einstein's explanation of the relationship between matter and energy in ordinary chemical reactions is called the **law of conservation of matter and energy**. According to this law,

Defining a scientific law

Connecting matter and energy

1. Neither matter nor energy can be created or destroyed, but either can be changed into other forms of matter or energy.

2. Matter can be changed into energy; energy can be changed into matter.

3. Therefore, the total amount of matter and energy in the universe is always the same.

This law requires lots of time to think about. Einstein quantified the relationship between matter and energy with his famous *special theory of relativity*, expressed in the equation $E = mc^2$. In this equation, E stands for the amount of energy, m for the amount of matter, and c for the immense speed of light (about 186,000 miles/second, or 300,000 kilometers/second). The equation indicates that the transformation of even a tiny amount of matter will release an enormous amount of energy. I invite you to think about this matter-energy relationship as we explore changes in matter and energy in the following sections.

Defining matter and energy

Matter is anything that takes up space and has mass. Air, water, rocks, wood, and metals are examples of matter. People, other animals, plants, the sun, and other stars and planets are also examples of matter. In contrast, **energy** is the ability to move other matter or to produce a change in other matter. We can also think of energy as the ability to do work. (Remember, *work* is defined as the process of applying a force to move something through a distance.) Now let's explore the interactions of various forms of energy with various forms of matter.

Heat Energy and Matter

Stored-up energy is called *potential energy,* whereas the energy of moving objects is called *kinetic energy.* As we begin the study of heat energy, you will see that it is, in fact, a form of kinetic energy.

What is heat?

Heat energy is really the energy of moving particles. The more heat energy a substance has, the faster its particles move, and the hotter the substance becomes. Remember that there are three states of matter on Earth: solids, liquids, and gases. (Plasma, the fourth state of matter, is the "stuff" stars are made of.) On Earth, the state of matter with the most heat energy is the gaseous state. The particles move fastest in a gas. In liquids, the particles move more slowly, and in solids they move very slowly.

It may be difficult to believe that solids, like your desk, are made of matter that is moving, but indeed that is so. We cannot see the motion, but we know that all matter is made up of atoms and molecules and their own subatomic particles, and that these particles are always in motion.

Water   When heat energy is added to water, the water becomes hotter and hotter—its particles move faster and faster—until it reaches its boiling point, and then it can change from a liquid into a gas, known as water vapor or steam. This water vapor has a greater amount of heat energy than the liquid. In fact, hot steam can cause a more severe burn than hot water because, to become steam, it had to absorb so much heat energy! Steam itself is not visible. We know that steam is present because as it meets the cooler air, it condenses. It is the condensed particles of water vapor that are visible.

Can you see steam?

Conversely, if we remove enough heat energy, we can cool water and produce a solid. The more heat energy we remove, the slower the particles move, and eventually the water becomes ice. The point at which this happens is the freezing point of water.

Physical change

When we change water from a solid into a liquid to a gas, we are creating a **physical change.** That is, we are changing only the water's *physical properties*—the properties that we can readily observe with our senses. The distance between the molecules changes: the molecules are closest together in the solid and farthest apart in the gas. But the basic composition of the water does not change: it is still made up of the same arrangement of atoms of hydrogen and oxygen that chemists designate as H_2O.

Similarly, if we tear a piece of paper in half using the force of our muscles, we are changing the size of the paper but not its composition. This is another example of an interaction of matter and energy that produces a physical change.

Sugar   Sugar is a compound made up of hydrogen, oxygen, and carbon; but its properties do not resemble the properties of hydrogen, oxygen, or carbon. When these three elements combine to form the compound sugar, the elements lose their original properties. In fact, sugar can be thought of as a system in which the parts and the whole do not have features in common.

When sugar is granulated or formed into cubes, we say it is undergoing a physical change; its composition has not changed. If we add heat energy to sugar so that it slowly caramelizes, we are changing it from a solid into a liquid in a process called melting, and that also is a physical change. The sugar still retains the same chemical composition.

Chemical change

But when we add enough heat energy to sugar, we will notice steam escaping from it, and a black carbon-like substance forms. This breakdown in the composition of sugar is called a **chemical change** or a *chemical reaction*. This particular type of chemical reaction is called *decomposition*.

The *chemical properties* of a substance are those characteristics that have to do with its composition and the way it behaves with other substances. Chemical changes usually produce new substances that have no resemblance to the original substances.

A balloon experiment

Bottles and Balloons   Imagine that you have two empty (except for air, of course) soda bottles, exactly the same size. Pour 100 milliliters of water into one bottle and 100 milliliters of vinegar into the other bottle. Place 2 tablespoons of baking soda into deflated balloons. Hang a balloon over each bottle like a stocking cap. With the help of a friend, simultaneously raise the balloon over each bottle so that the baking soda drops into the liquid.

Hold on! These two bottle-balloon systems produce different reactions when the baking soda reaches the liquid. In the vinegar bottle, there are lots of bubbles, and the balloon inflates. In the water bottle, the baking soda drops to the bottom, and nothing happens to the balloon. If you wanted to get the baking soda back, you could slowly allow the water to evaporate. In the vinegar bottle, however, a new substance has formed. Baking soda and vinegar combine to produce bubbles of carbon dioxide gas. The balloon inflates when the carbon dioxide is produced in the reaction.

In what ways are these systems the same? Different? Do you think they look the same initially? How could you tell that one bottle had water and one had vinegar?

Thinking About **INTERACTIONS**

Chemical and Physical Changes

We come across chemical and physical changes all the time in our daily lives. For example, when an iron nail rusts, it has changed its composition and undergone a chemical reaction; this is an example of a chemical change. A new substance is formed: iron oxide—the chemical name for rust.

See if you can figure out whether the following are examples of physical or chemical changes or both. Remember science is messy, and neat categories often elude us.

1. Sour milk

2. Burnt toast

3. A ripped skirt

4. A mowed lawn

5. A stained shirt

6. A flowing river

7. Eroded rock particles

8. A weathered building

9. Digestion

Some questions you may ask yourself include:

■ Was a new substance formed?

■ Was there a change in form, not content?

■ How did the change occur?

The answers are provided below.

Sources of Heat Energy   In order to better understand heat energy, you may want to think about the various sources of heat energy on our planet:

Where does heat come from?

■ Solar energy, or energy from the sun, produces heat energy. In fact, the sun-Earth system provides us with our main source of heat.

■ The mechanical force of friction produces heat energy. For instance, rub your hands or two sticks together, and you will produce heat. This is a transformation from mechanical energy of motion into heat energy.

■ Heat energy can also be produced by converting chemical energy. The burning of oil, gas, coal, or wood is a chemical process that releases heat energy.

■ Electrical energy can produce heat energy when an electric current flows through thin wires, such as the filament of a light bulb or a toaster.

■ The energy stored in the nucleus of an atom, or nuclear energy, can produce a vast amount of heat energy.

1. Chemical change, because the composition of the milk is changed.

2. Chemical change and physical change: the bread loses some of its water when toasted and changes color.

3. Physical change: there is a tear in the material.

4. Physical change: the grass is shorter.

5. It depends on the stain! If it is an acid stain, then it could change the composition of the materials; otherwise, it is a physical change in the fabric.

6. Physical change: the water moves but it is still water!

7. Physical change: the particles of rock are the same, only smaller.

8. Physical and chemical change: the composition of the surface is changed, and the color appears different as well.

9. Physical and chemical change, because the food changes in both size and composition as it goes through the digestive system.

Heat Energy on the Move   Heat energy travels in three basic ways, through the processes of radiation, conduction, and convection.

1. Radiation. *Radiation* is the method of heat transfer that occurs when the sun's energy is transferred to the Earth. This heat energy travels to us by radiating through space in invisible energy waves. Heat waves, also known as infrared waves, are part of the *electromagnetic spectrum*. This is a family of energy waves that includes radio waves, light rays, ultraviolet rays, x-rays, gamma rays, and cosmic rays. They all travel at the speed of light.

Heat traveling through space

Radiation as a form of heat transfer should not be confused with other types of radiation, such as radioactive emissions, some of which can be very harmful. The type of radiation that is emitted from high-energy nuclear reactors, for example, is harmful.

2. Conduction. Every time we use a potholder or wear shoes on a hot beach, we are protecting ourselves from getting burned by the process of *conduction*. As a substance takes in heat energy, its particles (molecules) move faster and faster and bump into each other. They can also collide with particles of another substance, such as the surrounding air or your own skin. The heat energy is passed along or *conducted* from molecule to molecule.

Heat transfer at the molecular level

In order for heat to move by conduction, two things with different temperatures must be touching. A material that passes heat along well is a good conductor. Metals are good heat conductors. Materials that do not allow heat through are insulators. Wool, down jackets, wood, plastic, and rubber are good insulators.

3. Convection. The heat transfer that occurs in fluids is known as *convection*. A *fluid* is any substance that flows. Liquids are fluids, and so are gases such as air.

When a gas or liquid is heated, the molecules move more rapidly and spread farther and farther apart. The greater the space between the particles, the more volume the fluid occupies, and the less dense it becomes (see the discussion of density in the chapter "Spiraling Curriculum"). For example, air or water that is warmed expands and becomes less dense.

Heat transfer in fluids

Think of a pot of water heated on a stove (Figure 13.5). The water on the bottom of the pot absorbs heat from the burner and becomes less dense. The water near the top of the pot remains colder and denser. The denser water then sinks, pushing the warmed water upward. Convection, then, is a process by which warmed gases or liquids are pushed upward by cooler, denser gases and liquids. The continuous cycling of these fluids is called a *convection current*.

Does heat rise?

Lots of people like to say that "heat rises." I remember how surprised I was to learn that heat itself did not magically rise, but that some *thing*— a gas or a liquid—was actually rising. Convection was at work in the story of "The Bottle and the Balloon," in the chapter "The Teacher as Mediator," where we saw a balloon inflated above a bottle that was placed in a pot of hot water. If you have a radiator in your house, you will notice how the

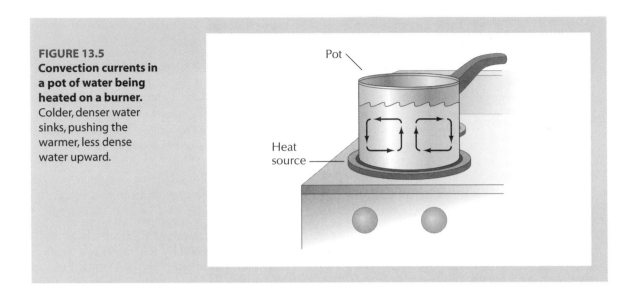

FIGURE 13.5
Convection currents in a pot of water being heated on a burner. Colder, denser water sinks, pushing the warmer, less dense water upward.

warm air rising from the radiator heats up an entire room by setting up a convection current. Some ovens are designed specifically to take advantage of convection currents.

Convection, in fact, is the basis for the Earth's system of air and water currents. Uneven heating of the Earth's curved surface causes some ocean waters to heat and cool at different rates. The air above these ocean waters heats and cools at different rates as well. The resulting convection currents explain many of our ocean and weather patterns. Even magma, the fluid rock beneath the Earth's surface, is heated unevenly. This results in convection currents that contribute to the formation of mountains, earthquakes, volcanoes, and even the spreading of the ocean floor.

Thinking About INTERACTIONS

Links Between Interactions and Systems

Interactions and systems are linked. When we think of systems, we may ask ourselves, "What are the interactions at work?" When we think of interactions, we may ask, "What system contains these interactions?"

For example, you have just read about convection currents, which are interactions between heat energy and liquids or gases. We could also be describing the operation of a system, for example, a convection oven. All systems rely on interactions between matter and energy.

Electricity

In an earlier chapter, you read two stories about teachers engaging their classes in investigations with electrical circuits. You may recall that **electricity** is a flow of electrons. In this section, we will try to delve more deeply into the following:

Questions about electricity

■ What is an electron?

■ How is electrical energy a form of matter-energy interactions?

■ How do other forms of energy produce electricity?

■ How does a generator work?

The Structure of Matter and the Electron   Much of the history of science has involved the search for the structure of matter. Matter, as you learned in an earlier chapter, is made up of tiny particles called atoms. An *atom* is the basic structural unit of matter—the smallest part of an element (a pure substance) that still has the properties of that element.

Atoms

We know a great deal now about the complex structure of the atom itself. There are three basic subatomic particles—protons, neutrons, and electrons— and scientists have broken these down into even smaller particles.

Molecules

Earlier in the book you also read about *molecules,* the smallest particles of a compound that still have the properties of the compound. The tiniest particle of water that still has the properties of water is a molecule of water. There are literally billions of molecules in a drop of water. Compounds are made up of two or more elements. Hence, molecules are usually made up of two or more atoms. Sometimes substances are made up of only one element, and the atoms of these elements form single-atom or diatomic (two-atom) molecules. Oxygen, nitrogen, and neon are examples of elements that can form molecules by themselves, without any other type of atom.

Electrons

Atoms, of course, are tinier than molecules, and electrons are much smaller than any given atom. An *electron* is a particle with a negative (–) electrical charge. Although they have very little mass, electrons have a lot of energy, and they move around the nucleus (center) of an atom with great speed, approximately the speed of light.

Protons

A *proton* is a particle with a positive (+) electrical charge. It is much heavier than an electron, about 1,840 times the mass of an electron, but it also has a lot of energy. Because of its mass, though, it does not move as fast as an electron. The positive charge of a proton is equal in strength to the negative charge of an electron, and the two charges are considered opposite to each other. When many electrons are near each other, they repel each other—that is, push each other away. When protons are near each other, they also repel each other. Protons and electrons, however, having opposite charges, are attracted to each other. When a proton and electron are near each other, the effects of their charges are neutralized.

Because atoms have the same number of electrons and protons, the atom is neutral, without electric charge. But if there is a loss or gain of electrons, the charge is out of balance, and the atom is no longer neutral. If there are excess electrons, we say the atom is negatively charged; if there are too few electrons, we say the atom is positively charged. An atom with an electrical charge is called an *ion*. Notice that the atom can gain or lose electrons, but the number of protons and neutrons usually remains stable. This is because the neutrons and protons are closely packed together in the nucleus of the atom.

Neutrons

Neutrons are subatomic particles that have neither a positive nor a negative charge. The mass of a neutron is about the same as the mass of a proton and an electron combined. Scientists believe that a neutron is, in fact, a proton and an electron held together by a small bundle of energy called a neutrino, which has no electrical charge and no mass.

Neutrons and protons are held together in the nucleus of the atom by enormous amounts of energy, sometimes called binding energy. The electrons move around the nucleus of the atom at different distances, called energy levels or orbitals. Thus, an atom's electrons form a sort of hazy electron cloud as they move around the nucleus. Sometimes they are near the nucleus and sometimes they are farther away, depending upon how much energy they have at the moment. (See the chapter "Expanding the Science 'Box'" for more on electron clouds.)

Static and Current Electricity   From the structure of the atom, you can see that all matter is electrical in nature. This brings us to the role of the electron in the form of energy called electricity.

Sometimes you can rub certain materials with another material and actually remove electrons from some of the atoms. When the electrons of one material pass to the atoms of another material as they are being rubbed, we may get a "shock." This happens, for instance, when you rub a balloon on a wool sweater. The kind of electricity that has been produced from the force of rubbing is called *static electricity*. Sometimes we say that our clothes feel "static-y."

Why does static hold a balloon to a wall?

You've probably also noticed that, after a balloon has been rubbed on a wool sweater, it can adhere to a wall. What is going on? Wool and fur tend to lose electrons when they are rubbed, giving them a net positive charge. The balloon, in contrast, gains electrons and has a net negative charge. When you hold the balloon against the wall, the electrons in the layer of paint on the wall are repelled by the balloon's extra electrons. The paint's electrons move away along the surface, leaving the spot where they originated with a net positive charge. The negatively charged balloon then "sticks" to the wall because opposites attract! For the same reason, little bits of paper will be attracted to the charged balloon.

Electricity on the move

When electricity moves, it is called *current electricity*. Scientists believe that when an electric current is flowing through a material, the electrons flow from atom to atom inside the material. Materials, such as copper wire, that allow an electric current to flow freely through them are called conductors. Most metals are good electrical conductors, just as they are good heat conductors. Carbon, although a nonmetal, can also conduct electricity. Materials that do not allow electrons to flow freely though them are called nonconductors or insulators. Examples of insulators are rubber, many plastics, wood, glass, porcelain, and cloth.

Energy Transformations and Generators   Electricity is a form of energy and can therefore be produced from other forms of energy. Chemical energy stored in a battery can be changed into electrical energy. Light energy can be transformed into electricity using a photoelectric cell or solar cell. You can even twist two wires together and heat them to produce an electric current; this device is called a thermocouple.

From magnetism to electricity

How is the electricity you use in your home produced? In most cases, it comes from a generating plant that takes advantage of the relationship between electricity and magnetism. The basic principle of an electrical *generator* is that electricity is produced by moving magnets around a wire coil—or, alternatively, moving a wire coil between the poles of a U-shaped magnet. A typical generating plant uses a source of heat energy to boil water. The steam from the boiled water turns large wheels called turbines, which then turn the wire coils or the huge magnets of the generator.

Notice that the electrical generator is a system that produces electrical energy as a result of many interactions between matter and other forms of energy. The mechanical energy of the turbines is needed to produce the electricity. The heat energy of the steam is used to produce the mechanical energy. Electrical power plants use different materials to heat the water; some use nuclear power, while others burn coal or oil. Some power plants use the mechanical energy of running water to turn the turbines. You may want to visit a local electrical power plant to learn more about how it works.

There are concerns about the ways in which utility plants operate. For example, coal-burning electrical plants may pollute the atmosphere in harmful ways. Nuclear-powered electrical plants may give off harmful radiation in the event of an accident. These systems are often not fully understood by the public, but they present issues that affect the quality of your life.

Light

Light is a form of energy that is given out, or radiated, from the sun and other light-producing objects in the form of waves. These light waves are sometimes referred to as radiant energy. Light, like heat energy, is part of a group of radiant energy waves called the electromagnetic spectrum. Among these waves, light rays are the only ones that we can see.

The speed of light

All electromagnetic waves, including light waves, travel at the same speed, approximately 186,000 miles/second (300,000 kilometers/second). You may recall that earlier in this chapter we referred to this enormous speed

Electrical power plants may use materials that pollute the atmosphere.

Mary Messenger/Stock Boston

when we explored the conservation of matter and energy. Light travels so quickly that it crosses earthly distances in what appears to be an instant. Light energy makes it possible for us to see the things around us—and to see them without any noticeable delay.

Measured against the vastness of outer space, however, the passage of light is not so instantaneous. Even at its enormous speed, the sun's light takes eight minutes to reach the Earth. This is useful for us to reflect on, because it helps us imagine the immensity of space. If the sun were to stop shining, it would not go dark in our sky for eight minutes!

The distance light travels in a year is a called a *light-year,* and it equals about 6 trillion miles, or 9.5 trillion kilometers. The light-year is used as a measure of distance when we are referring to the great expanses of the universe.

Like waves in water, light waves move up and down as they move forward. But light requires no medium to travel in; it can travel in a vacuum, such as the vacuum of outer space. In addition to its wavelike nature, light also acts like a stream of particles. Scientists have dubbed these particles *photons,* and they have learned that photons are a lot like little bundles of energy.

Sources of Light   The sun is our natural source of light. It produces energy by changing the atomic nuclei of its atoms. This process of *nuclear fusion* produces enormous amounts of solar energy. The energy is released as light and as all the other waves of the electromagnetic spectrum.

Is the sun on fire?   One common alternative conception about the sun is that it is "burning." In fact, there is no fire, but there is enormous heat (10,000 degrees Fahrenheit, or 5,538 degrees Celsius) and explosive activity. The sun is made of plasma, like other stars, and it produces its energy in the same way as other stars. The moon and planets do not produce their own light. Rather, they shine by the process of reflection—the sun's light bounces off their surfaces.

Besides the sun's natural light, we have many artificial sources of light. These include candles, kerosene or gasoline lamps, and various forms of electric light.

Thinking About **INTERACTIONS**

Making Connections: From Electricity to Heat and Light

Many everyday household objects work by converting electricity into heat energy. These include electric hair dryers, toasters, coffeemakers, irons, ranges, and heaters.

You may notice that wires get warm when electric current flows through them. Often, the thinner the wire, the hotter it gets, until it begins to glow. Can you think of how this phenomenon is applied? A common light bulb works on just this principle, converting electricity into heat and light energy.

The filament in a light bulb is made of tungsten, which will not melt when it gets very hot. Instead, it will glow, in a process called incandescence. Hence, in the system of a light bulb, there are interactions between electrical and heat energy and metal wires to produce light energy.

Oxygen in the air reacts with metals, as in the process of rusting. If this occurred with the tungsten in a light bulb, the bulb would not last long. Therefore, in the space inside the bulb, there is no regular air, just a gas such as argon, which does not react with the tungsten.

Light Energy and Matter   For us to see an object that does not produce its own light, there must be a source of light, the light must strike the object, and the light must bounce off or be *reflected* from the object and then travel to our eyes.

Opaque materials do not allow light to pass through them; instead, they reflect most of the light that strikes them. *Transparent* and *translucent* materials, in contrast, allow most of the light striking them to pass through. Still, some light is reflected and some is absorbed by the material.

Reflection and refraction of light

Light travels in straight lines; it does not go around corners. When light is reflected, its direction changes, but it still travels in a straight line. A mirror is a good example of a shiny, reflective surface that allows us to experiment with beams of light and watch the direction of reflected beams. Try shining a light at a mirror and studying the way it reflects (Figure 13.6a). Enough experiments of this sort will lead you to believe that the angle at which the incoming light ray hits the mirror is equal to the angle at which it is reflected. This happens only on smooth, polished surfaces, however. Rough surfaces reflect rays of light in an irregular way so the light scatters.

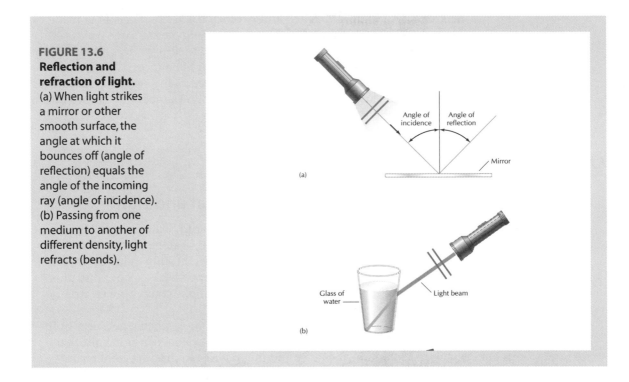

FIGURE 13.6
Reflection and refraction of light.
(a) When light strikes a mirror or other smooth surface, the angle at which it bounces off (angle of reflection) equals the angle of the incoming ray (angle of incidence). (b) Passing from one medium to another of different density, light refracts (bends).

When light rays travel at a slant or angle from one transparent medium, like air, into another, like water, the rays are bent or *refracted*; that is, they change direction. If you shine a narrow beam of light into a clear glass of water at an angle (Figure 13.6b), you can see the light beam bending as it passes through the glass and water. If you look closely at the surface of the water, you will notice that the beam bends at the point where the medium through which it is traveling changes.

When light rays are bent, they can magnify an image, making it appear closer. Conversely, if they bend differently, they can make an image seem farther away. This is one of the principles behind the construction of eyeglass lenses, as well as microscope, binocular, and telescope lenses. By refracting light in a precise way, lenses can help us see distant objects or bring blurry ones into better focus.

Color   Have you ever held up a glass or plastic prism to a narrow beam of light? If you do so, you will notice a band of colored lights called the **spectrum.** The spectrum of visible light includes red, orange, yellow, green, blue, indigo, and violet. White light is actually a mixture of these colored lights of the spectrum.

How does wavelength relate to color?

The colors that make up the spectrum have different wavelengths. *Wavelength* refers to the distance between corresponding parts of two of the light waves (Figure 13.7a). Violet light has the shortest wavelength, and red light the longest. When white light enters a prism, the colors with the shorter waves are refracted (bent) more than are the colors with the longer waves (Figure 13.7b). The seven colors of white light thus are separated according to how much they are refracted as they go through the prism.

A rainbow is a spectrum that is sometimes produced when the sun shines immediately after a rain shower. The water droplets in the air act as tiny prisms, breaking the sunlight into a spectrum in the form of a beautiful arch. If you create a spray with a garden hose, standing with your back to the sun, you can make an artificial rainbow.

Sound

Sound is a form of energy that is produced by objects moving back and forth or vibrating. The vibrations of material objects cause sound, so when the vibrations stop, the sound stops. Here we see an intricate interaction between matter and energy.

Like light, sound energy travels in waves. Unlike light, however, sound cannot travel in a vacuum. When your alarm clock rings across the room, the vibration of the ringer causes molecules in the air to vibrate. The air molecules pass the energy along, coming closer together and then stretching farther apart in a wave motion until the vibrating air molecules reach your ears. Because sound travels quickly, you hear the alarm clock in a fraction of a second.

The Speed of Sound   Sound usually reaches us by traveling though the air, but it can also travel though liquids and solids. Sound travels best through materials that have more closely packed particles—in other words,

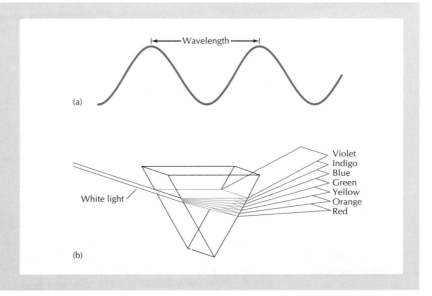

FIGURE 13.7
Color properties of light.
(a) The meaning of *wavelength*.
(b) Refracting different wavelengths by different amounts, a prism separates white light into its component colors.

How fast is sound?

through denser materials. Sound travels through air at a speed of about 1,100 feet/second, or about one mile in 5 seconds (one kilometer in 3 seconds). In ocean water, sound travels more than four times faster than in air (about 4,800 feet/second). In steel, sound travels more than 15 times faster than in air!

You can see why sound cannot travel in a vacuum; there are no molecules in a vacuum to carry the vibrations. You can also notice the huge difference between the speed of sound in air and the speed of light: approximately 1,100 feet per second versus approximately 186,000 *miles* per second. Think about how we notice this difference during a thunderstorm. The sound we know as thunder is caused by lightning passing through the air. The lightning makes the air heat up and expand, and this produces giant vibrations in the air that travel toward us as sound waves. But even though the thunder and lightning happen at virtually the same time, we always see the lightning first and then hear the thunder. This is because light travels so much faster than sound.

Characteristics of Sound   Experiments with sound reveal that you can vary the properties of materials to produce different types of sounds. For example:

■ *Amplitude or intensity.* The loudness or softness of a sound, called its amplitude or intensity, depends on the strength with which the sound-producing object is vibrating.

What causes changes in pitch?

■ *Pitch.* The highness or lowness of a sound, known as the pitch, depends on the rate at which the object is vibrating. The more vibrations per second, the higher the pitch of a sound. The fewer vibrations per second, the lower the pitch. The rate of vibrations is also called the *frequency.* The normal human ear can hear sounds with frequencies ranging between 20 and 20,000 vibrations per second. Dogs can hear higher sounds—that is, sounds with a frequency of more than 20,000 vibrations per second.

■ *Quality.* When objects vibrate, they generally send out a mixture of frequencies, and the particular mix determines what is called the quality of the sound. That is why a trumpet sounds different from a violin even when they both are playing the same note. In addition to the main frequency, each instrument is actually producing a set of overtones, or additional frequencies, that combine to give the sound its quality.

The Human Voice   Humans produce sound by using the larynx or voice box, which is located at the top of the trachea (windpipe). Stretched over the top of the larynx are two thin but strong bands of tissue called the vocal cords. When air from the lungs is blown through the narrow slit between the vocal cords, the cords vibrate and produce sounds.

How our vocal cords control pitch

Muscles attached to the vocal cords make them tight or loose, and in this way they control the pitch of your voice. The tighter the cords, the faster they vibrate, and the higher the pitch of the sound you produce. The same is true for a tighter violin string; it, too, will have a higher pitch from vibrating at a greater frequency.

Men's vocal cords are usually longer and thicker than women's, and they do not vibrate as fast. This explains why men tend to have deeper voices than women.

Thinking About INTERACTIONS

Sound Energy and Musical Instruments

Consider a wind instrument—what interactions does it use to create a sound? Basically, the instrument holds a column of air that is made to vibrate, either by blowing into it, as with a saxophone or clarinet, or by blowing across it, as with a flute or piccolo.

In a woodwind instrument like a clarinet, you blow on a thin piece of wood or plastic, called the reed, which is used to make the column of air vibrate. Pressing the keys or covering the holes changes the length of the column of air and therefore changes the vibrations per second and the pitch of the sound produced. A shorter column of air will vibrate faster than a longer column of air. Hence, the shorter the column of air, the higher the pitch.

How do you think the amplitude of the clarinet is changed? That's right—by blowing harder into the mouthpiece and causing the reed to vibrate with greater intensity.

In a percussion instrument—drum, xylophone, wood block, triangle, or cymbals—striking the instrument with another object produces sound. For the xylophone, the shorter the bar, the greater the number of vibrations and the higher the pitch. For drums, the thinner and tighter the covering, the greater the number of vibrations and the higher the pitch. Think about this: Can a drummer change the pitch of a drum's sound without altering the drum's covering? (Hint: Is the membrane that covers the drum equally tight all the way across?)

Magnetism

Earlier in this chapter you saw that a force is essentially a push or a pull. Usually a force causes a change in the position or motion of an object. Gravity, for example, is the force of attraction between objects in the universe. The gravitational attraction between objects is one of the causes of the kinetic energy that keeps the planets in motion around the sun.

Magnetism is another important type of force. It is produced when an object exerts an attraction for materials made of certain metals—iron, steel, cobalt, and nickel. These metals are called magnetic materials. There are two kinds of magnets, human-made and natural:

■ Natural magnets, found in the ground, are called lodestones. They contain a mineral called magnetite and look like irregularly shaped rocks.

■ Human-made magnets are made from iron, steel, cobalt, and nickel and are named for their shapes: bar magnets, rod magnets, horseshoe magnets, and U-shaped magnets.

This student observes the effects of magnetism passing through paper.

Tony Freeman/PhotoEdit

The force of a magnet is strongest at its ends, which are called the poles of the magnet. When magnets are allowed to swing freely, their poles are attracted to the north or the south of the Earth and therefore are called north-seeking or south-seeking poles. When the poles of two magnets are brought near each other, like poles repel each other and opposite poles attract. That is, two north poles will tend to push each other away. So will two south poles. But a north and a south pole will tend to pull each other closer. This is similar to the attraction and repulsion of electrical charges. In fact, magnetism and electricity are closely related.

From electricity to magnetism

Electromagnets   When an electric current passes through a wire, a *magnetic field* is created around the wire. This means that the space around the wire can act like a magnet. This effect is strengthened if the wire that carries the electricity is wrapped into a coil. If you then place a piece of iron inside the coiled wire, you make an even stronger magnet, called an *electromagnet*. The strength of this system can be increased by increasing the number of coils of the wire and by raising the strength of the electric current through the wire.

Like other magnets, an electromagnet has two poles, and it will attract magnetic materials such as iron and steel. But an electromagnet is a temporary magnet—its magnetism can be turned off by breaking the electric circuit.

The ability to create magnetic force with an electromagnet has many practical applications. We use electromagnets in devices ranging from telephones to radios, televisions, computers, motors, cranes, and generators (see the explanation of an electrical generator earlier in this chapter), to name a few. When you see large steel beams being lifted for the construction of a building, you know the crane is using giant electromagnets.

What Causes Magnetism?   What, you may wonder, are the causes for magnetism? Where does this mysterious force of attraction come from? Scientists are not sure, but they believe the answer lies with the movement of electrons in the atoms of magnetic materials.

The mystery of magnetism

Electrons spin as they revolve around the nucleus of the atom. Each spinning electron acts as a tiny magnet. In nonmagnetic materials, the number of electrons that spin in one direction is equal to the number of electrons that spin in the opposite direction. This cancels out their magnetic effects. In magnetic materials, there are more electrons spinning in one direction than in the opposite direction. It is believed that this imbalance of electrons spinning in opposite directions gives rise to magnetism in the material. This also explains why few naturally occurring materials are magnetic.

The Earth as a Magnet   The Earth behaves as if it were a huge magnet, with a north magnetic pole and a south magnetic pole. This is because the deep interior of the Earth, known as the inner core, is made up of iron and nickel. The magnetic field of the Earth even extends beyond the planet itself.

Why is the Earth magnetic?

When you use a compass to discover which direction you are going, you are relying on the Earth's magnetism. Because the compass needle is magnetized, one end will point toward the Earth's north magnetic pole. Although the Earth's north and south magnetic poles do not correspond exactly to the north and south geographic poles, they are close enough for most purposes—especially when you are lost in the woods.

From Content to Curriculum

From the sampling of science content in this chapter, you can see the richness of the topics that students explore and the importance of the "big ideas" they investigate. But how, you may be wondering, do schools and teachers fit all these topics and ideas into a specific curriculum that meets the needs of students?

What is a curriculum?

The word *curriculum* derives from a Latin term meaning "running course." In science teaching, we usually think of the **curriculum** as a plan of studies that includes the ways in which the science content is organized and presented at each grade level. It is not merely a list of topics, but an organizational scheme that describes the activities used to facilitate the presentation of the content. Often schools use a list of topics as a *summary* of the science curriculum.

In addition to this *formal* science curriculum, good teachers make use of an *informal* curriculum based on the students' daily lives, as you saw in the chapter "Making Connections." The informal curriculum includes everyday, often unexpected, topics that arise as a result of living in a given geographic environment or of exposure to a newsworthy science topic. Often, formal and informal science curriculum topics merge. For example, if a class in a seaside community is studying the oceans as a formal unit, the teacher and students can find many opportunities to incorporate aspects of their daily lives into the formal study.

Merging formal and informal curriculum

A few years ago, I saw a fifth-grade geology curriculum designed by a school in a shore community of Long Island, New York. It had an extensive section on sand, including required reading about the sands of the Sahara Desert. This reading segment was part of the science textbook that had been purchased by this school. Certainly, the Sahara, being the world's largest desert, was of interest, but it was unlikely that students could explore it directly. Unfortunately, the curriculum offered the students no direct access to sand, even though there was a beach full of it— directly accessible and relevant—down the street from the school.

This story illustrates the importance of using many criteria to design a curriculum. Also remember the key question, "Who are my students?" Whatever the formal curriculum dictates, answering this question will help you to make connections to the lived experiences of your students.

Who Creates the Curriculum? National Influence and Local Control

Growing national concern

In American public education, matters of curriculum have traditionally been the prerogative of local school districts. During the past two decades, however, there has been a great deal of national concern about the competencies and academic performance of students. The publication in the 1980s of reports like *A Nation at Risk* and *Educating Americans for the 21st Century* alerted the public to the perceived need to address higher standards in American public education. The subsequent "standards movement" has resulted in national standards for several areas of education, including science.

STANDARDS ✔

The Benchmarks and the National Standards   As we saw in the chapter, "An Invitation to Teaching Science," science education has been particularly influenced by two major national reform efforts. They have been represented by two documents that are useful tools for fashioning science curriculum: the *Benchmarks for Science Literacy* (1993), a publication of the American Association for the Advancement of Science, and the *National Science Education Standards* (1996), a publication of the National Research Council.

Both documents represent the work of teacher educators, scientists, and classroom science teachers from all over the world. The intent is to provide educators with a way of thinking about the importance of scien-

*Scientific
literacy defined*

tific literacy in today's world. **Scientific literacy** refers to an individual's ability to use scientific information to make choices and to "engage intelligently in public discourse and debate about important issues that involve science and technology" (National Research Council, 1996, p. 1). Both documents argue that such literacy should be the major goal of science education. The documents also agree on these two overarching themes:

Shared themes

■ A sound science program needs to engage students in inquiry—that is, real problem-solving and design experiences that help them to shape meaning from experience.

■ Students should focus on a smaller number of concepts than they do in traditional curricula, and these concepts should be integrated across disciplines.

The *Benchmarks* include statements of what students should know and be able to do in science, mathematics, and technology by the end of grades 2, 5, 8, and 12. Similarly, the National Science Education Standards (NSES) present standards for eight basic categories of content (described earlier in this chapter) for grades K–4, 5–8, and 9–12. The NSES also include principles to guide methods of teaching and assessment, as well as general standards for science education programs.

STANDARDS ☑

Frameworks

State and Local Interpretations   Individual states have also become involved in science curriculum decisions. Some states have provided their own documents, sometimes referred to as **frameworks,** that offer guiding principles for elementary and secondary science curricula. Recent state frameworks have usually been aligned with the content standards of the NSES. These state frameworks tend to dictate content standards—the science topics that should be addressed at each grade level.

Although the national standards and state frameworks have a great deal to say about what science curriculum should look like, local schools and school districts still have the final word in defining their own curricula. The standards movement should be seen as a guide to influence the development of curriculum. None of the standards or frameworks documents is a curriculum in itself.

Keep in mind, too, that topic selection is only part of curriculum construction. To develop a curriculum, educators also need to explore related activities, such as connections with literature, mathematics, technology, and social studies.

MST (Mathematics, Science, and Technology) Curriculum

STANDARDS ☑

In addition to connecting science firmly with technology, the NSES discuss coordinating the science program with the mathematics program (National Research Council, 1996, pp. 214, 218). Recently, in fact, a great deal of attention has been given to the links among math, science, and technology.

Blending
math, science,
and technology

One movement in curriculum transformation, which we can call the **MST initiative,** involves truly integrating the disciplines of mathematics, science, and technology in curriculum planning. MST stresses the fact that mathematics, science, and technology are interdependent human enterprises. To promote this integration, the MST approach often uses computer technology as a tool for brainstorming, doing research, and presenting information.

The important thing is not to stop questioning.
—ALBERT EINSTEIN

Students who are engaged in MST activities tend to be involved in some form of project-based learning in which they use science ideas and/or mathematics ideas to solve a problem. Often this problem relates to a *design challenge*, like the one you read about in the chapter "Expanding the Science 'Box,'" where the students in Ms. Murray's class were asked to design and build models of atoms.

MST and the Group Process   MST is a special way of engaging students in doing their own thinking and giving them the chance to direct their own learning. Central to MST is the understanding that students become active learners when they are engaged in experiences related to a meaningful context—a larger purpose that stimulates a need to know and encourages the students to acquire skills to solve a problem.

Emphasis on
cooperative learning

MST also emphasizes a group process. Working in cooperative learning groups, students engage in brainstorming and do background research in order to plan for the implementation of their design. This group process is very important to MST learning. It requires that students work together to reach the best solution to their design challenge.

Exploring MST Curriculum

If you want to begin exploring an MST curriculum, the following resources can help you to develop ideas.

The Invention Convention. http://www.eduplace.com/science/invention/. The Invention Convention is a science event aimed at integrating design throughout the curriculum. Think about the liquid-display toys that the students invented in the chapter "Spiraling Curriculum." Students are always thinking up new ways of doing old things. Why not put their ideas to work and enter them into the Invention Convention? You can hold a local Invention Convention and enter the winner in the national convention. Get all the details at the web site.

Synergy Learning: Math, Science, and Design Technology for Grades K–8. http://www.synergylearning.org/. *Connect* is a wonderful magazine for K–8 teachers who are engaged with innovations in science, mathematics, and technology. Each issue features project-based activities that use inquiry, design, and mathematical analyses. Visit the web site to download sample articles and to find out how to subscribe.

Technology and Children. http://www.iteawww.org/. This journal for elementary school technology education is produced by the International Technology Education Association. Subscription information is available on the web site.

When students or student groups present their designs, they are asked to discuss the process they used as well as the solutions they reached. Remember: in MST work, process *is* content! Students describe their process as they talk about the science and math ideas that are part of their design project.

The Impact of MST   The MST initiative is having an important impact on the development of school curricula and state frameworks. In New York State, for example, teachers are urged to explore their science curriculum and "MST" it. That means reviewing the problem-solving investigations with respect to the following criteria:

MST criteria

- What is the nature of the problem-solving activities in science?

- Where does mathematics present itself in these activities?

- Are students expected to design a process or a product as part of their investigations?

- What is the nature of students' access to computer information systems during their investigations?

- How are science ideas linked to mathematics and technology ideas?

In Part Two of *Science Stories*, you saw several examples of MST investigations. In the chapter "Spiraling Curriculum," when Ms. Drescher's students used their understanding of the differing densities of three liquids to design a liquid-display toy, all three components of problem solving—mathematics, science, and technology—came into play. In the chapter "Making Models," when students designed a model solar system, they used their analysis of the planets' relative sizes and distances to construct a model that accurately represented the planets in relation to the sun. The students also accessed the Internet to gather data about the nine planets. As a final example, some of Ms. Travis's students in the chapter "Expanding the Science 'Box'" designed a shoebox house and planned the wiring for ceiling lights in the rooms. They used the science ideas behind series and parallel circuits to light their model house, and they used mathematics to construct model furniture in an appropriate size.

Other Interdisciplinary Trends

Aside from MST initiatives, many schools are moving toward interdisciplinary units in order to make connections between science and other areas of study, such as social studies and literature. Often called *thematic* or *integrated* units, these segments of the curriculum emphasize an overarching topic that may or may not be rooted in the study of science.

Thematic and integrated units

For example, a social studies unit on Native Americans can explore how they designed their tepees, longhouses, or wigwams. This design reveals the Native American understanding of convection and insulation, which can lead to a scientific exploration of these topics. Mathematics, art, and other disciplines can be similarly integrated into the unit, so students develop knowledge in many fields while pursuing their understanding of Native Americans.

Stressing inquiry

Remember that, for an inquiry approach to learning, you should engage students in asking their own questions and seeking their own answers. Students need to be encouraged to question the phenomena under study and invent their theories for why something works. Hence, in the example of Native American tepees, students might be encouraged to do activities that demonstrate heat convection in order to understand why tepees were designed with an opening at the top.

As another example, one interdisciplinary middle school activity on making music in Brazil engaged students in building a Brazilian instrument known as a *cuica* (pronounced kwee-kah) (Bazin et al., 2002). Similar to a drum, a *cuica* is a metal cylinder with a skin stretched over one end. It differs from a drum in that a stick, fixed at the center of the skin and extending inside the metal cylinder, produces sound when it is rubbed by a piece of wet cloth or leather (pp. 18–20). The sound depends on how quickly the stick is rubbed. The *cuica* is a fascinating subject, but studying it will not necessarily engage the students in scientific inquiry. To make this a scientific investigation, we might consider the following challenges for the students:

■ How is sound produced?

■ How does the *cuica* in particular produce sound?

■ Why do different speeds of rubbing produce sounds of different pitch and quality?

■ What exactly do we mean by the pitch and quality of a sound?

In sum, when you plan an integrated or thematic unit, it is wise to consider the following questions:

Questions for a thematic unit

■ Where is the study of science in my unit?

■ What are the science ideas behind this topic?

■ What type of science experiences are students engaged in?

■ Is the nature of science represented here? In other words, do the students understand what counts for "evidence" in this scientific activity?

Developing Curriculum Units

After reading about standards, frameworks, and the creation of curricula, you may still be puzzled about how schools and teachers get from these broad definitions of expected learning to specific plans for classroom teaching. Usually, this is done by developing curriculum units.

In the chapter on lesson plans, I drew the usual distinction between a lesson and a unit. Typically, a **unit of study** includes several lessons that are designed around a central theme or topic. An individual lesson on snails, for example, could fit within a third-grade unit on classifying vertebrates and invertebrates.

A unit plan usually consists of the following:

Elements of
a unit plan

- The science ideas behind the unit

- The activities included in the unit

- The lesson plans for the unit

Sometimes, unit plans also include a description of the assessment strategy for each unit. We will address several types of assessments in the next chapter.

Aligning a Unit of Study with the Standard

STANDARDS

More and more, teachers are expected to link their units of study to specific content standards. This process involves the following steps:

Steps in
developing a unit

1. Identifying the topic and its relationship to the standard.

2. Identifying the science ideas behind this topic.

3. Exploring activity books and other resources relating to the topic.

4. Designing lessons that allow students to explore their own ideas and permit the teacher to extend the activities as needed.

5. Indicating connections with mathematics, technology, literature, and social studies.

Selecting Activities

If you are selecting activities for a unit, you should follow the same criteria described throughout this book for individual lessons. Ask yourself questions like these:

Questions
for selecting
unit activities

- Does the activity lend itself to individual thinking and problem solving?

- Does the activity match the science idea expressed by the unit?

- Are the materials accessible?

- Is the activity student-centered or teacher-centered?

You are looking for science activities that encourage individual explorations of phenomena. Commercial materials and kits can be useful as long as you frame the activity in a way that allows students to make decisions about the plan for their investigations.

The Resources for Further Exploration at the end of this chapter offer some starting points for selecting activities. The activity guides listed there contain an array of topics that explore all the areas in life, physical, and earth and space science. And as you gain experience, you will find your own activity books as well as Internet resources.

What Is Missing?

When you rely solely on a national or state standard to guide your school's or your class's science curriculum, you miss a great deal of the local influence that ought to contribute to the students' science experiences. Who your students are, how they experience nature, where they live, what region of the country your school is located in—all of these considerations should help you to frame your units of study.

Incorporating local and personal links

Remember, also, to learn about what kinds of personal lives your students have. Are they hungry? Poor? Overindulged? Disabled? Middle class? How will you use science curriculum to help students make meaning in the context of their own lives? That is the major role of your science curriculum: to engage students in their own learning, to relate science experiences to their lives, and to help them explore and draw conclusions. Certainly, national and state documents should help you to understand the range of topics and ideas that are appropriate. But what is best for *your* students remains a local decision.

Curriculum—any curriculum—is a lifeless document. You, the teacher, give it life when you use it to guide your students' experiences.

A Checklist for the Science Curriculum

The following checklist may help you ask the right questions when evaluating a science curriculum:

Questions for curriculum evaluation

■ What is the role of scientific inquiry in the curriculum?

■ Are there earth science, life science, and physical science topics at each grade level?

■ Are technology and mathematics incorporated into the science activities?

■ Where are the connections to other subjects, such as social studies and literature?

■ Do the topics spiral from lower to higher grades?

■ Are there topics that have local geographic connections and personal relevance for the students?

■ Are the topics explored in depth?

■ Is there room for informal science experiences?

If you are involved in creating the curriculum, you should ensure that these questions are answered as you plan. If you as a teacher are working with a curriculum designed by others, these questions can help you to identify its strong points and weak points and to decide when and how to supplement the formal curriculum with informal experiences.

KEY TERMS

gravitation *(p. 309)*
inertia *(p. 309)*
digestive system *(p. 311)*
circulatory system *(p. 311)*
respiratory system *(p. 313)*
respiration *(p. 314)*
nervous system *(p. 315)*
work *(p. 317)*
force *(p. 317)*
interaction *(p. 322)*
scientific law *(p. 323)*
law of conservation of matter and energy *(p. 323)*
matter *(p. 323)*
energy *(p. 323)*
physical change *(p. 324)*
chemical change *(p. 324)*
electricity *(p. 329)*
light *(p. 331)*
spectrum *(p. 334)*
magnetism *(p. 337)*
curriculum *(p. 339)*
scientific literacy *(p. 341)*
framework *(p. 341)*
MST initiative *(p. 342)*
unit of study *(p. 345)*

RESOURCES FOR FURTHER EXPLORATION

In addition to the following resources, see the "Exploring MST Curriculum" box earlier in this chapter for suggestions pertaining to the MST initiative.

Electronic Resources

AllExperts.com. http://www.allexperts.com/. This web site allows you to enhance your scientific understanding about any topic. Your questions are directed to one of many categories of "experts" who can help you make meaning of scientific concepts.

Developing Educational Standards. http://edstandards.org/Standards. html. This site offers an annotated list of Internet sites for K–12 educational standards and curriculum frameworks, including a breakdown of frameworks by state.

How Stuff Works. http://www.howstuffworks.com/.   This site has a straight-forward answer to practically any question one could think of about the way things work. There is a section devoted specifically to science, and you can type in a topic of your own using the site's search feature.

Internet Public Library Kidspace. http://www.ipl.org/div/kidspace/.   Click on "Math and Science" for basic information about a variety of topics related to earth science, animals, and more. You'll find excellent links to a wide range of data as well as useful images. In addition to enhancing your own science background, you can use this site with students in grades 3 and higher.

Motion, Energy and Simple Machines. http://www.necc.mass.edu/MRVIS/MR3_13/start.htm.   This site investigates Newton's laws of motion through experimentation with simple machines. It provides information on potential and kinetic energy, and it explores the concepts of force, friction, and energy transfer, as well as how each is affected by the use of simple machines.

National Science Education Standards. http://www.nap.edu/readingroom/books/nses/.   This web site includes an online version of the *Standards*.

The Physics Classroom. http://www.glenbrook.k12.il.us/gbssci/phys/Class/Bboard.html.   Geared for high school students as a tutorial in physics, this site contains a breadth of information on topics such as Newton's laws of motion; work, energy, and power; circular and satellite motion; static and current electricity; and more. Because it is framed in a tutorial format, the information is very easy to follow.

Project 2061. http://project2061.org/tools/.   Includes an online version of *Benchmarks for Science Literacy*.

Science NetLinks. http://www.sciencenetlinks.com/.   Developed by MCI, the American Association for the Advancement of Science, and the National Geographic Society, among other groups, this web site offers activities and lesson ideas keyed to *National Science Education Standards* and *Benchmarks for Science Literacy*.

Simple Machines. http://www.fi.edu/qa97/spotlight3/.   Sponsored by the Franklin Institute, this site contains explanations of different types of simple machines, including the inclined plane, wedge, screw, lever, wheel and axle, and pulley. It also provides links to other sites that have information on simple machines.

Solar System Resource Toolkit. http://cse.ssl.berkeley.edu/sol/solarsyst/sol_solarsyst_solarsyst.html.   This site from Science On-Line provides excellent teacher resources. It includes a selection of maps, graphs, and diagrams, as well as lesson plans and classroom activities that relate to the solar system. It also contains movies, images, and interactive tools to assist in the development of Internet-based classroom activities.

Welcome to the Planets. http://pds.jpl.nasa.gov/planets/.   This site is a great source of information on the nine planets. If you click on a planet's image, you are transported to a page that supplies a profile of the planet and describes some of its more prominent characteristics, such as craters, canyons, and moons. The site also contains a glossary of terms, as well as information about various types of spacecraft that have been used to explore the planets.

Print Resources

American Association for the Advancement of Science. (1993). *Benchmarks for Science Literacy.* Washington, DC: AAAS.

Bazin, M., Tamez, M., & Exploratorium Teacher Institute. (2002). *Math and Science Across Cultures.* New York: The New Press.

Kessler, J. (1996). *The Best of WonderScience: Elementary Science Activities.* Albany, NY: Delmar Publishers.

National Research Council. (1996). *The National Science Education Standards.* Washington, DC: National Academy Press.

Curriculum Activity Books and Guides for Science

Great Expectations in Mathematics and Science: The GEMS Series. Available from the Lawrence Hall of Science, University of California, Berkeley, CA 94720-5200; (510) 642-7771; **http://lhs.berkeley.edu/GEMS/.**

Insights. A series of curriculum modules available from Education Development Center, 55 Chapel Street, Newton, MA 02458; (800) 225-4276; **http://main.edc.org/.**

Science and Technology for Children: The STC Series. Developed by the National Sciences Resource Center. Available from Carolina Biological Supply Co., 2700 York Road, Burlington, NC 27215; (800) 334-5551; **http://www.carolina.com/STC/.**

14 What's the Big Idea?

Assessing What Students Know and Are Able to Do

FOCUSING QUESTIONS

- How do you know if the students "got" the science idea?
- What do you think it means to "match assessment to instruction"?
- How can a "performance" be an assessment?
- What role can technology play in assessment?

When I was in southern Texas working with a group of third- and fourth-grade teachers, they invited me to spend some time with their students. I was interested in learning what the students thought about science—how they would define it, for instance, and how they felt about learning it in school. One day I brought a tape recorder to class and interviewed the students about what they thought science was. This is how it went:

ME: What do you study in science?

THIRD-GRADE BOY: (really thinking) Scienzz, scienzz—what we're learning about scienzz. . . . There are stop scienzz, one-way scienzz, and yield scienzz.

My northern accent was clearly unintelligible to this student. He thought I had asked about "signs."

This story reminds me of the many occasions when we are trying to find out what students know but the student misunderstands the very way we ask or write the question. We, as teachers, are seeking one kind of meaning, and our students, with the best intentions, offer another kind. How, then, can we design ways to understand what students really know and are able to do in science?

This is the central theme of this chapter. Teachers refer to this quest to determine students' understanding with terms like *assessment* and *testing*. Let's explore what these terms mean in theory and in practice.

Assessment and Testing

A ssessment is an activity that teachers and, in fact, everyone else, engage in. We constantly find ways to assess ourselves and others. In education, though, this term is used in specific ways.

Science assessment refers to a process of collecting information that is used to determine the quality and character of an individual or group performance in a science learning experience. As you might imagine, this process of collecting information about what your students know and are able to do includes many different techniques. As two experts in the field put it, "When we assess students, we consider the way they perform a variety of tasks in a variety of settings or contexts, the meaning of their performances in terms of the total functioning of each individual, and the likely explanations for those performances" (Salvia & Ysseldyke, 2004, p. 6).

Testing is a narrower term. It refers to the use of teacher-made tests as well as state and local tests designed by educational agencies or testing services. Even within these categories, as you are probably aware, tests come in almost infinite varieties. The phrase *paper-and-pencil tests* generally refers to tests made up of short-answer or multiple choice questions. Essay tests, in contrast, require longer responses involving students' reflective thinking. Although essay tests may be taken with paper and a pencil, the term *paper-and-pencil test* does not usually refer to an essay test.

Many current science achievement tests measure "inert" knowledge—discrete, isolated bits of knowledge—rather than "active" knowledge—knowledge that is rich and well-structured.
—National Science Education Standards

Short-answer and multiple-choice tests tend to assess small pieces of knowledge, asking students to recall some term or fact related to the unit of study. Typically, these tests assess knowledge in a fragmented way rather than in the context of the students' learning. As we noted earlier in the book, recalling a term or a piece of knowledge is quite different from constructing meaning. It should not surprise you, then, to learn that paper-and-pencil tests are not the best method for assessing the type of deep, contextual scientific learning that is addressed in this book. To assess that deeper level, educators have been turning to performance assessment.

In **performance assessment**, also known as **authentic assessment**, students demonstrate their understanding by solving a problem in the real-life context of their classroom or their world. As you have seen throughout this book, the act of doing science always occurs in context.

Science is not isolated bits of observing, inferring, comparing, or recording; it is instead a contextual whole in which skills are employed because of a need to know. The skills are not important solely for their own sake. In the same way, a performance assessment sets up a need-to-know scenario that encourages the student to employ the skills that the assessment is intended to measure.

Performance assessments, as this chapter will show, can take a variety of forms. Whatever form you use, it should be appropriate to the context in which you are teaching. In other words, it has to *match the instruction*. In fact, a good assessment usually looks like a good instructional task. For example, as we teach science, we engage students in science journal writing. The journals can then also be used for assessment.

Finally, I like to use the term **evaluation** to refer to the process of making value judgments, based on the results of assessments, about a student's or a group's achievement in a science learning area (Doran, Lawrence, & Helgeson, 1993). When teachers evaluate their students' progress, they examine the assessment results and then make a judgment about how well the students understand a concept and use their science skills. Typically, evaluations relate students' progress to their own prior performance and to that of their peers within the class.

Value judgments

Today, many educators define this type of evaluation as part of assessment. In fact, when you hear the term *assessment*, it may even include the decisions that teachers go on to make after they have gathered their information and made their value judgments. For instance, deciding whether a student or a class should move on to the next unit could be considered a final step in assessment. In practice, be aware that assessment is a multifaceted process, and the word can mean different things to different people.

So much for definitions and qualifications. The question remains, How do we find out what our students know and are able to do in a given area of science? The next stage in answering that question is realizing that assessment is not separate from instruction. Rather, the two join naturally together in the instructional context.

Assessment and the Instructional Context

Whenever we are doing science with students, we are engaged in assessment. We wonder, "How are they doing? Do they work well together? What science skills are they using? Are they solving a problem? Do they get the science idea? What kind of model are they constructing?" Assessment and instruction may be thought of as siblings. They "live" in the same classroom, have the same parent (you, the teacher), and interact with the same people in their daily lives. Assessment is an integral part of instruction.

A family relationship

As you have noticed throughout this book, understanding a science concept often takes time, and there are alternative conceptions along the path to full understanding. You need to know where the students are in their thinking about an idea before you proceed to the next idea. Hence, you are always assessing as a natural part of creating meaningful science experiences.

If you follow the constructivist approach to instruction recommended by this textbook, you will want to explore your students' understanding in terms of their ability to employ knowledge to make sense of a situation or a problem. In other words, you will be looking at their learning in context, rather than just their "possession" of a certain item of knowledge. The following sections discuss several useful techniques: journals, portfolios, conversations, drawings, as well as other types of performances. We will also look at methods for using technology in assessment.

Using Science Journals for Assessment

Student journals

There are many ways to invite students to record a description of the science ideas and activities in which they are engaged. I encourage the use of **science journals,** which the chapter "Locating Your Scientific Self" described as a personal account of science experiences. Student science journals typically have a more specific structure than the science journal you may be keeping yourself. This structure directs students to the type of information they need to provide. Within this structure, though, the students' personal ideas about their science experiences have plenty of room to emerge.

A Sample Structure for a Science Journal

One way to structure a science journal is to use a list of questions as a guide. Students respond to the questions both by writing and by drawing illustrations. Here is a sample list of questions:

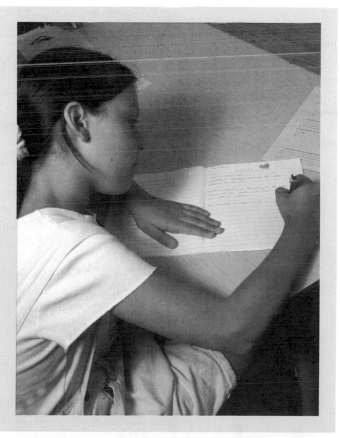

This student is recording data in her science journal, an important step as she draws conclusions about her investigations.

Mary Kate Denny/PhotoEdit

1. What do I know about _____?

*Expressing
prior knowledge*

For a particular lesson, you would fill in the blank with an appropriate word, such as *"snails," "electricity,"* or *"seeds."* This question is one for the students to answer *before* they begin a particular investigation or experiment. In this phase of journal writing, they express their prior knowledge; they process their existing ideas and understandings.

For example, in the fourth-grade snails lesson, described in the chapter "Sustained Inquiry," a student might write the following:

Snails are like slugs with shells. Snails move slowly. They live in the dirt.

2. What am I trying to find out?

*Defining
the problem*

This phase of journal writing prompts students to define one or more problems relating to the investigation. The students express the main problem they are trying to solve, formulate any other questions they may have, and perhaps think about extensions to the primary activity. By extensions to the primary activity we mean ideas that come up as students formulate the question. For example, in this section, a student might write:

How do snails move? What do they do when you shine a light on them? What happens when you put water near them? What happens when you put a piece of food near them?

3. What materials do I need?

*Listing
the materials*

Here the students list their materials. In the snails lesson, they would note a flashlight for testing the snails' response to light, lettuce for testing the response to food, and so on.

4. What did I do?

*Recording
the activities*

Once students have answered the first three questions, they proceed with their investigation. Afterward, in question 4, they describe their own activities. In some ways this section is like a log. It provides students with a record of what they did that led to their understandings. It can be written in a series of steps or in a narrative form.

5. What happened?

*A record
of findings*

In this phase of journal writing, the students document their observations. In the higher elementary and middle school grades, this section may be a formal record of findings, and the students may arrange their data in chart form or in graphs. In earlier grades, when the teacher has done a demonstration, this "what happened" section relates to what the class and the teacher have noticed together.

Even after a demonstration activity, the science journal should express the *individual* student's experience with the event. Students may draw or write their observations, or both. Figure 14.1 illustrates first graders' journal records of three ducklings' hatching in the classroom and what happened when they were taken outside by the teacher.

6. What did I find out?

Inferences and understandings

In this section of the journal, students express the inferences and understandings they have arrived at as a result of their investigation. For example, in the snails journal, students might write:

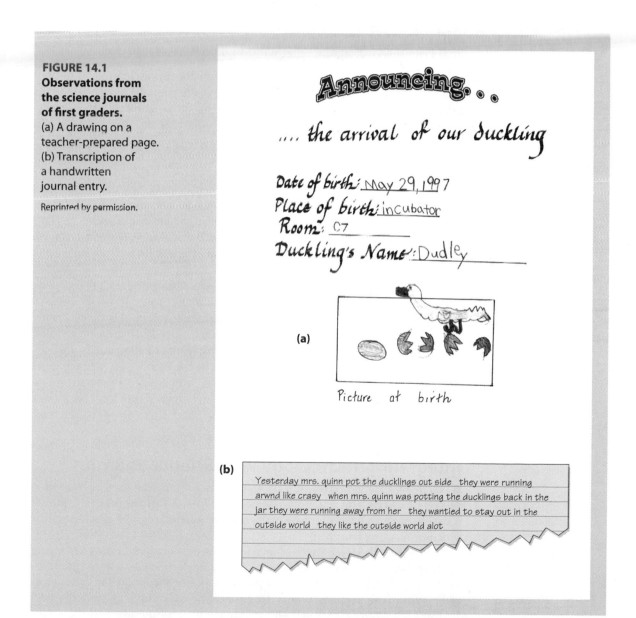

FIGURE 14.1
Observations from the science journals of first graders.
(a) A drawing on a teacher-prepared page.
(b) Transcription of a handwritten journal entry.

Reprinted by permission.

Announcing...
.... the arrival of our duckling

Date of birth: May 29, 1997
Place of birth: incubator
Room: C7
Duckling's Name: Dudley

(a)

Picture at birth

(b)

Yesterday mrs. quinn pot the ducklings out side   they were running arwnd like crasy   when mrs. quinn was potting the ducklings back in the jar they were running away from her   they wantied to stay out in the outside world   they like the outside world alot

The snails do not like the light.

The snails like to eat.

My snail moved very slowly.

7. What do I think about this experiment [or investigation or activity]?

Expressing opinions

In this section, students offer their opinions or ideas about the investigation. Sometimes they make connections to the real world—for example,

I like this experiment. It reminds me of how my mom says I move just like a snail.

8. If I did this over again, what would I do differently?

Planning modifications

This section invites students to analyze the investigation and plan modifications. Sometimes, they start the investigation all over again. This analysis and documentation of their thinking often leads them to important findings. After the snails lesson, one student wrote:

Next time, I would try this experiment by putting drops of water on the table. My snail didn't do anything when I put the water out in a dish.

Variant journal forms

Overall, a structure of this sort guides students' science writing as well as their science thinking. Journal entries do not always have to take the same form, however. Sometimes you might choose a more general question to prompt your students' thinking. For instance, during a unit on electricity, you might ask them to write in their journals on the topic, "What I wonder about electricity is. . . ."

A stimulus for further thinking

Besides encouraging students to keep a record of their science experiences, a science journal integrates their personal voice with their observations and inferences. Adult scientists maintain notebooks that become important sources for their research. Architects, artists, inventors, writers, and others keep journals and sketchbooks that record their ideas and observations and inspire further discoveries. In the same way, science journals do more than record students' emerging science ideas; they stimulate additional thinking and investigation. And when students look back over their science experiences as they have described them in their journals, they feel a considerable sense of pride.

Integrating Technology with Science Journals

If science journals are written by hand, they should always be kept in a bound notebook, not as separate sheets of paper. As an alternative, though, like other creative writing products, science journals can be created with a word processing program.

Advantages of computer journals

Students who keep their science journals on a computer disk can easily add, update, and correct. Moreover, if they have ready access to the Internet or CD-ROMs, they can insert pictures and other images in their journals. When the teacher wants to assess the students' knowledge and learning, the journals are usually printed out as hard copy and the pages are stapled together.

Drawing Pictures and Telling Stories

Importance of nonverbal expression

Students can record their observations in drawings as well as in words. Often I ask students to draw pictures in their journals of what they have observed or experienced during a science activity. Drawing gives them an opportunity to express themselves in a modality other than the verbal-analytic, and this can be an important consideration in our classrooms of increasingly diverse learners.

This form of assessment is not limited to the early grades. In fact, older students are often pleased and challenged when they are invited to draw what they have experienced. Older students usually place captions on their drawings and explain their understandings in writing as well.

Need for specific criteria

Remember that we are not telling the students *what* to draw. Rather, we are creating an opportunity for them to express their own ideas through the drawing. Nevertheless, we have to know why we are asking them to draw and what we expect their drawings to contain so as to demonstrate their understanding. In other words, we need to establish criteria for judging the students' performance, just as we would with any other assessment technique.

A clash of expectations

In this context, I'm reminded of a third-grade teacher who took her students on a "tree walk" and then asked them to draw a tree and label its "most important" parts. Her minimum expectation was that the students would properly identify trunk, leaves, bark, and roots. Many of her students, however, did not draw the roots because they were underground. Instead, they drew the trees as they had seen them on the tree walk. This clash of expectations can be avoided when the teacher establishes assessment checklists that match the context of the students' experiences.

Stories about drawings

With young children, it is useful to have them tell a story about their drawings. As they elaborate and evaluate what they drew on their paper, the teacher gets an excellent idea of what they know about the topic. This combination of drawing pictures and telling stories is a wonderful assessment tool for early childhood science education.

Evaluating Student Journals

For some purposes, you may want to use a specific scoring **rubric** or set of criteria to evaluate your students' understanding on the basis of their science journals. The following checklist is an example of such a rubric (modified from Shepardson & Britsch, 1997):

A sample rubric

Assessing for Conceptual Understanding

1. Evidence of conceptual understanding

2. Use of information, facts, and appropriate vocabulary

3. Evidence of changes in understanding

4. Drawings represent a realistic model

Assessing for Science Processes

1. Problem stated clearly

2. Expresses procedure for investigation

3. Observations recorded

4. Variable identified (where applicable)

5. Ideas and inferences based on observations and data

6. Analyzes the investigation with possibilities for change

Scoring systems

These categories of analysis lend themselves to various types of scoring. For example, we might allow up to 10 points for each of the ten criteria just listed, so the maximum score would be 100. Using this system, some teachers would give each student a numerical score. Other teachers use qualitative terms for science journals—for instance, "unacceptable," "acceptable," or "excellent," depending on the number of scoring points. In younger grades, labels like "budding scientist," "scientist," and "super scientist" can be useful.

Whatever system you use to evaluate science journals, you'll find that they give you many insights into the ways in which your students construct meaning. You'll see what the students understand and how they have come to understand it. You'll also discover what, if any, alternative conceptions need to be addressed in subsequent activities. Science journals are a good example of assessment techniques that provide a window into students' thinking.

Using Science Portfolios for Assessment

A selection of student work

A science portfolio is a selection of student work produced during a semester or a unit. The work included in the portfolio may take several forms—for example, a report, a drawing, a poem, or a letter that represents what the student has learned in science over a specific period of time. What is important about the portfolio is that the student selects its contents and reflects on his or her reasons for that selection.

Portfolios are more often created in writing, art, and math than in science. They would be used more often in science if more teachers understood their value. As an example of assessment activities that might form the basis for a portfolio, think back to the electricity lessons in the chapter "Expanding the Science 'Box.'" Ms. Travis might offer her students the following activities:

Sample assignments for portfolio assessment

■ Write a letter to a relative explaining how a simple circuit works.

■ Build a five-question game card using hidden electrical circuits. (The game card would be made with materials like aluminum foil, a manila folder, and a circuit tester consisting of a battery, three wires, a bulb, and a bulb holder. Only the card would go into the student's portfolio.)

■ Describe the reason that houses should be wired with parallel circuits.

■ Explain why circuit breakers are important.

■ Using the letters in the word *electric,* write one statement about electricity beginning with each letter.

■ Describe an activity that you have done with static electricity. What did you find out?

Each student would select and carry out three of these assignments to include in the science portfolio on electricity. As a guide to the portfolio, the students would explain the reasons for their choices. Of course, they could include any additional materials they chose. With an assessment technique like this, students become actively engaged in representing their understanding to the teacher.

Guide and cover sheets

Some teachers use ordinary folders in which a guide sheet has been stapled. These folders act as the students' portfolios, and the guide sheet includes a list of the contents under headings like these:

Description of Selection   *Why I Included This Item in My Science Portfolio*

Accompanying each selection is a cover sheet that may contain the following statements to complete:

Doing this assignment helped me:

_____

My favorite part of this assignment was:

_____

What I learned from this assignment was:

_____

Evaluating Student Portfolios

As with science journals, scoring systems for portfolios vary from teacher to teacher. Some teachers assign points; others use qualitative ratings.

Collaborating on a rating system

In the higher elementary and middle school grades, the portfolio rating system is usually developed through collaborative efforts by the class and the teacher. The teacher facilitates a discussion about what the class should look for in a science portfolio. Here is one example of a guide that a class and their teacher agreed to adopt:

Guide for Evaluating My Science Portfolio

■ It contains all required items.

■ It demonstrates my understanding of the science ideas behind the unit.

- It contains my reflections about the science experiences.

- It shows my ability to use science process skills.

Using Science Conversations for Assessment

Not all students can demonstrate what they know in writing as well as they can in "telling." An oral **science conversation,** sometimes called a **science interview**—that is, a direct communication between an individual student and the teacher—can overcome the problems that are created when we assess students solely on what they can explain in writing.

The chapter "Planning for Science" stressed the importance of how teachers question their students. But the usual questioning process, even something as simple as, "What do you think about this?" or "Why do you think this happened?" may leave out some members of the class. In personalized communication, you can engage a particular student one on one, find out what he or she is thinking, and negotiate the meanings of any terms that are problematic.

Personalized communication

Consider the story at the beginning of this chapter about my visit to southern Texas. After the student and I straightened out the pronunciation difficulty and we both understood that we were talking about science rather than street signs, we had the following conversation:

A sample science conversation

ME: What do you do when you do science?

STUDENT: We do experiments.

ME: What is an experiment like?

STUDENT: Well, one time we measured how much popcorn we had in a cup. Then we popped the popcorn and measured it again.

ME: How did you measure it?

STUDENT: We filled up other plastic cups with the popcorn and counted how many cups we had.

ME: What did you find out?

STUDENT: We got over twenty cups of popcorn from one cup!

ME: Wow, that's a lot of popcorn.

STUDENT: Yeah, the whole class ate it.

ME: Why do you think there was so much popcorn after you popped it?

STUDENT: Not sure. . . . I think it was something about how big each kernel got when it popped.

You can see that in a science conversation teachers can ask students to elaborate on statements, and in this way they can determine the depth of a student's understanding. Oral interviews such as these have proved to

Assessment: How Do We Know What the Students Know?

The following story is told by a teacher who discovers that her niece has a rather astonishing alternative conception about the phases of the moon. Think about what this anecdote reveals about the process of assessing students' knowledge.

My five-year-old niece Victoria and I were traveling south on the parkway after a family gathering in New York. The late spring day was warm, clear, and unusually colorful for that time of year. Victoria and I had noticed both the moon and the sun above us when she chuckled and asked, "Do you think the moon is going to follow us?"

I shrugged my shoulders in question, "Do you think it will?"

Victoria nodded her head up and down. "Yeah . . . it follows us all the time."

We watched the moon follow us, and as it hid behind a cloud my niece exclaimed, "Uh-oh. Maybe another moon will come out soon." As we drove, we discussed the "other moon."

AUNT LISA: What do you mean?

VICTORIA: Well, you know the other moons . . .

AUNT LISA: Victoria, how many moons are there?

VICTORIA: There's a lotta moons! There's eight moons, right?

AUNT LISA: Oh. Eight moons? How many suns are there?

VICTORIA: One.

AUNT LISA: How many stars do you see in the sky at night?

VICTORIA: So many!

AUNT LISA: How many moons do you see?

VICTORIA: Eight.

AUNT LISA: Really? You see eight moons when you look up at the sky?

VICTORIA: Yeah!

Victoria cupped her hand in the shape of a letter "C" and said, "Sometimes it looks like this." She reversed her "C"-shaped hand by flipping her cupped hand around and said, "Sometimes it looks like this." Victoria then held her finger in the air and traced a circle in the air. "Sometimes the moon looks like a circle."

"You see," she said with assurance as she threw her hands in the air, "there are a lot of moons!"

As this story illustrates, conversations are often vital for understanding what students really believe, and why.

be an effective way for both teachers and students to communicate what is known (Dana et al., 1991; Gallas, 1995). Teachers gain important clues about how students construct personal meaning, and these clues then influence their future instruction.

Using Technology to Assess Understanding

Technology-rich environments provide students with many additional ways to express their understanding to others. For example, as mentioned earlier, science journals kept on a computer can incorporate images as well as words. Students easily access web sites to "cut and paste" pictures or other graphic material that enhance their science journals.

Many presentation formats available

Even more dramatically, technology offers students the opportunity to be authors of their own meaning making by creating and designing products on the computer that indicate and sometimes demonstrate what they know about a given topic. Almost daily, it seems, new software products are emerging that are designed to reveal students' understanding of a topic. Many students, particularly those who may have difficulty expressing themselves in typical oral or written forms or in traditional test formats, embrace technology-based assessments as a way to express themselves creatively. These activities are also a good way to challenge gifted and creative students to expand their horizons.

Electronic portfolios

Products of technological assessment can be printed out and added to the student's portfolio. In many cases, too, students may be ready to create **electronic portfolios,** in which the portfolio and all its contents are stored in digital form. In addition to word-processed documents, an electronic portfolio might include photographs, data spreadsheets, scanned drawings, and more (Garthwait & Verrill, 2003).

The possibilities for technology-supported assessment are endless, but in this section we will look at technology that facilitates the use of three specific tools: concept maps, concept cartoons, and student presentations.

Concept Maps

You may recall that in the chapter "The Teacher as Mediator," Ms. Parker used a concept map to help develop and scaffold the complex understanding of the surface tension of water. This type of concept map, with arrows and circles, may be created by students as a form of assessment.

A concept map for the moon unit

Think about how you might use concept maps for the sixth-grade unit on the moon described in the chapter "Making Models." You might give students this assignment: "Placing the term *Moon* in the center of a concept map, demonstrate your understanding of how the moon shines and how it moves. The terms you may use include, but are not limited to, *Rotation, Revolution,* and *Reflection.*"

Using Inspiration software

Now, combine this with a handy authoring tool called Inspiration® (see the Electronic Resources at the end of the chapter), and the students can easily be creative in expressing their understanding of certain features of the moon. Using Inspiration, students can readily create the sort of concept map shown in Figure 14.2. Notice how the ovals relate to two different kinds of concepts about the moon and how the arrows demonstrate their linkage. This structural representation of understanding gives students another way of expressing meaning. The more ways in which we ask students to demonstrate what they know, the more possibility there is for students to actively engage in thinking deeply about a concept.

Concept maps may be saved and developed further as students continue to build their knowledge. You can make a concept map assignment open ended by asking students, for instance, to link "everything you have

FIGURE 14.2
Sample concept map for a sixth-grade unit on the moon

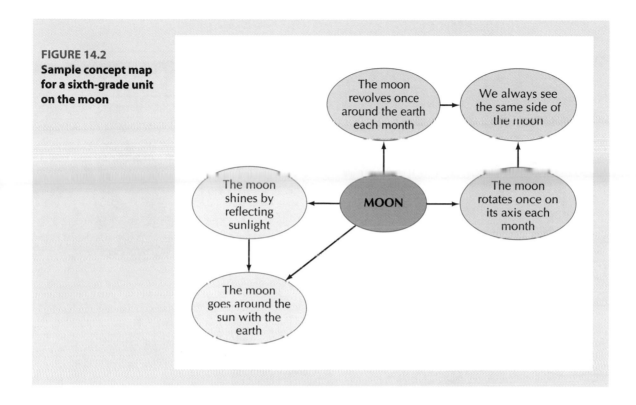

learned about the moon to the center circle." With Inspiration or a similar program, they can easily create links and arrows and build confidence in organizing information, understanding concepts, and expressing their thoughts. Remember, though, that just as a concept map shows what students know, misdirected links or wrong connections reveal what they don't understand.

Concept Cartoons

Concept Cartoons (Keogh and Naylor, 1999) were created to intrigue, provoke discussion, and stimulate scientific thinking among students. They feature cartoon-style drawings showing different characters arguing about an everyday situation. As students examine the cartoon, they are challenged with the question, "What do you think?" Often, the cartoons do not have a single right answer, but they all contain a visual representation of scientific ideas in a dialog form. They offer alternative viewpoints about a situation, and usually the most scientifically acceptable viewpoint is one of the alternatives. It is a wonderful way to stimulate discussion at the beginning of a unit or to assess understanding during the course of a unit (Naylor et al., 2001). Figure 14.3 is a sample Concept Cartoon that relates to a popular misconception about heating and cooling.

Cartoon drawings that challenge students to think

FIGURE 14.3
Concept Cartoon for a discussion of heat energy
What Do You Think?

Source: Reprinted from *Concept Cartoons,* http://www.conceptcartoons.com/.

Do you remember how the surface tension exploration in the chapter "The Teacher as Mediator" started with a student's wondering about the water strider insect? Figure 14.4 is a Concept Cartoon created with the software program Inspiration that could be used to assess students' understanding. Students can respond to this cartoon, in writing, to show their understanding of the surface tension of water. This is an excellent kind of assessment to use before students conclude their study of a topic. Many concept maps in science are readily available (see the Electronic Resources at the end of this chapter), and you can also create your own, either electronically or with pen and ink.

Electronic Presentations

Another kind of software that allows students to express their understanding is *presentation software.* This general category includes various programs that combine text, graphics, video, and sound in a single presentation. Microsoft's PowerPoint, widely used in business, is the most common example.

Using PowerPoint

PowerPoint presentations consist of a series of "slides" that appear on the computer screen and can be projected onto a larger screen. Teachers can provide rubrics that explain the framework and then ask students to

FIGURE 14.4
Concept Cartoon for the lesson on the surface tension of water

create their own presentations. For a PowerPoint presentation on land snails, the class might be asked to design four slides that explain how snails move, what they eat, what their habitat is like, and how they respond to stimuli. One slide might display a drawing of a land snail along with a short, descriptive passage of text. Students might design this slide so that, with the click of mouse on an on-screen button, the snail would appear to move slowly across the screen, accompanied by a recording of a student's voice offering observations about the speed of snails. Creating such a personal design package and presenting it to the class is an excellent way for students to use computer technology for assessment.

As with all other types of nontraditional performance-based tasks, technology design efforts must be evaluated according to an assessment checklist and rubric. If the students in Ms. Travis's fourth-grade class were asked to work in groups to design a PowerPoint presentation to compare series and parallel circuits, the following assessment checklist might guide them:

■ Does your presentation state the goal of the program?

■ Does your presentation include the materials that are part of electric circuits?

A third-grade student demonstrates a PowerPoint presentation she created for a science unit about bats.

Elaine Acker/BCI

■ Does your presentation show drawings of the two types of circuits?

■ Does your presentation offer real-life examples in which both types of circuits are used?

■ Does your presentation analyze the strengths of both types of circuits?

Regardless of the form your students' presentations take, the students themselves must be aware of the criteria for success if you are using their performances to measure the level of their understanding. Remember, the more varied the types of assessment you use, the more authentic information you will gain about students' understandings.

Multiple Types of Performances

The options described so far in this chapter, including science journals, portfolios, and presentations, are all useful methods for performance assessment. That is, they all can engage students in carrying out an assessment task that is relevant to the instructional context. These methods are far from the only possibilities, however. The following stories describe different ways in which students exhibit their understanding through performance.

SCIENCE STORY

Third Graders Enact the Water Cycle

The students'
experiences

In Ms. Nelson's third-grade classroom, the students have been exploring the water cycle and weather. On several days they have gone outside to observe the sky and make drawings of different clouds. They have been heating water and watching what happens. One day, Ms. Nelson places a pan of ice cubes over a pot with steam rising from it, and the students observe water droplets forming on the bottom of the pan. As these water droplets grow in size, they become so heavy that they fall back into the pot.

Many "big ideas" have emerged during the students' investigations of what happens to water when it is heated, what happens to steam when it is cooled, and the connections between their classroom models and the weather outside:

Ideas that
have emerged

When water is heated, it changes into steam.

You can see the steam rising from the pot. It looks like smoke.

When steam is cooled, it turns back to water.

The water falls back to the pot, filling it up again.

The water becomes steam again when it is heated.

When I see my breath in the winter, it is like a cloud.

Steam is really a gas called water vapor.

Toward the end of a week of exploration, Ms. Nelson introduces three terms: *evaporation, condensation,* and *precipitation.* She asks the students to think about how these terms describe some of the big ideas they have gathered.

Pondering new
terminology

The students have heard the term *evaporation* often. They know that the word applies to what happened when they washed the blackboard and the water seemed to disappear. Also, they have heard the term *precipitation* in weather reports, so they can connect it with their water droplets' falling back into the pot. But they are not sure about the term *condensation.*

At this point, Ms. Nelson draws a chart with arrows depicting water evaporating, becoming part of the clouds, and then precipitating back down to the Earth. The students reason that condensation must be the process of the gas's turning back into the water droplets. Ms. Nelson is impressed with their reasoning.

The students'
own ideas for
assessment projects

After some time, Ms. Nelson asks, "How shall we express what we know about the water cycle and weather?" The students come up with a variety of ideas:

Make a mural   Write a song

Write a poem   Write a story

Do a dance

Ms. Nelson asks, "What should all of our water cycle and weather projects have in common?" The students decide that their projects have to explain their understanding of *all* the big ideas about the water cycle they have listed that week.

Forming interest groups

Now Ms. Nelson guides the students to form groups that reflect their various talents and interests. Class time is set aside for group meetings, and resources are made available. The dance group, for example, needs a tape recorder; the art group needs brown butcher paper, pencils, and colored markers.

Eventually, all of the groups present their projects to the class. The song group sings a song they have composed about the water cycle, with instrumental accompaniment provided by one of the members who has brought in his guitar. The members of the dance group, except for the student playing the role of the sun, mime raindrops in the water cycle. They start out crouched on the floor like water particles, reach up to the sky like gas particles, shiver and huddle together to form a cloud, and gracefully fall down to the ground as rain—all to the background music of "Raindrops Keep Falling on My Head." Some students have opted to write personal water cycle stories, which they read to the class. One student has imagined that she is a drop in the water cycle, and she describes her journey through evaporation, condensation, and precipitation.

The dance group's interpretation

Students' deep engagement

In Ms. Nelson's class, all of the students have become engaged in the experience, thought deeply about it, made personal choices, and reflected a high level of understanding about the water cycle. The multiple assessment modes have allowed them to use various talents and means of presentation to express what they know. This is one way to implement what Brooks and Brooks (1999) refer to as "assessment in service to the learner."

 SCIENCE STORY

Second Graders Do a Station Assessment for a Unit on Matter

Setting up work stations around the classroom, similar to those described in the chapter on the science circus, is one way to design unit assessments. This format is often called a **station assessment.** The students use an answer sheet to respond to the questions at each assessment sta-

*Stations that present
challenging tasks*

tion. You must be sure that these workstations create a genuine context for the students to perform a task. Each station must challenge them to create meaning based on their prior knowledge and on the experiences in which they were engaged during their science study.

Consider this station assessment developed by second-grade teachers for a science unit on matter. Their school is in the Northeast, and it has been a snowy winter. The children will visit three stations.

*Station 1: Comparing,
contrasting, describing*

At Station 1 they find a plastic bag of air, a plastic bag of water, and a plastic bag of ice. The children are encouraged to examine these bags, but not to open them. The card on the table reads:

> **Look at the plastic bags of ice cubes, air, and water. In what ways are they the same? In what ways are they different?**

*Station 2:
Predicting*

At Station 2 are two identical glasses of water. One is covered, the other uncovered. The card reads:

> **What do you think will happen to the water in the glass that has no cover on it if we leave it out on a sunny day?**

*Station 3:
Sequencing, describing*

At Station 3, the students discover sheets of paper for them to take. Each sheet has three boxed pictures on it. The pictures represent different stages of a snowman melting. The card reads:

Take one sheet and cut the pictures out. Paste the pictures in order. What is happening in each picture?

Developing an assessment rubric for the stations

When the second-grade teachers designed these stations, they knew they also needed an assessment checklist and rubric, so they developed the one shown in Figure 14.5. After using the assessment in their classes, all of the teachers felt it had worked well. For the students, it was an important experience. For the teachers, the tallies of the class's performance led to a useful evaluation of the science lessons. The results of this assessment helped the teachers modify the curriculum and instruction to meet the students' needs.

To develop station assessments, you need to do the following:

Steps in creating a station assessment

1. State the goal of the assessment.

2. Describe the format of the assessment tasks, making sure that they match the instructional activities.

3. Develop a scoring rubric for measuring student competence.

4. Evaluate the students' responses to the experience.

Assessment and National Standards

STANDARDS ☑️

Assessment and learning are two sides of the same coin.
—NATIONAL SCIENCE EDUCATION STANDARDS

The National Science Education Standards support the importance of creating assessments that have a real-world relevance and context. This type of authentic assessment is the mirror image of the authentic instruction model that the NSES promote and this book describes. If we engage students in meaningful science experiences that relate to real-world contexts, then we need to assess them with meaningful experiences that relate to real-world contexts. To put it another way, when we allow students to be active participants in their own learning, we should assess their understanding with tasks that actively demonstrate what they know and are able to do—tasks that match the instruction.

NSES criteria for authentic assessment

The NSES state that assessment tasks are authentic when they ask students to apply their science knowledge and reasoning to "situations similar to those they will encounter in the world outside the classroom, as well as to situations that approximate how scientists do their work" (Na-

FIGURE 14.5
Sample checklist and scoring rubric for a station assessment

The following hands-on assessment of the second-grade unit on matter will provide us with a better understanding of what students know and are able to do as a result of their experiences with the matter unit.

1. Stations 1 and 2 invite observation, comparing, classifying, and describing.

2. Station 2 asks students to predict an outcome that they cannot observe at the moment.

3. Station 3 asks students to place events in their proper time sequence and describe the event in each picture.

Scoring Rubric—Matter Assessment

	YES	NO

1. Uses scientific terms such as:
   solid, liquid, gas, evaporation.

2. Accurately describes the water.

3. Accurately describes the ice.

4. Accurately describes the air.

5. Makes reasonable predictions about the
   glass of water that is uncovered:
   Water will get warm.
   Water will disappear.

6. Correctly sequences events.

7. Describes pictures accurately.

The following categories reflect the number of "yes" checks:

Budding scientist	Scientist	Super scientist
2–3	4–6	all 7

tional Research Council, 1996, p. 78). This chapter has advocated extensive and multiple means of performance assessment, including problem solving, creative writing, drawing, drama, technology applications, and other original forms of presentation.

The technology-enhanced assessments we have mentioned also help students meet performance indicators in the National Educational Technology Standards (NETS). For example, by the end of eighth grade, according to the NETS, students should be able to "design, develop, publish, and present products . . . using technology resources that demonstrate and communicate curriculum concepts" (International Society for Technology in Education, 2000, p. 22).

When to use paper-and-pencil tests

After contemplating all these performance-based and high-tech assessment measures, you may wonder whether there aren't any traditional paper-and-pencil tests that would be useful. You can indeed use paper-and-pencil tests, with multiple-choice or fill-in questions, to assess your students' familiarity with terminology and their recall of particular bits of science knowledge. Also, paper-and-pencil assessments have been constructed to measure students' science process skills (Smith & Welliver, 1990). In the example shown in Figure 14.6, developed for fourth graders, the test questions were matched to specific science process skills. Looking at

FIGURE 14.6
A paper-and-pencil test that invites students to use process skills

Look carefully at these students.

1   2   3   4

4. Which of the following statements about these students is correct?
  A. Students 1, 2 and 3 all have long hair
  B. Students 2, 3 and 4 all have long pants
  C. Students 1, 2 and 4 are all smiling
  * D. All of the answers A, B and C are correct

5. A. One student has short hair
  B. One student is wearing a dress
  C. One student is not smiling
  * D. All of the answers, A, B and C are correct

FIGURE 14.6
Continued

From *Journal of Research in Science Teaching*, 27(8), pp. 727–738. Excerpted with permission from the *Science Process Assessment for Fourth Grade Students*, © 1986 Kathleen A. Smith. Revised 1995. Reprinted by permission of Wiley-Liss, Inc. a subsidiary of John Wiley & Sons, Inc.

TANK 1
Guppy swimming -- student drops an alka-seltzer tablet in the tank. The bubbles are carbon dioxide.

TANK 1
After one minute, guppy stopped swimming and had trouble breathing.

TANK 2
Guppy swimming -- Plain water.

TANK 2
Guppy swimming -- Plain water after one minute.

8. Which sentence would best describe what effect alka-seltzer has on a guppy?
    * A. Guppies may not be able to survive long when carbon dioxide is in the water.
       B. Guppies become active when carbon dioxide is in the water.
       C. Guppies show no change in behavior when carbon dioxide is in the water.
       D. All of the answers A, B and C are correct.

the figure, you should be able to identify questions that relate to the skills of observation, inference, comparing, contrasting, and so on. But notice that although each question engages the student in using a process skill, there is no apparent reason to do so. There is no real-world context. Hence, tests of this type may have limited usefulness for teachers who want an active demonstration of their students' understanding.

Teaching, Learning, and Assessing

Carefully designing the assessment

Since educational data profoundly influence the lives of students, the design of assessments requires careful consideration. The drive to support authentic instruction with authentic assessment requires that teachers state the purpose and design of the assessment as well as the ideas and processes it is intended to measure (National Research Council, 1996, pp. 78–79).

As you have seen throughout this chapter, a good assessment task fits into the science experience and is a good instructional task as well. The students do not feel judged or threatened, and the teacher discovers what they know and understand about a science idea. Understanding what your students know about a topic will then influence your science instruction. Hence, assessment and instruction are interactive.

Assessment in a diverse environment

Remember that your class will probably include diverse groups of students with different learning styles and multiple ways of communicating their ideas. If you vary the types of assessments you employ, you create a more equitable learning environment. The chances are that using multiple modes of assessment, you will find a match for the mode of expression that each student feels most comfortable with. When you use a single assessment approach, you place students who are not comfortable with that selected way of expressing themselves—or students who have disabilities in a specific mode of communication—at an unfair disadvantage.

Remember that assessment is ongoing. It is embedded in all the work you do with your students. Keep asking yourself questions like these:

Questions to ask yourself about assessments

- Who are my students?

- How can I learn about what they understand?

- In what ways do they express themselves?

Assessing your students' learning can also lead you toward an assessment of your efforts as a science teacher. The next chapter will discuss how you can reflect on your own teaching as you engage students in science.

KEY TERMS

science assessment *(p. 351)*
testing *(p. 351)*
performance assessment *(p. 351)*
authentic assessment *(p. 351)*
evaluation *(p. 352)*
science journal *(p. 353)*
rubric *(p. 357)*
science portfolio *(p. 358)*
science conversation *(p. 360)*
science interview *(p. 360)*
electronic portfolio *(p. 362)*
station assessment *(p. 368)*

RESOURCES FOR FURTHER EXPLORATION

Electronic Resources

Assessments. http://intranet.cps.k12.il.us/Assessments/.   This page of the Instructional Intranet of the Chicago Public Schools will guide you to a variety of resources. Check the "Ideas and Rubrics" section for a bank of rubrics and instructions for creating a rubric from scratch.

Classroom Assessment.   http://www.enc.org/topics/assessment/classroom/. A web page where a number of teachers share strategies for assessing their students' work and their own teaching.

Concept Cartoons.   http://www.conceptcartoons.com/.   This site offers examples of excellent Concept Cartoons in science as well as ideas for helping students evaluate existing ones and generate their own.

ERIC Clearinghouse on Assessment and Evaluation.   http://ericae.net/.   A site that offers links to resources on a variety of assessment topics, including performance and portfolio assessment.

Inspiration Software.   http://www.inspiration.com/.   From the home page of this company, you can download a free trial of Inspiration software or its companion product, Kidspiration.

PowerPoint.   http://www.microsoft.com/office/powerpoint/.   This is Microsoft's home page for information about PowerPoint presentation software.

Print Resources

Gallas, K. (1995). *Talking Their Way into Science: Hearing Children's Questions and Theories, Responding with Curricula.* New York: Teachers College Press.

Hein, G., & Price, S. (1994). *Active Assessment for Active Science.* Portsmouth, NH: Heinemann.

Keogh, B., & Naylor, S. (1999). Concept Cartoons, teaching and learning in science: An evaluation. *International Journal of Science Education,* 21(4): 431–446.

Moline, S. (1995). *I See What You Mean: Children at Work with Visual Information.* York, ME: Stenhouse.

Shepardson, D. P., & Britsch, S. (1997). Children's science journals: Tools for teaching, learning, and assessing. *Science and Children* 5(34):13–17, 46–47.

15 Pulling It All Together:

Reflection and Self-Assessment

FOCUSING QUESTIONS

- Have you started a science journal?
- Have you been exploring science web sites?
- Have you examined one or more science lessons?
- Have you located your scientific self?

When you set up a plan for doing science with your students, you need a way to pull the lesson together. This chapter is my way of pulling this book's ideas together for you as you continue to develop as a teacher of elementary or middle school science.

We close *Science Stories* where we began—with our own scientific selves. You may wonder why I return so regularly to our scientific selves. It is because we do our best science teaching when we *model inquiry* to students.

Your Scientific Self

You would like, I'm sure, to show your students what it looks like to wonder, to be curious, to get messy, to explore nature, to yearn to find out about the natural world, and to be thrilled at the prospect of experimenting. In order to convey these feelings to our students, we need to feel them authentically inside ourselves.

My definitions of science change. Do yours?

My own feelings about science are not static. My definitions of science change as I grow and develop, and I am always adding to my list. I invite you to develop your own definitions of science as you have opportunities to do science with students. The following list of definitions contains statements that are true for me at different times. I usually do not believe all these definitions at the same time. They change as I change, as I interact with nature and with students.

*Some of the ways
I define science*

- Science is a way of exploring nature.

- Science is a method, a set of ideas, and a set of attitudes.

- Science is a subject in which you expect the unexpected.

- Science is an area of study that can be frustrating.

- Science is a way to explore students' thinking.

- Science is a dynamic area of study, ever changing, always revealing new evidence, and its practitioners are always changing their minds.

- Science is a joyous activity when shared with students.

- Science is not about knowing but about trying to find out.

Which of these definitions do you agree with now? Have your definitions changed as you read this book? What other definitions can you add?

*Getting comfortable
with your scientific self*

A large part of your journey toward becoming a successful science teacher involves locating your scientific self and becoming comfortable with it. Find ways in which you are comfortable exploring nature, write about them in your science journal, think about the characteristics of exploration, and come up with *your own* ideas and test them. Remember that we use process skills in our daily life, so look for experimentation in

Everyday Wonderings

In the course of your daily life, what do you wonder about? Do you write your questions and your discoveries in your science journal? The following excerpts from the science journals of preservice teachers illustrate how many ordinary things you can find to wonder about.

The ocean is beautiful in the Gulf of Mexico. The water is so blue; the sand is soft. There really weren't any shells. How come some beaches are just plain sand with a few shells, and other beaches have a ton of shells? Do some places have more shells to be washed on shore? Or is there a rougher tide at the beaches with shells? I am curious. Are there more shells after a hurricane or a big storm?

Every time I bake cookies, I jump as I hear the noise of the bending pans come from the oven. I've never understood why they warp like that. If heat causes things to expand, wouldn't the pan spread yet still lie flat?

Today some of my friends and I celebrated their graduation. We all got champagne with a strawberry in it. I watched this strawberry. When it was first put into the champagne, it sank to the bottom of the glass. But as the bubbles in the glass were dwindling, some of them stuck to the strawberry. The strawberry then floated to the top of the glass. I wonder what caused this.

Well, the weather is terrible today (as usual). The humidity is definitely the worst. It makes my hair look terrible. Why is that? I mean, I know what humidity is, but why does it affect my hair so much?

Reprinted by permission.

The teacher is exploring a natural environment with his students.

Arthur Tilley/i2i Images/
PictureQuest

everyday places. Watch for opportunities to observe, infer, predict, classify, and experiment. Some adults experiment in the kitchen or the garage or the garden. Ever curious about your environment, take these multiple opportunities to ask yourself:

■ Where is "nature"?

■ What do I notice?

■ What do I wonder about?

Write down your thoughts, and then share them with your students.

When you find your scientific self, you can no longer view science as just a subject taught in school. As you open your eyes to nature, you also

Looking around for science opportunities

feel a sense of confidence about exploring the scientific reasons for natural events. Look in your newspaper for items of interest that relate to scientific discovery; share these with your students, and encourage them to do the same. Ask yourself: What contemporary scientific issues especially engage me? Are they environmental issues? Or do they relate to health and nutrition?

Similarly, take time to visit local community resources. Look around for zoos, museums, botanical gardens, science and technology centers, bird sanctuaries, and other informal science learning sites. Watch even for dandelions in the cracks in the sidewalk. Being alert to all these opportunities to do science will help you become a successful science teacher as well as a lifelong science learner.

Becoming a Reflective Teacher

Reflection is active, not passive

Locating your scientific self takes time, and it often requires that you reflect on nature and the way nature presents itself in your world. This reflection is an *active process*. That is, it takes active, deliberative thinking, not passive musing. Further, it often leads to additional action to consolidate your understanding. When you reflect on an aspect of nature, you may be impelled to ask questions about it, to learn more about it, to make sense of it. The bird story early in this book—the entries from my science journal about the birds in the tree behind my house—is an example of how reflection stimulates further learning.

Being a reflective teacher requires frequent reflections on your students' thinking and on your own teaching practices. These reflections, too, lead to further action. Reflecting on how your students are responding to a lesson may require you to alter your lesson plan and change the course of subsequent lessons. On a larger scale, being reflective about your teaching practice will prompt you to seek out additional means for professional development, such as workshops and contacts with other teachers.

Developing a Personal Philosophy

As you begin your teaching career and engage students in scientific experiences, you will develop your own personal philosophy of teaching. By thinking about what you firmly believe and what you remain unsure about, you can promote your development as a teacher.

One useful technique is to develop a personal philosophy statement. It should contain your thoughts and feelings and indicate their connection to your actions as a teacher. As one such exercise, try completing the following statements (adapted from Kochendorfer, 1994):

A personal philosophy statement

I am the kind of science teacher who thinks that . . .

When I do science with students, I feel . . .

The science experiences that I believe are most worthwhile include . . .

If you can complete those sentences, you already have a rough draft of your philosophy statement. But it undoubtedly will change over time. Consider engaging in this sort of reflection during every school year, and keep track of your philosophy statements. You may be amazed at your own growth as a scientist and as a teacher.

Professional Development

Growing evidence suggests that ongoing professional development not only makes teachers feel better about their practice, but it also reaps learning gains for students.
—LINDA DARLING-HAMMOND (1998)

Professional development is the process by which teachers strive to improve their work as teachers, to grow in their profession. Your professional development is based, most of all, on inquiry into your own teaching—inquiry that leads to research and action. Reflection is part of that inquiry process, but there are numerous additional activities and resources to which you can turn. Many of them involve interactions with your professional colleagues, either within your school or in more extended networks.

Networking in the Profession

As you teach science, you will have many opportunities to interact with colleagues and join networks of teachers whose personal philosophy about teaching and learning is similar to your own. Local teacher centers and science organizations offer workshops and courses that create such networking opportunities for you.

Value of networking

Why should you spend time on professional networking? Research tells us that teachers who engage in professional communication with colleagues refine their practice throughout their careers (Darling-Hammond, 1998). Networking activities can include experiential learning—for example, working with colleagues on concrete tasks, such as developing a science station assessment. They can also include working with a mentor teacher in your own school, observing an exemplary teacher, and attending teacher discussion groups centered on teaching practice.

Look for such opportunities in your own school and district. Be alert for opportunities to attend science teaching workshops. Inquire whether your school or district will offer funding for you to attend national or regional conferences.

Joining NSTA

As a first step, you can join your state science teachers' association and the National Science Teachers Association (NSTA). Membership in the NSTA includes a subscription to *Science and Children*, a journal devoted to preschool through middle-level science teaching. The contact information is listed in the Resources for Further Exploration at the end of this chapter.

Promotion and Certification Requirements

Increasingly, teachers are being required to show evidence of their professional development in order to earn promotions, or even to have their teaching certificates renewed. Since requirements vary from state to state, you should explore the criteria in your own locale.

STANDARDS ☑

On the national level, certification is being offered by the National Board for Professional Teaching Standards (NBPTS). Established in 1987, The NBPTS is a nonprofit organization governed by a sixty-three-member board of directors. Most of the directors are classroom teachers; others are school board leaders, governors, and business and community leaders. The mission of the NBPTS is to establish high and rigorous standards for what accomplished teachers should know and be able to do, and to operate a national, voluntary system for assessing and certifying teachers who meet these standards. By the beginning of 2003, over 24,000 teachers were National Board certified in more than twenty certificate areas. For elementary and middle school teachers, there are generalist certification standards for teaching students in early childhood (ages 3–8), and middle childhood (ages 7–12), and early adolescence (ages 11–15). For science teaching in particular, there are certificates for teaching students in adolescence (ages 14–18) and early adolescence (ages 11–15). Some elementary school teachers become so interested in engaging students in science that they return to school part-time and take more science courses for higher-level certifications.

NBPTS certification

The five major propositions around which the National Board has organized its standards are the following:

■ Teachers are committed to students and their learning.

■ Teachers know the subjects they teach and how to teach those subjects to students.

Teachers learn with and from each other. Formal and informal teacher networks help teachers share strategies for doing science with students.

Carol Palmer

■ Teachers are responsible for managing and monitoring student learning.

■ Teachers think systemically about their practice and learn from experience.

■ Teachers are members of learning communities.

Advocates of the national board believe that offering professional credentials brings prestige to the teaching profession, and they hope that schools and school districts will see NBPTS certification as a valuable teaching qualification. You may want to visit the NBPTS web site, listed in the Resources at the end of this chapter, and explore the requirements for certification. You must have been teaching for a minimum of three years and have completed your baccalaureate degree to be eligible to take the series of assessments that lead to an NBPTS certificate.

Further Means of Professional Development

Besides networking with colleagues and fulfilling state and local requirements for advancement in the field, there are many other ways that you can promote your own professional development as a science teacher. Here are some ideas:

Doing your own science research

■ Do research on science topics. If there is a topic that you wish you knew more about, turn to the library, the Internet, and science trade books to research it. Be sure to gain confidence in the science content areas that you will be exploring with your students.

■ For exemplary science instructional materials, refer to the curriculum guides listed in the Resources for Further Exploration of the chapter "Science and Science Curriculum," as well as the other resources mentioned throughout this book.

■ Trust your own judgment. If you come across a scientific investigation that does not appeal to you, most likely it won't appeal to your students either.

■ Keep a science journal, for both in-class and outside-of-class science activities.

Doing your own research on teaching

■ Do your own research on what is happening in your classroom. **Action research,** also known as **teacher research,** involves research projects in which classroom teachers explore some area of their teaching or some aspect of the students' learning. For example, they may study how their students are experiencing a science unit, lesson, or activity. The goal of action research is to improve your own or a colleague's teaching. Sometimes an action research project is a questionnaire you distribute to students to learn what they thought about an investigation or a unit. Sometimes the research design is more extended, depending on what you want to find out. Doing research in your own classroom is not complicated, and the Resources at the end of the chapter can help you get started.

How Am I Doing? A Guide to Self-Evaluation

Science teaching, like all other teaching, is a commitment to becoming a lifelong learner. As you reflect on what you have learned and how you teach, the checklist in Figure 15.1 may help you to evaluate your professional growth. Revisit the table's questions from time to time.

If you are unsure of your progress in any of the areas listed in Figure 15.1, ask a colleague to videotape you as you teach. Videotapes are often useful as personal guides for developing professionally. Use the checklist to review the videotape and assess your own progress.

Using a video to review your progress

But don't let the checklist—or any other teaching guidelines—intimidate you. Go easy on yourself at first. Be prepared to fumble now and again. You are traveling in what may often be uncharted territory. Do not be discouraged—science takes time.

Looking Back to Look Ahead: A New Chapter in Your Science Autobiography

Science Stories has been an attempt to have a conversation with you about science teaching and learning—about yourself as a science learner and a science teacher. As one of the goals for the book, I hoped to engage you

**FIGURE 15.1
A Checklist for
Self-Evaluation**

1. Am I providing *opportunities* for my students to explore natural phenomena?
   Yes_____No_____Comments_____

   _____

2. Do I allow my students enough *time* to complete their explorations?
   Yes_____No_____Comments_____

   _____

3. Whose *voice* is dominant during science explorations: mine or the students'?
   Theirs_____Mine_____Comments_____

   _____

(continued)

FIGURE 15.1
Continued

4. Do I encourage children students to ask *questions?* How do I do that?

   Yes _____ No _____ Comments _____

   _____

5. Do I *coach* students to find their own answers?

   Yes _____ No _____ Comments _____

   _____

6. Do I *record my students' questions* to save until another day if there is no time to help them find the answers when the question is asked?

   Yes _____ No _____ Comments _____

   _____

7. Do I encourage the use of *technology* for communication, presentation, and research?

   Yes _____ No _____ Comments _____

   _____

8. Do I *let go of my prepared plan* if the students' own ideas generate a new direction?

   Yes _____ No _____ Comments _____

   _____

9. Do I use *diverse techniques* to assess what the students know about a topic?

   Yes _____ No _____ Comments _____

   _____

10. Does my classroom have a *student-directed science corner?*

    Yes _____ No _____ Comments _____

    _____

11. Am I *having a good time* doing science with my students?

    Yes _____ No _____ Comments _____

    _____

in the stories of real students and real teachers who were learning science together and separately. To encourage your professional growth, I've also tried to connect you with some of the research that has influenced this way of doing science with students.

These are the major themes that we have addressed:

This book's major themes

- The nature of science
- Constructivism
- Prior knowledge
- Activity-based learning
- Science as inquiry
- Integrating technology with science
- Alternative conceptions
- Lesson planning
- Working with cooperative learning groups
- Developing curriculum
- Creating assessments
- Science in your—and your students'—everyday life
- Locating your own scientific self!

Everyone deserves to share in the excitement and personal fulfillment that can come from understanding and learning about the natural world.
—NATIONAL SCIENCE EDUCATION STANDARDS

Science teaching needs to encourage, invite, engage, excite, interrogate, and challenge. I also like to say that it should shine like a beacon, signaling that science is truly for everyone. Science teaching can make connections to students' lived experiences and help them to frame their own questions about natural phenomena as a way of making meaning of their world. I always hope that students will take ownership of their own knowledge and gain autonomy as they seek their own answers. But everything I hope for the students, I also hope for you, their science teacher.

Draw yourself

When you have your own classroom, take a moment after the first hectic months and draw a picture of yourself as you are teaching a "typical" science lesson. Drawing skill is not important—just try to portray what is going on. Place a caption under your drawing and have a look at it. You can interrogate your drawing by asking: What am I doing? What are the students doing? What is my position in the room? How confident do I feel in my science teaching? This exercise will help you continue to develop as a science teacher.

Your next chapter

Right now, as a result of your own journey toward science teaching, you may be ready to begin the next chapter of your science autobiography. You may even want to start writing your own science stories. One teacher summarized her feelings about doing science with students in a poem; the first letters of the lines spell out the word *inquiry:*

Investigate and you will find,
New information of some kind,
Question all your observations,
Understand through your explanations,

Integrate what you have discovered,
Reflect and share what you have uncovered.
You are doing science! (Carol Federico, 2002)

KEY TERMS

professional development *(p. 380)*
action research *(p. 382)*
teacher research *(p. 382)*

RESOURCES FOR FURTHER EXPLORATION

Electronic Resources

National Academies Press.   http://www.nap.edu/.   A source for many publications relevant to professional development.

National Board for Professional Teaching Standards.   http://www.nbpts.org/. This web site is a guide to the teacher-assessment process and the standards that inform that process. It is both a resource and a "how-to" site.

National Science Teachers Association.   http://www.nsta.org/.   At this site you can learn about membership in the association and sample some of the resources offered to members.

Networks: An On-line Journal for Teacher Research.   http://www.oise. utoronto.ca/~ctd/networks/.   This site provides articles by teachers about their own classroom research as well as useful links and a discussion forum. It is an excellent site for your own professional development.

Teachers.Net.   http://www.teachers.net/.   A web site that offers chat opportunities, a reference desk, and more—many different resources to use in your teaching.

Print Resources

Darling-Hammond, L. (1998). Teacher learning that supports student learning. *Educational Leadership*, 55 (5):6–11.

Darling-Hammond, L. (1999). *Reshaping Teaching Policy, Preparation, and Practice: Influences of the National Board for Professional Teaching Standards.* Washington, DC: AACTE Publications.

Elliot, J. (1991). *Action Research for Educational Change.* Philadelphia: Open University Press.

Kockendorfer, L. (1994). *Becoming a Reflective Teacher.* Washington, DC: National Education Association.

More Resources for Teachers

Organizations and Associations for Professional Development

- Organizations and Associations for Professional Development
- Useful Equipment, Materials, and Suppliers
- Safety Tips for Science in Elementary Schools
- Trade Books About Nature and Science

This list includes both educational and scientific organizations, as well as some groups that are specifically devoted to science teaching. By contacting the ones most suited to your own interests and needs, you can find ways to broaden your perspectives and further your own professional development as a teacher of science.

American Association for the Advancement of Science (AAAS)
1200 New York Avenue NW, Washington, DC 20005
(202) 326-6400; **http://www.aaas.org**

American Chemical Society (ACS)
1155 16th Street NW, Washington, DC 20036
(202) 872-4600; **http://www.acs.org**

American Indian Science and Engineering Society (AISES)
P.O. Box 9828, Albuquerque, NM 87119-9828
(505) 765-1052; **http://www.aises.org**

American Physical Society
One Physics Ellipse, College Park, MD 20740-3844
(301) 209-3200; **http://www.aps.org**

American Zoo and Aquarium Association
8403 Colesville Road, Suite 710, Silver Springs, MD 20910-3314
(301) 562-0777; **http://www.aza.org**

Association for Supervision and Curriculum Development (ASCD)
1703 North Beauregard Street, Alexandria, VA 22311-1714
(703) 578-9600 or 1-800-933-ASCD; **http://www.ascd.org**

Association for Women in Science (AWIS)
1200 New York Avenue NW, Suite 650, Washington, DC 20005
(202) 326-8940; http://www.awis.org

Association of Science-Technology Centers
1025 Vermont Avenue NW, Suite 500, Washington, DC 20005-3516
(202) 783-7200; http://www.astc.org

Council for Elementary Science International (CESI)
Betty Burchett, Membership Director, 511 Marion Drive,
Columbia, MO 65203
(573) 874-1038; http://unr.edu/homepage/crowther/cesi.html

**ERIC Clearinghouse for Science, Mathematics, and
Environmental Education**
1929 Kenny Road, Columbus, OH 43210-1080
(800) 276-0462 or (614) 292-6717; http://www.ericse.org

**ERIC Clearinghouse on Elementary and Early Childhood Education
Children's Research Center, University of Illinois at Urbana-
Champaign,** 51 Gerty Drive, Champaign, IL 61820-7469
(800) 583-4135 or (217) 333-1386; http://www.ericeece.org

Harvard-Smithsonian Center for Astrophysics
60 Garden Street, Cambridge, MA 02138
(617) 495-7461; http://cfa-www.harvard.edu

International Technology Education Association (ITEA)
1914 Association Drive, Reston, VA 20191-1539
(703) 860-2100; http://www.iteawww.org

JASON Project
The JASON Foundation for Education,
11 Second Avenue, Needham Heights, Massachusetts 02494-2808
(781) 444-8858; http://www.jasonproject.org

Lawrence Hall of Science (LHS)
University of California, Centennial Drive, Berkeley, CA 94720-5200
(510) 642-5132; http://www.lhs.berkeley.edu

National Academies Center for Education
500 5th Street NW, Washington, DC 20001
(202) 334-2353; http://www7.nationalacademies.org/cfe

National Assessment of Educational Progress (NAEP)
1990 K Street NW, 8th Floor, Washington, DC 20006
(202) 502-7400; http://nces.ed.gov/nationsreportcard

National Association for the Education of Young Children
1509 16th Street NW, Washington, DC 20036-1426
(800) 424-2460; http://www.naeyc.org

National Association for Research in Science Teaching (NARST)
http://www2.educ.sfu.ca/narstsite

National Association for Science, Technology and Society (NASTS)
Mail Stop 282, Department of Curriculum and Instruction,
University of Nevada, Reno, NV 89557
(775) 784-4961; http://www.nasts.org/

National Board for Professional Teaching Standards
1525 Wilson Boulevard, Suite 500, Arlington, VA 22209
(703) 465-2700; http://www.nbpts.org/

National Oceanic and Atmospheric Administration (NOAA)
14th Street and Constitution Avenue NW, Room 6217,
Washington, DC 20230
(202) 482-6090; http://www.noaa.gov

National Science Foundation (NSF)
4201 Wilson Boulevard, Alexandria, VA 22230
(703) 292-5111; http://www.nsf.gov

National Science Resources Center (NSRC)
901 D Street SW, Suite 704B, Washington, DC 20560-0952
(202) 287-3750; http://www.si.edu/nsrc

National Science Teachers Association (NSTA)
1840 Wilson Boulevard, Arlington, VA 22201-3000
(703) 243-7100; http://www.nsta.org

**National S.E.E.D. Project on Inclusive Curriculum:
Seeking Educational Equity and Diversity**
Dr. Peggy McIntosh, Center for Research on Women,
Wellesley College, Wellesley, MA 02481
(781) 283-2520; http://www.wcwonline.org/seed

National Wildlife Federation
11100 Wildlife Center Drive, Reston, VA 20190-5362
(703) 438-6000 or (800) 822-9919; http://www.nwf.org

Network for Portable Planetariums
c/o Ms. Sue Button, Planetarium Specialist, Onondaga-
Cortlandt-Madison BOCES, P.O. Box 4754, Syracuse, NY 13221
(315) 433-2671

Operation SMART
Girls Incorporated, 30 East 33rd Street, New York, NY 10016
(212) 689-3700; http://www.rit.edu/~easi/easisem/girls95.html

Project WILD
5555 Morningside Drive, Suite 212, Houston, TX 77005
(713) 520-1936; http://www.projectwild.org

School Science and Mathematics Association (SSMA)
Arthur L. White, Executive Director, The Ohio State University, School
of Teaching and Learning, 238 Arps Hall, 1945 North High Street,
Columbus, OH 43210-1172
(614) 292-7695; **http://www.ssma.org**

Smithsonian Center for Education and Museum Studies
900 Jefferson Drive SW, Room 1163, Washington, DC 20560-40402
(202) 357-2425; **http://educate.si.edu**

Society for Advancement of Chicanos and Native Americans in Science
P.O. Box 8526, Santa Cruz, CA 95061-8526
(831) 459-0170; **http://www.sacnas.org**

Triangle Coalition for Science and Technology Education
1840 Wilson Boulevard, Suite 201, Arlington, VA 22201
(800) 582-0115; **http://www.triangle-coalition.org**

U.S. Geological Survey
509 National Center, Reston, VA 20192
(703) 648-4748; **http://www.usgs.gov**

Young Astronaut Council
5200 27th Street NW, Washington, DC 20015
(301) 617-0923; **http://www.yac.org/yac**

Useful Equipment, Materials, and Suppliers

The science stories in this book demonstrate that you don't need a great
deal of fancy equipment to do science with students. Often, though,
some basic supplies are extremely useful. This section lists handy materials and equipment, then the names and addresses of suppliers.

Materials and Equipment

Aluminum foil

Aluminum foil pie pans

Baby food jars

Baking soda

Balloons

Batteries: AA and D

Beakers: 250 ml

Bell wire

Bottles: juice and soda

Buttons

Cages

Candles

Corn oil

Cornstarch

Corn syrup

Drinking straws

Flashlights

Food coloring

Funnels

Glass jars (especially large ones)

Graduated cylinders

Hot plates: safety-approved for schools

Land snails

Magnets: all shapes and sizes

Magnifying lenses

Matches

Meter sticks

Metric measuring cups

Mirrors

Modeling clay

Owl pellets

Paper towels

Plastic bags: resealable "zip-lock" style, both sandwich size and food storage size

Plastic containers: quart size or larger

Plastic cups (10 ounces, 12 ounces)

Plastic spoons

Plastic tubing

Pocket microscopes

Poster paper and paper tape

Potting soil

Prisms

Rock collections

Salt

Sand

Scales: double-pan primer balances with uniform masses for elementary school; triple-beam balances for middle school; one electronic (digital) scale per classroom

Seeds: many types, including grass, mustard, radish, red kidney beans, lima beans, pumpkin, corn

Shells

Shoeboxes

String

Sugar

Tape

Thermometers

Toothpicks

Trowels

Tuning forks

Vinegar

Wire strippers

Sources of Supplies and Equipment

Arbor Scientific
P.O. Box 2750, Ann Arbor, MI 48106-2750
(800) 367-6695; **http://www.arborsci.com**

Carolina Biological Supply Company
2700 York Road, Burlington, NC 27215-3398
(800) 334-5551; **http://www.carolina.com**

Connecticut Valley Biological Supply Company
P.O. Box 326, Southampton, MA 01073
(800) 628-7748; **http://www.ctvalleybio.com**

Delta Education
P.O. Box 3000, Nashua, NH 03061-3000
(800) 258-1302; **http://www.delta-ed.com**

ETA/Cuisenaire
500 Greenview Court, Vernon Hills, IL 60061
(800) 445-5985

Fisher Scientific International
2000 Park Lane Drive, Pittsburgh, PA 15275
(800) 766-7000; **http://www.fishersci.com**

Nasco
901 Janesville Avenue, Fort Atkinson, WI 53538-0901
(800) 558-9595; **http://www.nascofa.com**

Radio Shack (for pocket microscopes)
200 Taylor Street, Suite 600, Fort Worth, TX 76102
(800) 843-7422; **http://www.radioshack.com**

Science Kit and Boreal Laboratories
P.O. Box 5003, Tonawanda, NY 14151-5003
(800) 828-7777; **http://sciencekit.com**

Safety Tips for Science in Elementary Schools

The following safety suggestions are general guides for doing science in the classroom. Many of these ideas are adapted from a National Science Teachers Association booklet, *Safety in the Elementary Science Classroom*, available directly from the NSTA (see the list of Organizations and Associations for Professional Development).

Learning About Safety Policies

■ Know your school's policies regarding:
Live animals in the classroom
Use of electrical hot plates
Procedures in case of an accident
Outdoor walks and field trips

■ Check state and federal regulations about school safety.

■ Be sure to obtain appropriate consent from parents and guardians for out-of-classroom activities and extended investigations of living organisms.

Preparing for Classroom Safety

■ When stored, all equipment and materials should be labeled clearly to avoid mistakes.

■ Maintain cooperative learning groups of manageable size, and make certain that the students are responsible for returning materials to designated storage spaces.

- Be sure your classroom has a fire extinguisher and a fire blanket.

- Glassware can be dangerous. Whenever possible, use plastic instead. When you must use glassware, be sure careful procedures are followed. Have a whisk broom and dustpan handy for sweeping up broken pieces of glass.

- Use thermometers that are filled with alcohol, not mercury.

- Keep a first-aid kit in the classroom; check that it is fully supplied.

- Caution students never to taste, touch, or inhale unknown substances.

- Minimize the use of chemicals.

- Substances that are potentially harmful should be handled only by the teacher.

- Instruct students that all accidents or injuries—no matter how small— must be reported to you immediately.

- Explain to students that it is unsafe to touch their faces, mouths, eyes, and other parts of their bodies while they are working with plants, animals, or chemical substances. They must wash their hands and clean their nails after handling these materials.

- When working on an electricity unit, warn students not to experiment with the electric current in their home circuits.

- Hands should be dry when working with electrical cords, switches, or appliances.

- In general, if any materials or procedures may present a danger, explore the possible hazards carefully, and then train students in the proper methods.

Providing for Students with Special Needs

- Take steps to ensure that students with special needs or disabilities have safe and easy access to science facilities, to the extent that is advisable according to their circumstances.

- Anticipate any special needs that these students may have in emergency situations, and be sure that these requirements can be met.

Trade Books About Nature and Science

The following are some of my favorite trade books that can help you learn about science and scientists. Some are written for children, some for adults, but all may be useful as you develop your own scientific self.

Amato, I. (1997). *Stuff: The Materials the World Is Made Of*. New York: Basic Books.

Brenneman, R. J., ed. (1984). *Fuller's Earth: A Day with Bucky and the Kids*. New York: St. Martin's Press.

Bryson, B. (2003). *A Short History of Nearly Everything*. New York: Random House.

Carson, R. (1956). *The Sense of Wonder*. New York: Harper & Row.

Carson, R. (1970). *Silent Spring*. Introduction by Paul R. Ehrlich. Greenwich, CT: Fawcett.

DuQuette, K. (2002). *They Call Me Woolly: What Animal Names Can Tell Us*. New York: G. P. Putnam's Sons.

Ferris, T. (1998). *The Whole Shebang: A State-of-the-Universe Report*. New York: Touchstone Books.

Feynman, R. P., as told to R. Leighton. (1985). *Surely You're Joking, Mr. Feynman: Adventures of a Curious Character*. Edited by Edward Hutchings. New York: Norton.

Feynman, R. P., & Freeman, D. (2000). *The Pleasure of Finding Things Out: The Best Short Works of Richard P. Feynman*. New York: Perseus Book Group.

Fuller, R. B. (1992). *Cosmography: A Posthumous Scenario for the Future of Humanity*. Adjuvant, Kiyoshi Kuromiya. New York: Macmillan.

Gould, S. J. (1980). *The Panda's Thumb: More Reflections in Natural History*. New York: Norton.

Gould, S. J. (1991). *Bully for Brontosaurus: Reflections in Natural History*. New York: Norton.

Greene, B. (2000). *The Elegant Universe: Superstrings, Hidden Dimensions, and the Quest for the Ultimate Theory*. New York: Vintage Books.

Hawking, S., ed. (1992). *Stephen Hawking's A Brief History of Time: A Reader's Companion*. Prepared by Gene Stone. New York: Bantam Books.

Hazen, R. M., & Trefil, J. (1991). *Science Matters: Achieving Scientific Literacy*. New York: Doubleday.

James, S. M. (2002). *Dolphins*. New York: Mondo.

Keller, E. F. (1983). *A Feeling for the Organism: The Life and Work of Barbara McClintock*. New York: W. H. Freeman.

Lerner, C. (2002). *Butterflies in the Garden*. New York: HarperCollins.

Logan, C. (2002). *The 5,000-Year-Old Puzzle: Solving a Mystery of Ancient Egypt*. New York: Farrar, Straus and Giroux.

Morrison, G. (2002). *Pond*. New York: Houghton Mifflin.

Negroponte, N. (1995). *Being Digital*. New York: Knopf.

Old, W. (2002). *To Fly: The Story of the Wright Brothers*. St. Louis, MO: Clarion.

Peterson, R. T. (1979). *A Field Guide to the Birds of Texas and Adjacent States*. Boston: Houghton Mifflin.

Peterson, R. T. (1998). *Peterson Field Guide to Eastern Birds* (4th ed.). Boston: Houghton Mifflin.

Peterson, R. T. (1998). *Peterson Field Guide to Western Birds* (3d ed.). Boston: Houghton Mifflin.

Pipe, J. (2002). *What Does a Wheel Do?* Brookfield, CT: Copper Beech Books/Millbrook.

Trefil, J. (1992). *Sharks Have No Bones: 1001 Things Everyone Should Know About Science*. New York: Simon & Schuster.

Winter, Y. (2002). *Birds Build Nests*. Watertown, MA: Charlesbridge.

Zemlicka, S. (2002). *From Egg to Butterfly*. Minneapolis, MN: Lerner.

Glossary

action research   Refers to research projects in which classroom teachers explore some area of their teaching or some aspect of the students' learning with the goal of improving their own or a colleague's teaching. Also called *teacher research* or *classroom research*.

alternative conception   An idea that is not scientifically accurate, but represents a step toward full understanding of a concept.

angiosperm   A seed plant; one that produces flowers that eventually form fruits with seeds.

Animalia   The scientific name for the animal kingdom. It is commonly divided into two broad groups: animals with backbones and animals without backbones.

aphelion   The point in a planet's orbit when it is farthest from the sun.

arthropod   An invertebrate animal with a skeleton on the outside of its body—for example, lobsters, crayfish, crabs, shrimp, spiders, and all insects.

assessment   *See* Science assessment.

asteroid   A tiny chunk of planet-like material that moves around the sun. Between Mars and Jupiter, there is a belt of several thousand asteroids of different sizes.

atom   The smallest part of an element that retains the properties of that element. There are 92 different kinds of atoms found naturally on earth. The atoms of each element are exactly the same as one another and different from those of any other element.

authentic assessment   A process of judging how well students execute a task as part of solving a problem in a larger context. Often the execution of the task involves a type of student performance. Hence, this type of assessment is also called *performance assessment*.

Benchmarks for Science Literacy   A document published by the American Association for the Advancement of Science that provides guidelines for science, technology, and mathematics education. *Benchmarks* is part of a larger science education reform movement called Project 2061, named for the year of the next return of Halley's comet to earth's orbit. *Benchmarks* addresses what students should know and be able to do in science, mathematics, and technology by the end of grades 2, 5, 8, and 12.

bivalve mollusk   Mollusks with two shells connected by a muscular hinge. Clams, oysters, scallops, and mussels are all bivalve mollusks.

buoyancy   The lifting force that water exerts on objects. All objects appear to be lighter in water because of the buoyancy of water.

chemical change   A change in the chemical properties of a substance, that is, in the composition of the substance and the way it behaves with other substances; also called a *chemical reaction.*

chlorophyll   The substance in leaves that allows the chemical reaction of photosynthesis to take place and that gives leaves their green color.

circuit   *See* Electric circuit.

classifying   Sorting objects or ideas into groups on the basis of similar properties.

comparing and contrasting   Discovering similarities and differences among objects or events.

compound   A combination of two or more elements in a definite proportion. For example, water is H_2O—two parts hydrogen to one part oxygen.

Concept Map   A diagram for exploring knowledge by developing an understanding of relationships between ideas. A concept map consists of circles or boxes that are called cells and that contain an idea, a selected term or a question. The links between cells are labeled and denote direction with an arrow symbol. The labeled links explain the relationship between the cells.

constant   An experimental condition that remains the same throughout a scientific investigation.

constructivism   A family of theories about knowledge and learning whose basic tenet is that all knowledge is constructed by synthesizing new ideas with what we have previously come to know. This means that knowledge is not passively received. Rather, knowledge is actively built up by the learner as he or she experiences the world.

cooperative learning   An instructional approach in which students work together in groups to accomplish shared learning goals.

cooperative learning group   An arrangement in which a group of students, usually of mixed ability, gender, and ethnicity, work toward the common goal of promoting each other's and the group's success.

cotyledon   The part of the seed that has food stored in it for the tiny plant. Also called the *seed leaf.*

current *See* Electric current.

curriculum A plan of studies that includes the ways in which the instructional content is organized and presented at each grade level. *See also* Formal science curriculum; Informal science curriculum.

density Mathematically defined as the mass of an object divided by its volume (expressed numerically in grams per cubic centimeter). Roughly, density can be conceived as how closely packed together the particles of an object are, or as the relative number of particles that can fit into a given amount of space.

design challenge In design technology, a specific problem that students are asked to solve by designing and constructing a product.

design technology The technological counterpart to the science-as-inquiry process. For students, the design process typically involves solving a problem by constructing a product that meets a set of established criteria.

dicot Seed-producing plant with two seed leaves or cotyledons. Dicots include most flowers, vegetable shrubs, bean plants, and flowering trees.

differentiating instruction Adapting instructional techniques to suit the needs of specific children or groups of children in a classroom.

discovery learning A phrase popularized by learning theorist Jerome Bruner, who suggested that at any given stage of cognitive development, teaching should proceed in a way that allows children to discover ideas for themselves.

electric circuit A pathway for an electric current. A circuit requires some source of electrical power, such as a battery or generator, and a material through which electrons can travel, such as copper wire. In elementary school science, circuits usually include some simple appliance that uses electricity, like a light bulb or a bell.

electric current A flow or motion of electrons. Electric currents in wires are caused by electrons moving along the wire.

electricity A form of energy produced by a flow of electrons.

electron A negatively charged particle found in the atoms of all elements. Electrons revolve around the nucleus of the atom in different orbitals or "shells"; each shell represents a distinct energy level. Each electron is thought to be a particle of negative electricity.

electron cloud A term for the general area occupied by each "shell" or energy level where electrons orbit the nucleus of an atom. The metaphor of a "cloud" emphasizes the fact that we cannot know exactly where an electron is at a particular time; we just know that it is somewhere within that general area.

electronic portfolio   A portfolio of student work saved in digital form; *see* Science portfolio.

element   A substance made up of only one type of material. The simplest form of matter, elements are the building blocks of all other substances. There are 92 naturally occurring elements in the universe, and 14 others that have been produced by scientists in laboratories. Iron, nickel, gold, silver, oxygen, hydrogen, helium, carbon, and mercury are all elements.

ellipse   An oval shape with no center but with two points of reference called *foci*. Planets travel in elliptical orbits around the sun, which is located at one of the foci of the orbits.

emerging relevance   A perception by students that questions or ideas arising from an investigation have personal significance to them. The key part of this concept is that certain matters become relevant to students as they engage in learning activities. By helping them explore these emerging questions and ideas, teachers can help students construct their own meaning.

energy   The ability to do work.

evaluation   The process of making value judgments, based on the results of assessments, about a student's or a group's achievement in a learning area. Many educators include this process as part of the definition of assessment. *See* Science assessment.

fair test   An investigation in which all the experimental conditions remain the same (constant) except for the one being tested (the variable).

family science night   A community-involvement activity in which students bring a significant adult or adults to the school to participate in inquiry-based science activities, typically set up at stations in a large classroom or in the school cafeteria.

faults   Large cracks or breaks in the earth's crustal plates. Earthquakes are most common in areas where there are major faults.

focus   One of two points (foci) used to construct an ellipse.

focusing questions   Questions that prompt students to come up with their own ideas about a specific topic or investigation. Teachers also use focusing questions to probe their students' understandings of a particular concept related to the investigation.

force   A physical agency (such as a push or a pull) that tends to cause a change in the position or motion of an object.

formal science curriculum   The explicit statement by a school or a school district of the science topics and methodologies to be implemented at each grade level.

framework   A document, usually prepared at the state level, that offers guiding principles for elementary and secondary curricula. In science, recent state frameworks have usually been aligned with the content standards of the *National Science Education Standards*. These state frameworks tend to dictate science content, specifying the topics that should be addressed at each grade level.

fruit   A ripened ovary of a seed plant; a container for the plant's seeds.

fungi   A kingdom of living things containing tiny plantlike organisms. Fungi do not have chlorophyll and cannot make their own food. Fungi include molds, mildews, yeast, and mushrooms.

gas   A state of matter that has no definite shape or size. When a gas is poured into a container, it spreads out until it has the same size as the container and takes the shape of the container.

germination   The process by which a seed sprouts and begins to grow into a new plant.

graduated cylinder   A device used for measuring liquid volume. In essence, it is a scientific measuring cup—a glass or plastic cylinder that is calibrated in milliliters. It is a handy tool in the elementary classroom.

gravitation   The attraction of any two objects that have mass. According to the *law of gravitation*, every body in the universe attracts every other body with a force that increases when the masses of the objects increase and decreases as the objects move farther away from each other.

high tide   High level of ocean waters, when the waters reach farthest onto land. On the side of the earth facing the moon, high tide occurs because the waters bulge out from the moon's gravitational pull. At the same time, on the opposite side of the earth, there is also a high tide, because the moon's gravitational force has pulled the solid earth as well, leaving the waters bulging out on that side.

hypothesis   An inference or a guess that is tested through a planned investigation or experiment.

inclusion model   The practice of placing students with disabilities in regular classrooms to the greatest extent possible.

inference   Reasonable explanation that we construct on the basis of our observations. Inferences sometimes lead us to set up further investigations.

informal science curriculum   Science learning experiences that go beyond the formal science curriculum of the school or school district to include other topics and methodologies that connect to students' daily life outside the school. The topics might arise, for example, from spontaneous natural occurrences, local news events, or materials the students bring from home.

inquiry   The type of exploration that lies at the heart of scientific activity. According to the *National Science Education Standards,* inquiry is "a multifaceted activity that involves making observations; posing questions; . . . planning investigations; . . . using tools to gather, analyze, and interpret data; proposing answers, explanations, and predictions; and communicating the results" (National Research Council, 1996, p. 23).

instructional technology tools   Materials that aid instruction and learning. Examples include computers with Internet access, video camcorders, and authoring software such as HyperStudio and PowerPoint.

interfacing instruments   Laboratory instruments that come with a means to connect them to the personal computer. The most common such devices are probes with related software.

interview, for assessment   *See* Science interview.

interviewing a scientist   A learning activity in which students or teachers have a formal encounter with a research scientist. The interview provides the opportunity to explore the scientist's reasons for choosing a scientific career and the nature of his or her work. It is a way to change the culturally constructed "mad scientist" image that many adults and children hold.

invertebrate   An animal without a backbone. Invertebrates are the most numerous of all animals.

journal   *See* Science journal.

kinetic energy   The energy of motion; that is, the energy that an object has because it is moving.

kingdom   The broadest division of classification of living things. There are five kingdoms of living organisms: Animalia, Plantae, Protista, Fungi, and Monera.

learning cycle   An approach to teaching science that typically includes five phases of science teaching and learning: engagement, exploration, explanation, elaboration, and evaluation.

lesson   In science instruction, the process of engaging students in a meaningful science experience and in reflections on the experience.

lesson plan   A document describing a teacher's plans for a particular lesson, including the ideas presented in the lesson, the activities that students will engage in, and the ways in which the teacher will help students reflect on their experiences.

light   A form of energy radiated by the sun and stars. Light is only the visible part of the electromagnetic spectrum, which also includes many types of electromagnetic waves that we cannot see.

liquid   A state of matter with a definite size but no definite shape. A liquid takes the shape of its container.

low tide   Low level of ocean waters that occurs because, as the waters bulge on two sides of the earth, the remaining waters flatten.

magnetism   A force produced when an object exerts an attraction for materials made of certain metals, such as iron, steel, cobalt, and nickel.

mass   The amount of matter that is in an object, typically measured in grams and kilograms.

matter   Anything that has mass and takes up space.

meaningful science experience   An activity that engages students in the key processes of science, such as observing and predicting, inferring and hypothesizing, manipulating objects, investigating, and imagining; that relates to the students' everyday lived experiences; and stimulates the students to reflect on what they are exploring and to come up with their own ideas.

measuring   Determining distance, volume, mass, or time by using instruments that indicate these properties (e.g., centimeter sticks, graduated cylinders, scales, stopwatches).

mediator   A teaching role in which the teacher helps students to learn by reflecting their own ideas back to them and guiding them in sorting out the inconsistencies. As a mediator, the teacher helps students delve deeply into their thoughts and expand their own thinking about an idea.

mixture   Any combination of elements, compounds, or other mixtures. Because there are only 92 naturally occurring elements, most matter consists of either compounds or mixtures.

model   A representation of a system or object: for example, a physical structure that imitates a smaller or larger structure, a mental construct that represents an object or process, or a computer program that parallels the workings of a larger system.

molecule   The smallest part of a compound that still has the properties of that compound. Molecules are made up of atoms.

mollusk   An invertebrate animal that has a soft, fleshy body and a protective shell made of lime—for example, clams, oysters, scallops, snails, octopuses, and squids.

monera   A kingdom of living things consisting of bacteria, tiny organisms that do not have chlorophyll and cannot make their own food. All bacteria are made up of just one cell. Blue-green algae are also a part of the monera kingdom.

monocot A type of seed-producing plant with just one cotyledon or seed leaf—for example, lilies, tulips, irises, onions, and grasses and grains. Also called *monocotyledon plants*.

MST initiative A curriculum transformation project that strives to integrate mathematics, science, and technology by promoting the use of inquiry and design in problem-solving activities.

National Educational Technology Standards A set of standards prepared by the International Society for Technology in Education and published in a series of books and brochures. These standards cover both what students should know and be able to do with technology and how teachers should prepare to teach with technology.

National Science Education Standards A set of standards prepared by the National Research Council and published in book form in 1996. It offers guidelines for teachers, teacher educators, curriculum developers, and school districts for establishing science education programs. The overall theme is that acquiring scientific knowledge, understanding, and abilities should be a central aspect of education, just as science has become a central aspect of our society.

national standards Guidelines written by national agencies and members of professional organizations for establishing comprehensive programs of study. Such guidelines have been published for precollege education in several discipline areas, including science, mathematics, technology, language arts, and social studies.

neutron A particle with no electrical charge found in the nucleus of an atom.

observation Perceptions of an object or an event, using as many senses as possible.

open-ended questions Questions that lead to multiple answers. They are especially important because they help students think critically about their science experiences.

orbit The path of one heavenly body as it travels around another heavenly body.

parallel circuit An electric circuit in which each device has a separate pathway, its own separate branch of the circuit.

performance assessment See Authentic assessment.

perihelion   The point in a planet's orbit when it is closest to the sun.

phases of the moon   The various aspects of the moon as seen from earth, such as the full moon and new moon. These phases reflect changes in the amount of the lighted surface of the moon that we can see from earth.

photosynthesis   The process by which green plants use carbon dioxide from the air and water from the soil, in the presence of sunlight, to manufacture molecules of glucose. Glucose is a simple sugar that the cells of the plant then use to make energy for the plant to carry on its functions, including growth.

physical change   Change in the physical properties of a substance, that is, in the properties we can readily observe with our senses.

physical science   The branch of elementary school science that includes the exploration of nonliving materials, their interactions, and interactions between matter and energy.

planets   Principal members of the solar system that move around the sun. In order of their distance from the sun, the planets are Mercury, Venus, Earth, Mars, Jupiter, Saturn, Uranus, Neptune, and Pluto. Planets shine by reflecting the light of the sun or other stars.

planning an investigation   Determining a reasonable procedure that could be followed to test an idea. This includes listing the materials needed, writing out the procedure to be followed, and identifying which variables will be kept the same and which will be changed.

portfolio   *See* Science portfolio.

potential energy   The energy an object has because of its position; stored-up energy. When potential energy is set free, it is changed into kinetic energy.

predicting   Estimating the outcome of an event on the basis of observations and, usually, prior knowledge of similar events.

prior knowledge   What an individual has learned from all his or her previous experiences. This plays a crucial role in determining how the person integrates a new concept.

process skills   Abilities that help people gain information about nature and natural phenomena: observing, inferring, classifying, recording data, predicting, and planning investigations. These skills are employed on a planned and regular basis by those engaged in scientific activity. Also called *inquiry skills.*

professional development   The process by which teachers strive to improve their work as teachers in order to grow in their profession. It is generally based on inquiry into their own teaching practices, active engagement in their own research, and teacher workshops and courses.

property words   The basic words we use to describe the material world, referring to common properties of objects such as size, shape, color, odor, texture, taste, composition, and hardness.

protista   A kingdom of simple organisms, consisting mainly of algae, except for blue-green algae. Other protists are protozoans like ameba, paramecium, and euglena.

proton   A positively charged particle in the nucleus of an atom.

questions   *See* Focusing questions; Open-ended questions.

recording data   Writing down (in words, pictures, graphs, or numbers) the results of observations of an object or an event.

reflective teacher   A teacher who thinks deeply about his or her teaching practices, the needs and identities of the students, and what the teaching is intended to accomplish.

rubric   A set of criteria used to determine the scoring value of an assessment task.

satellite   Any heavenly body that travels around another heavenly body. The moon is a satellite of the earth, and the earth-moon system is a satellite of the sun.

science assessment   A process of collecting information that is used to determine the quality and character of an individual or group performance in a science learning experience.

science autobiography   A personal description of one's experience with science, in or out of school.

science circus   A science activity that consists of several stations at which the visitors are asked to perform certain tasks and record their results or reactions.

science conversation (or science interview)   A direct discussion between a teacher and an individual student about a science learning experience. This activity allows teachers to ask students to elaborate on their ideas—a good way to determine the depth of a student's understanding. Through such conversations, teachers gain important clues about how students construct personal meaning, and these clues then influence future instruction.

science interview   A conversation between student and teacher that is designed to assess concept understanding.

science journal   A personal journal in which the writer focuses on nature and natural events in his or her daily experiences.

science portfolio   A selection of a student's work during a semester or a unit. The work in the portfolio might include one or more reports, drawings, poems, or other products representing what the student has learned in science over a defined period of time. The most important feature of a portfolio is that the student selects its contents and reflects on his or her reasons for this selection.

scientific literacy   The ability to use the processes of science to make important life decisions; in particular, the ability to explore a problem through careful reasoning.

scientific law   A statement about principles or patterns in nature, indicating relationships between or among facts. Laws have endured over time and have consistently been tested; but, like theories, they are not absolutely "proved."

scientific method   The typical process that scientists use in the course of studying natural phenomena, including steps such as observation, forming a hypothesis, and experimentation to test the hypothesis.

scientific theory   *See* Theory.

seed   The part of the plant that can grow into a new plant.

seed plant   *See* Angiosperm

series circuit   An electric circuit in which the current has only a single pathway through the entire circuit.

solar system   The sun and the group of heavenly bodies that move around it. The sun is the only member of our solar system that is a star.

solid   A state of matter with a definite size and shape.

spiraling of curriculum   Engaging students in the same topic of study at different grade levels, so that the topic is explored at greater depth in later grades.

star   A heavenly body that produces its own light. There are billions of stars in the universe, including our sun. About 3,000 stars are visible with the naked eye.

states of matter   The basic forms in which matter is found: solid, liquid, and gas (and a state that is rare on earth, plasma).

station assessment   An assessment activity in which work stations are set up around the room to create a genuine context for the students to perform tasks. The students typically use an answer sheet to respond to the questions at each station. Each work station assesses a different aspect of the science unit.

suspension   A mixture in which solid particles do not dissolve, but literally are suspended in a liquid.

sustained inquiry   Prolonged investigation of a scientific phenomenon. For elementary school science, this typically means an investigation that includes multiple activities over the course of several days or weeks.

taxonomy   An entire classification system, such as the scientific classification of all living things into categories ranging from kingdom to species.

teacher research   *See* Action research.

testing   Assessment of students' learning by means of teacher-made tests or state and local tests designed by educational agencies or testing services.

theory   An idea that has been tested and (to some significant degree) corroborated—in other words, the best explanation we currently have for why something is so. Although theories can be strongly supported, they can never be absolutely "proved." As evidence for one theory grows, the credibility of others may be disputed.

tide   *See* High tide; Low tide.

unit of study   A segment of the curriculum that includes several lessons designed around a central theme or topic.

univalve mollusk   Mollusks with one shell, usually shaped in a spiral. Snails, slugs, and conches are univalve mollusks.

variable   The property or condition of a scientific investigation that will change when experimental conditions are changed.

vegetable   An edible plant part that is the root, stem, leaf, or flower of the plant.

vertebrate   An animal with a backbone. There are five vertebrate groups: fish, amphibians, birds, reptiles, and mammals.

volume   The amount of space an object takes up. Liquid volume is typically measured in milliliters and liters; solid volume, in cubic centimeters and cubic meters. When we refer to the *size* of an object, we usually mean its volume.

wait time   The time that elapses between the moment a teacher asks a question and the moment the teacher selects a student to respond, offers a clue, rephrases the question, or otherwise moves ahead with the lesson.

weathering   The wearing away of rocks on the earth by the action of the sun, air, and water.

WebQuest   An inquiry-oriented activity in which most or all of the resources used by learners come from the World Wide Web.

weight   The gravitational pull that the earth has on an object. The weight of an object increases when its mass increases; but weight in scientific terms is not the same as mass, because weight is dependent on the gravitational pull that is exerted on the object.

work   The act of applying a force to move an object through a distance.

year   The time needed for a planet to make one complete turn or revolution about the sun.

References

Abder, P. (1990). Elementary science process circus. Paper presented at the National Science Teachers Association Regional Meeting, San Juan, Puerto Rico.

American Association for the Advancement of Science. (1993). *Benchmarks for Science Literacy.* Washington, DC: Author.

Australian Academy of Sciences (1996). *Primary Investigations: The Science Program for Primary Schools.* Canberra, ACT: Australian Academy of Sciences.

Barba, R. H. (1998). *Science in the Multicultural Classroom: A Guide to Teaching and Learning.* (2nd ed.) Needham Heights, MA: Allyn and Bacon.

Barman, C. (1997). Students' views of scientists and science: Results from a national study. *Science and Children,* 35(1):18–24.

Barman, C., Barman, N., Berglund, K., & Goldston, M. (1999). Assessing students' ideas about animals. *Science and Children,* 37(1):44–49.

Barman, C., Barman, N., Cox, M., Berglund, K., & Goldston, M. (2000). Students' ideas about animals: Results of a national study. *Science and Children,* 38(1):42–47.

Barton, A. C. (1998). Teaching science with homeless children: Pedagogy, representation and identity. *Journal of Research in Science Teaching,* 35(4): 379–394.

Bazin, M., Tamez, M., & Exploratorium Teacher Institute. (2002). *Math and Science Across Cultures.* New York: The New Press.

Biological Science Curriculum Study. (1996). *Primary Investigations.* Dubuque, IA: Kendall/Hunt.

Brooks, J. G. (2002). *Schooling for Life: Reclaiming the Essence of Learning.* Reston, VA: Association for Supervision and Curriculum Development.

Brooks, J. G., & Brooks, M. (1999). *In Search of Understanding: The Case for Constructivist Classrooms.* Alexandria, VA: Association for Supervision and Curriculum Development.

Bruner, J. S. (1960). *The Process of Education.* Cambridge, MA: Harvard University Press.

Bruner, J. S. (1966). *Toward a Theory of Instruction.* Cambridge, MA: Harvard University Press.

Campbell, P. B., & Clewell, B. C. (1999). Science, math, and girls. *Education Week,* 19(2):50, 53.

Chancer, J., & Rester-Zodrow, G. (1998). *Moon Journals: Writing, Art and Inquiry*. Portsmouth, NH: Heinemann.

Chapman, A. (1997). *A Great Balancing Act: Equitable Education for Girls and Boys*. Washington, DC: National Association of Independent Schools.

Chuska, K. R. (1995). *Improving Classroom Questions*. Bloomington, IN: Phi Delta Kappa.

Clewell, B. C., Anderson, B. T., & Thorpe, M. E. (1992). *Breaking the Barriers: Helping Female and Minority Students Succeed in Mathematics and Science*. San Francisco: Jossey-Bass.

Cobb, V. (1972). *Science Experiments You Can Eat*. Philadelphia: Lippincott.

Conant, J. B. (1966). *Science and Common Sense*. New Haven: Yale University Press.

Dana, T. M., Lorsbach, A.W., Hook, K., & Briscoe, C. (1991). Students showing what they know: A look at alternative assessments. In G. Kulm & S. M. Malcom (Eds.), *Science Assessment in Service to Reform*. Washington, DC: American Association for the Advancement of Science.

Darling-Hammond, L. (1998). Teacher learning that supports student learning. *Educational Leadership*, 55(5):6–11.

Darling-Hammond, L. (1999). *Reshaping Teaching Pol-icy, Preparation, and Practice: Influences of the National Board for Professional Teaching Standards*. Washington, DC: AACTE Publications.

Dewey, J. (1904). The relation of theory to practice in education. In C. McMurray (Ed.), *The Relation of Theory to Practice in the Education of Teachers: Third Yearbook for the National Society of the Scientific Study of Education*. Chicago: University of Chicago Press.

Dewey, J. (1933, 1988). *How We Think*. Boston: Houghton Mifflin.

Doran, R., Lawrenz, F., & Helgeson, S. (1994). Research on assessment in science. In D. Gabel (Ed.), *Handbook of Research on Science Teaching and Learning*. A project of the National Science Teachers Association. New York: Macmillan.

Driver, R. (1989). Students' conceptions and the learning of science. *International Journal of Science Education*, 11:481–490.

Driver R., Asoko, H., Leach, J., Mortimer, E., & Scott, P. (1994). Constructing scientific knowledge in the classroom. *Educational Researcher*, 23(7): 5–12.

Dublin, P., Pressman, H., & Barnett, E. (1994). *Integrating Computers in Your Classroom: Elementary Science*. New York: HarperCollins.

Duckworth, E. (1996). *The Having of Wonderful Ideas and Other Essays on Teaching and Learning*. (2nd ed.) New York: Teachers College Press.

Duckworth, E., Easley, J., Hawkins, D., & Henriques, A. (1990). *Science Education: A Minds-on Approach for the Elementary Years.* Hillsdale, NJ: Erlbaum.

Elliot, J. (1991). *Action Research for Educational Change.* Philadelphia: Open University Press.

Eltgeest, J. (1985). The right question at the right time. In W. Harlen (Ed.). *Primary Science: Taking the Plunge.* Portsmouth, NH: Heinemann.

Feynman, R. P. (1968). What is science? *Physics Teacher,* 7(6):313–320.

Fort, D., & Varney, H. (1989). How students see scientists: Mostly male, mostly white and mostly benevolent. *Science and Children,* 26:8–13.

Gallas, K. (1995). *Talking Their Way into Science: Hearing Children's Questions and Theories, Responding with Curricula.* New York: Teachers College Press.

Garthwait, A., & Verrill, J. E-portfolios: Documenting student progress. *Science and Children,* 41(6):22–27.

Gilster, P. (1998). *Digital Literacy.* New York: Wiley.

Gould, S. J. (1981). *Hen's Teeth and Horse's Toes.* New York: Norton.

Grabe, M., & Grabe, C. (2000). *Integrating the Internet for Meaningful Learning.* Boston: Houghton Mifflin.

Grabe, M., & Grabe, C. (2004). *Integrating Technology for Meaningful Learning.* (4th ed.) Boston: Houghton Mifflin.

Grumet, M. (1991). The politics of personal knowledge. In C. Witherell & N. Noddings (Eds.), *Stories Lives Tell: Narratives and Dialogue in Education.* New York: Teachers College Press.

Hawkins, D. (1965). Messing about in science. *Science and Children,* 2(5).

Healy, J. M. (1998). *Failure to Connect: How Computers Affect Our Children's Minds—and What We Can Do About It.* New York: Touchstone Books.

Heller, R. (1999). *Chickens Aren't the Only Ones.* New York: Penguin Putnam Books for Young Readers.

Hilbert, D. (1902). Mathematical problems. Trans. M. W. Newson. *Bulletin of the American Mathematical Society,* 8:437–479.

Hopkins, D. (1993). *A Teacher's Guide to Classroom Research.* Philadelphia: Open University Press.

Howe, E. (2002). *Connecting Girls and Science: Constructivism, Feminism, and Science Education Reform.* New York: Teachers College Press.

Hubbard, R., & Wald, E. (1993). *Exploding the Gene Myth.* Boston: Beacon Press.

International Society for Technology in Education. (2000). *National Educational Technology Standards for Students: Connecting Curriculum and Technology.* Eugene, OR: Author.

International Society for Technology in Education. (2002). *National Educational Technology Standards for Teachers: Preparing Teachers to Use Technology.* Eugene, OR: Author.

International Technology Education Association. (2000). *Standards for Technological Literacy: Content for the Study of Technology.* Reston, VA: Author.

Irvine Belson, Sarah. *Technology for Exceptional Learners: Choosing Instructional Tools to Meet Students' Needs.* Boston: Houghton Mifflin, 2003.

Johnson, D., & Johnson, R. (1999). *Learning Together and Alone: Cooperative, Competitive, and Individualistic Learning.* (5th ed.) Boston: Allyn and Bacon.

Jones, C., & Levin, J. (1994). Primary/elementary teachers' attitudes toward science in four areas related to gender differences in students' science performance. *Journal of Elementary Science Education,* 6(1):46–65.

Kagan, S. (1997). *Cooperative Learning.* San Clemente, CA: Kagan Cooperative Books.

Kahle, J. B., & Meece, J. (1994). Research on girls and science: Lessons and applications. In D. Gabel (Ed.), *Handbook of Research in Science Teaching and Learning.* Washington, DC: National Science Teachers Association.

Kaner, E. (1989). *Balloon Science.* Reading, MA: Addison-Wesley.

Keogh, B., & Naylor, S. (1999). Concept Cartoons, teaching and learning in science: An evaluation. *International Journal of Science Education,* 21(4):431–446.

Koballa, T. R., & Crawley, F. E. (1985). The influence of attitude on science teaching and learning. *School Science and Mathematics,* 85(3):222–232.

Kober, N. (1993). *Edtalk: What We Know About Science Teaching and Learning.* Washington, DC: Council for Educational Development and Research.

Koch, J. (1990). The science autobiography project. *Science and Children,* 28(3):42–44.

Koch, J. (1993). *Lab Coats and Little Girls: The Science Experiences of Women Majoring in Biology and Education at a Private University.* Ann Arbor, MI: University Microfilms International No. 5712.

Koch, J. (2002a). Gender issues in the classroom. In W. R. Reynolds & G. E. Miller (Eds.), *Educational Psychology.* Volume 7 of the *Comprehensive Handbook of Psychology.* New York: Wiley.

Koch, J. (2002b). Who eats the mango? In D. Tippins, T. Koballa, & B. Payne (Eds.), *Learning from cases: Unraveling the complexities of elementary science teaching.* Needham Heights, MA: Allyn & Bacon.

Kochendorfer, L. (1994). *Becoming a Reflective Teacher*. Washington, DC: National Education Association.

Lederman, N. G. (1992). Students' and teachers' conceptions of the nature of science: A review of the research. *Journal of Research in Science Teaching*, 29(4):331–359.

Logan, J. (1997). *Teaching Stories*. New York: Kodansha International.

Loucks-Horsley, S. (1990). *Elementary School Science for the 90s*. Andover, MA: The Network, Inc.

Margulis, L., & Schwartz, K. V. (1982). *Five Kingdoms: An Illustrated Guide to Phyla of Life on Earth*. New York: Freeman.

McIntosh, M. (1983). *Interactive Phases of Curricular Re-Vision: A Feminist Perspective*. (Working Paper No. 124.) Wellesley, MA: Wellesley College Center for Research on Women.

Mintzes, J., Wandersee, J., and Novak, J. (1998). *Teaching Science for Understanding: A Human Constructivist View*. San Diego, CA: Academic Press.

National Commission on Excellence in Education. (1983). *A Nation at Risk*. Washington, DC: U.S. Government Printing Office.

National Research Council. (1996). *The National Science Education Standards*. Washington, DC: National Academy Press.

National Science Board. (1983). *Educating Americans for the 21st Century*. Washington, DC: National Science Foundation.

Naylor, S., Keogh, B., de Boo, M., & Feasey, R. (2001). Formative assessment using Concept Cartoons: Initial teacher training in the UK. In R. Duit (Ed.), *Research in Science Education: Past, Present and Future*, pp. 137–142. Dordrecht: Kluwer.

Noddings, N. (1990). Constructivism in mathematics education. *Journal for Research in Mathematics Education*, no. 4.

Nussbaum, J., & Novak, J. D. (1976). An assessment of children's concepts of the earth utilizing structured interviews. *Science Education*, 60:535–550.

Perkes, V. A. (1975). Relationship between a teacher's background to sensed adequacy to teach elementary science. *Journal of Research in Science Teaching*, 12(1):85–88.

Perkins, D. (1993). Teaching for understanding. *American Educator*, 17(3):8, 28–35.

Perkins, D. (1999). The many faces of constructivism. *Educational Leadership*, 57(3):6–11.

Phillips, D. C. (1995). The good, the bad, and the ugly: The many faces of constructivism. *Educational Researcher*, 24(7):5–12.

Piaget, J. (1964). *The Construction of Reality in the Child*. New York: Basic Books.

Piaget, J. (1974). *To Understand Is to Invent: The Future of Education*. New York: Grossman.

President's Committee of Advisors on Science and Technology (1997). *Report to the President on the Use of Technology to Strengthen K–12 Education in the United States*. Washington, DC: Executive Office of the President of the United States.

Pyramid Film & Video. (1988). *A Private Universe: An Insightful Lesson on How We Learn*. Video and booklet. Santa Monica, CA: Author.

Reynolds, K., & Barba, R. (1996). *Technology for the Teaching and Learning of Science*. Needham Heights, MA: Allyn and Bacon.

Rowe, M. B. (1974). Wait-time and rewards as instructional variables: Their influence on language, logic and fate control: Part One— Wait-time. *Journal of Research in Science Teaching*, 11(2):81–94.

Rowe, M. B. (1987). Wait-time: Slowing down may be a way of speeding up. *American Educator*, 11(1):38–47.

Rutherford, F. J., & Ahlgren, A. (1990). *Science for All Americans*. New York: Oxford University Press.

Sadker, M., & Sadker, D. (1994). *Failing at Fairness: How America's Schools Cheat Girls*. New York: Charles Scribner's Sons.

Salvia, J., & Ysseldyke, J. E. (2004). *Assessment: In Special and Inclusive Education*. 9th ed. Boston: Houghton Mifflin.

Sanders, J., Koch, J., & Urso, J. (1997). *Gender Equity Right from the Start: Instructional Activities for Teacher Educators in Mathematics, Science and Technology*. Hillsdale, NJ: Erlbaum.

Schon, D. A. (1983). *The Reflective Practitioner: How Professionals Think in Action*. New York: Basic Books.

Schon, D. A. (1986). *Educating the Reflective Practitioner*. San Francisco: Jossey-Bass.

Schon, D. A. (1991) *The Reflective Practitioner*. San Francisco: Jossey-Bass.

Shepardson, D. P., & Britsch, S. (1997). Children's science journals. *Science and Children*, 35(2):13ff.

Shrigley, R. (1983). The attitude concept and science teaching. *Science Education*, 67(2):425–442.

Shrigley, R. (1990). Attitude and behavior are correlates. *Journal of Research in Science Teaching*, 27(2):97–113.

Siegler, R. S. (1998). *Children's Thinking.* (3rd ed.) Upper Saddle River, NJ: Prentice-Hall.

Slavin, R. E. (1987). Cooperative learning and the cooperative school. *Educational Leadership,* 45(3):7–13.

Slavin, R. E. (2003). *Educational Psychology: Theory and Practice.* (7th ed.) Boston: Allyn and Bacon.

Smith, K., & Welliver, P. (1990). The development of a science process assessment for fourth-grade students. *Journal of Research in Science Teaching,* 27(9):727–738.

Snowman, J., & Biehler, R. *Psychology Applied to Teaching,* 10th ed. Boston: Houghton Mifflin, 2003.

Songer, N. B., & Linn, M. C. (1991). How do students' views of science influence knowledge integration? *Journal of Research in Science Teaching,* 28(9):761–784.

Stefanich, G. (2001). *Science Teaching in Inclusive Classrooms: Models and Applications.* Cedar Falls, IA: Wolverton Printing Co.

Stefanich, G., Fetters, M., Pyle, E., Pickard, D., & Ellis, J. (2003). "Making Science Accessible and Inclusive: Strategies for Teachers in Science Education." Preconference workshop presented at the Association for the Education of Teachers of Science International Conference, St. Louis, MO, January.

Tobin, K. (1986). Effects of teacher wait time on discourse characteristics in mathematics and language arts classes. *American Educational Research Journal,* 23:191–200.

Tomlinson, C. A. (1999). *The Differentiated Classroom: Responding to the Needs of All Learners.* Reston, VA: Association for Supervision and Curriculum Development.

The University of the State of New York, The State Education Department (1996). *Learning Standards for Mathematics, Science and Technology.* Albany, NY: Author.

U.S. Department of Education, National Center for Education Statistics. (2000). *Educational Equity for Girls and Women.* NCES 2000-030. Washington, DC: U.S. Government Printing Office.

U.S. Department of Education, National Center for Education Statistics. (2001). *The Condition of Education 2001.* NCES 2001-072. Washington, DC: U.S. Government Printing Office.

Valenza, J. K. (1997, August 21). Teachers can mine net for lesson plans, other kinds of help. *Philadelphia Inquirer.*

Valenza, J. K. (2000, August 31). Two gateway sites help teachers retrieve just what they need. *Philadelphia Inquirer.*

VanCleave, J. P. (1993). *200 Gooey, Slippery, Slimy, Weird and Fun Experiments*. New York: Wiley.

von Glasersfeld, E. (1995). *Radical Constructivism: A Way of Knowing and Learning*. London: Falmer Press.

Vygotsky, L. (1962). *Thought and Language*. Cambridge, MA: MIT Press.

Walberg, H. J. (1969). Social environment as a mediator of classroom learning. *Journal of Educational Psychology*, 60:443–448.

Whitney, D. (1995). The case of the misplaced planets. *Science and Children*, 32(5):12–14ff.

Yager, R. (1991). The constructivist learning model: Towards real reform in science education. *Science Teacher*, 58(6):52–56.

Index

Abder, P., 87
Accessibility, 273, 274, 394.
    See also Disabilities
Action research, 382–383
Active learner, 11
Active reflection, 379
Activities, 254–255,
    256–257, 260, 261.
    See also Concrete
    experiences
    are not lessons, 255,
        266, 269
    journal entries on, 354
    multistation, 86–103
    selecting, 345–346
Air, 59, 60, 62
    gases in, 134
    weight of, 129–130
Alienation from science,
    105, 107–108, 125
Alimentary canal, 311, 316
Alternative conceptions,
    18–19, 63–64, 70,
    73–74
    asking questions
        about, 84, 263,
        361
    about breathing, 314
    changing, 74, 200
    about electricity, 226
    lesson plan and, 261
    about science educa-
        tion, 223–224
    about sun, 332
Amato, Ivan, 132
American Association for
    the Advancement
    of Science
    (AAAS), 7, 20,
    104, 387
Americans with Disabili-
    ties Act (ADA),
    271–272
Amplitude of sound, 336,
    337
Angiosperms, 153
Animalia, 153
Animals. See also Snails
    alternative concep-
        tions about, 73–74

in classroom, restric-
    tions on, 146, 162,
    393, 394
dissection of, 295
invertebrates, 146,
    162
as living things,
    142–143, 144–145,
    146, 310
marine organisms,
    291–294
in science corner, 146
taxonomy of, 153
vertebrates, 146, 162
Aphelion, 214
Apples, Potatoes, and
    Density (Science
    Story), 190–199
Applying concepts, 89
Arachnids, 167
Arteries, 312
Arterioles, 312
Arthropods, 167
Assessment, 350–374. See
    also Evaluation
    careful designing of,
        373–374
    checklists for, 357–358,
        370, 371
    concept cartoons in,
        363–364
    concept maps in,
        362–363
    conversations in,
        360–361
    definitions of, 351,
        352
    evaluation based on,
        352
    forms of, 351
    instructional context
        of, 351–352, 366,
        370, 374
    journals in, 258, 352,
        353–358
    in learning cycle
        approach, 18
    in lesson plan, 258
    multiple modes of,
        366–370, 374

national standards
    and, 370–373
paper-and-pencil tests
    in, 351, 372–373
portfolios in, 358–360,
    362
presentation software
    in, 364–366
stations in, 368–370,
    371, 380
stories about, 366–370
technology in,
    361–366, 372
in unit plan, 345
for WebQuest,
    292–293
Associations, for profes-
    sional develop-
    ment, 387–390
Associative neurons, 315
Asteroids, 209, 308
Astronomical unit (AU),
    205, 208
Atoms
    defined, 136, 238
    history of atomic
        theory, 238,
        239–241
    of magnetic materials,
        339
    models of, 243–249
    motion of, 324
    Periodic Table and,
        243
    size of, 238–239, 248
    structure of, 238,
        241–242, 243, 248,
        329–330
Attention-deficit/hyperac-
    tivity disorder
    (ADHD), 276
Attitudes
    of parents about
        science, 102
    scientific, 3, 6, 7
    of teachers about
        science, 36–38,
        44–46
Authentic assessment, 351,
    370–371, 373

Autobiography, science,
    45–46, 385
Avocado pit, 158, 159
Axle, 317, 318–319, 320,
    321

Balloons, 33–35, 57–60, 61,
    62, 64, 325
Barba, R. H., 4, 267, 289
Barman, C., 38, 39
Bartholomew and the Oobleck
    (Dr. Seuss), 134
Bascom, Florence, 89
Batteries, Bulbs, and Wires
    (Science Story),
    224–226
Batteries, Bulbs, and Wires
    Revisited (Science
    Story), 226–236
Bazin, M., 344
Beliefs. See Attitudes
Benchmarks for Science
    Literacy (AAAS),
    20, 104, 305, 316,
    322, 340–341
Bicycle, 321
Biehler, R., 73
Big ideas, 303
Biological Science Curricu-
    lum Study, 192,
    268
Bird watching, 47–51, 379
Bivalve mollusks, 167
Blind scientist, 271
Blind students, 273
Blood, 312–313
Body systems, 310–315,
    316, 320
Bohr, Niels, 239, 240, 243
A Book of Snails (Science
    Story), 163–168
Books
    connections to litera-
        ture, 111–112, 341,
        343, 345, 346
    in science corner,
        111–112
    selected list on nature
        and science,
        394–396

Bose-Einstein condensate, 134
Boys. *See also* Gender
    computer use by, 27, 28
Brain, 315, 316
Brain stem, 315
Breathing, 314
Britsch, S., 357
Brooks, J. G., 11, 13, 59, 60, 67, 75, 125, 184, 200, 368
Brooks, M., 11, 13, 59, 60, 67, 184, 368
Bruner, Jerome, 8, 9–10, 13, 190
Buoyancy, 183, 197

Capillaries, 312, 314
Cartoons, 363–364
Categories. See Classifying
Central nervous system, 315
Central neurons, 315
Cerebellum, 315
Cerebrum, 315
Certification, 380–382
Challenging authority, 35, 36
Change. *See also* Interactions; Variables
    chemical, 324–326
    of living things over time, 141, 144, 145
    patterns of, 5–6, 305, 322–339
    physical, 324, 325–326
Change of state, 70–72, 324
Charge, electrical, 329–330
Chemical changes, 324–326
Chemical composition, 136, 329
Chemical energy, 331
Chemical properties, 325
Chemical reactions, 324
Chickens Aren't the Only Ones (Heller), 114
Children. *See also* Students
    instincts for exploration, 1, 2–3
Chlorophyll, 152, 155
Chuska, K. R., 263
Circuits, electric, 224–236, 365–366
Circulatory system, 310, 311–313, 316

Circumference, 185, 188
Circus, science, 87–100, 101
The Circus Comes to Mount Holly (Science Story), 88–100
Classifying
    development of skills in, 126–127, 139–140
    of living things, 153
    messiness in, 126, 137, 138–140
    of nonliving materials, 126–135, 136, 137, 138–140
    as process skill, 5, 97, 98, 99, 101, 126–127
    questions about, 262
    of science ideas, 5–6, 304, 305
Classroom, accessibility of, 273, 274
Closed systems, 316
Cobb, V., 24
Cognitive development, stages of, 8–10
Collaboration. *See also* Groups
    in cooperative learning groups, 264–270, 342–343, 393
    diversity of students and, 23
    by email, 27, 294
    national standards and, 20, 167, 168, 265, 282
    as scientific attitude, 6, 7
    by scientists, 264, 267
    in sustained inquiry, 141–142, 167, 168, 170
    in Web-based projects, 290–294
Color, 334–335
Comets, 308
Communication. *See also* Language
    students' different styles of, 362, 374
    technology in, 282
    two-way, 63

Comparing and contrasting, 98, 99, 101
    living vs. nonliving things, 142–143
    properties of materials, 127
    questions about, 262
Compass, 339
Compound machines, 320–321
Compounds, 136, 329
Computer models, 202
Computers. *See also* Internet; Technology; Web sites
    access of students to, 27, 281
    in assessment, 361–366
    checklist for use of, 283
    educational software, 295–296, 297, 300
    email with, 27, 283, 286, 288, 294
    gender differences in use of, 27–28
    integrating with instruction, 24–27, 283–285
    interfacing instruments with, 284, 288–289
    journals kept with, 356
    lesson plans kept with, 277
    MST curriculum and, 342, 343
    process skills with, 98
    in science corner, 110
    students with disabilities and, 110, 272, 273
Conant, James B., 4
Concept cartoons, 363–364
Concept maps, 77–79, 82, 362–363
Concepts. *See also* Alternative conceptions; Ideas
    applying, 69
    curriculum standards and, 341
    as prior knowledge, 61

Concrete experiences, 13–14, 23, 60, 73, 84, 266. *See also* Activities
Concrete operations stage, 10
Condensation, 122, 367
Conduction, of heat, 59, 327
Conductors, electrical, 331
Connections to other subjects, 111–113, 341, 343–344, 345, 346
Connections to students' lives. *See also* Everyday life
    curriculum and, 340, 346
    learning cycle and, 18
    lesson plan and, 257, 258
    in lessons on liquids, 173–174, 178, 184
    rationale for, 13, 105–108, 121–122, 385
    reflection on, 277
    Science Story about, 117–121
Connections to world through field trips, 115–117, 125, 393
Conservation of matter and energy, 323
Constants, 71, 76, 175, 176, 178
Construction of meaning
    assessment of, 361
    computer technology in, 284
    from concrete experiences, 13
    by diverse students, 22
    helping students with, 56–57, 60–64, 84
    lesson plan and, 255, 257, 258
    vs. memorizing, 16
    models in, 211
    social, 63
    by teacher, 303
    understanding and, 12

Constructivism
    alternative concep-
        tions and, 18, 19
    assessment and, 352
    basic concepts of, 8–12
    diversity of students
        and, 22–23
    implications for teach-
        ing, 12–14, 19,
        60–61, 84
    national standards
        and, 89
    reflection after lesson
        and, 276
    small-group learning
        and, 264, 265–267
    summary of approach,
        19
    three roles of, 11–12
Content standards, 304,
    305. See also
    National Science
    Education Stan-
    dards (NSES);
    Science ideas
Contrasting. See Comparing
    and contrasting
Controlling variables, 98,
    101
Convection, 59, 327–328
    343–344
Convection current,
    327–328
Conversations, for assess-
    ment, 360–361
Cooperative learning
    groups, 264–270,
    342–343, 393. See
    also Collaboration
Cotyledons, 149, 152, 155
Crawley, F. E., 36
Creative learner, 11–12, 89
Crick, Francis, 202
Crustaceans, 167
Cultural diversity, 21–22,
    23, 106, 107, 160,
    266–267
Curiosity, 2, 6, 43, 59, 96
Current
    convection, 327–328
    electric, 229, 234, 326,
        330–331, 333, 338
Curriculum, 339–347. See
    also Lesson plans
    approach to, 303
    checklist for, 346–347

defined, 339
developing units of,
    344–347
extending, 184–185,
    260–261
formal, 104, 121, 340
informal, 69, 104–105,
    111, 117–121, 125,
    340, 346, 347
interdisciplinary
    trends, 341–344
local influences on, 340,
    341, 346
MST initiative,
    341–343
national standards
    and, 104, 340–341
spiraling of, 9, 190,
    200, 346
state influence on, 341,
    343, 346
technology and,
    341–343, 345, 346
time pressure for
    covering, 15–16
web site resources for,
    297
Cylinder, graduated, 178

Dalton, John, 239, 240
Dana, T. M., 361
Darling-Hammond, L.,
    380
Data gathering, 204, 208,
    210
    from Internet, 282,
        283, 285–288
Data recording, 98, 99, 101
Day, of a planet, 308
Deaf students, 275
Decomposition, 324
Definitions in science, 5
Delving Deeper into Den-
    sity (Science
    Story), 181–184
Democritus, 239, 240
Density, 172–173, 176–184
    of common materials,
        179
    defined, 179
    floating and, 181–183,
        188, 189, 190–199
    spiraling approach to,
        190
Design challenge, 247–248,
    250–251, 342–343

Design portfolio, 243–244,
    250
Design technology, 180,
    249, 250–251
Dewey, John, 8, 44, 45, 61,
    73
Diaphragm, 314, 316
Dicots, 155
Difference. See Comparing
    and contrasting;
    Variables
Differentiating instruction,
    23, 270, 271
Digestive system, 310, 311,
    316
Director, 82, 192, 268
Disabilities
    classroom safety,
        394
    classroom strategies,
        272–276
    constructivism and,
        22–23
    inclusion model,
        271–272
    science corner accessi-
        bility, 110
    of successful scientists,
        271
Discovery learning, 9
Dissection, simulations of,
    295
Diversity in nature, 105,
    126, 132, 136
Diversity of scientists,
    41
Diversity of students,
    21–24, 105. See
    also Disabilities;
    Gender
    in cooperative learn-
        ing, 266–267, 268,
        270
    cultural, 21–22, 23,
        106, 107, 160,
        266–267
    email buddies and,
        294
    inclusive science
        education,
        270–276
    modes of assessment
        and, 374
DNA, 202
Dodge, Bernie, 290
Doran, R., 352

Drawings
    of scientist, 38–39, 40,
        41
    in student journals,
        357
    in student portfolios,
        358
    of yourself, 385
Driver, R., 303
Duckworth, Eleanor, 47,
    62, 139, 184, 190
Dyslexia, 275

Earth
    as magnet, 339
    as satellite, 306
Earthquakes, 120, 122–123,
    285, 290
Earth science, 5, 55, 304,
    305, 346
An Edible Solar System
    (Science Story),
    203–210, 211
Educating Americans for the
    21st Century, 19,
    340
Education. See Teaching
    science
Einstein, Albert, 74, 323
Elaboration phase, 18, 62,
    256, 257, 258
Electric charge, 329–330
Electric circuits, 224–236,
    365–366
Electric current, 229, 234,
    330–331, 333, 338
Electricity, 329–331
    defined, 234
    heat energy from, 333
    light energy from,
        333
    safe use of, 394
    Science Stories about,
        16–17, 224–234
    static, 330
    student's portfolio on,
        358–359
Electromagnetic spectrum,
    327, 331, 332
Electromagnets, 338–339
Electron clouds, 243, 246,
    248, 330
Electronic appearances,
    294
Electronic mentoring, 294
Electronic portfolios, 362

Electronic presentations, 364–366
Electrons, 234, 243, 248, 329–330, 339
Elements, 136, 329
Ellipse, 212–214, 307
Email, 27, 283, 286, 288, 294
Embryo, plant, 149, 155
Emerging relevance, 184–185, 260
Endocrine system, 310
Energy
    as abstract concept, 223, 226–227
    conservation of matter and, 323
    defined, 5, 136, 323
    of electricity, 329–331, 333
    forms of, 136, 223
    of heat, 59, 71, 323–328, 332–333, 344, 363
    interactions with matter, 322–323
    of light, 331–335
    of living things, 145, 311, 314
    of sound, 335–337
Energy levels, 330
Engagement phase, 17, 256, 257
Environment. See also Nature
    awareness of, 125
    interactions with living things, 144–145, 161, 168
Equipment, 390–393
    for outdoor activities, 116
    safe use of, 393–394
Esophagus, 311
Ethnicity. See also Diversity of students
    cooperative learning and, 264, 267, 268
    success in science and, 270
Evaluation. See also Assessment
    based on assessment, 352
    of student journals, 357–358

of student portfolios, 359–360
teacher's self-evaluation, 383–384
Evaluation phase, 18, 256, 257, 258, 270
Evaporation, 367
Everyday life. See also Connections to students' lives
    process skills in, 5, 101, 377–378
    of teacher's scientific self, 377–379
Evolution
    studied by Geerat Vermeij, 271
    taxonomy and, 153
Excel, 283
Experiments
    to change alternative conceptions, 74
    constants and variables in, 71, 76, 98, 101, 175, 178, 358
    in everyday life, 378
    extended over time, 141–142, 155, 167, 168, 169–170
    failed, 146–147, 154
    freedom in, 67, 70
    national standards on, 98
    in science corner, 111
    in scientific process, 4–5, 35
    thought experiments, 94–95, 96, 98
Explanation phase, 18, 62, 256, 257, 258
Explanations, 5, 35, 88, 199. See also Inference; Theories
Exploration phase, 18, 256, 257, 259
Exploring Solids, Liquids, and Gases (Science Story), 127–131
Extended investigations, 141–142, 155, 167, 168, 169–170
Extending curriculum, 184–185, 260–261

Extensions to primary activity, 354

Fair test, 71, 98. See also Experiments
Family science night, 101–102
Faults, 123
Federico, Carol, 386
Fee, Elizabeth, 108
Feynman, Richard P., 4
Field trips, 115–117, 125, 393
Fish, 146
Floating and Sinking Fruits (Science Story), 185–189
Fluids. See also Gases; Liquids
    defined, 327
    heat transfer in, 327–328
Foci of ellipse, 212, 214
Focusing questions, 262
Force. See also Gravity
    machines and, 317–320
    magnetic, 337–339
    work and, 136, 317
Formal cooperative learning, 265
Formal operations stage, 10
Formal science curriculum, 104, 121, 340
Fort, D., 38
Frameworks, state, 341, 343, 346
Franklin, Rosalind, 202
Freedom to experiment, 67, 70
Frequency, 336
From Seed to Plant: A Failed Experiment (Science Story), 146–147, 154
Fruits, 158–160, 161
Fulcrum, 317, 318, 319, 320
Fungi, 153

Gallas, K., 361
Garthwait, A., 362

Gases, 127–131, 133, 134, 136
    heat energy of, 324, 327–328
Gateway sites, 296–297
Gears, 321
Gender
    computer use and, 27–28
    cooperative learning and, 264, 266–267, 268
    enrollment in science courses and, 39, 41
    in stereotype of scientist, 38, 39, 107–108, 270–271
    student diversity and, 21, 22, 23, 24
Generator, electrical, 331
Germination, 151, 154–155, 156, 158, 289
Germination bags, 150–152, 154, 289
Girls. See also Gender
    alienation from science, 107–108
    computer use by, 27–28
    encouraging science participation of, 23, 24, 270
    enrollment in science courses, 39, 41
The Giving Tree (Silverstein), 112
Global classrooms, 294
Goals, 256, 257, 258, 259
Gould, Stephen Jay, 153
Grabe, C., 266, 284, 294, 296
Grabe, M., 266, 284, 294, 296
Graduated cylinder, 178
Gravity
    as a force, 317
    law of, 308–309
    and potential energy, 136
    and tides, 119
    and weight, 66

Groups. *See also* Collaboration
  for cooperative learning, 264–270, 342–343, 393
  lesson plan and, 258, 259
  mediating for, 269–270
  MST curriculum and, 342–343
  structure of, 82, 192, 267–269
Grumet, Madeleine, 51
Guide for Making a Science Lesson Plan, 256–258

Hands-on experiences. *See* Concrete experiences
Healy, J. M., 285, 299
Hearing impairments, 275
Heart, 311–313, 316
Heat energy, 323–328. *See also* Temperature
  change of state and, 71, 324
  concept cartoon about, 363
  convection of, 59, 327–328, 343–344
  from electricity, 333
  interdisciplinary curriculum and, 344
  of sun, 326, 327, 332–333
Helgeson, S., 352
Hierarchies, 127
High tide, 119
Hook, 256, 257
Horrible Harry and the Green Slime (Kline), 134
Hubbard, Ruth, 4
Human body systems, 310–315, 316, 320
Human voice, 336–337
Hydrogen bonding, 82
Hyperactivity, 276
Hypothesis, 35–36, 97, 101

Icicles (Science Story), 64–72
Ideas. *See also* Alternative conceptions;
Concepts; Construction of meaning; Prior knowledge; Science ideas
  construction of, 10, 11, 13
  scaffolding of, 22, 77, 79, 255, 257, 258, 362
  valuing students' ideas, 10, 12, 22, 61–62, 63
Inclined plane, 317, 319, 320
Inclusion model, 272
Individualized education plan (IEP), 272
Individuals with Disabilities Education Act (IDEA), 271–272
Inertia, 308, 309
Inference, 5, 35, 36, 97, 99, 101
  journal entries on, 355–356, 358
  questioning and, 262
Informal cooperative learning, 265
Informal science curriculum, 69, 104–105, 111, 117–121, 125, 340, 346, 347
Inquiry
  collaboration in, 264, 267
  curriculum evaluation and, 346
  defined, 86, 88
  in interdisciplinary curricula, 344
  modeling for students, 376
  national standards and, 59, 88, 98–99, 123, 141–142, 188–189, 199, 210, 219, 235, 304, 341
  sustained, 141, 155, 161, 169–170
  technological tools of, 281, 284
Inquiry skills. *See* Process skills

Insects, 167
  water strider, 75, 76, 79, 81, 82, 84
Inspiration (software), 362–363, 364
Instructional technology tools, 282, 284, 299. *See also* Computers; Internet
Insulators, 331
Integrated units, 343–344
Intensity of sound, 336, 337
Interactions. *See also* Energy; Matter
  categories of, 5–6, 305
  chemical changes, 324–326
  defined, 322
  between electricity, heat, and light, 333
  of living things with environment, 144–145, 161, 168
  between matter and energy, 322–323
  physical changes, 324, 325–326
  in systems, 328
Interdisciplinary units, 343–344
Interfacing instruments, 284, 288–289
International Society for Technology in Education (ISTE), 25–26, 282
Internet. *See also* Email; Web sites
  images from, for journals, 356, 362
  need to know and, 25, 284, 285
Interview
  for assessment, 360–361
  of scientist, 41–43
Invertebrates, 146, 162. *See also* Snails
Ions, 183, 330
Irvine Belson, S., 273

Johnson, D., 264, 268, 269
Johnson, R., 264, 268, 269

Jones, C., 37
Journals
  for assessment, 258, 352, 353–358
  bound notebook for, 356
  evaluation of, 258, 357–358
  for family science night, 102
  lesson plan as part of, 259
  moon-phase, 215–217, 218, 221
  pictures in, 356, 357, 362
  questioning students about, 263
  reflective, 46–47
  structure for, 353–356
  teacher's science journal, 46–52, 377–378, 382
  technology integrated with, 356

Kagan, S., 264, 269
Kahle, J. B., 23
Keogh, B., 363
Kinetic energy, 136, 323
Kingdoms, 153
Knowledge. *See* Ideas; Learning
Koballa, T. R., 36
Kober, N., 102
Koch, Janice, 23, 24, 36, 37
Kochendorfer, L., 379

Laboratory instruments, interfacing, 284, 288–289
Language
  in cooperative learning groups, 266
  learning disabilities and, 275
  of learning environment, 11
  non-native English speakers, 22, 173
  property words, 127, 131, 147
  of science, 5
Lanier, Judith, 12
Law, scientific, 323

Law of conservation of matter and energy, 323
Law of gravitation, 308–309. *See also* Gravity
Lawrenz, F., 352
Learning. *See also* Construction of meaning; Constructivism; Teaching science; Understanding
classroom research about, 382–383
by concrete experience, 13–14, 23, 60, 73, 84, 266
cooperative, 264–270, 342–343
integrating technology into, 283–285, 299–300
replacement of understandings in, 200
social context of, 11, 13, 21–22, 63, 266
theory of, 8–12
Learning cycle, 17–18, 62, 256, 258
Learning disabilities, 22, 271, 275–276
Lederman, N. G., 6
Lesson
is not activity, 255, 266, 269
reflection about, 276–277
unit and, 345
Lesson plans, 254–261. *See also* Curriculum
checklist for, 259
defined, 255
evaluating, 297, 299, 300
guide for, 256–258
importance of, 254
modifying, 255, 259, 260–261, 269, 379
reflections on, 277
time allotment for, 259–260
for unit of study, 345
on the Web, 297–299
writing it down, 259
Lever, 317–318, 320

Levin, J., 37
Life science, 5, 55, 304, 305, 346
Light, 331–335
interactions with electricity, 331, 333
reflection of, 218, 307, 333, 334, 362
speed of, 323, 327, 329, 331–332, 336
Lighting, of classroom, 274
Lightning, 336
Light-year, 332
Liquids. *See also* Water
heat energy of, 324, 327–328
properties of, 127–129, 131–135, 136, 138, 173–184
temperature and, 90
Listening to students, 14–16
Listening to Students' Ideas (Science Story), 14–15
Literature, connections to, 111–112, 341, 343, 345, 346
Living things, 141, 142–145, 310. *See also* Animals; Human body systems; Microorganisms; Plants
national standards on, 143, 145, 146, 156, 161
Local control, 340, 341
Looking at Liquids (Science Story), 173–180
The Lorax (Dr. Seuss), 112
Low tide, 119
Lungs, 312–314

Machines
compound, 320–321
defined, 317
simple, 316–320
Magnetic field, 338
Magnetism, 337–339
generator and, 331
Making Connections, Inside and Out-

side the Classroom (Science Story), 117–123
Making Models of Atoms (Science Story), 238–249
Manager, group, 268
Margulis, L., 153
Marine organisms, 291–294
Mass
change of state and, 70–71
defined, 66
density and, 179, 195–197
weight and, 66
Materials and equipment, 390–393
journal entries on, 354
in lesson plan, 257
for outdoor activities, 116
safe use of, 393–394
Materials manager, 82, 192, 268, 269
Mathematics
connections to, 112, 341, 345, 346
MST curriculum initiative, 341–343
national standards for, 19–20, 199, 341
scale models and, 293
Matter, 136
change of state, 70–72, 324
classifying, 126–135, 136, 137, 138–140
conservation of energy and, 323
defined, 66, 129, 323
interactions with energy, 322–323
states of, 129, 132–133, 134, 135, 323–324, 369–370
structure of, 329–330
Mayer, Maria Goeppert, 239, 240
McClintock, Barbara, 3, 271
Meaning. *See* Construction of meaning
Meaningful science experiences, 14, 18, 20, 254–255, 352

Measuring, 97–99, 101
graduated cylinder for, 178
of water displacement, 197, 198
Mediator
of group learning, 269–270
lesson plan and, 258
role of, 16, 18, 56–57, 62–64, 68, 70, 84, 237
Mental models, 202, 238, 241
Mentoring, electronic, 294
Mentor teacher, 380
Messiness, 126, 128, 133, 137–140
Meteorites, 308
Meteors, 308
Microorganisms
taxonomy of, 153
video-microscope and, 289
Microscope
lenses of, 334
with video camera, 289
Microsoft PowerPoint, 283, 364–366
Minority groups. *See also* Diversity of students
alienation from science, 107–108
Mintzes, J., 16
Misconceptions. *See* Alternative conceptions
Mixtures, 136
A Model Orbit (Science Story), 212–215
Models
of atoms, 243–248
Internet resources for, 286
kinds of, 202
of marine organisms, 293
mental, 202, 238, 241
of moon phases, 217–218
MST initiative and, 343
national standards and, 210

of orbits, 212–215
of solar system, 203–211
usefulness of, 201–203, 211
Molecules
compounds and, 329
defined, 136, 329
motion of, 324
of water, 78–79, 82, 329
Mollusks, 167
Molds in, 155
Monocots, 155
Moon
exploration of, 281
light reflection by, 218, 333
other planets' moons, 308, 309
phases of, 215–221, 361, 362–363
as satellite, 306
Moon-phase journal, 215–217, 218, 221
Motion
of atoms and molecules, 324
work and, 317
Motivation, of students, 256
Motor neurons, 315
Motor/orthopedic disabilities, 273
MST initiative, 341–343
Multimedia presentations, 27, 282, 284
Multiple-choice tests, 351, 372–373
Multistation science activities, 86–103
Muscular system, 310, 317
Musical instruments, 337, 344
Mysterious Matter (Science Story), 132–135

National Board for Professional Teaching Standards (NBPTS), 381–382, 389
National Educational Technology Standards (NETS), 25, 282–283

assessment and, 372
on collecting information, 83, 99
on pedagogical strategies, 71, 83
on student diversity, 21
National Science Education Standards (NSES), 20
on assessment, 370, 371
on collaboration, 20, 167, 168, 265
content standards, 304, 305
curricula based on, 104, 340–341
on earth and space science, 210, 214, 219, 304
on environment of organisms, 161, 168
on excitement of science, 385
on extended investigations, 168
on history and nature of science, 249, 304
key themes of, 20, 182
on life science, 143, 145, 146, 156, 161, 168, 304
on mathematics, 199, 341
on personal and social perspectives, 123
on physical science, 59, 71–72, 83, 135, 180, 183, 198, 235, 304
on safety, 138
on scientific inquiry, 59, 88, 98–99, 123, 141–142, 188–189, 199, 210, 219, 235, 304, 341
on teacher attitudes, 36
on teaching strategies, 170, 183, 233

on technological design, 180, 249, 250–251
on testing, 351
National Science Teachers Association (NSTA), 380, 389
National standards. See Standards
A Nation at Risk, 19, 340
Nature. See also Environment
objects from, 105, 108, 110
teacher's observation of, 47, 51, 52, 377–379
Naylor, S., 363
Nervous system, 310, 315, 316
Networking, 380
Neurons, 315
Neutrons, 241–243, 248, 330
Newton, Isaac, 309
Newton's first law of motion, 309
Noddings, N., 13
Novak, J., 16
Nuclear energy, 326, 327, 331
Nuclear fusion, 332
Nucleus
of atom, 241–242, 243, 248, 330
of cell, 241
Numbered heads together, 269–270

Observation
compared to prediction, 98
as process skill, 5, 97, 99, 101, 262
as scientific activity, 4, 5, 35, 36
student's journal entries on, 354–355, 358
teacher's journal entries on, 47, 51, 52
Oobleck, 134
Opaque materials, 333
Open-ended questions, 261

Open systems, 316
Orbitals, 248, 330
Orbits, 209, 212–215, 307, 309, 317
Organisms. See Living things
Organizations, for professional development, 387–390
Orthopedic disabilities, 273
Outdoor trips, 116, 393

Paper-and-pencil tests, 351, 372–373
Parallel circuits, 224, 225–226, 230, 231, 232–233
assessment of understanding, 365–366
explanation of, 235
Parents
attitudes about science, 102
consent for activities, 116, 393
Patterns of change, 5–6, 305, 322–323. See also Interactions
Peer assistant, for student with disability, 273, 275
People of color. See also Diversity of students
alienation from science, 23, 107–108
as successful scientists, 270–271
Performance assessment, 351–352, 366. See also Assessment
stories about, 366–370, 371
Perihelion, 214
Periodic Table, 243
Perkes, V. A., 36
Perkins, D., 12, 16
Personal journals, 46–47. See also Journals
Phases of the moon, 215–221, 361, 362–363
Phillips, D. C., 11
Photons, 332

Photosynthesis, 152–153, 155–156, 286
Physical changes, 324, 325–326
Physical models, 202
Physical properties, 324
Physical science, 5, 55, 136, 304, 305, 346
    national standards for, 59, 71–72, 83, 135, 180, 183, 198, 235, 304
Piaget, Jean, 8–10, 11, 13
Pictures. *See also* Drawings
    in journals, 356, 357, 362
Pitch, 336–337, 344
Planetoids, 308
Planets, 306–308. *See also* Solar system
    light reflection by, 333
    orbits of, 209, 212–215, 307, 309, 317
Planning a lesson. *See* Lesson plans
Planning an investigation, 5, 98, 99, 101, 262
Plantae, 153
Planting in a Vacant Lot (Science Story), 157–158, 160–161
Plants
    from avocado pit, 158, 159
    edible, 158–160, 161
    as living things, 143–144, 145
    photosynthesis by, 152–153, 155–156, 286
    in science corner, 146
    seeds of, 146–152, 153, 154–155, 157–158, 159–160
    structures of, 161
    taxonomy of, 153
Plasma
    of blood, 312
    as state of matter, 134, 136, 323–324, 333
Platelets, 312
Portfolios
    for assessment, 358–360, 362

for design, 243–244, 250
Potential energy, 136, 323
Power plant, 331
PowerPoint, 283, 364–366
Precipitation, 367
Predicting, 5, 98, 99, 101, 262
Preoperational stage, 8, 10
Prescientific conceptions. *See* Alternative conceptions
Presentation software, 364–366
Prior knowledge
    acquired in earlier grades, 172, 189–190, 193, 200
    journal entry about, 354
    teaching strategy and, 10–11, 18, 19, 61, 62, 63, 84
A Private Universe (Project STAR), 74
Problem solving. *See also* Inquiry
    in MST activities, 342, 343
Process, scientific, 3–5, 6, 7
Process skills. *See also names of specific skills*
    building over time, 101
    in everyday life, 5, 101, 377–378
    in family science night, 102
    on field trip, 116
    lesson plan and, 258
    names of, 97–98, 99
    paper-and-pencil assessments of, 372–373
    questioning students and, 261–262
    in science circus, 86–87, 96–98, 100, 101
    value in other fields, 7
Professional development, 380–383
    organizations for, 387–389

Project 2061, 20
Projectors, 274
Property words, 127, 131, 147
Protista, 153
Protons, 241–243, 248, 329–330
Pulley, 317, 319
Pulling it together, 257, 258, 261

Quality of sound, 336, 344
Questions
    for reflection by teacher, 276–277
    scientific, 4–5
    for students, 255, 258, 261–264

Radiation, 327
Rainbow, 335
Recorder, 82, 192, 268
Recording data, 98, 99, 101
Red blood cells, 312
Reflection
    cooperative learning and, 266, 269
    lesson plan and, 255, 257, 258, 259, 260
    of light, 218, 307, 333, 334, 362
    by teacher after lesson, 276–277
Reflective journals, 46–47
Reflective teachers, 44, 45–47, 259, 379–380
Refraction, 334, 335
Relativity, special theory of, 323
Relevance, emerging, 184–185, 260
Reproductive system, 310
Research by teacher
    about classroom learning, 382–383
    science journal and, 51
Resistance, electrical, 235
Respiration, 314
Respiratory system, 310, 313–314, 316
Responses, of organisms, 256, 257, 258

Revolution, of heavenly body, 306, 308, 362
Reynolds, K., 289
Rosenblum, Meryl, 4
Rotation
    of moon, 362
    of planets, 307–308
Rowe, M. B., 263
Rubrics
    for atomic design project, 245–246
    for electronic presentations, 364–365
    for station assessment, 370, 371
    for student journal evaluation, 357–358
    for WebQuest assessment, 291, 292–293
Rules, for science corner, 110–111
Rutherford, Ernest, 239, 240

Sadker, D., 23
Sadker, M., 23
Safety, 138, 274, 393–394
Salvia, J., 351
Same. *See* Comparing and contrasting; Constants
Sanders, J., 23, 24
Satellites, 214, 306, 308
Scaffolding, 22, 77, 79, 255, 257, 258, 362
Schneier, Lisa, 139
Schon, Donald, 44
Schwartz, K. V., 153
Science. *See also* Teaching science
    alienation from, 105, 107–108, 125
    definitions of, 3, 4, 377
    major areas of, 5, 55, 304, 305, 346
    messiness of, 126, 128, 133, 137–140
    nature of, 3–7
    teachers' beliefs about, 36–38, 44–46
    technology and, 281

Science and Children (journal), 296, 380
Science assessment. *See* Assessment
Science autobiography, 45–46, 385
Science centers. *See* Science corners
Science circus, 87–100, 101
Science content. *See* Science ideas
Science conversation, 360–361
Science corners, 108–115, 117, 118, 120, 122, 125
  plants and animals in, 146, 163
Science Curriculum Improvement Study (SCIS), 17
Science education. *See* Teaching science
Science ideas, 3, 5–6, 7. *See also* Interactions, Systems
  big, 303
  categorizing, 5–6, 304, 305
  curriculum and, 303, 339
  about interactions, 5–6, 305, 322–339
  in interdisciplinary curricula, 344
  of lesson plan, 256, 257, 258, 261
  making them your own, 303
  replaced by more complex ideas, 200
  about systems, 5, 305, 306–322
  teacher's research on, 382
  of unit plan, 345
Science interview, 360
Science journal. *See* Journals
Science portfolios, 358–360, 362
Science stories
  Apples, Potatoes, and Density, 190–199

Batteries, Bulbs, and Wires, 224–226
Batteries, Bulbs, and Wires Revisited, 226–236
A Book of Snails, 163–168
The Bottle and the Balloon, 57–60, 61, 62, 63–64
The Circus Comes to Mount Holly, 88–100
Delving Deeper into Density, 181–184
An Edible Solar System, 203–210, 211
  explanation of, 28–29
Exploring Solids, Liquids, and Gases, 127–131
Floating and Sinking Fruits, 185–189
Icicles, 64–72
Listening to Students' Ideas, 14–15
Looking at Liquids, 173–180
Making Connections, Inside and Outside the Classroom, 117–123
Making Models of Atoms, 238–249
A Model Orbit, 212–215
Mysterious Matter, 132–135
Planting in a Vacant Lot, 157–158, 160–161
The Search for Understanding: A Toaster Story, 16–17
Second Graders Do a Station Assessment for a Unit on Matter, 368–370, 371
From Seed to Plant: A Failed Experiment, 146–147, 154

Shapes of the Moon, 215–220
The "Skin" of Water, 75–83
Third Graders Enact the Water Cycle, 367–368
A WebQuest on Marine Organisms, 291–294
What Does It Mean to Be Alive?, 142–145
What's Inside a Seed, 148–156
When is a Vegetable a Fruit, 158–161
Why the Balloon Doesn't Pop: An Experience for New Teachers, 33–34, 35–36
Science tables. *See* Science corners
Science toys, 177–178, 180
Scientific inquiry. *See* Inquiry
Scientific law, 323
Scientific literacy, 19–20, 341
Scientific method, 3–5. *See also* Process skills
Scientific self, 1, 38, 46, 47, 52, 56, 303, 376–379
Scientific theories. *See* Theories
Scientists
  children as, 2–3, 41
  collaboration by, 264, 267
  drawings of, 38–39, 40, 41
  electronic appearances by, 294
  interviewing, 41–43
  stereotypes about, 38–41, 107–108, 267, 270–271
  teachers' beliefs about, 38, 41, 43
  web sites for contact with, 286, 287
Screw, 317, 319

The Search for Understanding: A Toaster Story (Science Story), 16–17
Seashores, 116, 118–120, 122
Seasonal changes, 108
Second Graders Do a Station Assessment for a Unit on Matter (Science Story), 368, 370, 371
Seedfolks (Fleischman), 157
Seed plant, 155
SEED (Seeking Educational Equity and Diversity) Project, 121, 389
Seeds, 146–152, 153, 154–155, 157–158, 159–160
Seesaw, 317, 318
Self-evaluation, by teacher, 383–384
Sensorimotor stage, 8, 10
Sensory neurons, 315
Series circuits, 224, 225, 230, 231, 232, 233
  assessment of understanding, 365–366
  explanation of, 235
Shapes of the Moon (Science Story), 215–220
Shepardson, D. P., 357
Shrigley, R., 36
Simple machines, 316–320
Simulation software, 295
Situated cognition, 73
Skeletal system, 310
The "Skin" of Water (Science Story), 75–83
Skin system, 310
Slavin, R. E., 264
Snails, 162–169
  assessment of understanding, 365
  blind scientist's studies of, 271
  design challenge with, 251
  lesson plan for, 256–258
  questions about, 262, 263

Snow, 118, 122
Snowman, J., 73
Social construction of meaning, 63
Social context of learning, 11, 13, 21–22, 63, 266
Social learner, 11
Social studies, connections to, 112, 341, 343–344, 345, 346
Software
    for concept cartoons, 364
    for concept maps, 362–363
    educational, 295–296, 297, 300
    for presentations, 364–366
Solar system. See also Moon
    edible model, 203–210, 211
    ideas about, 205, 208–209, 214, 306–309, 316, 320
    orbits of planets, 209, 212–215, 307, 309, 317
Solids, 127–129, 131–135, 136, 138
    heat energy of, 324
Sound, 335–337
    computer simulation about, 26
    in interdisciplinary unit, 344
    Science Story about, 14–15
Speaker, 82, 192, 268, 269
Special educator, 272
Special needs students, 22–23, 394. See also Disabilities
Special theory of relativity, 323
Spectrum
    of colors, 334–335
    electromagnetic, 327, 331, 332
Spinal cord, 315
Spiraling of curriculum, 9, 190, 200, 346
Spreadsheet, 283

Stages of cognitive development, 8–10
Standards. See also Benchmarks for Science Literacy (AAAS); National Educational Technology Standards (NETS); National Science Education Standards (NSES)
    curriculum and, 104, 340–341, 345, 346
    for science education, 19–20
    for technology in education, 25–26
    Web resource on, 297
Stars, 209, 306, 333
State frameworks, 341, 343, 346
State regulations on safety, 393
States of matter, 129, 132–133, 134, 135, 323–324, 369–370
Static electricity, 330
Stations
    for assessment, 368–370, 371, 380
    multistation activities, 86–103
Stefanich, G., 272, 273
Stereotypes. See also Diversity of students
    of scientists, 38–41, 107–108, 267, 270–271
Stimuli, 256, 257, 258
Stories. See also Science Stories
    told by children, 357
Strong force, 242
Students. See also Alternative conceptions; Connections to students' lives; Diversity of students; Prior knowledge
    beliefs about scientists, 38–41
    fear of being wrong, 96

as knowers, 61, 63, 70, 84, 236–237
    listening to, 14–16
    unexpected explorations by, 172
    valuing ideas of, 13, 19, 22, 61–62, 63
Style, Emily, 121
Sublimation, 107
Sugar, 324
Sun, 209, 306, 309, 316, 317. See also Solar system
    heat energy from, 326, 327, 332–333
    light from, 331, 332–333
Suppliers, of materials and equipment, 392–393
Surface tension, 76–83, 364
Suspension, 134
Sustained inquiry, 141, 155, 161, 169–170
Systems, 306–322. See also Solar system
    Benchmarks on, 322
    as conceptual category, 5, 305
    of human body, 310–315, 316, 320
    interactions in, 328
    interconnection of parts in, 309, 322
    meaning of, 316
    open or closed, 316
    questions about, 306
    simple machines, 316–321

Taxonomy, 153
Teacher. See also Mediator
    associations and organizations for, 387–390
    beliefs about science, 36–38, 44–46
    beliefs about science teaching, 236–237
    beliefs about scientists, 38, 41, 43
    certification, 380–382
    Internet resources for, 296–299
    personal philosophy, 379–380

professional development, 380–383, 387–390
    promotion, 380
    reflective, 44, 45–47, 259, 379–380
    science autobiography of, 45–46, 385
    science journal of, 46–52
    scientific self of, 1, 38, 46, 47, 52, 56, 303, 376–379
    as scientist, 35–36
    self-evaluation, 383–384
    technology standards for, 282–283
Teacher game, 62
Teacher research, 382–383
Teaching science. See also Curriculum; Learning; Lesson plans; Standards
    alternative conceptions about, 223–224
    constructivism and, 12–14, 19, 60–61, 84
    cooperative learning groups, 264–270, 342–343, 393
    equipment for, 390–393
    inclusion in, 270–276
    integrating technology with, 283–285, 299–300
    learning cycle in, 17–18, 62, 256, 258
    listening in, 14–16
    major themes about, 385
    mediating in. See Mediator
    prior knowledge and, 10–11, 18, 19, 61, 62, 63, 84
    questioning in, 255, 258, 261–264
    reflecting on lesson, 276–277
    safety in classroom, 138, 274, 393–394

traditional methods, 12, 106–107
for understanding, 16–17, 59, 60
value of, 7–8
Technological design, 180, 249, 250–251
Technology, 24–28, 280–301. *See also* Computers; Email; Internet; National Educational Technology Standards (NETS); Web sites
in assessment, 361–366, 372
critical evaluation of, 284–285
curriculum and, 341–343, 345, 346
defined, 281
design technology, 180, 249, 250–251
integrating with instruction, 283–285, 299–300
interfacing instruments, 284, 288–289
for journal writing, 356
process skills with, 98
for students with disabilities, 272–273
video cameras, 289
Temperature. *See also* Heat energy
computerized probe, 289
heat conduction and, 327
liquids and, 90
Testing
defined, 350, 351
of a hypothesis, 35–36, 101
paper-and-pencil tests, 351, 372–373
Textbooks, 155
The Bottle and the Balloon (Science Story), 57–60, 61, 62, 63–64

Thematic units, 343–344
Theories
defined, 62, 97
nature of science and, 6, 7
of students, 62–63, 263
Thermoform, 273
Third Graders Enact the Water Cycle (Science Story), 367–368
Thomson, J. J., 239, 240
Thought experiments, 94–95, 96, 98
Tides, 119
Tobin, K., 263
Tomlinson, C. A., 23
Translucent materials, 333
Transparent materials, 333
Tutoring, electronic, 294

Understanding. *See also* Assessment; Construction of meaning; Ideas; Learning
journal entries on, 355–356
levels of, 200
meaning of, 16–17, 59, 60
prior knowledge as, 61
Unit of study, 345–346
Univalve mollusks, 167
Urso, J., 23, 24

Valenza, J. K., 296, 297
Variables, 71, 76, 175, 178
controlling, 98, 101
identified in journal, 358
Varney, H., 38
Vegetables, 158–160, 161
Veins, 312
The Velveteen Rabbit (Williams), 142
Venules, 312
Vermeij, Geerat, 271
Verrill, J., 362
Vertebrates, 146, 162
Video cameras, 289

Video-microscope, 289
Videotaping teachers, 383
Visual impairments, 271, 273
Voice, 336–337
Volume, 174, 176, 179. *See also* Density
von Glaserfeld, Ernst, 8, 60
Vygotsky, Lev, 8, 11, 13

Wait time, 263–264
Walberg, H. J., 37
Wald, Elijah, 4
Wandersee, J., 16
Water
buoyancy of, 183, 197
chemical composition of, 136, 324
displacement of, 197–198
floating on, 181–183, 185–199
heat energy and, 324, 327–328
as a liquid, 127–129, 131–135
molecules of, 78–79, 82, 329
surface tension, 75–83, 364
Water cycle, 322, 367–368
Watson, James, 202
Wavelength, 334–335
Waves
light, 331–332, 334–335
sound, 335–337
Weather
water cycle and, 322, 367–368
web sites, 95–96, 98, 99, 100, 285
Weathering, 122
WebQuest, 283, 290–294
A WebQuest on Marine Organisms (Science Story), 291–294
Web sites. *See also* Internet
evaluating, 286–288, 297, 299

information from, 283, 285–288
lesson plans on, 297–299
need to know and, 25
projects based on, 290–294
teachers' resources, 296–299
on weather, 95–96, 98, 99, 100, 285
young children and, 280–281
Wedge, 317, 319, 320
Weight. *See also* Density
of air, 129–130
explanation of, 66
of liquid, 131
What Does It Mean to Be Alive? (Science Story), 142–145
What's Inside a Seed (Science Story), 148–156
Wheel and axle, 317, 318–319, 320, 321
Wheelchairs, 274
When is a Vegetable a Fruit (Science Story), 158–161
White blood cells, 312
Whitney, D., 205
Why the Balloon Doesn't Pop: An Experience for New Teachers (Science Story), 33–34, 35–36
Wilkins, Maurice, 202
Women as scientists, 270–271. *See also* Girls
Work, 136, 317, 323
Workshops, 380
World Wide Web. *See* Web sites
Writing. *See also* Journals
by students, 26–27

Yager, R., 59, 60, 73
Year, of a planet, 214, 308
Ysseldyke, J. E., 351

About the Author

Janice Koch is a Professor of Science Education for the Department of Curriculum and Teaching at Hofstra University on Long Island, New York. Dr. Koch teaches courses in elementary and middle school science methods, gender issues in the classroom, and techniques of classroom research. She has several chapters in edited texts on issues relating to the lives of girls and women in schools and has recently co-edited on gender equity in education. She is the author of the Gender Issues in the Classroom chapter for the *Handbook of Psychology*, Volume 7(2002). Dr. Koch consults broadly to schools all over the country and in Australia addressing issues in science education as they connect to other academic disciplines. She is currently directing IDEAS—the Institute for the Development of Education in the Advanced Sciences—at Hofstra University. This outreach institute fosters the public understanding of science as well as furthering professional development in science and technology.